Electrical Wiring
Residential

NELSON EDUCATION

Based on the 2008
NATIONAL ELECTRICAL CODE®

Electrical Wiring Residential

SIXTEENTH EDITION

Ray C. Mullin

NELSON EDUCATION

NELSON EDUCATION

Printed and bound in USA
1 2 3 4 12 11 10 09

For more information contact
Nelson Education Limited
1120 Birchmount Road,
Toronto, Ontario, M1K 5G4.
Or you can visit our internet site
at http://www.nelson.com

This textbook is a Nelson custom publication. Because your instructor has chosen to produce a custom publication, you pay only for material that you will use in your course.

Cover Photo Credit:
© Eric Vega/iStockphoto

ISBN-13: 978-0-17-649219-9
ISBN-10: 0-17-649219-4

Consists of selections from:

Electrical Wiring – Residential, 16th Edition
Ray C. Mullin
ISBN-10: 1-4180-5095-5

NOTICE TO THE READER

Publisher does not warrant or guarantee any of the products described herein or perform any independent analysis in connection with any of the product information contained herein. Publisher does not assume, and expressly disclaims, any obligation to obtain and include information other than that provided to it by the manufacturer.

The reader is expressly warned to consider and adopt all safety precautions that might be indicated by the activities herein and to avoid all potential hazards. By following the instructions contained herein, the reader willingly assumes all risks in connection with such instructions.

The publisher makes no representation or warranties of any kind, including but not limited to, the warranties of fitness for particular purpose or merchantability, nor are any such representations implied with respect to the material set forth herein, and the publisher takes no responsibility with respect to such material. The publisher shall not be liable for any special, consequential, or exemplary damages resulting, in whole or part, from the readers' use of, or reliance upon, this material.

Contents

CHAPTER 1

General Information for Electrical Installations

OBJECTIVES

After studying this chapter, you should be able to

- **understand the basic safety rules for working on electrical systems.**
- **access the Internet to obtain a virtual unlimited source of safety and technical related information.**
- **become familiar with important electrical codes, safety codes, and building codes such as NFPA 70, 70A, 70B, 70E, 73, OSHA, NIOSH, ADA, NRTL, and the ICC.**
- **learn about licensing, permits, plans, specifications, symbols, and notations.**
- **understand the role of the electrical inspector and the International Association of Electrical Inspectors.**
- **understand the metric system of measurement.**

SAFETY IN THE WORKPLACE

Electricity is great when it is doing what it is intended to do, and that is to stay in its intended path. But electricity out of its intended path is dangerous, often resulting in fire, serious injury, or death.

Before getting into residential wiring and the *National Electrical Code*® (*NEC*®), we need to discuss on-the-job safety. Safety is not a joke! Electricians working on new construction, remodel work, maintenance, and repair work find that electricity is part of the work environment. Electricity is all around us, just waiting for the opportunity to get out of control. Repeat these words: **Safety First** . . . **Safety Last** . . . **Safety Always**!

Working on switches, receptacles, luminaires, or appliances with the power turned on is dangerous. Turn off the power! In addition, check with a voltmeter to be sure the power is off.

The voltage level in a home is 120 volts between one "hot" conductor and the "neutral" conductor or grounded surface. Between the two "hot" conductors (line-to-line), the voltage is 240 volts.

An electrical shock is received when electrical current passes through the body. From basic electrical theory, you learned that line voltage appears across an open in a series circuit. Getting caught "in series" with a 120-volt circuit will give you a 120-volt shock. For example, open-circuit voltage between the two terminals of a single-pole switch on a lighting circuit is 120 volts when the switch is in the "OFF' position and the lamp(s) are in place. See Figure 1-1. Likewise, getting caught "in series" with a 240-volt circuit will give you a 240-volt shock.

Working on equipment with the power turned on can result in death or serious injury, either as a direct result of electricity (electrocution or burns) or from an indirect secondary reaction, such as falling off a

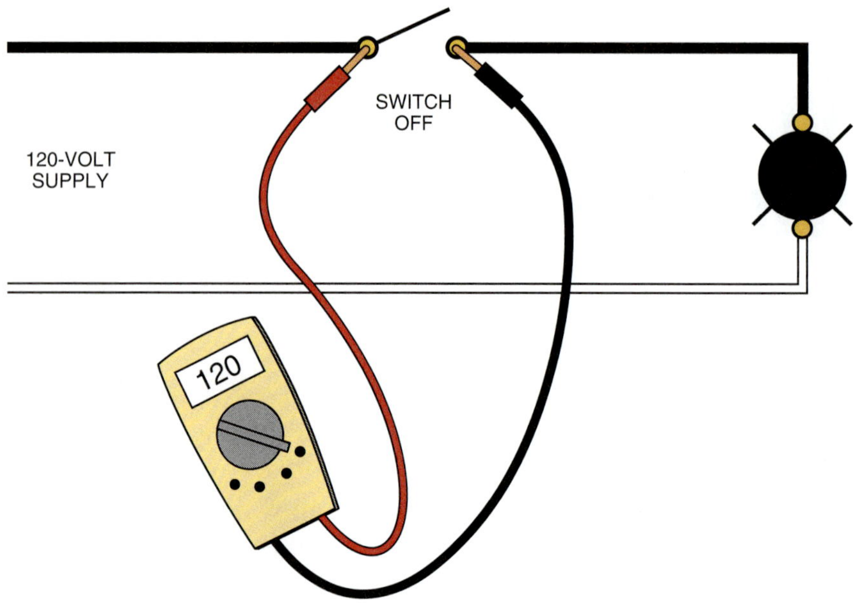

Figure 1-1 The voltage across the two terminals of the single-pole switch is 120 volts.

ladder or jerking away from the "hot" conductor into moving parts of equipment such as the turning blades of a fan. For example: A workman was seriously injured while working a "live" circuit that supplied a piece of equipment. He accidentally came into contact with a "hot" terminal, and reflex action caused him to pull his hand back into a turning pulley. The pulley cut deeply into his wrist, resulting in a tremendous loss of blood.

Dropping a metal tool onto live parts, allowing metal shavings from a drilling operation to fall onto live parts of electrical equipment, cutting into a "live" conductor and a "neutral" conductor at the same time, or touching the "live" wire and the "neutral" conductor or a grounded surface at the same time can cause injury directly or indirectly.

A short circuit or ground fault can result in a devastating arc flash that can cause serious injury or death. The heat of an electrical arc has been determined to be hotter than the sun. Tiny hot "balls" of copper can fly into your eye or onto your skin. Figure 1-2 shows a disconnect switch that has been locked and tagged.

Lockout/tagout (sometimes called LOTO) is the physical restraint of all hazardous energy sources that supply power to a piece of equipment. It simply means putting a padlock on the switch and applying a warning tag on the switch.

Dirt, debris, and moisture can also set the stage for equipment failure and personal injury. Neatness and cleanliness in the workplace are a must.

What about Low-Voltage Systems?

Although circuits of less than 50 volts generally are considered harmless, don't get too smug when working on so-called low voltage. Low-voltage circuits are not necessarily low hazard. A slight "tingle" might cause a reflex. A capacitor that is discharging can give you quite a "jolt," causing you to jump or pull back.

In commercial work, such as telephone systems with large battery banks, there is extreme danger even though the voltage is "low." Think of a 12-volt car battery. If you drop a wrench across the battery terminals, you will immediately see a tremendous and dangerous arc flash.

It is the *current* that is the harmful component of an electrical circuit. *Voltage* pushes the current through the circuit. If you're not careful, you might become part of the circuit.

Figure 1-2 A typical disconnect switch with a lock and a tag attached to it. In the OSHA, ANSI, and NFPA standards, this is referred to as the *lockout/tagout* procedure.

Higher voltages can push greater currents through the body. Higher voltages like 240, 480, and 600 volts can cause severe skin burns and possibly out-of-sight injuries such as internal bleeding and/or destruction of tissues, nerves, and muscles.

It's the Law!

Not only is it a good idea to use proper safety measures as you work on and around electrical equipment, it is **required** by law. Electricians and electrical contractors need to be aware of these regulations. Practicing safety is a habit—like putting on your seat belt as soon as you get into your car.

The *NEC*® is full of requirements that are safety related. For example, *430.102(B)* requires that a disconnecting means be located in sight from the motor location and the driven machinery location. This section also has "in-sight" and "lock-off" requirements, discussed in detail in Chapter 19.

▶The *NEC*® defines a qualified person as: *One who has skills and knowledge related to the construction and operation of the electrical equipment and installations and has received safety training to recognize and avoid the hazards involved.*◀ Merely telling someone or being told to "be careful" does not meet the definition of "proper training" and does not make the person qualified. An individual "qualified" in one skill might very well be "unqualified" in other skills.

According to *NFPA 70E, Electrical Safety in the Workplace*, circuits and conductors are not considered to be in an electrically safe condition until all sources of energy are removed, the disconnecting means is under lockout/tagout, and the absence of voltage is verified by an approved voltage tester.

The U.S. Department of Labor **Occupational Safety and Health Administration** (**OSHA**) regulations (Standards – 29 CFR) is the law! This entire standard relates to safety in the workplace for general industry. Specifically, Part 1910, Subpart S involves electrical safety requirements. The letters *CFR* stand for *Code of Federal Regulations*.

Key topics in the standard are: electric utilization systems, wiring design and protection, wiring methods, components and equipment for general use, specific purpose equipment and installations, hazardous (classified) locations, special systems, training, selection and use of work practices, use of equipment, selection and use of work practices, use of equipment, safeguards for personnel protection, and definitions (a mirror image of definitions found in the *NEC*®).

A direct quote from 1910.333(a)(1) states that "Live parts to which an employee may be exposed shall be deenergized before the employee works on or near them, unless the employer can demonstrate that de-energizing introduces additional or increased hazards or is infeasible due to equipment design or operational limitations. Live parts that operate at less than 50 volts to ground need not be deenergized if there will be no increased exposure to electrical burns or to explosion due to electric arcs."

OSHA 1910.333(c)(2) states that "Only qualified persons may work on electric circuit parts or equipment that have not been deenergized under the procedures of paragraph (b) of this section. Such persons shall be capable of working safely on energized circuits and shall be familiar with the proper use of special precautionary techniques, personal protective equipment, insulating and shielding materials, and insulated tools."

OSHA 1910.399 defines a *qualified person* as "One familiar with the construction and operation of the equipment and the hazards involved," almost the same definition as that of the *NEC*.®

For the most part, turning the power off then locking and tagging the disconnecting means is the safest. As the OSHA regulations state, "A lock and a tag shall be placed on each disconnecting means used to de-energize circuits and equipment."

Part 1926 in the OSHA regulation (Standards – 29 CFR) deals with *Safety and Health Regulations for Construction*. Here we find the rules for anyone involved in the construction industry, not just electrical. A few of the topics are: medical services and first aid, safety training and education, recording and reporting injuries, housekeeping, personal protective equipment, means of egress, head protection, hearing protection, eye and face protection, ladders, scaffolds, rigging, hand and power tools, electrical requirements (a repeat of Part 1910, Subpart S), fall protection, and required signs and tags.

PERSONAL PROTECTIVE EQUIPMENT

Safety courses refer to personal protective equipment (PPE). These include such items as rubber gloves, insulating shoes and boots (footware suitable for electrical work are marked with the letters "EH"), face shields, safety glasses, hard hats, ear protectors, Nomex™, and similar products. OSHA 1910.132(f)(1) requires that "The employer shall provide training to each employee who is required by this section to use PPE."

Working on electrical equipment while wearing rings and other jewelry is not acceptable. OSHA states that "Conductive articles of jewelry and clothing (such as watch bands, bracelets, rings, key chains, necklaces, metalized aprons, cloth with conductive thread, or metal headgear) may not be worn if they might contact exposed energized parts. However, such articles may be worn if they are rendered nonconductive by covering, wrapping, or other insulating means."

ARC FLASH

Don't get too complacent when working on electrical equipment.

A major short circuit or ground fault at the main service panel or at the meter cabinet or base can deliver a lot of energy. On large electrical installations, an arc flash (also referred to as an arc blast) can generate temperatures of 35,000°F (19,427°C). This is hotter than the surface on the sun. This amount of heat will instantly melt copper, aluminum, and steel. The blast will blow hot particles of metal and hot gases all over, resulting in personal injury, fatality, and/or fire. An arc flash also creates a tremendous air pressure wave that can cause serious hearing damage and/or memory loss due to the concussion. The blast might blow the victim away from the arc source.

Don't be fooled by the size of the service. Typical residential services are 100, 150, and 200 amperes. Larger services are found on large homes. Electricians seem to feel out of harm's way when working on residential electrical systems and seem to be more cautious when working on commercial and industrial electrical systems. A fault at a small main service panel can be just as dangerous as a fault on a large service. The available fault current at the main service disconnect for all practical purposes is determined by the kVA rating and impedance of the transformer. Other major limiting factors for fault current are the size, type, and length of the service-entrance conductors. Available fault current can easily reach 22,000 amperes, as is evident by panels that have a 22,000/10,000-ampere series rating.

Short-circuit calculations are discussed in Chapter 28.

Don't be fooled into thinking that if you cause a fault on the load side of the main disconnect that that main breaker will trip off and protect you from an arc flash. An arc flash will release the energy that the system is capable of delivering for as long as it takes the main circuit breaker to open. How much current (energy) the main breaker will "let through" is dependent upon the available fault current and the breaker's opening time.

Although not required for house wiring, *NEC® 110.16* requires that switchboards, panelboards, industrial control panels, meter socket enclosures, and motor control centers in commercial and industrial installations that are likely to be worked on while energized be field marked to warn qualified personnel of potential arc-flash hazard. More information on this subject is found in *NFPA 70E* and in the ANSI Standard Z535.4, *Product Safety Signs and Labels*.

TIP: When turning a standard disconnect switch "ON," don't stand in front of the switch. Instead, stand to one side. For example, if the handle of the switch is on the right, then stand to the right of the switch, using your left hand to operate the handle of the switch, and turn your head away from the switch. That way, if an arc flash occurs when you turn the disconnect switch "ON," you will not be standing in front of the switch. You will not have the switch's door fly into your face, and the molten metal particles resulting from the arc flash will fly past you.

Classifying Electrical Injuries

OSHA recognizes the four main types of electrical injuries as:

- Electrical shock (touching "live" line-to-line or line-to ground conductors) (ground-fault circuit interrupters are discussed in Chapter 6)
- Electrocution (death due to severe electrical shock)
- Burns (from an arc flash)
- Falls (an electrical shock might cause you to lose your balance, pull back, jump, or fall off a ladder)

What to Do If You Are Involved with a Possible Electrocution

The following is taken in part from the OSHA, NIOSH, NSC regulations, and the American Heart Association recommendations. These are steps that should be taken in the event of a possible electrocution (cardiac arrest). You need to refer to the actual cardiopulmonary resuscitation (CPR) instructions for complete and detailed requirements, and to take CPR training.

- First of all, you must recognize that an emergency exists. Timing is everything. The time between the accident and arrival of paramedics is crucial. Call 911 immediately. Don't delay.
- Don't touch the person if he or she is still in contact with the live circuit.
- Shut off the power.
- Stay with the person while someone else contacts the paramedics, who have training in the basics of life support. In most localities, telephoning 911 will get you to the paramedics.
- Have the caller verify that the call was made and that help is on the way.
- Don't move the person.
- Check for bleeding; stop the bleeding if it occurs.
- If the person is unconscious, check for breathing.
- The *ABCs* of CPR are: *a*irway must be clear; *b*reathing is a must, either by the victim or the rescuer; and *c*irculation (check pulse).
- Perform CPR if the victim is not breathing—within 4 minutes is critical. If the brain is deprived of oxygen for more than 4 minutes, brain damage will occur. If it is deprived of oxygen for more than 10 minutes, the survival rate is 1 in 100. CPR keeps oxygenated blood flowing to the brain and heart.
- Defibrillation may be necessary to reestablish a normal heartbeat. Ventricular fibrillation is common with electric shock, which causes the heartbeat to be uneven and unable to properly pump blood.
- By now, the trained paramedics should have arrived to apply advanced care.
- When it comes to an electrical shock, *timing is everything!*

Electrical Equipment

For safety, it is very important that electrical equipment be "listed" by a Nationally Recognized Testing Laboratory (NRTL). This is a requirement of *NEC® 90.7*.

NEC® 110.3(B) ***Installation and Use***: states that "*Listed or labeled equipment shall be installed and used in accordance with any instructions included in the listing or labeling.*"

OSHA rules state that "All electrical products installed in the work place shall be listed, labeled, or otherwise determined to be safe by a Nationally Recognized Testing Laboratory (NRTL)."

Who Is Responsible for Safety?

You are!

The electrical inspector inspects electrical installations for compliance to the *NEC*.® He or she is not really involved with on-the-job safety.

For on-the-job safety, OSHA puts the burden of responsibility on the employer. OSHA can impose large fines for noncompliance with its safety rules. But since it's your own safety that we are discussing, you share the responsibility by applying safe work practices, using the proper tools and PPE equipment the contractor furnishes, and installing "Listed" electrical equipment. Be alert to what's going on around you! Do a good job of housekeeping!

Tools

Using the proper tools for a job is vital to on-the-job safety.

OSHA Standard 1926.302 specifically covers the requirements for hand and power tools. The American National Standards Institute (ANSI) also has standards relating to tools.

If you want to learn more about tools, visit the Web site of the Hand Tools Institute at www.hti.org. The institute has a number of excellent safety education materials available. Of particular interest is its 90-plus-page publication *Guide to Hand Tools* that includes topics for selecting, proper use, maintaining, hazards involved, as well as special emphasis on eye protection using all types of hand tools.

Electrical Power Tools

You will be using portable electric power tools on the job. Electricity is usually in the form of temporary power, covered by *Article 590* of the *NEC*.®

NEC® 590.6(A) requires that *"All 125-volt, single-phase, 15-, 20-, and 30-ampere receptacle outlets that are not a part of the permanent wiring of the building or structure and that are in use by personnel shall have ground-fault circuit interrupter protection for personnel."*

Because this requirement is often ignored or defeated on job sites, you should carry and use as part of your tool collection a portable GFCI of the types shown in Figure 1-3—an inexpensive investment that will protect you against possible electrocution. Remember, *"The future is not in the hands of fate, but in ourselves."*

Digital Multimeters

Some statistics show that more injuries occur from using electrical meters than from electric shock.

For safety, electricians should use quality digital multimeters that are *category rated*. The International Electrotechnical Commission (IEC) Standard 1010 for *Low Voltage Test, Measurement, and Control Equipment* rates the ability of a meter to withstand voltage transients (surges or spikes). This standard is very similar to UL Standard 3111. When lightning strikes a high line, or when utilities are

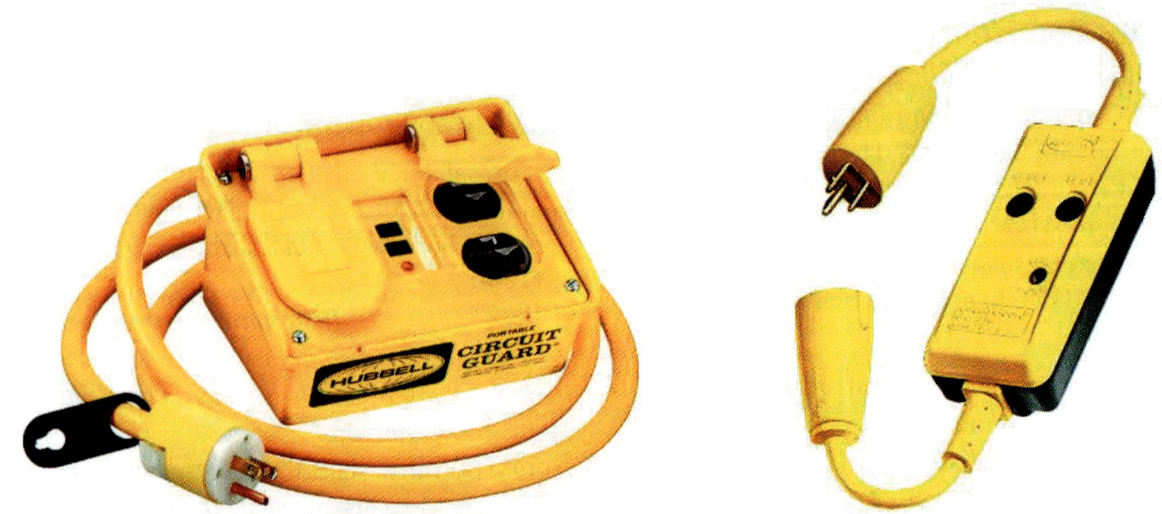

Figure 1-3 Two types of portable plug-in cord sets that have built-in GFCI protection.

performing switching operations, or when a capacitor is discharging, a circuit can "see" voltage transients that greatly exceed the withstand rating of the digital multimeter. The meter could explode, causing an arc flash (a fireball) that in all probability will result in personal injury. A properly selected category-rated digital multimeter is able to withstand the spike without creating an arc blast. The leads of the meter are also able to handle high transient voltages.

Digital multimeters also are category rated based on the location of the equipment to be tested, because the closer the equipment is to the power source, the greater the danger from transient voltages.

Cat IV multimeters are used where the available fault current is high, such as a service entrance, a service main panel, service drops, and the house meter.

Cat III multimeters are used for permanently installed loads such as in switchgear, distribution panels, motors, bus bars, feeders, short branch circuits, and appliance outlets where branch-circuit conductors are large and the distance is short.

Cat II multimeters are used on residential branch circuits for testing loads that are plugged into receptacles.

Cat I multimeters are used where the current levels are very low, such as electronic equipment. Note that the lower the category rating, the lower is the meter's ability to withstand voltage transients. If you will be using the multimeter in all of the above situations, select the higher category rating.

Category-rated digital multimeters also contain fuses that protect against faults that happen when the meter is accidentally used to check voltage while it is inadvertently set in the current reading position.

To learn more about meters, visit the Web site of Fluke Corporation, http://www.fluke.com, for a wealth of technical information about the use of meters and other electrical and electronic measuring instruments.

Ladders

To learn more about ladders, visit the Web site of Werner Ladder Company, http://www.wernerladder.com. You can download their pamphlet entitled *Ladder Safety Tips*. You will learn about the right and wrong ways to use a ladder such as: Never work on a step ladder in which the spreaders are not fully locked into position; the 4:1 ratio, which means that the base of an extension ladder should be set back (S) one-fourth the length (L) of where the upper part of the ladder is supported (S = 1⁄4 L); the duty ratings, such as do not stand higher than the second step from the top for step ladders, and do not stand higher than the fourth rung from the top for extension ladders; plus many more safety tips.

Ladders are labeled with their duty rating. Medium-duty commercial (Type II—225#), heavy-duty industrial (Type I—250#), and extra-heavy-duty (Type IA—300#) ladders bear an OSHA compliance label. Light-duty household (Type III—200#) ladders do not bear an OSHA logo.

Hazardous Chemicals

You will find more and more hazardous chemicals on the job. What do you do if you get a spilled chemical on your skin or in your eyes, or if you breathe the fumes?

Every manufacturer of this type of product is required to publish and make available a comprehensive data sheet called the **m**aterial **s**afety **d**ata **s**heet (MSDS). There are supposedly over 1.5 million of these data sheets. They contain product identification, ingredients, physical data, fire and explosion hazard data, health-hazard data, reactive data, spill or leak procedures, protection information, and special precautions.

The least you can do is to be aware that this information is available. Apprenticeship programs include some training about MSDS.

You can learn more about MSDS by checking any search engine for the letters MSDS.

TRAINING

If you want to learn more, visit manufacturers' Web sites. For example, Bussmann's Web site is http://www.Bussmann.com. It is easy to use and has a computer program for making arc-flash and fault-current calculations. This Web site also has a technical publication *Selecting Protective Devices*, or bulletin SPD, a 190-plus-page publication about overcurrent protection selection, application, *NEC*,® and safety. You can order a hard copy of the publication from them.

The OSHA Training Institute offers outreach training programs of interest to electricians, contractors, and instructors. The basic safety courses for general construction safety and health are the OSHA

10-hour and OSHA 30-hour courses. Instructors interested in becoming an outreach trainer for the 10- and 30-hour courses must complete the OSHA 500 course entitled "Trainer Course in Occupational Safety and Health Standards for the Construction Industry." To become an outreach trainer, a test must be passed. Before the end of 4 years, outreach trainers must take the OSHA 502 update course for the construction industry or the OSHA 502 update course "Update for Construction Industry Outreach Trainers." Completion cards are issued upon completion of these courses.

Other courses, publications, "free loan" videos, schedules of upcoming safety training seminars, and other important information relating to safety on the job are available from OSHA for electricians, contractors, and trainers.

Visit the OSHA Web site at http://www.OSHA.gov for everything there is to know about OSHA safety requirements in the workplace. The OSHA Web site is a virtual gold mine of information relating to safety on the job.

Another valuable source of safety information is the National Institute for Occupational Safety and Health (NIOSH), a division of the Department of Health and Human Services Centers for Disease Control and Prevention (CDC). Check out its Web site at http://www.cdc.gov/niosh. NIOSH offers an excellent downloadable 80-plus-page manual on *Electrical Safety*.

The National Safety Council has a vast amount of information relative to all aspects of safety. Check out its Web site at http://www.nsc.org.

The Consumer Product Safety Commission offers many safety publications for downloading. Visit its Web site at http://www.cpsc.gov, click on Library, click on CPSC Publications, click on By General Category, and then click on Electrical Safety. Here you will see a list of CPSC publications about GFCIs, AFCIs, metal ladder hazards, home wiring hazards, repairing aluminum wiring, and others.

The *National Fire Protection Association* offers many publications, videos, and a training course relating to safety. Browse its Web site at http://www.nfpa.org.

NFPA 70E Standard for Electrical Safety in the Workplace and *NFPA 70B Recommended Practices for Electrical Equipment Maintenance* present much of the same text regarding electrical safety as does the OSHA regulation.

Accredited apprenticeship training programs incorporate safety training as an integral part of their curriculum.

SAFETY CANNOT BE COMPROMISED!

It is impossible to put a dollar value on a life.

Don't take chances! Use the right tools! Turn off the power. Follow a lockout/tagout procedure. Mark the tag with a description of exactly what that particular disconnect controls.

How many times have we heard "The person would not have been injured (or electrocuted) had he turned the power OFF"? How many more times can we say it? **Turn OFF the power before working on the circuit!**

Visit the Web sites of the various organizations mentioned earlier. The Web site list can also be found in the back of this text. These organization have a wealth of information about on-the-job safety educational material and safety training courses.

Check out the Web site of the Electrical Safety Foundation International (ESFI) at http://www.electrical-safety.org. This organization has a tremendous amount of down to earth, simple to understand electrical safety material. Some of their educational material is free, other items are priced. Certain items are downloadable. The bottom line is to reduce deaths and injuries from preventable electrical accidents.

LICENSING AND PERMITS

Most communities, counties, and/or states require electricians and electrical contractors to be licensed. This usually means they have taken and have passed a test. To maintain a valid license, many states require electricians and electrical contractors to attend and satisfactorily complete approved continuing education courses consisting of a specified number of classroom hours over a given period of time. Quite often, a community will have a "Residential Only" license for electricians and contractors that limits their activity to house wiring.

Permits are a means for a community to permanently record electrical work to be done, who is doing the work, and to schedule inspections during and after the "rough-in" stage and in the "final" stages of construction. Usually, permits must be issued prior to starting an electrical project. In most cases, homeowners are allowed to do electrical work in their own home where they live but not in other properties they might own.

Figure 1-4 is a simple application for an electrical permit form. Some permit application forms are much more detailed.

If you are not familiar with licensing and permit requirements in your area, it makes sense to check this out with your local electrical inspector or building department before starting an electrical project. Not to do so could prove to be very costly. Many questions can be answered: You will find out what tests, if any, must be taken; which permits are needed; which electrical code is enforced in your community; minimum size electrical service; and so on. Generally, the electrical permit is taken out by an electrical contractor who is licensed and registered as an electrical contractor in the jurisdictional area.

APPLICATION FOR ELECTRICAL PERMIT

VILLAGE OF ANYWHERE, USA 1-234-567-8900, EXT. 1234

Date ________________ Permit No. ________________

Owner ________________ Job Address ________________

Telephone No. ________________ Job Start Date ________________

CONTRACTOR INFORMATION AND SIGNATURE

Electrical Contractor ________________ Tel. No. ________________

Address ________________ City ________________ State ______ Zip ______

Registration No. ________________ City of Registration ________________

Supervising Electrician (Please Print Name) ________________

Supervising Electrician's Signature ________________

Insurance Bond ________________ Village Business License ________________

SERVICE INSPECTIONS OR REVISIONS

Existing Service Size: Amps ______ Volts ______ No. of Circuits ______ No. Added ______

New Service Size: Amps ______ Volts ______ No. of Circuits ______

Type: Overhead ______ Underground ______

Service Installation Fees: 100-200 amps $50 ______ over 200 amps $75 ______

MOTORS AND AIR-CONDITIONING EQUIPMENT

No. of Motors: up to 1 HP @ $50 ______ Over 1–10 HP @ $50 ______

11–25 HP @ $25 ______ Over 25 HP @ $25 ______

Air Conditioner/Heat Pump:

No. of Tons ______ ($20 for first ton, $5 for each additional ton) ______

Furnace (electric): kW ______ Amps ______ ($25) ______

Dryer (electric): kW ______ Amps ______ ($10) ______

Range, oven, cooktop (electric): Total kW ______ Amps ______ ($10 each) ______

Water Heater (electric): kW ______ Amps ______ ($10) ______

TYPE OF MISCELLANEOUS ELECTRIC WORK

____

____

Minimum Inspection Fee: $40.00 ______

Escrow Deposit, if applicable ______

TOTAL DUE ______

Figure 1-4 A typical Application for Electrical Permit.

For new construction or for a main electrical service change, you will also need to contact the electric utility.

Temporary Wiring

There is an ever-present electrical shock hazard on construction sites. The *NEC®* addresses this in *Article 590*. This is covered in Chapter 6.

Construction Terms

Electrical Wiring—Residential covers all aspects of typical residential wiring, with focus on the *NEC®*. Electricians work with others on construction sites. Knowing construction terms and symbols is, therefore, a key element to getting along with the other workers. A rather complete dictionary of construction terms can be found on http://www.constructionplace.com/glossary.asp. Architectural symbols are found in the Appendix of this text.

PLANS

An architect or electrical engineer prepares a set of drawings that shows the necessary instructions and details needed by the skilled workers who are to build the structure. These are referred to as **plans**, **prints**, **blueprints**, **drawings**, **construction drawings**, or **working drawings**. The sizes, quantities, and locations of the materials required and the construction features of the structural members are shown at a glance. These details of construction must be studied and interpreted by each skilled construction craftsperson—masons, carpenters, electricians, and others—before the actual work is started.

The electrician must be able to: (1) convert the two-dimensional plans into an actual electrical installation, and (2) visualize the many different views of the plans and coordinate them into a three-dimensional picture, as shown in Figure 1-5.

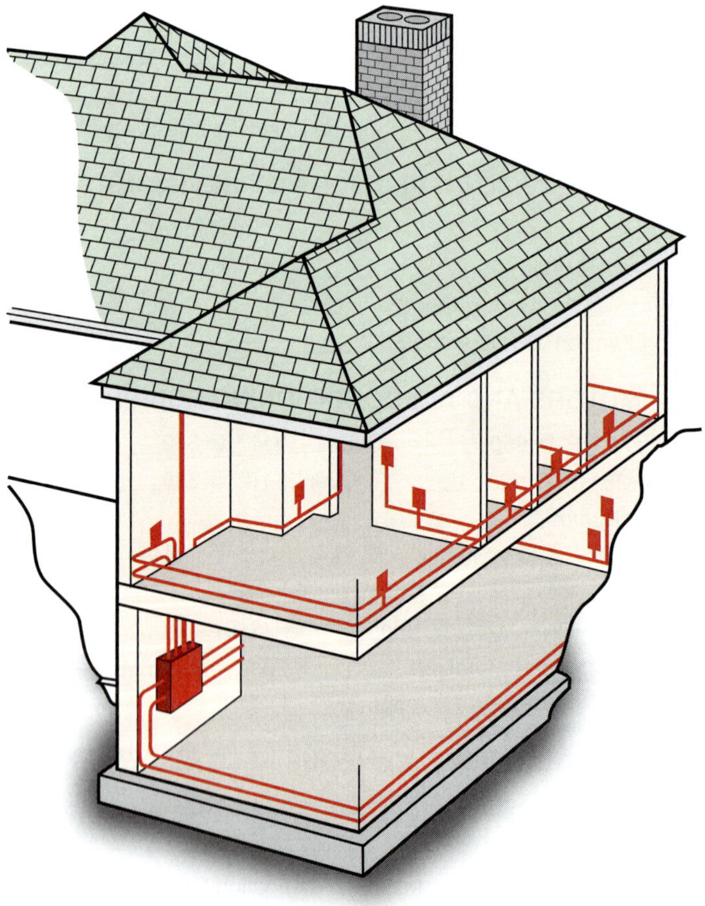

Figure 1-5 Three-dimensional view of house wiring.

The ability to visualize an accurate three-dimensional picture requires a thorough knowledge of blueprint reading. Because all of the skilled trades use a common set of plans, the electrician must be able to interpret the lines and symbols that refer to the electrical installation and also those used by the other construction trades. The electrician must know the structural makeup of the building and the construction materials to be used

Plans might be **black line prints**, which are simply photocopies, or they might be computer-aided drawings (CAD). Although pretty much a thing of the past, we still have blueprints. Blueprints are created by running yellowish, light-sensitive paper and transparent Mylar® with black images on it through a blueprint machine, where the two sheets are exposed to a bright light for a short period of time. The light-sensitive paper turns white in all places except where the black images are. Where the black images are, the light-sensitive paper turns blue. That is why it is called a blueprint.

A tear-out/fold-out set of full-size plans for the residence referred to throughout this text is included in the back of the book.

SPECIFICATIONS

The **specifications** (specs, for short) for the electrical work indicated on the plans for the residence discussed throughout this text are found in the back of the book, before the Appendix.

Working drawings are usually complex because of the amount of information that must be included. To prevent confusing detail, it is standard practice to include with each set of plans a set of detailed written specifications prepared by the architect.

These specifications provide general information to be used by all trades involved in the construction. In addition, specialized information is given for the individual trades. The specifications include information on the sizes, the type, and the desired quality of the standard parts to be used in the structure.

Typical specifications include a section on "General Clauses and Conditions," which is applicable to all trades involved in the construction. This section is followed by detailed requirements for the various trades—excavating, masonry, carpentry, plumbing, heating, electrical work, painting, and others.

In the electrical specifications, the listing of standard electrical parts and supplies frequently includes the manufacturers' names and the catalog numbers of the specified items. Such information ensures that these items will be of the correct size, type, and electrical rating, and that the quality will meet a certain standard. To allow for the possibility that the contractor will not always be able to obtain the specified item, the phrase "or equivalent" is usually added after the manufacturer's name and catalog number.

The specifications are also useful to the electrical contractor in that all of the items needed for a specific job are grouped together and the type or size of each item is indicated. This information allows the contractor to prepare an accurate cost estimate without having to find all of the data on the plans.

If there is a difference between the plans and specifications, the specifications will take preference. The electrical contractor should discuss the matter with the homeowner, architect, and engineer. The cost of the installation might vary considerably because of the difference(s), so obtain any changes to the plans and/or specifications in writing.

SYMBOLS AND NOTATIONS

The architect uses **symbols** and **notations** to simplify the drawing and presentation of information concerning electrical devices, appliances, and equipment. For example, an electric range outlet symbol is shown in Figure 1-6.

Most symbols have a standard interpretation throughout the country as adopted by ANSI. Symbols are described in detail in Chapter 2.

A notation will generally be found on the plans (blueprints) next to a specific symbol calling attention to a variation, type, size, quantity, or other necessary information. In reality, a symbol might be considered to be a notation because symbols represent words, phrases, numbers, quantities, and so on.

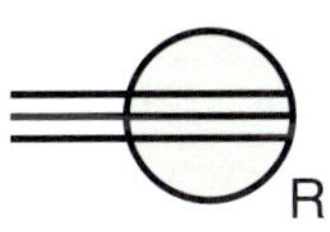

Figure 1-6 An electric range outlet symbol.

Another method of using notations to avoid cluttering up a blueprint is to provide a system of symbols that refer to a specific table. For example, the written sentences on plans could be included in a table referred to by a notation. Figure 2-10 is an example of how this could be done. The special symbols that refer to the table would have been shown on the actual plan.

NATIONAL ELECTRICAL CODE® (NEC®)

The *NEC®* is the electrical *Code* standard recognized by everyone in the electrical industry.

The first sentence in the *NEC®* is found in *90.1*. This sentence lays the foundation for all electrical installations. It states: "*The purpose of this Code is the practical safeguarding of persons and property from hazards arising from the use of electricity.*" It goes on to state that the *NEC®* "*contains provisions that are considered necessary for safety*" and that "*compliance therewith and proper maintenance will result in an installation that is essentially free from hazard but not necessarily efficient, convenient, or adequate for good service or future expansion of electrical use.*"*

As you study this text, you will learn how to "Meet Code" for wiring a typical house, not "Beat Code."

As *NEC®* requirements are discussed throughout this text, the sheer number of *Code* references can become mind boggling. To simplify using this text as a reference, in addition to the conventional "subject" index at the back of the text, there is a Cross Index, making it easy for you to pinpoint specific *Code* sections and articles found in this text.

The *NEC®* is published by the National Fire Protection Association and is referred to as *NFPA 70*. The *NEC®* was first published in 1897. It is revised every 3 years so as to be as up to date as possible. The *NEC®* does not become law until adopted by official action of the legislative body of a city, municipality, county, or state. Because of the ever-present danger of fire or shock hazard through some failure of the electrical system, the electrician and the electrical contractor must use listed materials and must perform all work in accordance with recognized standards.

*Reprinted with permission from NFPA 70-2008.

One- and Two-Family Dwelling Electrical Code

NFPA 70A is the *National Electrical Code® Requirements for One- and Two-Family Dwellings.* It is a condensed version of the *NEC®* that contains excerpts directly from the *NEC®-NFPA 70*. It includes requirements and tables that relate only to house wiring. It does not include *Code* requirements for other types of construction.

Other Electrical Codes

In addition to the *NEC,®* you must also consider local and state electrical codes.

Code Arrangement

It is important to understand the arrangement of the *NEC.®*

- Introduction, *Article 90* — An introduction to the *NEC.®* Explains what is and what is not covered in the *NEC,®* the arrangement of the *NEC,®* who has the authority to enforce the *Code*, what mandatory rules are, what permissive rules are, and the basics of metric vs. inch-pound measurements found throughout the *NEC.®*
- Chapter 1 — General
Article 100: Definitions
Article 110: Requirements for Electrical Installations
Applies to all electrical installations.
- Chapter 2 — Wiring and Protection
Articles 200–299
Applies to all electrical installations.
- Chapter 3 — Wiring Methods
Articles 300–399
Applies to all electrical installations.
- Chapter 4 — Equipment for General Use
Articles 400–499
Applies to all electrical installations.

- Chapter 5 Special Occupancies Articles 500–599
- Chapter 6 Special Equipment Articles 600–699
- Chapter 7 Special Conditions Articles 700–799
- Chapter 8 Communications Systems Articles 800–899 The articles in Chapter 8 are not subject to the requirements of Articles 1 through 7 unless specifically stated.
- Chapter 9 Tables showing dimensional data for raceways and conductors, resistance and reactance values of conductors, Class 2 and Class 3 circuit power limitations.
- Annex A Provides a comprehensive list of product safety standards from Underwriters Laboratories (UL).
- Annex B Provides data for determining conductor ampacity where there is engineering supervision.
- Annex C Has tables showing the maximum number of conductors permitted in various types of raceways.
- Annex D Examples of load calculations.
- Annex E Types of building construction.
- Annex F ▶Availability and Reliability of Critical Operations Power Systems◀
- Annex G Supervisory Control and Data Acquisitions (SCADA)
- Annex H Administration and Enforcement A comprehensive suggested typical electrical ordinance that could be adopted on a local level.
- Index The alphabetical index for the *NEC*®

Note: Annexes and fine print notes (FPN) are informational only. They are not mandatory.

Easy to Find Things!

Finding things in the current edition of the *NEC*® is much easier than in past editions. All articles in Chapter 3 of the *NEC*® cover wiring methods. In each article, the same section number has been assigned for a particular requirement. Here are a few examples:

- *Scope* is found in *Section XXX.1*
- *Permitted Uses* are found in *Section XXX.10.*
- *Uses Not Permitted* are found in *Section XXX.12.*
- *Securing and Supporting* is found in *Section XXX.30.*

This is referred to as "the parallel numbering system."

How to Spot Changes in the 2008 *NEC*®?

Highlighted text makes it easy to quickly spot where changes in the *NEC*® have been made from the previous edition.

Who Writes the *Code*?

For each *Code* cycle, the NFPA solicits proposals from anyone interested in electrical safety. Anyone may submit a proposal to change the *NEC*® using the Proposal Form found in the back of the *NEC*.® Proposals received are then given to a specific Code-Making Panel (CMP) to accept, reject, accept in part, accept in principle, or accept in principle in part. These actions are published in the Report on Proposals (ROP). There were 3,668 Proposals submitted for the 2008 *NEC*.® Individuals may send in their comments on these actions using the Comment Form found in the ROP. There were 3,206 Comments submitted for the 2008 *NEC*.® The CMPs meet again to review and take action on the comments received. These actions are published in the Report on Comments (ROC). Final action (voting) on proposals and comments is taken at the NFPA annual meeting.

However, before the *NEC*® is published, if there is disagreement on any specific Code requirement adopted through the above process, NFPA will consider an *Appeal* that is reviewed and acted upon by the NFPA Standards Council about 6 weeks after the annual meeting. After an *Appeal* is acted upon by the Standards Council, should there still be controversy, another step not often used in the *Code* adoption process is a Petition that is reviewed and acted upon by the NFPA Board of Directors.

Individuals who serve on CMPs are electrical inspectors, electrical contractors, electrical engineers, individuals from utilities, manufacturers, testing laboratories, the Consumer Product Safety Commission, insurance companies, and similar organizations. CMP members are appointed by the NFPA. The CMPs have ten to twenty principal members, plus a similar number of alternate members. All of the CMPs have a good balance of representation.

Which Edition of the *NEC*® to Use?

This text is based on the 2008 edition of the *NEC*.® Some municipalities, cities, counties, and states have not yet adopted this edition and may still be using older editions. Check with your local electrical inspector to find out which edition of the *Code* is in force.

Copies of the latest edition of the *NEC®-NFPA 70* may be ordered from the following:

Thomson Delmar Learning
P.O. Box 8007
Clifton Park, NY 12065
Phone: 800-998-7498
http://www.delmar.cengage.com

National Fire Protection Association
1 Batterymarch Park
Quincy, MA 02269-9101
Phone: 617-770-3000
http://www.nfpa.org

International Association of Electrical Inspectors
901 Waterfall Way, Suite 602
Richardson, TX 75080-7702
Phone: 800-786-4234
http://www.iaei.org

Electrical Inspection Code for Existing Dwellings

This code is published by the NFPA and is referred to as *NFPA 73*. It is a brief nine-page code that provides requirements for evaluating installed electrical systems within and associated with existing dwellings to identify safety, fire, and shock hazards—such as improper installations, overheating, physical deterioration, and abuse. This code lists most of the electrical things to inspect in an existing dwelling that could result in a fire or shock hazard if not corrected. It only points out things to look for that are visible. It does not get into examining concealed wiring that would require removal of permanent parts of the structure. It also does not get into calculations, location requirements, and complex topics as does the *NEC®-NFPA 70*.

This code can be an extremely useful guide for electricians doing remodel work and for electrical inspectors wanting to bring an existing dwelling to a reasonably safe condition. Many localities require that when a home changes ownership, the wiring must be brought up to some minimum standard, but not necessarily as extensively as would be the case for new construction.

Homes for the Physically Challenged

The *NEC*® does not address the wiring of homes for the physically or mentally challenged or disabilities associated with the elderly.

Each installation for the physically challenged must be based upon the specific need(s) of the individual(s) who will occupy the home. Some physically challenged people are bedridden, require the mobility of a wheelchair, have trouble reaching, have trouble bending, etc. There are no hard and fast rules that *must* be followed—only many suggestions to consider.

Some of these are:

- Install more ceiling luminaires instead of switching receptacles. Cords and lamps are obstacles.
- Install luminaires having more than one bulb.
- Go “overboard” in the amount of lighting for all rooms, entrances, stairways, stairwells, closets, pantries, bathrooms, and so on.
- Use higher wattage bulbs—not to exceed the wattage permitted in the specific fixture.
- Consider installing luminaires in certain areas (such as bathrooms and hallways) to be controlled by motion detectors.
- Consider installing exhaust fans in certain areas (such as laundries, showers, and bathrooms) that turn on automatically when the humidity reaches a predetermined value.
- Consider the height of switches and thermostats, usually 42 in. (1.0 m) or lower, instead of the standard 46–52 in. (1.15 to 1.3 m).
- Consider rocker-type switches instead of toggle type.

- Install pilot light switches.
- Consider "jumbo" switches.
- Be sure stairways and stairwells are well lit.
- Consider stair tread lighting.
- Position lighting switches so as not to be over stairways or ramps.
- Locate switches and receptacles to be readily and easily accessible—not behind doors or other hard-to-reach places.
- Consider installing wall receptacle outlets higher 24–27 in. (600 mm to 675 mm) than normal 12 in. (300 mm) height.
- Install lighted doorbell buttons.
- Chimes: consider adding a strategically located "dedicated" lamp(s) that will turn on when door bell buttons are pushed. The wiring diagram for this is found in Figure 25-25.
- Telephones: consider adding visible light(s) strategically located that will flash at the same time the telephone is ringing.
- Consider installing receptacle outlets and switches on the face of kitchen cabinets. Wall outlets and switches can be impossible for the physically challenged person to reach.
- Consider fire, smoke, and security systems directly connected to a central office for fast response to emergencies that do not depend upon the disabled to initiate the call.
- Consider installing the fuse box or breaker panel on the first floor instead of in the basement.
- Consider the advanced home systems concept of remote control of lighting, receptacles, appliances, television, telephones, and so on. The control features can make life much easier for a disabled person.

When involved with multifamily dwellings, check with your local building authority. They will have copies of the Americans with Disabilities Act (ADA) from the U.S. Department of Justice and the Fair Housing Act from the U.S. Department of Housing and Urban Development (HUD) that basically require that all units must have accessible light switches, electrical outlets, thermostats, and other environmental controls.

The ANSI publication *ANSI A117.1–2003, Standard for Accessible and Useable Buildings and Facilities,* contains many suggestions and considerations for buildings and facilities for the physically challenged. This and other standards can be ordered from:

American National Standards Institute
25 West 43rd Street
New York, NY 10036
Tel: 212-642-4900
Fax: 212-398-0023

The same standard is available from the International Code Council (ICC) under the publication number *ICC/ANSI A117.1-2003*.

Another virtually unlimited source of standards is:

Global Engineering Documents
15 Inverness Way East
Englewood, CO 80112
Phone: 800-624-3974 ext. 1950
303-792-2181 ext. 1950
Fax: 303-792-2192
http://www.global.ihs.com
e-mail: globalcustomerservice@ihs.com

BUILDING CODES

The majority of the building departments across the country have for the most part adopted the *NEC*® rather than attempting to develop their own electrical codes. As you study this text, you will note numerous references to the *NEC*,® the electrical inspector, or the authority having jurisdiction.

An authority's level of knowledge varies. The electrical inspector may be full-time or part-time and may also have responsibility for other trades, such as plumbing or heating. The heads of the building departments in many communities are typically called the Building Commissioners or Directors of Development. Regardless of title, they are responsible for ensuring that the building codes in their communities are followed.

International Code Council (ICC)

Rather than writing their own codes, most communities for the most part adopt the codes of the International Code Council (ICC). Over the years, the ICC has developed comprehensive and coordinated model construction codes. These include building, mechanical, plumbing, fire, energy conservation, existing building, fuel gas, sewage disposal, property maintenance, zoning, residential, and electrical codes. The ICC provides technical, educational, and informational products. Its address is:

ICC Headquarters
500 New Jersey Avenue, NW, 6th Floor
Washington, DC 20001
Phone: 888-422-7233
http://www.iccsafe.org

The *ICC International Residential Code* in Chapters 33 through 42 contains electrical provisions that were written and produced under the guidance of the NFPA. The material in these chapters is copyrighted by the NFPA. These provisions are similar to the *NEC*® other than the layout and numbering system.

The *ICC International Electrical Code* is a rather brief thirty-page administrative code. It contains only two pages of actual electrical provisions.

Electrical Wiring—Residential is based on the *NEC*.®

Because local electrical codes may differ from the *NEC*,® you should check with the local inspection authority to determine which edition of the *NEC*® is enforced, and what, if any, local requirements or amendments take precedence over the *NEC*.®

American National Standards Institute

The **American National Standards Institute (ANSI)** is an organization that coordinates the efforts and results of the various standards-developing organizations, such as those mentioned in previous paragraphs. Through this process, ANSI approves standards that then become recognized as American National Standards. One will find much similarity between the technical information found in ANSI standards, the UL standards, the International Electronic and Electrical Engineers standards, and the *NEC*.®

International Association of Electrical Inspectors

The International Association of Electrical Inspectors (IAEI) is a nonprofit organization. The IAEI membership consists of electrical inspectors, building officials, electricians, engineers, contractors, and manufacturers throughout the United States and Canada. The major goal of the IAEI is to improve the understanding of the *NEC*.® Representatives of this organization serve as members of the various CMPs of the *NEC*® and share equally with other members in the task of reviewing and revising the *NEC*.®

The IAEI publishes a bimonthly magazine—*The IAEI News*. It is devoted entirely to electrical code topics. Anyone in the electrical industry is welcome to join the IAEI. An application form is found after the Appendix of this text. Its address is:

International Association of Electrical
Inspectors
901 Waterfall Way, Suite 602
Richardson, TX 75080-7702
Phone: 800-786-IAEI
http://www.iaei.org

Code Definitions

The electrical industry uses many words (terms) that are unique to the electrical trade. These terms need clear definitions to enable the electrician to understand completely the meaning intended by the *Code*.

Article 100 of the *NEC*® is a "dictionary" of these terms. *Article 90* also provides further clarification of terms used in the *NEC*.® Here are a few examples:

Ampacity: The current, in amperes, that a conductor can carry continuously under the conditions of use without exceeding its temperature rating.

Approved: Acceptable to the authority having jurisdiction.

Authority Having Jurisdiction (AHJ): An organization, office, or individual responsible for enforcing the requirements of a code or standard, or for approving equipment, materials, an installation, or a procedure. See *NEC*® *90.4*.

Dwelling Unit: A single unit, providing complete and independent living facilities for one or more provisions for living, sleeping, cooking, and sanitation.

Fine Print Notes (FPN): Fine print notes (FPNs) are found throughout the *Code*. FPNs are "explanatory" in nature, in that they refer to other sections of the *Code*. FPNs also define things where further description is necessary. See *90.5*.

Listed: Equipment, materials, or services included in a list published by an organization that is acceptable to the authority having jurisdiction and concerned with evaluation of products or services, that maintains periodic inspection of production of listed equipment or materials or periodic evaluation of services, and whose listing states that either the equipment, material, or services meets appropriate designated standards or has been tested and found suitable for a specified purpose.

Shall: Indicates a mandatory rule, *90.5*. As you study the *NEC*®, think of the word "shall" as meaning "must." Some examples found in the *NEC*® where the word "shall" is used in combination with other words are: *shall be*, *shall have*, *shall not*, *shall be permitted*, *shall not be permitted*, and *shall not be required*.

Refer to Key Terms in the Appendix of this text.

Read *110.3(B)* Carefully!

One of the most far-reaching *NEC*® rules is *110.3(B)*. This section states that "*Listed or labeled equipment shall be installed and used in accordance with any instructions included in the listing or labeling*." This means that an entire electrical system and all of the system's electrical equipment must be *installed* and *used* in accordance with the *NEC*® and the numerous standards to which the electrical equipment has been tested.

METRICS (SI) AND THE *NEC*®

The United States is the last major country in the world not using the metric system of weights and measures as the primary system. For most of our lifetime, we have used the English system of weights and measures, also referred to as inch-pound and U.S. Customary. But this is changing!

Manufacturers are now showing both inch-pound and metric units in their catalogs. By law, plans and specifications for new governmental construction and renovation projects have used the metric system since January 1, 1994.

You may not feel comfortable with metric measurements, but metric measurements are here to stay. You might just as well become familiar with the metric system.

All measurements in the *NEC*® are shown in both inch-pound and metric values.

For more information about metrics, refer to the "Metric System of Measurement" section found in the Appendix of this text.

Trade Sizes

A unique situation exists. Strange as it may seem, what electricians have been referring to for years has not been correct!

Raceway sizes have always been an approximation. For example, there has never been a ½-in. raceway! Measurements taken from the *NEC*® for a few types of raceways are shown in Table 1-1.

You can readily see that the cross sectional areas, critical when determining conductor fill, are different. It makes sense to refer to conduit, raceway, and tubing sizes as *trade sizes*. The *NEC*® in *90.9(C)(1)* states that "where the actual measured size of a product is not the same as the nominal size, trade size designators shall be used rather than dimensions." This edition of *Electrical Wiring—Residential* uses the term *trade size* when referring to conduits, raceways, and tubing. For example, a ½-in. EMT is referred to as trade size ½ EMT. EMT is also referred to in the trade as "thinwall."

The *NEC*® also uses the term *metric designator*. A trade size ½ EMT is shown as *metric designator*

TRADE SIZE	INSIDE DIAMETER (I.D.)
½ Electrical Metallic Tubing	0.622 in.
½ Electrical Nonmetallic Tubing	0.560 in.
½ Flexible Metal Conduit	0.635 in.
½ Rigid Metal Conduit	0.632 in.
½ Intermediate Metal Conduit	0.660 in.

Table 1-1 Comparison of trade size vs. actual inside diameters.

16 (½). A trade size 1 EMT is shown as *metric designator 27 (1)*. The numbers 16 and 27 are the metric designator values; the (½) and (1) are the trade sizes. The metric designator is the raceway's inside diameter—in rounded-off millimeters (mm). Table 1-2 shows some of the more common sizes of conduits, raceways, and tubing. A complete listing is found in *NEC® Table 300.1(C)*.

For ease in understanding, this text uses only the term *trade size* when referring to conduit and raceway sizes.

Conduit knockouts in boxes do not measure up to what we call them. Table 1-3 shows some examples.

Outlet boxes and device boxes use their nominal measurement as their *trade size*. For example, a 4 in. × 4 in. × 1½ in. does not have an internal cubic-inch volume of 4 in. × 4 in. × 1½ in. = 24 in.^{3} *Table 314.16(A)* shows this size box as having 21 cubic-in. volume. This table shows *trade sizes* in two columns—millimeters and inches.

In this text, a square outlet box is referred to as trade size 4 × 4 × 1½. Similarly, a single-gang device box would be referred to as a trade size 3 × 2 × 3 box.

Trade sizes for construction material will not change. A 2 × 4 is really a *name*, not an actual dimension. A 2 × 4 will keep its name forever. This is its *trade size*.

In this text, most measurements directly related to the *NEC®* are given in both inch-pound and metric units. In many instances, only the inch-pound units are shown. This is particularly true for the examples of raceway and box fill calculations, load calculations for square foot areas, and on the plans (drawings).

Because the *NEC®* rounded off most metric conversion values, a calculation using metrics results in a different answer when compared to the same calculation done using inch-pounds. For example, load calculations for a residence are based on 3 volt-amperes per square foot or 33 volt-amperes per square meter.

For a 40 ft × 50 ft dwelling: 3 VA × 40 ft × 50 ft = 6000 volt-amperes.

In metrics, using the rounded off values in the *NEC®*: 33 VA × 12 m × 15 m = 5940 volt-amperes.

The difference is small, but, nevertheless, there is a difference.

To show calculations in both units throughout this text would be very difficult to understand and would take up too much space. Calculations in either metrics or inch-pounds are in compliance with the *NEC®* *90.9(D)*. In *90.9(C)(3)* we find that metric units are not required if the industry practice is to use inch-pound units.

It is interesting to note that the examples in *Chapter 9* of the *NEC®* use inch-pound units, not metrics.

METRIC DESIGNATOR AND TRADE SIZE	
Metric Designator	**Trade Size**
12	⅜
16	½
21	¾
27	1
35	1¼
41	1½
53	2
63	2½
78	3

Table 1-2 Trade sizes of raceways and their metric designator identification.

TRADE SIZE KNOCKOUT	ACTUAL MEASUREMENT
½	⅞ in.
¾	1³⁄₃₂ in.
1	1⅜ in.

Table 1-3 Comparison of knockout trade size vs. actual measurement.

Guide to Metric Usage

The metric system is a "base-10" or "decimal" system in that values can be easily multiplied or divided by 10 or "powers of 10." The metric system as we know it today is known as the International System of Units (SI), derived from the French term "le Système International d'Unités."

In the metric system, the units increase or decrease in multiples of 10, 100, 1000, and so on. For instance, one megawatt (1,000,000 watts) is 1000 times greater than one kilowatt (1000 watts).

By assigning a name to a measurement, such as

a *watt*, the name becomes the unit. Adding a prefix to the unit, such as *kilo*, forms the new name *kilowatt*, meaning 1000 watts. Refer to Table 1-4 for prefixes used in the metric system.

The prefixes used most commonly are *centi*, *kilo*, and *milli*. Consider that the basic unit is a meter (one). Therefore, a centimeter is 0.01 meter, a kilometer is 1000 meters, and a millimeter is 0.001 meter.

Some common measurements of length and equivalents are shown in Table 1-5.

Electricians will find it useful to refer to the conversion factors and their abbreviations shown in Table 1-6.

Refer to the Appendix of this text for a comprehensive metric conversion table. The table includes information on how to "round off" numbers for practical use on the job.

NATIONALLY RECOGNIZED TESTING LABORATORIES (NTRL)

How does one know if a product is safe to use?

Manufacturers, consumers, regulatory authorities, and others recognize the importance of independent, "third-party" testing of products in an effort to reduce safety risks. Unless you have all

PREFIX	SYMBOL	MULTIPLIER	SCIENTIFIC NOTATION (POWERS OF TEN)	VALUE
tera	T	1 000 000 000 000	10^{12}	one trillion (1 000 000 000 000/1)
giga	G	1 000 000 000	10^{9}	one billion (1 000 000 000/1)
mega	M	1 000 000	10^{6}	one million (1 000 000/1)
kilo	k	1 000	10^{3}	one thousand (1 000/1)
hecto	h	100	10^{2}	one hundred (100/1)
deka	da	10	10^{1}	ten (10/1)
unit		1	—	one (1)
deci	d	0.1	10^{-1}	one tenth (1/10)
centi	c	0.01	10^{-2}	one hundredth (1/100)
milli	m	0.001	10^{-3}	one thousandth (1/1 000)
micro	µ	0.000 001	10^{-6}	one millionth (1/1 000 000)
nano	n	0.000 000 001	10^{-9}	one billionth (1/1 000 000 000)
pico	p	0.000 000 000 001	10^{-12}	one trillionth (1/1 000 000 000 000)

Table 1-4 Metric prefixes, symbols, multipliers, powers, and values.

one inch	=	2.54	centimeters
	=	25.4	millimeters
	=	0.025 4	meter
one foot	=	12	inches
	=	0.304 8	meter
	=	30.48	centimeters
	=	304.8	millimeters
one yard	=	3	feet
	=	36	inches
	=	0.914 4	meter
	=	914.4	millimeters
one meter	=	100	centimeters
	=	1 000	millimeters
	=	1.093	yards
	=	3.281	feet
	=	39.370	inches

Table 1-5 Some common measurements of length and their equivalents.

inches (in) × 0.025 4	=	meters (m)
inches (in) × 0.254	=	decimeters (dm)
inches (in) × 2.54	=	centimeters (cm)
centimeters (cm) × 0.393 7	=	inches (in)
inches (in) × 25.4	=	millimeters (mm)
millimeters (mm) × 0.039 37	=	inches (in)
feet (ft) × 0.304 8	=	meters (m)
meters (m) × 3.280 8	=	feet (ft)
square inches (in^2) × 6.452	=	square centimeters (cm^2)
square centimeters (cm^2) × 0.155	=	square inches (in^2)
square feet (ft^2) × 0.093	=	square meters (m^2)
square meters (m^2) × 10.764	=	square feet (ft^2)
square yards (yd^2) × 0.836 1	=	square meters (m^2)
square meters (m^2) × 1.196	=	square yards (yd^2)
kilometers (km) × 1 000	=	meters (m)
kilometers (km) × 0.621	=	miles (mi)
miles (mi) × 1.609	=	kilometers (km)

Table 1-6 Useful conversions and their abbreviations.

of the necessary test equipment and knowledge of how to properly test a product for safety, the surest way is to accept the findings of a third-party testing agency.

Nationally recognized testing laboratories (NRTL) have the knowledge, wherewithal, and test equipment to test and evaluate products for safety.

A NRTL will perform tests on a product based on a specific nationally recognized safety standard. After the product has been tested and found to comply with the safety standard, the product is considered to be free from reasonably foreseeable risk of fire, electric shock, and related hazards. The product is then "listed" and will have a listing marking (label).

As you work with electrical products, make sure the product has a listing marked on it from a NRTL. If the product is too small to have a listing mark on the product itself, then look for the mark on the carton the product came in.

The following laboratories do a considerable amount of testing and listing of electrical equipment:

Underwriters Laboratories, Inc. (UL®)

Underwriters Laboratories, Inc. (UL), founded in 1894, is a highly qualified, nationally recognized testing laboratory. UL develops standards, and performs tests to these standards. Most reputable manufacturers of electrical equipment submit their products to UL where the equipment is subjected to numerous tests. These tests determine if the product can perform safely under normal and abnormal conditions to meet published standards. After UL tests and evaluates a product, and determines that the product complies with the specific standard, the manufacturer is then permitted to *label* its product with the UL Mark (Figure 1-7). The products are then *listed* in a UL Directory.

UL Marking. The UL marking is required to be on the product! The UL marking will always consist of four elements—UL in a circle, the word "LISTED" in capital letters, the product identity, and a unique alphanumeric control or issue number. If the product is too small or has a shape or is made of a material that will not accept the UL Mark to have the UL marking on the product itself, the marking is permitted on the smallest unit carton or container that the product comes in. Marking on the carton or box is nice but does not ensure that the product is UL listed!

Figure 1-7 The Underwriters Laboratories mark.

The letters will *always* be staggered: **UL**. They will *not* be side by side: **UL**.

Counterfeit Products. Be on the lookout for counterfeit electrical products. These products have not been tested and listed by a recognized testing laboratory. They can present a real hazard to life and property. Most counterfeit products as of this writing supposedly come from China. Counterfeit electrical products might also be referred to as "black market products."

Look for unusual logos or wording. For example, the UL logo might be illustrated in an oval instead of a circle, or the UL logo might not be encircled with anything, or the wording might say *approved* instead of LISTED. UL doesn't approve anything! It tests the product. If the product meets UL standards, the product is then LISTED. The UL marking might be on the carton and not on the product. Marking on the carton or box is nice, but it can be considered advertising! Absence of the manufacturer's name should raise the caution flag.

Currently, there is federal legislation in progress that would make it a criminal offense to traffic in counterfeit products and counterfeit trademarks. The legislation makes it mandatory that the counterfeit products and any tools that make the products or markings be seized and destroyed.

To learn more about counterfeits, check out http://www.ul.com, then search on (type in) the word "counterfeit." Also, check out http://www.nema.org, then type in the word "counterfeit."

UL *does not approve* a product. Rather, UL *lists* those products that conform to a specific safety standard. A UL Listing Mark on a product means that representative samples of the product have been tested and evaluated to nationally recognized safety standards with regard to fire, electric shock, and related safety hazards.

Do not confuse a UL marking in a circle with the markings found on *recognized components*. Recognized components that have passed certain tests are marked with the letters *RU* printed backwards (Figure 1-8). By themselves, recognized components are not to be field-installed. They are intended for use in end-use products or systems that would ultimately be tested and listed, with the final assembly becoming a UL listed product. Some examples of recognized components are relays, ballasts, insulating materials, special switches, and so on.

Useful UL publications are:

Electrical Construction Equipment Directory (Green Book)

Electrical Appliance and Utilization Equipment Directory (Orange Book)

Guide Information for Electrical Equipment Directory (White Book)

It is extremely useful for an electrician, an electrical contractor, and/or an electrical inspector to refer to these directories when looking for specific requirements, permitted uses, limitations, and others for a certain product.

Many times the answer to a product-related question that cannot be found in the *NEC*® can be found in one of these directories.

Figure 1-8 The *recognized components* mark.

The Green and Orange Directories provide technical information about a particular product, and they list the names and addresses of manufacturers and the manufacturers' identification numbers. The White Book provides technical information regarding a product but does not show manufacturers' names and addresses.

The best companion to the *NEC*® is probably the UL White Book (Figure 1–9).

These directories can be obtained by contacting:

Underwriters Laboratories, Inc.
333 Pfingsten Road
Northbrook, Illinois 60062-2096
Phone: 847-272-8800
http://www.ul.com

Underwriters Laboratories, Inc. and the Canadian Standards Association (CSA) have worked out an agreement whereby either agency can test, evaluate, and list equipment for the other agency. For example, UL might test and list an air conditioner unit to the requirements of UL Standard 1995 (Heat-

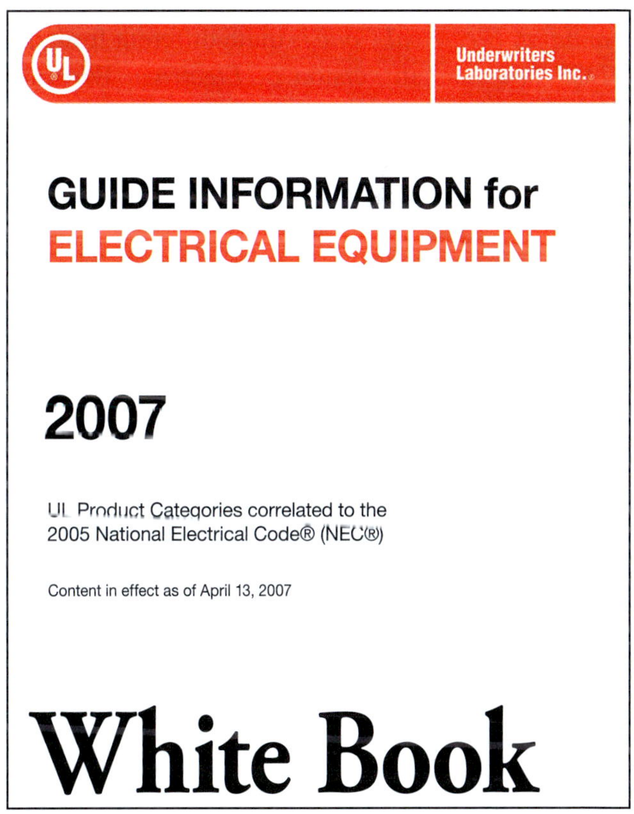

Figure 1-9 The Underwriters Laboratories White Book.

ing and Cooling Equipment) because the Canadian Standard C22.2 No. 236-M90 is a mirror image of UL Standard 1995. One by one, the UL and CSA Standards are becoming similar.

When UL tests and lists products that comply to the requirements of a particular CSA standard, the UL logo shown in Figure 1-10 will appear with a "C" outside of and to the left of the circle.

This means the product has been tested and evaluated for compliance *only* with Canadian requirements.

This harmonization of Codes and Standards is going on in the world today as a result of the North American Free Trade Act (NAFTA). Discussions are also going on with Mexico. When all of this is finalized, electrical equipment standards may be the same in the United States, Canada, and Mexico.

Figure 1-10 The mark indicating that UL has tested and listed a product for compliance *only* with Canadian requirements.

CSA International CSA INTERNATIONAL

CSA International is the Canadian counterpart of Underwriters Laboratories, Inc. in the United States. CSA International is the source of the *Canadian Electrical Code (CEC)* and of the Canadian Standards for the testing, evaluation, and listing of electrical equipment in Canada. The *Canadian Electrical Code* is quite different from the *NEC*.® A Canadian version of *Electrical Wiring—Residential* is available in Canada.

The *Canadian Electrical Code* and CSA standards can be obtained by contacting:

CSA International
178 Rexdale Boulevard
Toronto, Ontario, CANADA
M9W 1R3
Phone: 416-747-4044
800-463-6727
Fax: 416-747-2510
http://www.csa-international.org

Intertek Testing Services ITS

ITS is a nationally recognized testing laboratory. Its ETC SEMKO division provides testing, evaluation, labeling, listing, and follow-up service for the safety testing of electrical products. This is done in conformance to nationally recognized safety standards.

Information can be obtained by contacting:

Intertek Testing Services, NA, Inc.
ETL SEMKO
3933 US Route 11
Cortland, NY 13045
Phone: 607-753-6711
http://www.etlsemko.com

National Electrical Manufacturers Association NEMA

The National Electrical Manufacturers Association (NEMA) represents nearly 600 manufacturers of electrical products. NEMA develops electrical equipment standards, which, in many instances, are very similar to UL and other consensus standards. NEMA has representatives on the CMPs for the *NEC*.® Additional information can be obtained by contacting:

National Electrical Manufacturers Association
1300 North 17th Street, Suite 1847
Rosslyn, VA 22209
Phone: 703-841-3200
http://www.nema.org

World Wide Web Sites

A comprehensive list of World Wide Web sites for manufacturers, organizations, and inspection and testing agencies is provided in the back of this text.

REVIEW

Note: Refer to the *NEC*® or the plans in the back of this text where necessary.

1. What is the purpose of specifications? ______________________________

2. Refer to the specifications in the back of this text following Chapter 32.
   a. What electrical codes must be conformed to?
   ____
   b. What is the wiring method to be used in the workshop?
   ____
   c. What size conductors are to be used for:
   The lighting branch circuits: ____________ AWG
   The small-appliance branch circuits: ____________ AWG
   d. What section of the specifications tells us the size of the service entrance to be installed for this residence?
   ____

3. What is done to prevent a plan from becoming confusing because of too much detail?
   ____

4. Name three requirements contained in the specifications regarding material.
   a. ____________ c. ____________
   b. ____________

5. The specifications state that all work shall be done ______________________________.

6. What phrase is used when a substitution is permitted for a specific item? ______________________________

7. What is the purpose of an electrical symbol? ______________________________

8. What is a notation? ______________________________

9. Where are notations found? ______________________________

10. List at least twelve electrical notations found on the plans for this residence. Refer to the plans at the back of the text. ______

11. What three parties must be satisfied with the completed electrical installation?
    a. ______ b. ______ c. ______

12. What code sets standards for electrical installation work? ______

13. What authority enforces the requirements set by the *NEC*®? ______

14. Does the *NEC*® provide minimum or maximum standards? ______

15. What do the letters *UL* signify? ______

16. What section of the *NEC*® states that all listed or labeled equipment shall be installed or used in accordance with any instructions included in the listing or labeling? ______

17. When the word "shall" appears in a *NEC*® reference, it means that it (must)(may) be done. (Underline the correct word.)

18. What is the purpose of the *NEC*®? ______

19. Does compliance with the *NEC*® always result in an electrical installation that is adequate, safe, and efficient? Why? ______

20. Name two nationally recognized testing laboratories. ______

21. a. Do Underwriters Laboratories and the other recognized testing laboratories "approve" products? ______

b. What do these testing laboratories do? ______________________________________

____

____

____

22. a. Has the *NEC*® been officially adopted by the community in which you live? _____
    b. By the state in which you live? ______________________________________
    c. If your answer is YES to a. or b., are there amendments to the *NEC*®? __________
    d. If your answer is YES to c., list some of the more important amendments.

____

____

____

____

23. Does the *NEC*® make suggestions about how to wire a house that will be occupied by handicapped persons? ______________________________________

24. A junction box on a piece of European equipment is marked 200 cm^3. Convert this to cubic inches. ______________________________________

____

25. Convert 4500 watts to Btu/hour. ______________________________________

____

26. You will learn in Chapter 3 that residential lighting loads are based on 3 volt-amperes per ft^2 (33 volt-amperes per m^2). Determine the minimum lighting load required for an area of 186 m^2. Do calculations for both feet squared and meters squared so you can see the difference in answers. To convert meters squared to feet squared, refer to Table 1-6.

____

____

____

____

SAFETY RELATED QUESTIONS

27. What federal organization dictates requirements for work-related safety issues? Circle the correct answer.
    a. *NEC*®
    b. OSHA
    c. IAEI

28. What can you do to reduce or eliminate the possibility of receiving an electric shock when working on electrical circuits? Circle the correct answer.
    a. Turn off the power on the circuit you are working on.
    b. Turn off the power on the circuit you are working on, tag it, and lock the disconnect in the "OFF" position.
    c. Turn off the power on the circuit you are working on, then tell everyone else working with you not to turn the power back on.

29. What is the *NEC*® definition of a qualified person? ______

30. Are you a *qualified person*? Explain your answer. ______

31. Are low-voltage systems totally safe? Explain. ______

32. What NFPA standard specifically covers safety in the workplace? ______

33. What do the letters PPE stand for? ______

34. Explain briefly what an "arc flash" is. ______

35. Where might you obtain information about on-the-job safety and safety training? ______

36. a. Is it a safe practice to use a step ladder in which the spreaders have not been fully locked into position? ______
    b. If the ladder collapses, who is at fault? ______

CHAPTER 2

Electrical Symbols and Outlets

OBJECTIVES

After studying this chapter, you should be able to

- **identify and explain the electrical outlet symbols used in the plans of the single-family dwelling.**
- **discuss the types of outlets, boxes, luminaires, and switches used in the residence.**
- **explain the methods of mounting the various electrical devices used in the residence.**
- **understand the preferred way to position receptacles in wall boxes.**
- **understand issues involved in remodel work.**
- **understand how to determine the maximum number of conductors permitted in a given size box.**
- **understand the concept of fire-resistance rating of walls and ceilings.**

ELECTRICAL SYMBOLS

Electrical symbols used on an architectural plan show the location and type of electrical device required. A typical electrical installation as taken from a plan is shown in Figure 2-1.

The *NEC*® has many words unique to the electrical trade. For example:

A **device** is: *A unit of an electrical system that carries or controls electric energy as its principle function.*

An **outlet** is: *A point on the wiring system at which current is taken to supply utilization equipment.*

A **receptacle** is: *A contact device installed at the outlet for the connection of an attachment plug.*

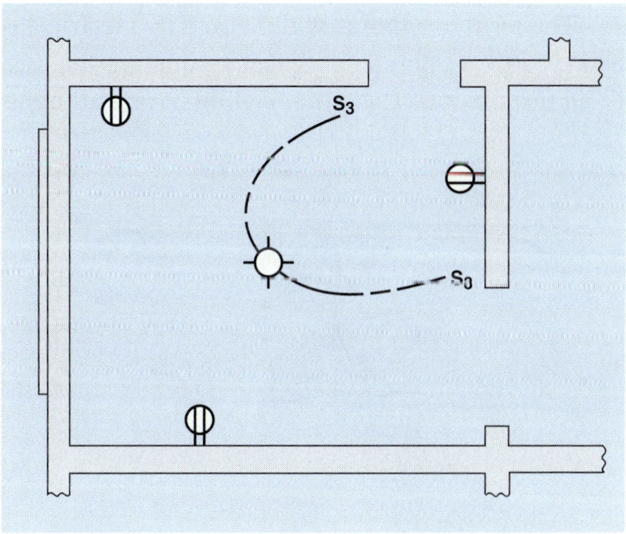

Figure 2-1 Use of electrical symbols and notations on a floor plan.

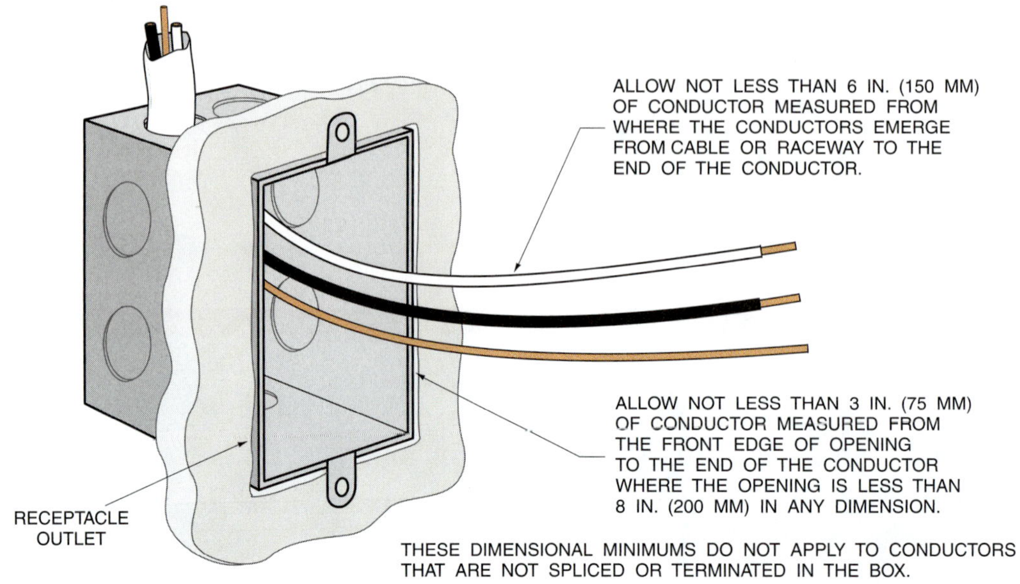

Figure 2-2 Where a receptacle is connected to the branch-circuit wires, the outlet is called a *receptacle outlet. NEC® 300.14* states the minimum length of conductors at an outlet, junction, or switch point for splices or the connection of luminaires or devices. Leaving the conductors too long can cause crowding of the wires in the box, leading to possible short circuits and/or ground faults.

A **receptacle outlet** is: *An outlet where one or more receptacles are installed,* Figure 2-2.

►A **lighting outlet** is: *An outlet intended for the direct connection of a lampholder or luminaire.* See Figure 2-3.◄

By definition, toggle switches and receptacles are devices because they carry current but do not consume power.

The term *opening* is widely used by electricians and electrical contractors when estimating the cost of an installation. The term *opening* covers all lighting outlets, receptacle outlets, junction boxes, switches, etc. The electrician and/or electrical contractor will estimate a job at "X dollars per lighting outlet," "X dollars per switch," "X dollars per receptacle outlet," and so on. These estimates will include the time and material needed to complete the job. Each type of electrical *opening* is represented on the electrical plans as a symbol. The electrical openings in Figure 2-1 are shown by the symbols in Figure 2-4.

ANSI recently published a totally revised standard entitled *Symbols for Electrical Construction Drawings*. This was the first revision in over 25 years. Figure 2-5, Figure 2-6, Figure 2-7, Figure 2-8, Figure 2-9, and Figure 2-10 show the electrical symbols most commonly found on architectural and

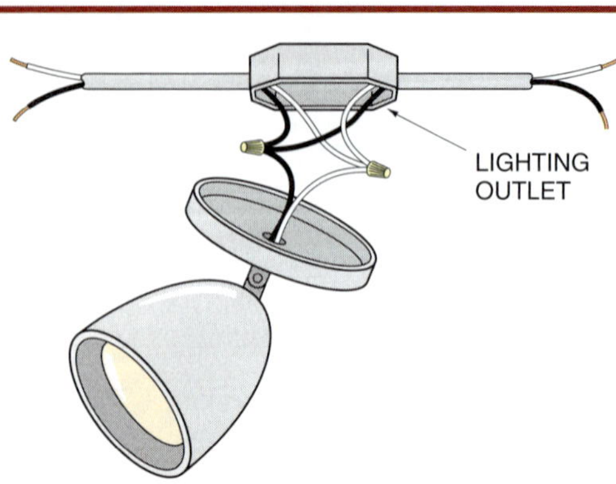

Figure 2-3 When a luminaire (lighting fixture) is connected to the branch-circuit wires, the outlet is called a *lighting outlet.*

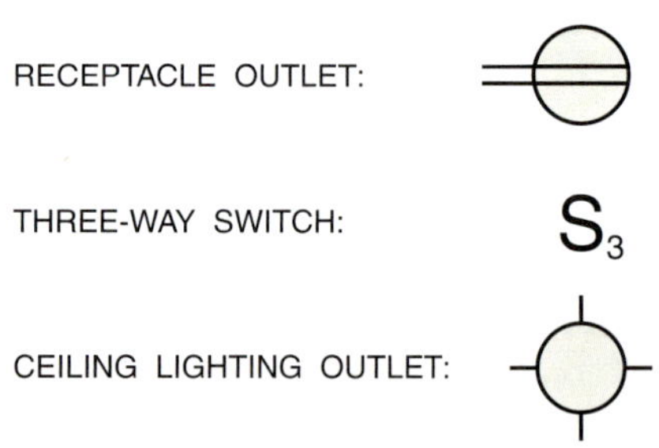

Figure 2-4 Some common electrical symbols.

OUTLETS	CEILING	WALL
SURFACE-MOUNTED INCANDESCENT	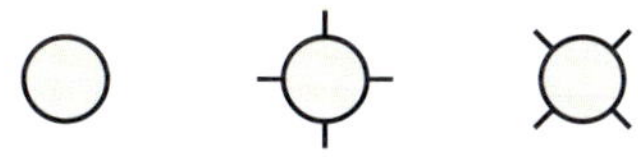	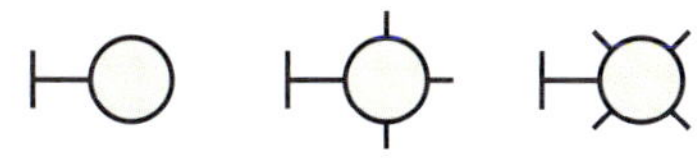
LAMPHOLDER WITH PULL SWITCH		
RECESSED INCANDESCENT		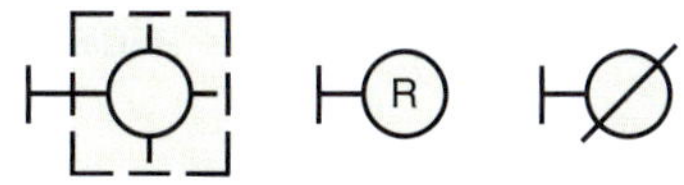
SURFACE-MOUNTED FLUORESCENT	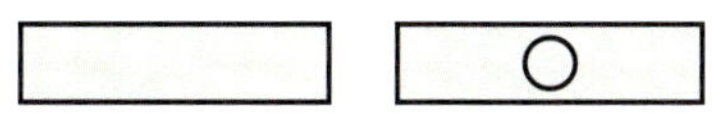	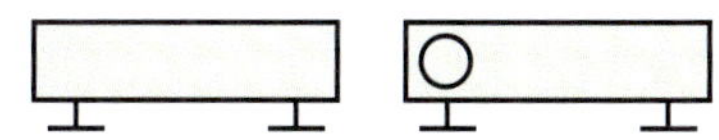
RECESSED FLUORESCENT		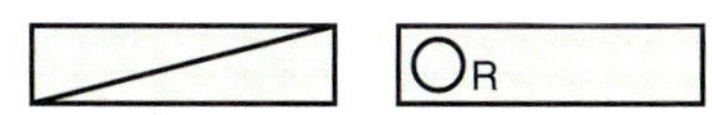
SURFACE OR PENDANT CONTINUOUS ROW FLUORESCENT	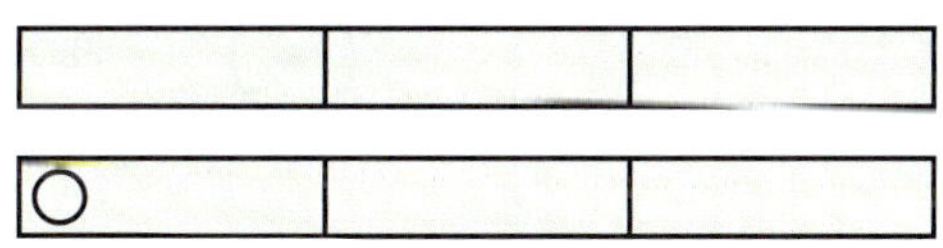	
RECESSED CONTINUOUS ROW FLUORESCENT	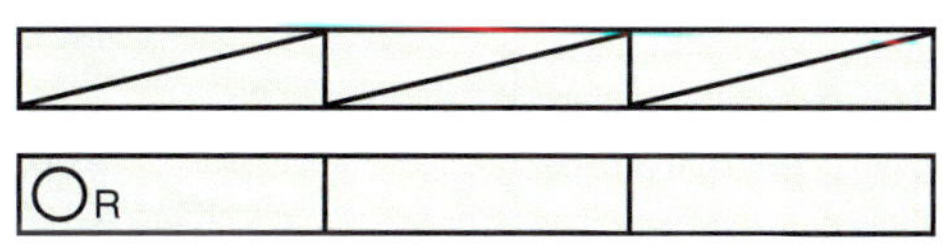	
BARE LAMP FLUORESCENT STRIP		
SURFACE OR PENDANT EXIT		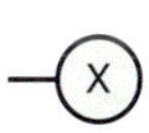
RECESSED CEILING EXIT		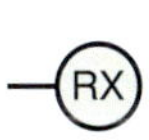
BLANKED OUTLET		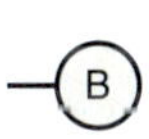
OUTLET CONTROLLED BY LOW-VOLTAGE SWITCHING WHEN RELAY IS INSTALLED IN OUTLET BOX		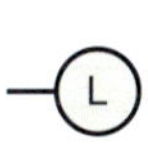
JUNCTION BOX		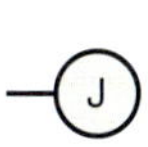

Figure 2-5 Lighting outlet symbols.

RECEPTACLE OUTLETS			
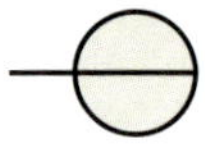	SINGLE RECEPTACLE OUTLET	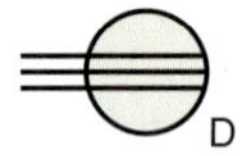	CLOTHES DRYER OUTLET
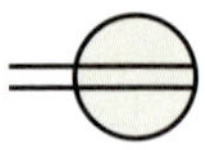	DUPLEX RECEPTACLE OUTLET	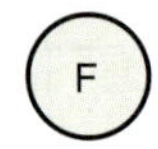	FAN OUTLET
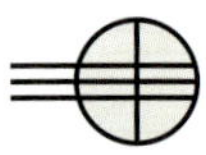	TRIPLEX RECEPTACLE OUTLET	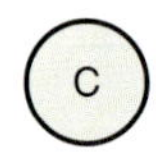	CLOCK OUTLET
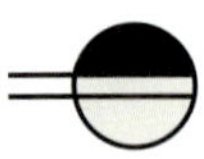	DUPLEX RECEPTACLE OUTLET, SPLIT-CIRCUIT	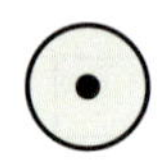	FLOOR OUTLET
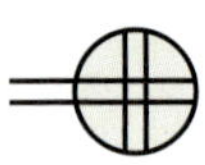	DOUBLE DUPLEX RECEPTACLE (QUADPLEX)	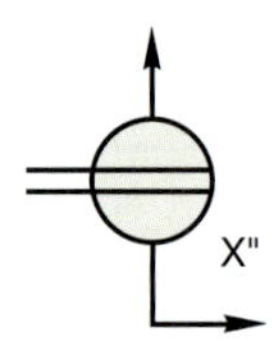	MULTIOUTLET ASSEMBLY; ARROW SHOWS LIMIT OF INSTALLATION. APPROPRIATE SYMBOL INDICATES TYPE OF OUTLET. SPACING OF OUTLETS INDICATED BY "X" INCHES.
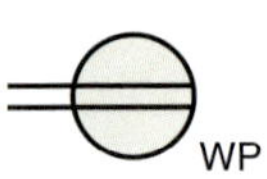	WEATHERPROOF RECEPTACLE OUTLET	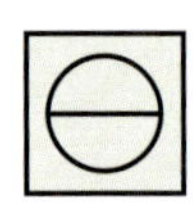	FLOOR SINGLE RECEPTACLE OUTLET
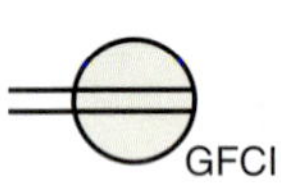	GROUND-FAULT CIRCUIT INTERRUPTER RECEPTACLE OUTLET	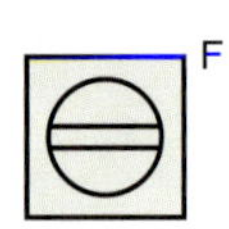	FLOOR DUPLEX RECEPTACLE OUTLET
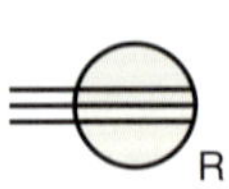	RANGE OUTLET		FLOOR SPECIAL-PURPOSE OUTLET
	SPECIAL-PURPOSE OUTLET (SUBSCRIPT LETTERS INDICATE SPECIAL VARIATIONS: DW = DISHWASHER. ALSO a, b, c, d, ETC. ARE LETTERS KEYED TO EXPLANATION ON DRAWINGS OR IN SPECIFICATIONS).		

Figure 2-6 Receptacle outlet symbols.

SWITCH SYMBOLS

S	SINGLE-POLE SWITCH
S_2	DOUBLE-POLE SWITCH
S_3	THREE-WAY SWITCH
S_4	FOUR-WAY SWITCH
S_D	DOOR SWITCH
S_{DS}	DIMMER SWITCH
S_G	GLOW SWITCH TOGGLE— GLOWS IN OFF POSITION
S_K	KEY-OPERATED SWITCH
S_{KP}	KEY SWITCH WITH PILOT LIGHT
S_{LV}	LOW-VOLTAGE SWITCH
S_{LM}	LOW VOLTAGE MASTER SWITCH
S_{MC}	MOMENTARY-CONTACT SWITCH
M	OCCUPANCY SENSOR—WALL-MOUNTED WITH "OFF-AUTO" OVERRIDE SWITCH
M P	OCCUPANCY SENSOR—CEILING-MOUNTED "P" INDICATES MULTIPLE SWITCHES WIRE-IN PARALLEL
S_P	SWITCH WITH PILOT LIGHT ON WHEN SWITCH IS ON
S_T	TIMER SWITCH
S_R	VARIABLE-SPEED SWITCH
S_{WP}	WEATHERPROOF SWITCH

Figure 2-7 Switch symbols.

CIRCUITING

A 1-2	HOME RUN TO PANEL. NUMBER OF ARROWS INDICATES NUMBER OF CIRCUITS. LETTERS AND NUMBERS INDICATE CIRCUIT(S). FULL SLASHES INDICATE UNGROUNDED "HOT" (OR SWITCH LEG) CIRCUIT CONDUCTORS. HALF SLASHES INDICATE GROUNDED NEUTRAL CIRCUIT CONDUCTOR(S). NO SLASHES INDICATE ONE "HOT" AND ONE NEUTRAL CONDUCTOR.
	BRANCH CIRCUIT. FULL SLASHES INDICATE UNGROUNDED "HOT" (OR SWITCH LEG) CIRCUIT CONDUCTORS. HALF SLASHES INDICATE GROUNDED NEUTRAL CIRCUIT CONDUCTOR(S). NO SLASHES INDICATE ONE "HOT" AND ONE NEUTRAL CONDUCTOR. DOTS INDICATE EQUIPMENT GROUNDING CONDUCTORS.
	WIRING CONCEALED IN CONSTRUCTION IN FINISHED AREAS, EXPOSED IN UNFINISHED AREAS
	CONDUIT CONCEALED IN OR UNDER FLOOR SLAB
	CONDUIT TURNING UP
	CONDUIT TURNING DOWN
CO	CONDUIT ONLY (EMPTY)
	SWITCH LEG; CONNECTS SWITCHED OUTLETS WITH CONTROL POINTS

Figure 2-8 Circuiting symbols.

electrical plans. Because some items may have more than one symbol, it is important to check the plans and specifications of any job you are working on for a symbol schedule to make sure you have interpreted the symbols correctly.

The dashed lines in Figure 2-1 run from the outlet to the switch or switches that control the outlet. These lines are usually curved so that they cannot be mistaken for invisible edge lines. Outlets shown on the plan without curved dashed lines are independent outlets and have no switch control.

A study of the plans for the single-family dwelling shows that many different electrical symbols are used to represent the electrical devices and equipment used in the building.

Be very careful when interpreting symbols because of the similarity between them, Figure 2-11.

When preparing electrical plans for commercial and industrial buildings, most architects and electrical engineers use symbols approved by ANSI wherever possible. For residential projects, usually only the basic symbols are used, showing the location of

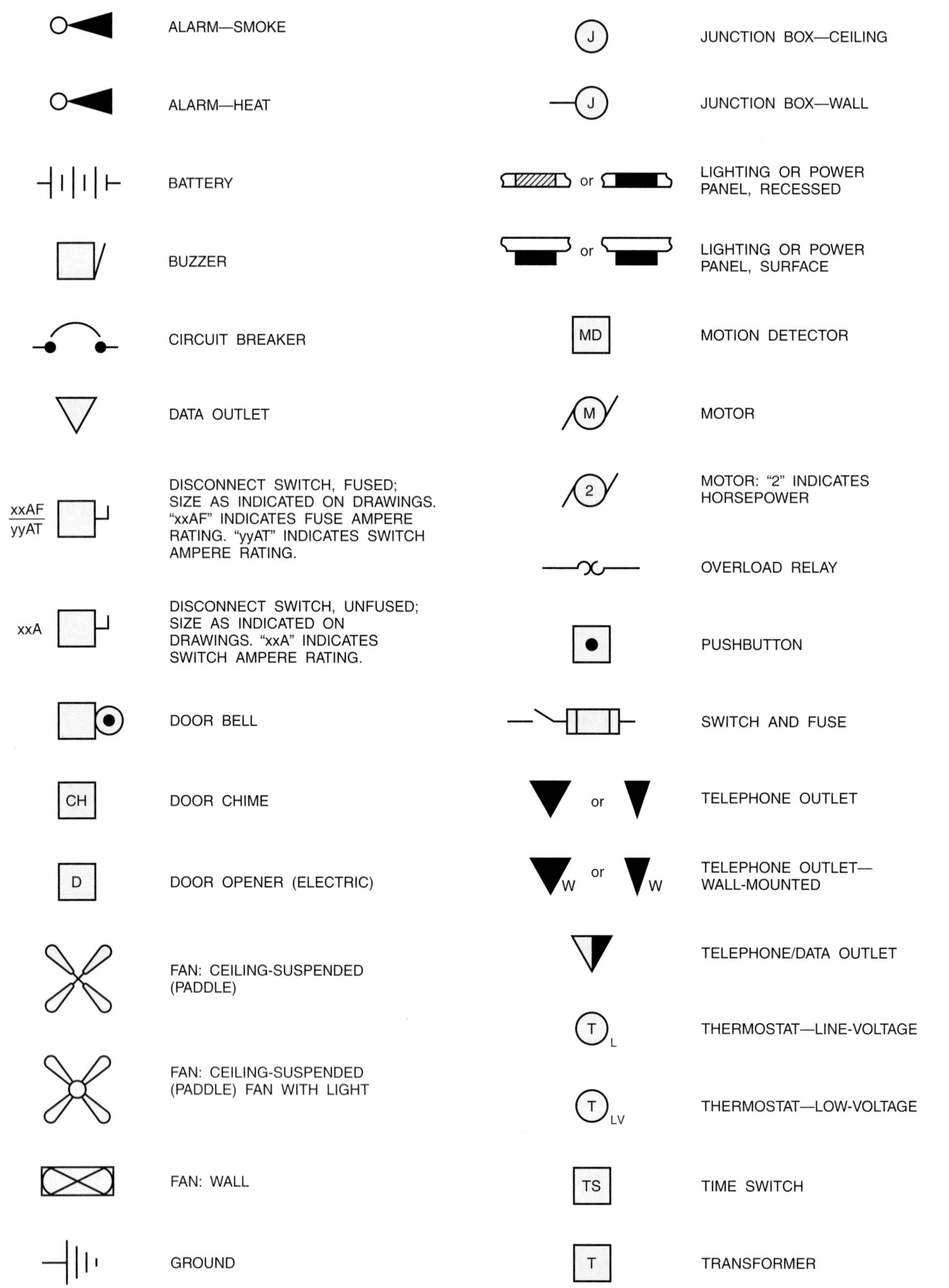

Figure 2-9 Miscellaneous symbols.

SYMBOL	NOTATION
1	PLUGMOLD ENTIRE LENGTH OF WORKBENCH. OUTLETS 18 IN. (457 mm) O.C. INSTALL 48 IN. (1.2 m) TO CENTER FROM FLOOR. GFCI PROTECTED.
2	TRACK LIGHTING. PROVIDE 5 LAMPHOLDERS.
3	TWO 40-WATT RAPID START FLUORESCENT LAMPS IN VALANCE. CONTROL WITH DIMMER SWITCH.

Figure 2-10 Example of how certain notations might be added to a symbol when a symbol itself does not fully explain its meaning. The architect or engineer has a choice of explaining fully the meaning directly on the plan if there is sufficient room; if insufficient room, then a notation could be used.

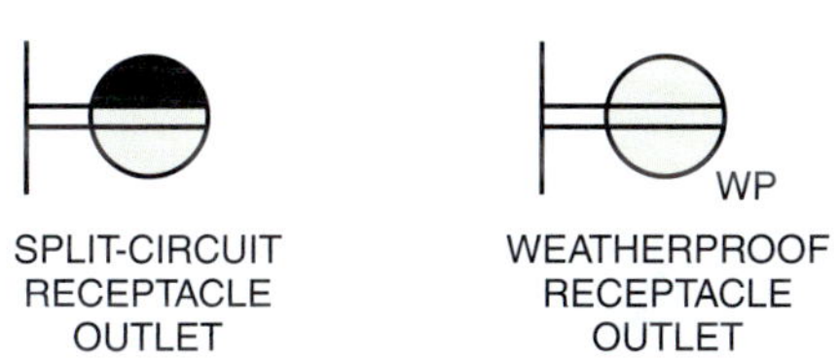

Figure 2-11 Variations in significance of outlet symbols.

receptacles, switches, appliances, and luminaires. Specific circuitry as shown in Figure 2-8 is generally left up to the electrician.

Later in this text, you will find suggested *cable layouts* for all of the branch circuits in this residence. These *cable layouts* show the required number of conductors between outlets and switches.

LUMINAIRES AND OUTLETS

The term *luminaire* is found in the *NEC*.® In the United States, we have used the term *lighting fixture* for years. But since the *NEC*® is an international code, we must become familiar with some new terms such as "luminaire." By definition, a *luminaire* is: ▶*A complete lighting unit consisting of a light source such as a lamp or lamps, together with the parts designed to position the light source and connect it to the power supply. It may also include parts to protect the light source, ballast, or distribute the light. A lampholder itself is not a luminaire.*◀

Simply stated for our purposes, a luminaire and a lighting fixture are one and the same.

The location of lighting outlets is determined by the amount and type of illumination required to provide the desired lighting effects. It is not the intent of this text to describe how proper and adequate lighting is determined. Rather, the text covers the proper methods of installing the circuits for such lighting.

Luminaire manufacturers publish catalogs that provide a tremendous amount of information regarding recommendations for residential lighting. These publications are available at electrical distributors, lighting showrooms, and home centers.

Architects often include a specific amount of money in the specifications, referred to as a *fixture allowance*. Electrical contractors include this amount in their bid, and the choice of luminaires is then left to the homeowners. If the owner selects luminaires whose total cost exceeds the fixture allowance, the owner is expected to pay the difference between the actual cost and the fixture allowance. If the luminaires are not selected before the rough-in stage of wiring the house, an electrician will usually install outlet boxes such as those illustrated in Figure 2-20.

How luminaires are handled varies by job and geographical area you are working in. Sometimes the recessed luminaire housings are included in the base bid, and the trims are included in the fixture allowance. Always read the specifications and study the plans carefully for important symbols and notations that might reference luminaires.

Surface-mounted luminaires are secured to an outlet box, a raised plaster (adapter) ring, or a device box using the mounting hardware (straps and No. 8-32 or No. 6-32 screws) furnished with the luminaire. Some outlet box/bar hanger assemblies have a fixture stud on which to fasten the luminaire. See Figure 2-12.

Symbols Used to Represent Lighting Outlets and Switches

Typical lighting outlet symbols are shown in Figure 2-12. Typical switch symbols are shown in Figure 2-13.

SYMBOL	TYPE OF LUMINAIRE OR OUTLET	BOXES THAT MAY BE USED
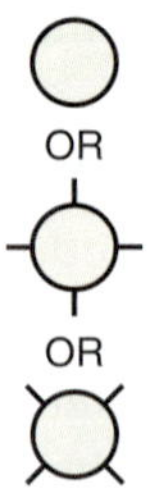 CEILING LIGHTING OUTLET	1.  SURFACE-MOUNTED LUMINAIRE	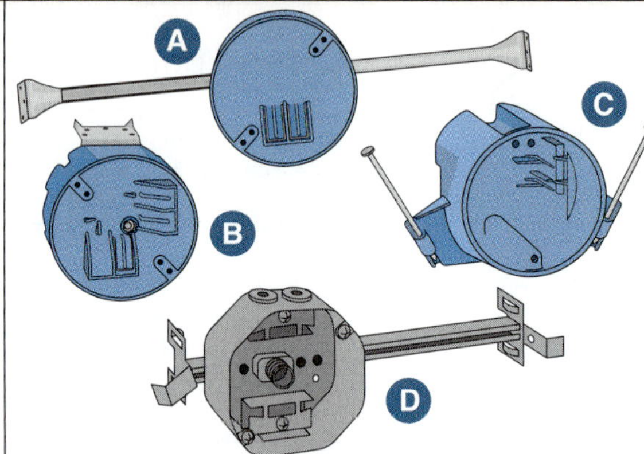 (A) ADJUSTABLE BRACKET WITH OUTLET BOX. (B) OUTLET BOX WITH BRACKET FOR JOIST MOUNTING. (C) OUTLET BOX WITH CAPTIVE NAILS/BRACKET FOR JOIST MOUNTING. (D) ADJUSTABLE OFFSET BAR HANGER WITH OUTLET BOX. NOTE LUMINAIRE STUD IN BOX. BOXES ARE "LISTED" FOR LUMINAIRE SUPPORT.
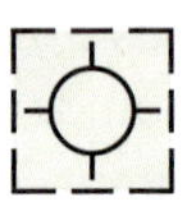 RECESSED CEILING LIGHTING OUTLET	2. 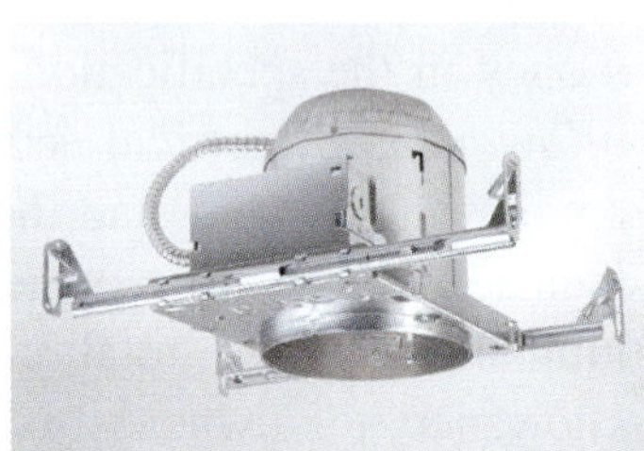 RECESSED LUMINAIRE	CABLE TERMINATES IN BOX THAT IS FURNISHED WITH LUMINAIRE. SPECIAL CODE RULES GOVERNING THE INSTALLATION ARE FOUND IN *410.110* THROUGH *410.122* OF THE *NATIONAL ELECTRICAL CODE®*. SEE CHAPTER 7.
 WALL LIGHTING OUTLET	3.  WALL-MOUNTED LUMINAIRE ALSO CALLED A "SCONCE"	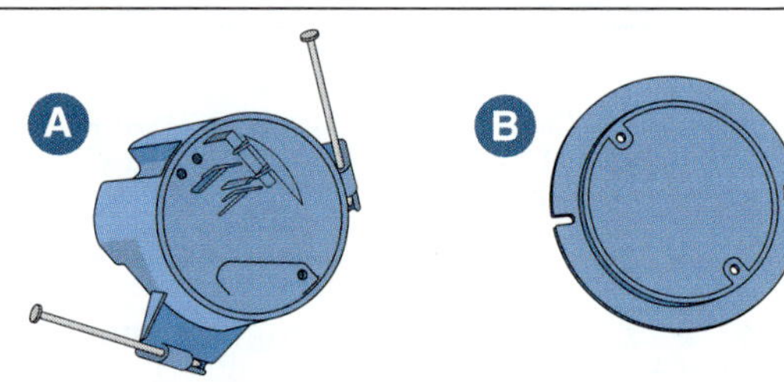 (A) OUTLET BOX WITH CAPTIVE NAILS/BRACKET FOR STUD MOUNTING. (B) ADAPTER RING FOR OUTLET BOX. BOX "LISTED" FOR LUMINAIRE SUPPORT.
 DUPLEX RECEPTACLE OUTLET  TRIPLEX RECEPTACLE OUTLET	4. 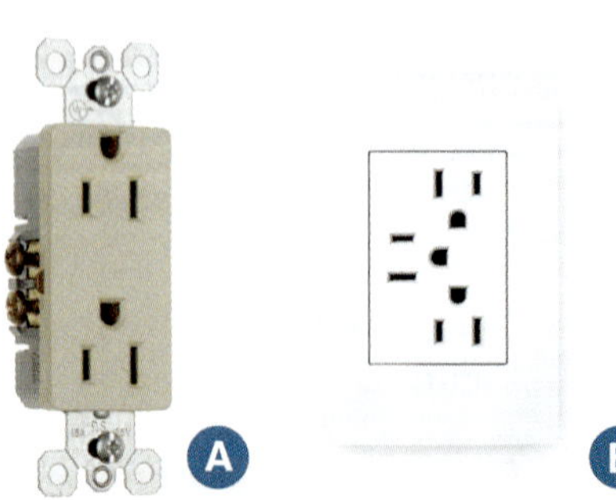	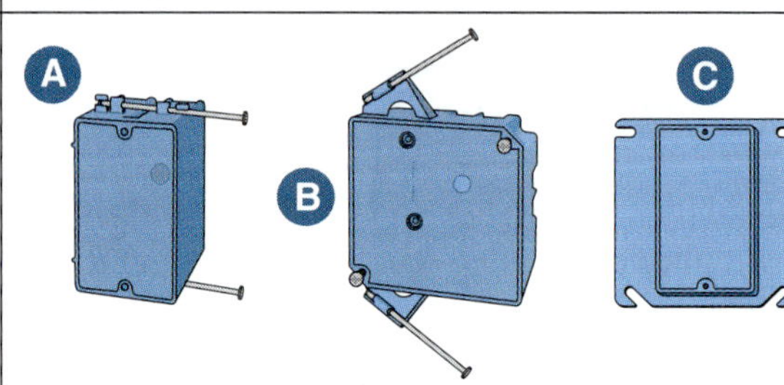 (A) SINGLE-GANG SWITCH (DEVICE) BOX. (B) 4-IN. SQUARE BOX WITH CAPTIVE NAILS FOR STUD MOUNTING. (C) 4-IN. SQUARE SINGLE-GANG RAISED ADAPTER RING.

Figure 2-12 Typical electrical symbols, items they represent, and boxes that could be used. ***Photos courtesy of Progress Lighting (1, 3), Halo/Cooper Lighting (2), Leviton Manufacturing Company (4A & 4B).***

SYMBOL	FLUSH TOGGLE SWITCH	OPERATION	CONNECTIONS
S SINGLE-POLE	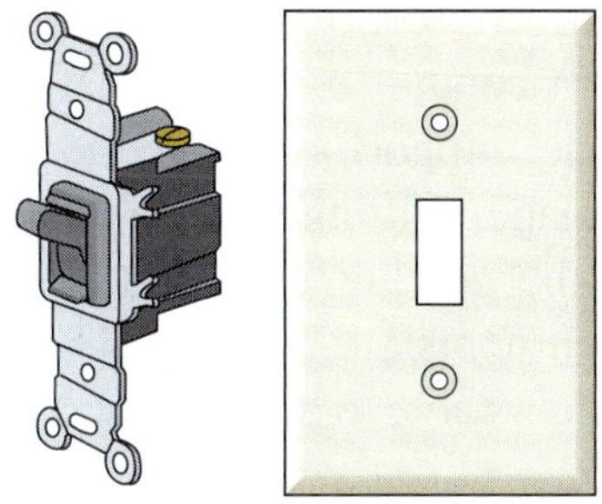	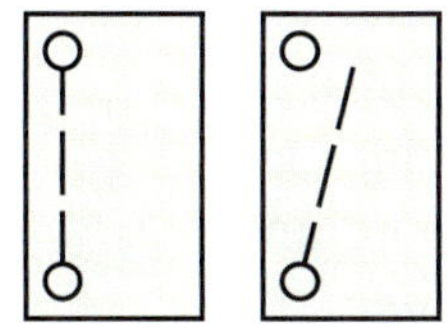 ON OFF	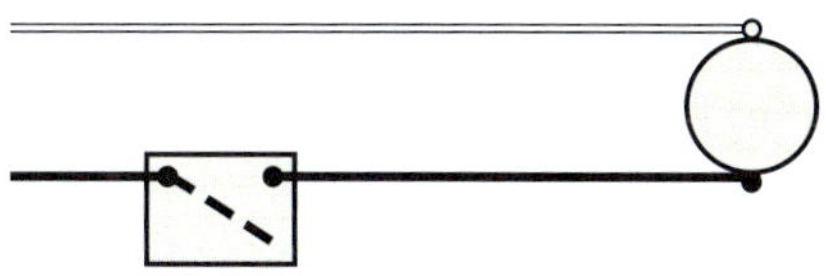
S_2 DOUBLE-POLE	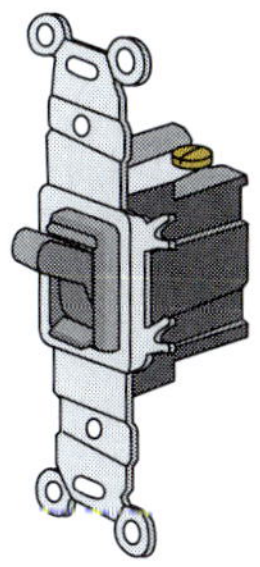	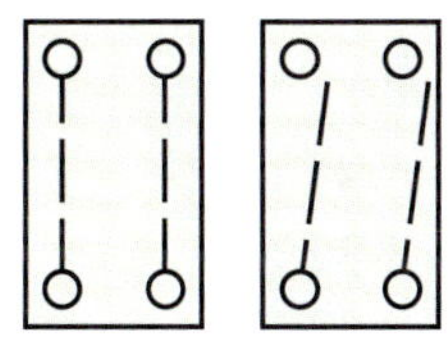 ON OFF	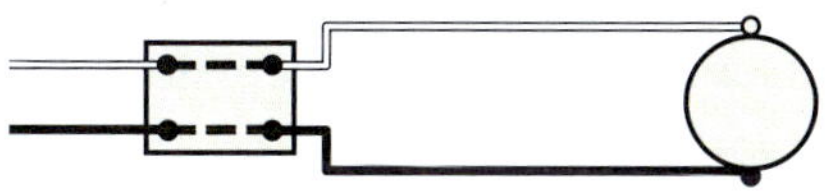
S_3 THREE-WAY	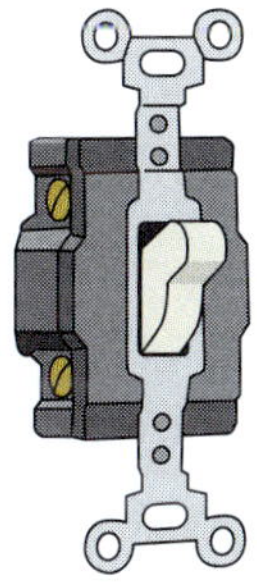	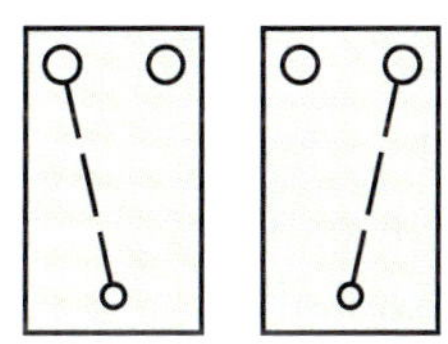 POSITION 1 POSITION 2	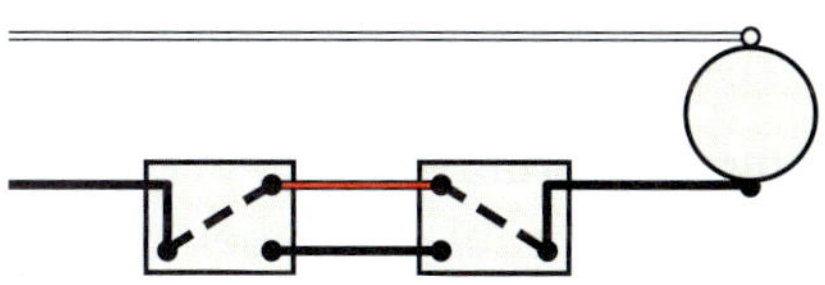
S_4 FOUR-WAY	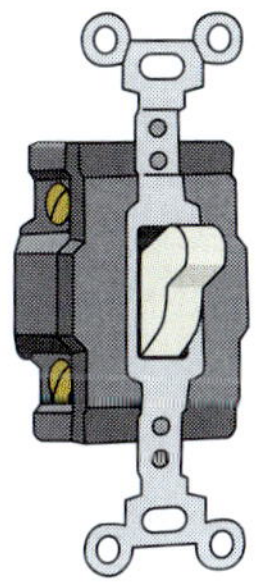	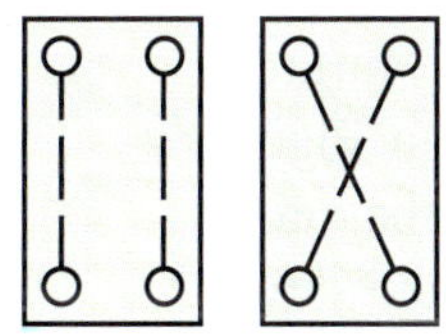 1 2	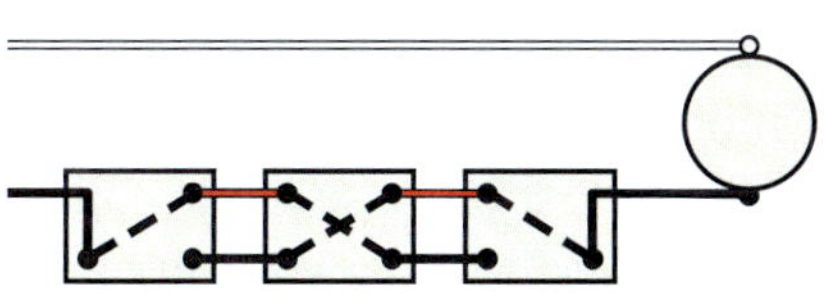
S_p SWITCH AND PILOT LIGHT	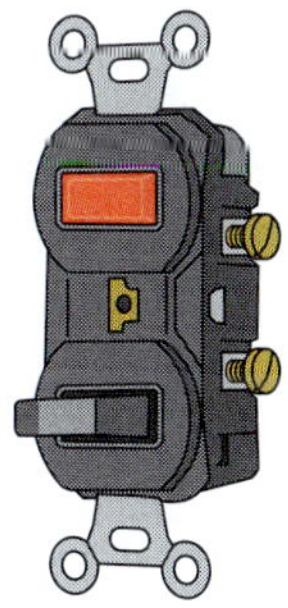	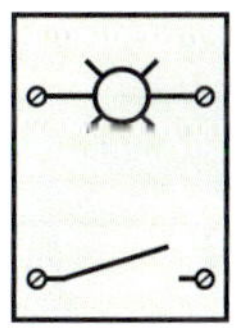 FOR CONTROLLING LIGHTS FROM ONE POINT WITH PILOT LIGHT INDICATION	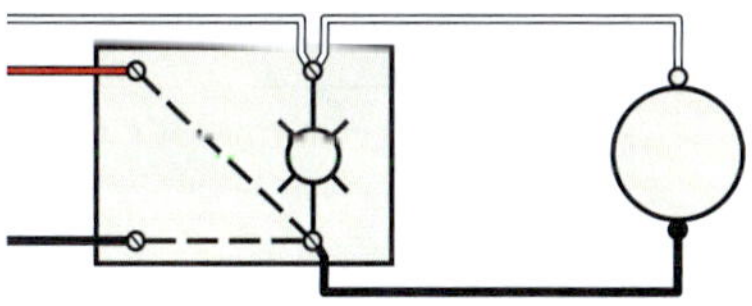 ALSO AVAILABLE IN THREE-WAY TYPE OF CONTROLLING LIGHT FROM TWO POINTS WITH PILOT LIGHT INDICATION

Figure 2-13 Standard switches and symbols.

OUTLET, DEVICE, AND JUNCTION BOXES

Article 314 contains much detail about outlet boxes, device boxes, pull boxes, junction boxes, and conduit bodies (LB, LR, LL, C, etc.), all of which are used to provide the necessary space for making electrical connections, contain wiring, and support luminaires, and so on. *Article 314* is quite lengthy. For the moment, we will focus on some of the basic *Code* requirements for outlet boxes, device boxes, and junction boxes. Additional *Code* requirements are covered on an "as needed" basis in this chapter and in later chapters.

Screw sizes for typical electrical boxes are:

Device boxes and faceplates	No. 6-32
Outlet boxes	No. 8-32
Ceiling fan boxes (two sets of holes)	No. 10-32 and No. 8-32

Some Basic *Code* Requirements

- *NEC® 300.11* and *314.23:* Boxes must be securely mounted and fastened in place.
- *NEC® 300.15*: Where conduit, electrical-metallic tubing, nonmetallic-sheathed cable, Type AC cable, or other cables are installed, a box or conduit body must be installed at each conductor splice connection point, outlet, switch point, junction point, or pull point. This requirement is illustrated in Figure 2-14. Exceptions to this are found in *300.15(A)* through *(M)*. Typical exceptions are surface-mounted strip luminaires, as shown in Figure 10-2. Most of these have a back plate that has a trade size ½ knockout intended for the direct entry of a cable without the need of a box behind the luminaire.
- *NEC® 300.15(C):* Where cables enter or exit from conduit or tubing that is used to provide cable support or protection against physical damage, a fitting shall be provided on the end(s) of the conduit or tubing to protect the cable from abrasion. Figure 2-15 shows a transition from a cable to a raceway.
- *NEC® 314.16:* Boxes must be large enough for all of the enclosed conductors and wiring devices. Installing boxes too small for the number of conductors, wiring devices, luminaire studs, and splices is a real problem! This topic is covered in detail later.
- *NEC® 314.17(C):* The exception allows multiple cables to be run through a single knockout opening in a nonmetallic box. This permission is not given for metallic boxes. See Figure 2-16.
- *NEC® 314.20:* In walls or ceilings where the surface material is noncombustible, boxes, plaster rings, domed covers, extension rings, or listed extenders shall be mounted so that they will be set back not more than ¼ in. (6 mm). In walls or ceilings where the surface material is combustible, boxes, plaster rings, domed covers, extension rings, or listed extenders shall be set flush with the surface.
- *NEC® 314.22:* A surface extension from a box of a concealed wiring system is made by mounting and mechanically securing an extension ring over the concealed box. An exception to this is that a surface extension is permitted to be made from the cover of a concealed box

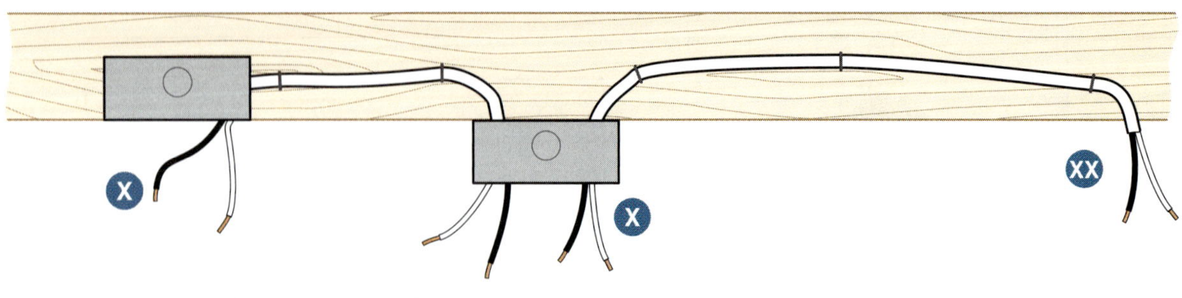

Figure 2-14 A box (or fitting) must be installed wherever there are splices, outlets, switches, or other junction points as indicated by the "X." Unless listed for use without a box, such as a typical surface-mounted strip luminaire that has a back plate with a trade size ½ knockout, point XX is a *Code* violation, *300.15*.

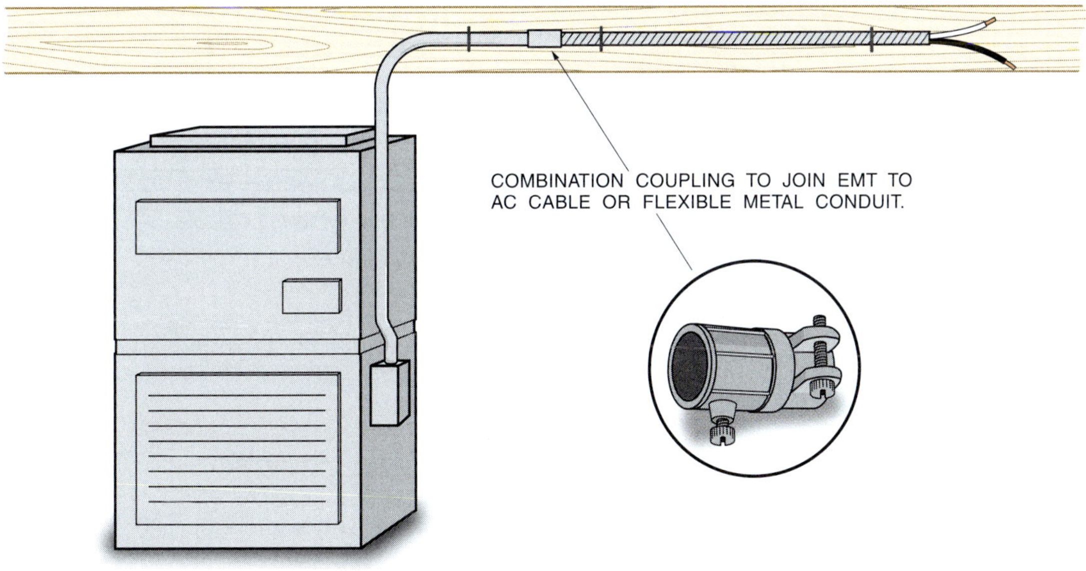

Figure 2-15 ***NEC® 300.15(C)*** **permits a transition to be made from one wiring method to another wiring method. In this case, the armor of the Type AC cable is removed, allowing sufficient length of the conductors to be run through the conduit. A proper fitting must be used at the transition point, and the fitting must be accessible after installation. The conductors in Type AC cable are THHN.**

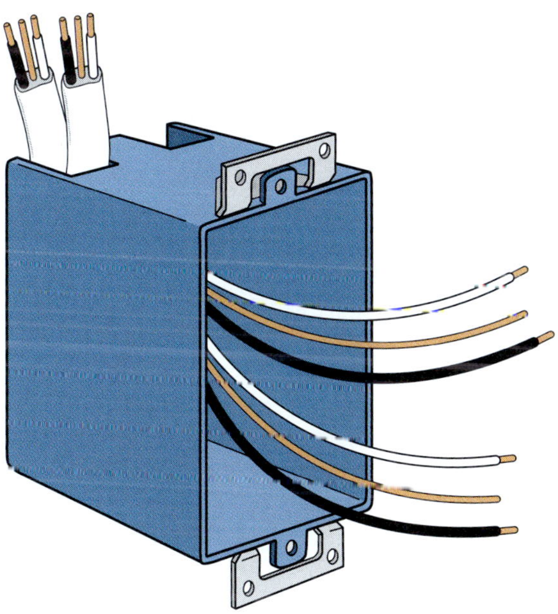

Figure 2-16 Multiple cables may run through a single knockout opening in a nonmetallic box, ***314.17(C), Exception.***

where the cover is designed so it is unlikely to fall off, or be removed if its securing means becomes loose. The wiring method must be flexible and arranged so that any required grounding continuity is independent of the connection between the box and cover. This is shown in Figure 2-17.

- *NEC® 314.24:* ▶Outlet and device boxes shall be deep enough so that conductors will not be damaged when installing the wiring device or equipment into the box. Merely calculating and providing the proper volume of a box is not always enough. The volume calculation might prove adequate, yet the size (depth) of the wiring device or equipment might be such that conductors behind it may possibly be damaged.◀
- *NEC® 314.25:* In completed installations, all boxes shall have a cover, faceplate, or luminaire canopy. Do not leave any electrical boxes uncovered.
- *NEC® 314.27(A):* Boxes used at lighting outlets must be designed or installed so that a luminaire may be attached to it.

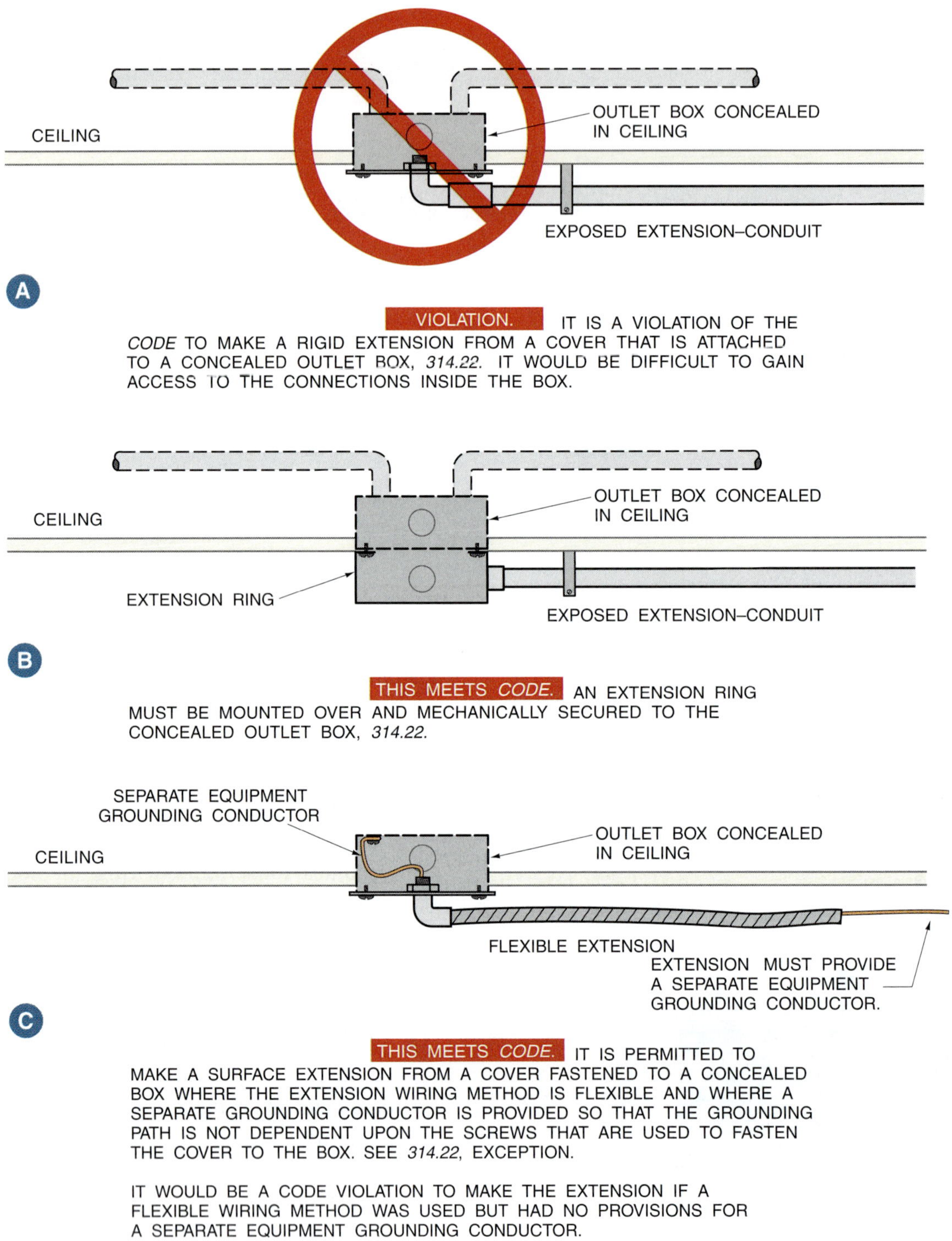

Figure 2-17 How to make an extension from a flush-mounted box.

- *NEC® 314.27(A)* and *(B)*: Listed outlet boxes are suitable for hanging luminaires that weigh 50 lb. (23 kg) or less. Luminaires that weigh more than 50 lb. (23 kg) must be supported independently of the outlet box, or the outlet box must be "listed" for the weight to be supported. Wall-mounted luminaires of not more than 6 lb. (3 kg) may be supported by a box, or by a plaster ring secured to a box, by not less than two No. 6-32 or larger screws, as in Figure 2-18.
- *NEC® 314.27(D):* Standard outlet boxes must

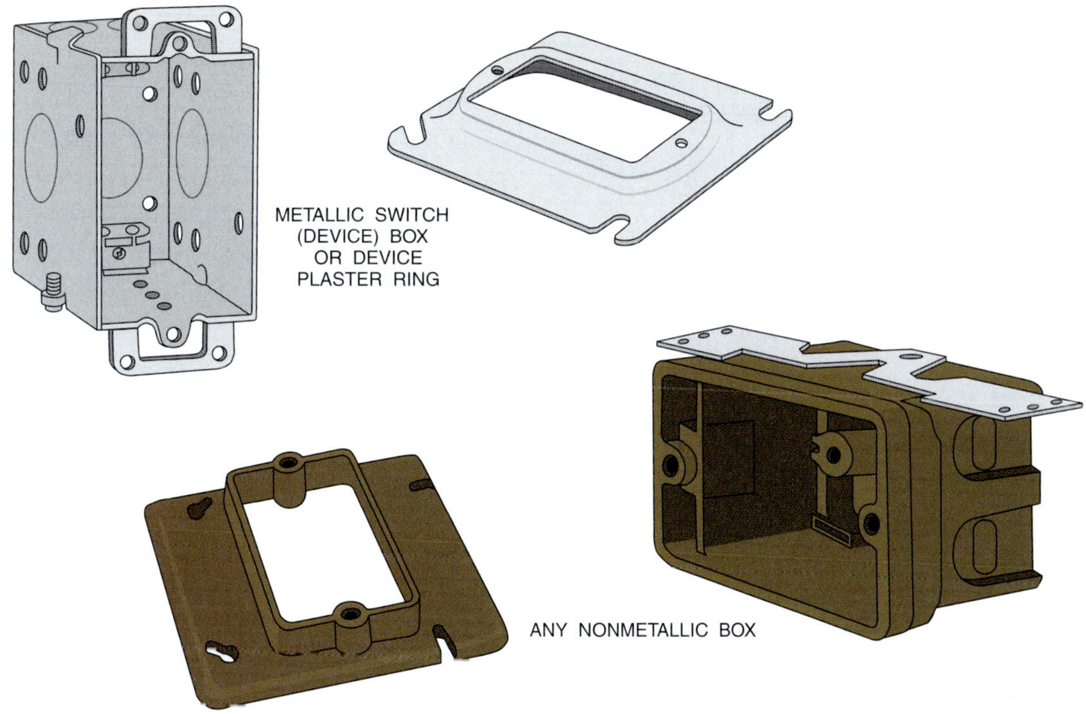

Figure 2-18 Wall-mounted luminaires (lighting fixtures) that do not weigh more than 6 lb. (3 kg) are permitted to be secured to these types of boxes and plaster rings by not less than two No. 6-32 or larger screws, *314.27(A), Exception*. For standard outlet boxes, the maximum weight is 50 lb. (23 kg), *314.27(B)*.

not be used as the sole support for ceiling-suspended (paddle) fans unless they are specifically listed for this purpose. See Chapter 9 for detailed discussion of this issue.

- *NEC® 314.29:* Conduit bodies, junction, pull, and outlet boxes must be installed so the wiring contained in them is accessible without removing any part of the building. Never install outlet boxes, junction boxes, pull boxes, or conduit bodies where they will be inaccessible behind or above permanent finished walls or ceilings. Should anything ever go wrong, it would be a nightmare, if not impossible, to troubleshoot and locate hidden splices. Wiring located above "lay-in" ceilings is considered accessible because it is easy to remove a panel(s) to gain access to the space above the ceiling. The *NEC®* definition of *accessible* is: *Capable of being removed or exposed without damaging the building structure or finish, or not permanently closed in by the structure or finish of the building.**

  The same accessibility requirement is true for underground wiring. Boxes must be accessible without excavating sidewalks, paving, earth, or other material used to establish the finished grade.

  The exception to *314.29* permits listed boxes to be covered with *gravel, light aggregate, or non-cohesive granulated soil* (not clay) if their location is clearly marked.

- *NEC® 314.71:* Pull and junction boxes must provide adequate space and dimensions for the installation of conductors, and they shall comply with the specific requirements of this section.
- *NEC® 410.22:* This is another repeat of the requirement that boxes must be covered. The "cover" could be a blank cover, a luminaire canopy, a lampholder, a switch or receptacle, or similar device with faceplate.
- ▶*NEC® 410.36(A):* Here we find permission to use outlet boxes and fittings to support luminaires provided the requirements found in *314.27(A)* and *(B)* are met.◀

*Reprinted with permission of NFPA 70-2008.

What to Do Where Recessed Luminaires Will Be Installed. This topic is covered in detail in Chapter 7.

GROUNDING/BONDING

As you study this text, you will come across many terms unique to the electrical industry. For now, let us explain the meaning of *grounding* and *bonding*.

What Does Grounded (Grounding) Mean?

▶The definition of *grounded (grounding)* found in *NEC® Article 100* is: *Connected to ground or to a conductive body that extends the ground connection.*◀

What Does Bonded (Bonding) Mean?

▶The definition of *bonded (bonding)* found in *NEC® Article 100* is: *Connected to establish electrical continuity and conductivity.*◀

Take a look at Figure 27-17A, Figure 27-17B, Figure 27-26, and Figure 27-27 to see the meanings of these terms. Other terms are explained and illustrated as they appear.

NONMETALLIC OUTLET AND DEVICE BOXES

Today, most house wiring is done using nonmetallic boxes as permitted by *314.3*. Although not often done, *NEC® 314.3 (Exceptions)* allows metal raceways and metal-jacketed cables (BX) to be used with nonmetallic boxes provided all metal raceways or cables entering the box are bonded together to maintain the integrity of the grounding path to other equipment in the installation.

The house wiring system usually is formed by a number of specific circuits. Each circuit consists of runs of cable from outlet to outlet or from box to box. The residence plans show many branch circuits for general lighting, appliances, electric heating, and other requirements. The specific *Code* rules for each of these circuits are covered in later chapters.

GANGED SWITCH (DEVICE) BOXES

Multiple-Gang Boxes

Where more than one wiring device is to be installed at one location, multiple-gang boxes are used. Nonmetallic boxes for wiring devices are available in two-gang, three-gang, and four-gang.

Metal device boxes can be ganged together by removing and discarding one side from both the first and third boxes, and both sides from the second (center) box.

Multiple-gang boxes are shown in Figure 2-19.

Box Fill

Figure 2-20 shows the dimensions of typical metal boxes and the number of conductors permitted in a given size box. This figure replicates *Table 314.16(A)* of the *NEC®*

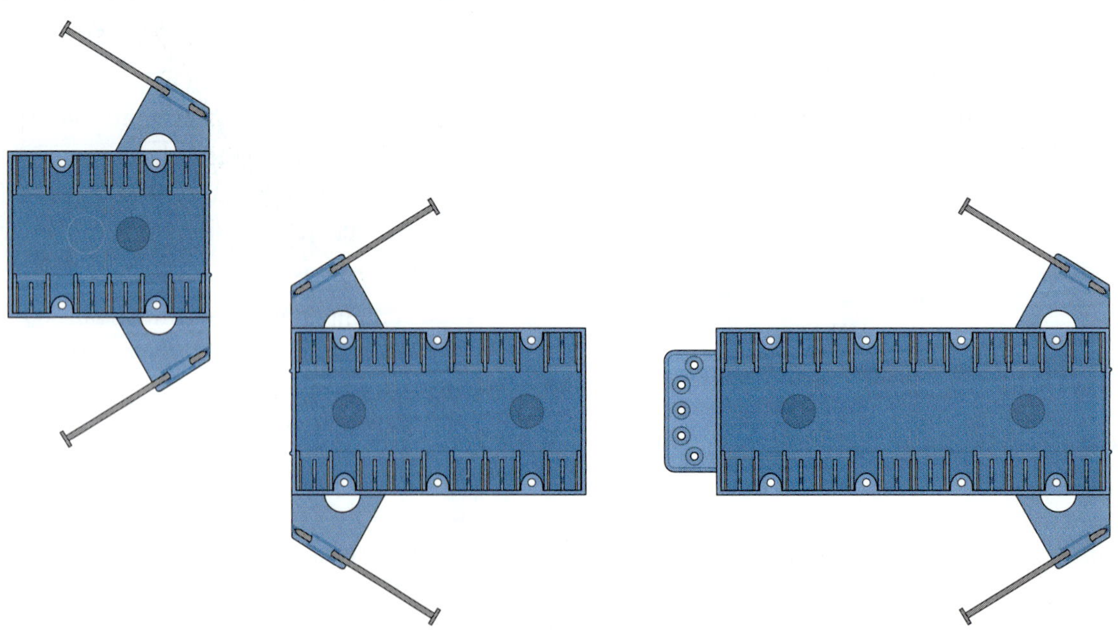

Figure 2-19 Examples of multiple-gang device boxes.

QUIK-CHEK BOX SELECTION GUIDE
FOR BOXES GENERALLY USED FOR RESIDENTIAL WIRING

DEVICE BOXES

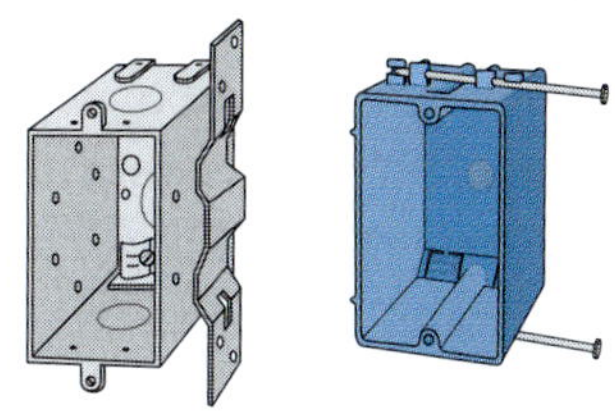

WIRE SIZE	3x2x1$\frac{1}{2}$ (7.5 in.^{3})	3x2x2 (10 in.^{3})	3x2x2$\frac{1}{4}$ (10.5 in.^{3})	3x2x2$\frac{1}{2}$ (12.5 in.^{3})	3x2x2$\frac{3}{4}$ (14 in.^{3})	3x2x3 (16 in.^{3})	3x2x3$\frac{1}{2}$ (18 in.^{3})
14 AWG	3	5	5	6	7	8	9
12 AWG	3	4	4	5	6	7	8

THE NUMBER OF CONDUCTORS IS "PER GANG"

SQUARE BOXES

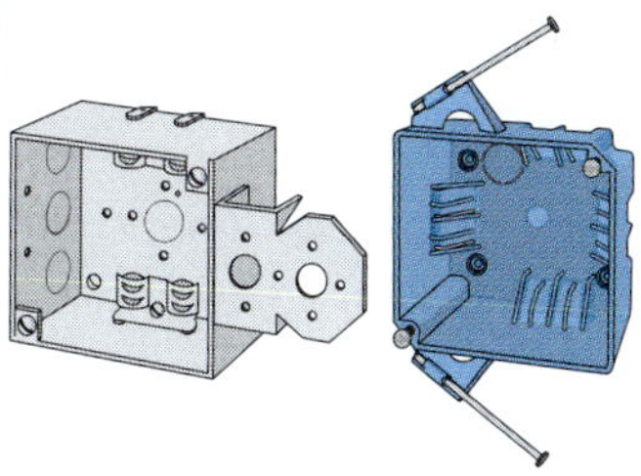

WIRE SIZE	4x4x1$\frac{1}{2}$ (21 in.^{3})	4x4x2$\frac{1}{8}$ (30.3 in.^{3})
14 AWG	10	15
12 AWG	9	13

OCTAGON BOXES

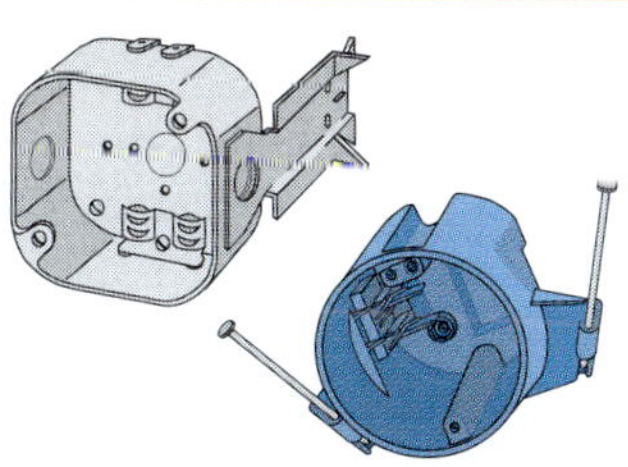

WIRE SIZE	4x1$\frac{1}{2}$ (15.5 in.^{3})	4x2$\frac{1}{8}$ (21.5 in.^{3})
14 AWG	7	10
12 AWG	6	9

HANDY BOXES

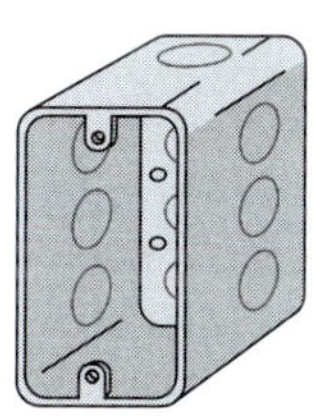

WIRE SIZE	4x2$\frac{1}{8}$x1$\frac{1}{2}$ (10.3 in.^{3})	4x2$\frac{1}{8}$x1$\frac{7}{8}$ (13 in.^{3})	4x2x2$\frac{1}{8}$ (14.5 in.^{3})
14 AWG	5	6	7
12 AWG	4	5	6

RAISED COVERS

WHERE RAISED COVERS ARE MARKED WITH THEIR VOLUME IN CUBIC INCHES, THAT VOLUME MAY BE ADDED TO THE BOX VOLUME TO DETERMINE MAXIMUM NUMBER OF CONDUCTORS IN THE COMBINED BOX AND RAISED COVER. NONMETALLIC RAISED COVERS ARE AVAILABLE.

MASONRY BOXES

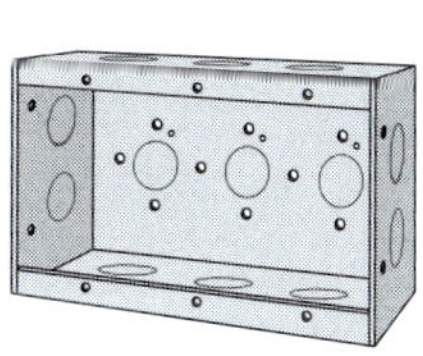

3-GANG BOX

WIRE SIZE	3$\frac{3}{4}$x2x2$\frac{1}{2}$ (14 in.^{3})	3$\frac{3}{4}$x2x3$\frac{1}{2}$ (21 in.^{3})
14 AWG	7	10
12 AWG	6	9

MASONRY BOXES HAVE LOTS OF ROOM. AVAILABLE UP TO 6 GANG. THE CONDUCTOR FILL IS FOR EACH GANG. REFER TO *TABLE 314.16(A)* AND *(B)*.

NOTE: BE SURE TO MAKE DEDUCTIONS FROM THE ABOVE MAXIMUM NUMBER OF CONDUCTORS PERMITTED FOR WIRING DEVICES, CABLE CLAMPS, FIXTURE STUDS, AND GROUNDING CONDUCTORS. THE CUBIC-INCH (IN.^{3}) VOLUME IS TAKEN DIRECTLY FROM *TABLE 314.16(A)* OF THE *NEC.®* NONMETALLIC BOXES ARE MARKED WITH THEIR CUBIC-INCH CAPACITY.

Figure 2-20 Quik-chek box selection guide.

Nonmetallic boxes are marked with their cubic-inch volume. *Table 314.16(B)* shows the cubic-inch volume allowance required for different size conductors.

BOX MOUNTING

NEC® 314.20 states that where noncombustible surface material (tile, gypsum, plaster, and like material) is used on walls or ceilings, boxes, plaster rings, domed covers, extension rings, or listed extenders must be mounted so that they will be set back not more than 1/4 in. (6 mm) from the face of the surface material. Where combustible surface material (wood paneling) is used on walls or ceilings, boxes, plaster rings, domed covers, extension rings, or listed extenders must be set flush with the surface material, Figure 2-21.

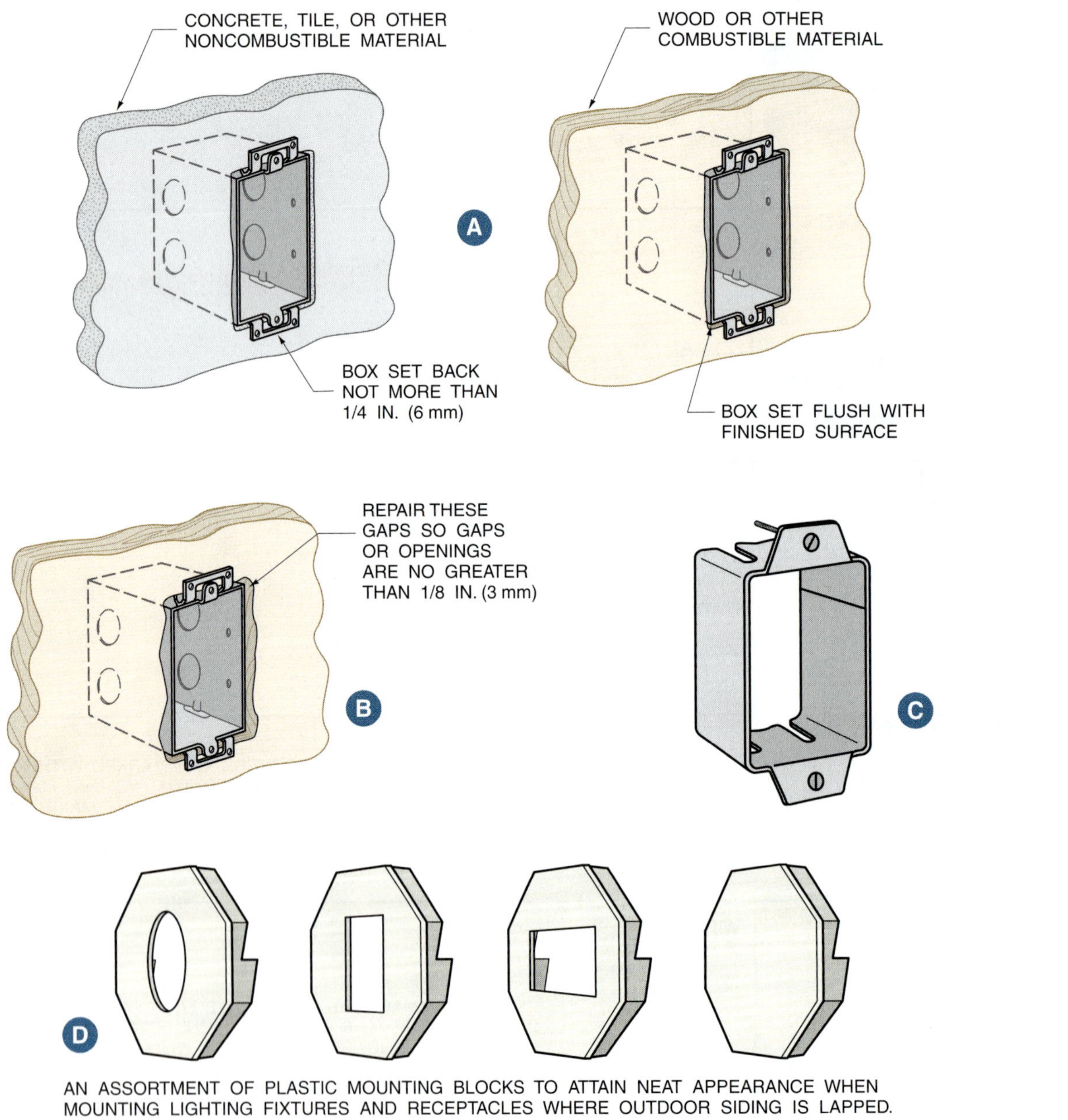

Figure 2-21 Box position requirements in walls and ceilings constructed of various materials. If the box is not flush with the finished surface (as a result of improper installation) or if paneling, drywall, tile, or a mirror is added, then install a box extender, sometimes referred to as a "goof ring." One type is shown in (C). Box extenders that are 1/4 in., 3/8 in., 1/2 in., or 3/4 in. deep are also available for one- and two-gang boxes. Refer to *314.20* and *314.21*. For set-back requirements for panelboards, see *312.3* and *312.4*.

These requirements hold back, retard, and slow down the spread of fire caused by arcing at a loose connection, a short circuit, or a ground fault that might occur within the box. This significantly reduces the supply of oxygen needed to keep a fire burning. Closing the gaps around boxes further reduces the spread of fire.

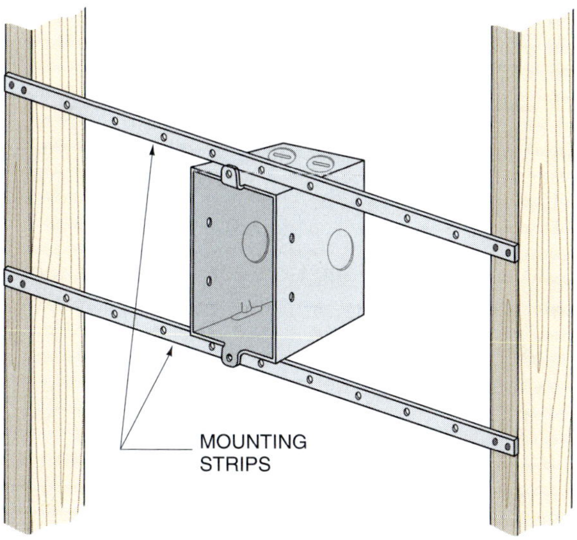

Figure 2-22 Switch (device) boxes installed between studs using metal switch box supports, often referred to as "Kruse strips." If wood strips are used, they must have a cross-sectional dimension of not less than 1 in. × 2 in. (25 mm × 50 mm), *314.23(B)(2)*.

Ganged sectional switch (device) boxes can be installed using a pair of metal mounting strips. These strips are also used to install a switch box between wall studs, Figure 2-22. When an outlet box is to be mounted at a specific location between joists, as for ceiling-mounted luminaires, an adjustable bar hanger is used, as in Figure 2-12.

NEC® 314.23(B)(1) requires that mounting nails or screws through a box shall not be more than ¼ in. (6 mm) from the back or ends of the box, as shown in Figure 2-23. This ensures that the nails or screws will not interfere with the wiring devices in the box. Furthermore, you are not allowed to use screws through a box unless the threads are protected by an approved means to avoid abrasion of conductor insulation.

Why bother with these *Code* requirements that take up valuable wiring space and could lead to conductor damage? It is much better to use boxes that have external mounting means.

Most residences are constructed with wood framing. However, metal studs and joists are being used more and more. Figure 2-24 shows a few types of boxes for use with metal framing members.

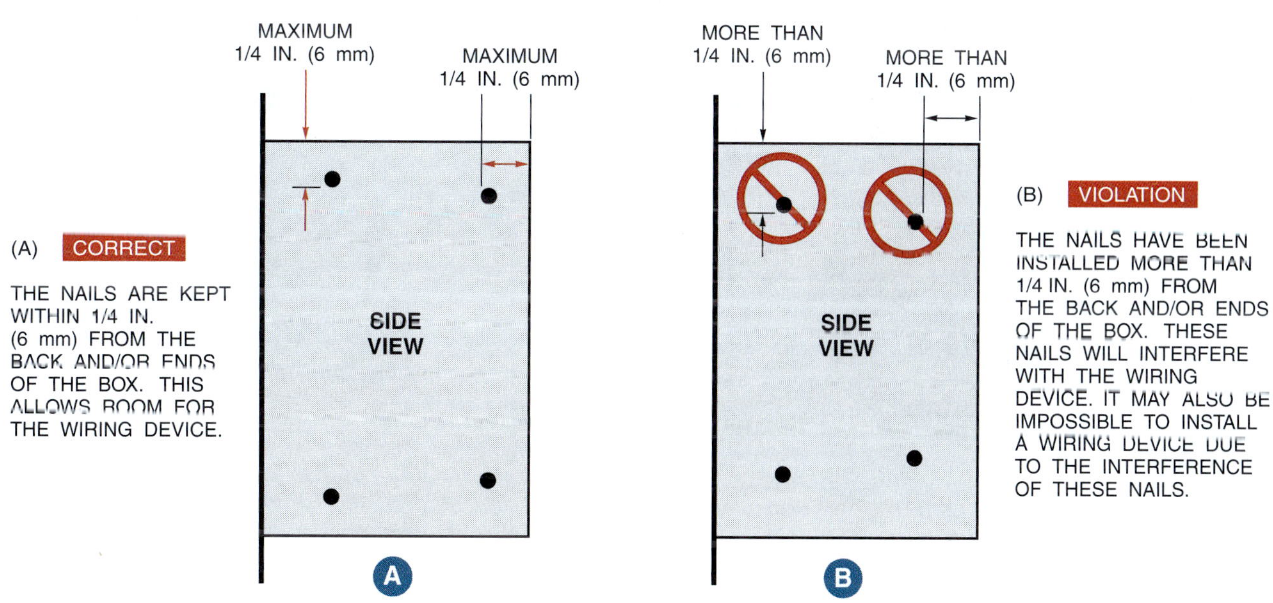

Figure 2-23 Using nails or screws to install a sectional switch box, *314.23(B)(1)*. UL listed boxes will have nail mounting holes positioned to meet the requirements of the *NEC®* A better choice is to use boxes that have external brackets or external nail mounting fixtures.

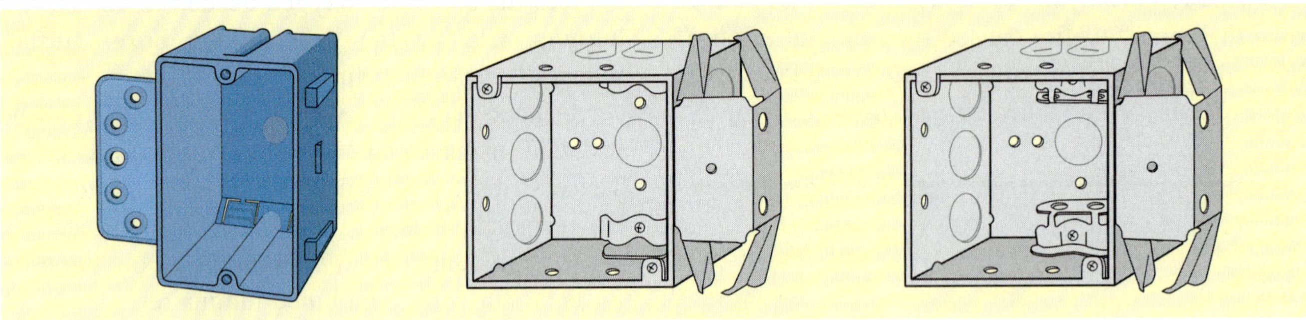

Figure 2-24 Types of boxes that can be used with steel framing construction. Note the side clamps that "snap" directly onto the steel framing members.

The first one is a single-gang nonmetallic device box that can be riveted or screwed to the metal stud. The second is a 4-in. square steel box with nonmetallic sheathed cable (Romex) clamps. The third is a 4-in. square steel box with armored cable (BX) clamps. The second and third boxes "snap" onto the metal stud, and do not require drilling the metal studs and fastening the box with nuts and bolts or screws. See Chapter 4 for *Code* requirements about running cables through metal framing members.

Another type of device used for fastening electrical boxes to steel framing members is shown in Figure 2-25. The bracket is screwed to the steel framing members, then the box or boxes are attached to the bracket.

Figure 2-25 A bracket for use on steel framing members. The bracket spans the space between two studs. Note that more than one box can be mounted on this bracket. ***Courtesy of*** **ERICO,® Inc.**

Damage Control!

One of the most common problems electricians face is what happens to conductors in boxes during the construction stage of a job. It's a major problem. In an attempt to minimize conductor damage, a new requirement was proposed for the 2008 *NEC®* in *300.4(G)*:

▶ *Conductors, inside electrical boxes, subject to physical damage from router bits, sheet rock saws, and knives, and nonconductive coatings, such as drywall mud, paint, lacquer and enamel, shall be protected during the construction process by means of a rigid cover, plate, or insert of a thickness and strength as to prohibit penetration by the above mentioned items.* ◀

This proposal was put on "HOLD," and will be brought up again for the *2011 NEC®* cycle. In the meantime, do everything possible to avoid damaging conductors in electrical boxes. Pushing the conductors deep into the box and using deeper boxes can reduce damage to conductors.

Remodel (Old Work)

When installing switches, receptacles, and lighting outlets in remodel work where the walls and ceilings (paneling, drywall, sheetrock and plaster, or lath and plaster) are already in place, first make sure you will be able to run cables to where the switches, receptacles, and lighting outlets are to be installed. After making sure you can get the cables through the concealed spaces in the walls and ceilings, you can then proceed to cut openings the size of the specific type of box to be installed at each outlet location. Cables are then "fished" through the stud and joist spaces behind or above the finished walls and ceilings to where you have cut the openings. Then boxes having plaster ears and snap-in brackets, Figure 2-26, can be inserted from the front, through the holes already cut at the locations where the wall or ceiling boxes are to be installed. After the boxes are snapped into place through the hole from the front, they become securely locked into place.

Another popular method of fastening wall and ceiling boxes in existing walls and ceilings is to use boxes that have plaster ears. Insert the box through the hole from the front. Then position a metal support into the hole on each side of the box. Be careful not to let the metal support fall into the hole. Next, bend the metal support over and into the box (Figure 2-27). Two metal supports are used. These metal switch box supports are known as Madison Hold-Its.™*

*Hold-It™ is a brand name trademark owned by Madison Equipment Co., Cleveland, OH.

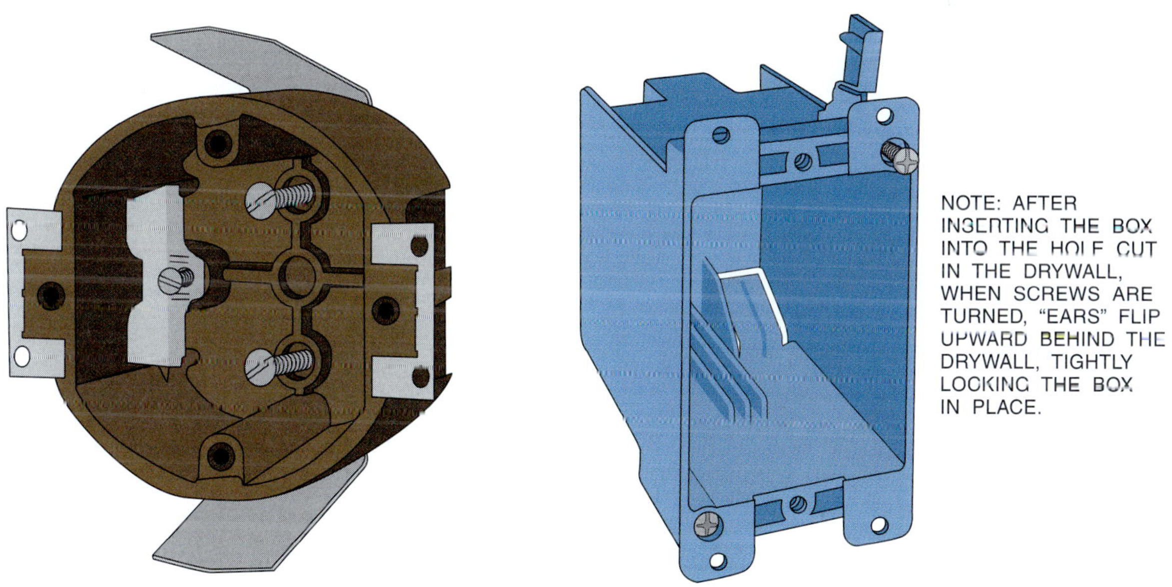

Figure 2-26 Nonmetallic boxes are commonly used for remodel work. When boxes are inserted into the hole cut in the drywall, they securely lock into place. This type of box is not for use in new work.

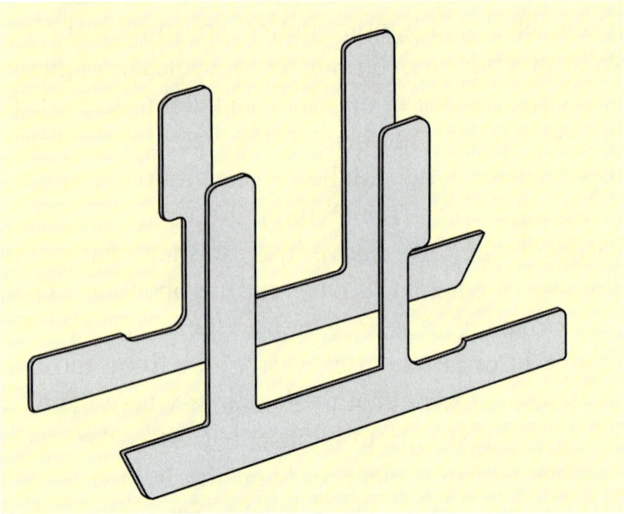

Figure 2-27 Metal device box supports referred to as Madison Hold-Its™.

Also available for old work are boxes that have a screw-type support on each side of the box, as in Figure 2-28. This type of box has plaster ears. It is inserted through the hole cut in the wall or ceiling, then the screws are tightened. This pulls up a metal support tightly behind the wall or ceiling, firmly holding the box in place. The action is very similar to that of Molly screw anchors.

Because these types of remodel boxes are supported by the drywall or plaster, as opposed to new work where the boxes are supported by the framing members, be careful not to hang heavy luminaires from them. Be sure that there is proper support if a ceiling fan is to be installed. This is covered in Chapter 9.

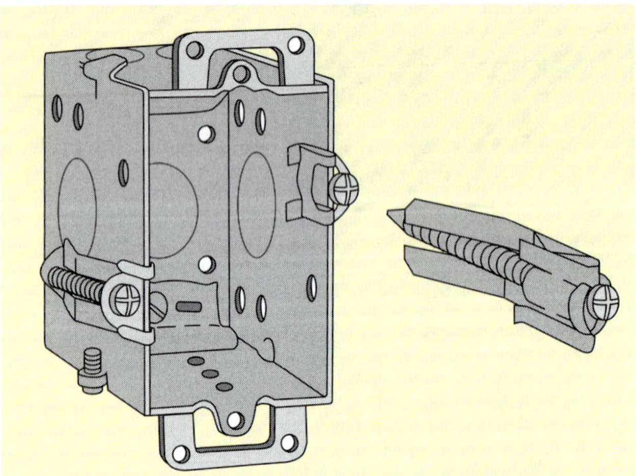

Figure 2-28 These boxes are commonly used in remodel work. The box is installed from the front, then the screws are tightened. The box is adequately supported.

Spread of Fire

To protect lives and property, fire must be contained and not be allowed to spread.

In addition to the *NEC*,® you must also become familiar with building codes.

Building codes such as the International Code Council (ICC) *International Residential Code* generally do not require fire-resistance-rated walls and ceilings in one- and two-family buildings. Some communities have amendments to the basic building codes, such as requiring ⅝-in. (16-mm) gypsum wallboard [instead of the normal ½-in. (13-mm)] on the ceilings and on the walls between the garage and living areas and requiring *draft stopping* where ducts, cables, and piping run through bottom (sole) and top plates. Draft stopping is generally done by the insulation contractor. Townhouses, condominiums, and other multi-occupancy buildings do have fire-resistance rating requirements. To avoid costly mistakes, check with your local building officials to determine exactly what the requirements are!

In walls, partitions, and ceilings that are fire-resistance-rated, special consideration must be given when installing wall and ceiling electrical boxes "back to back" or in the same stud or joist space of common walls or ceilings, as might be found in multifamily buildings. Electrical wall boxes installed back to back or installed in the same stud or joist space defeat the fire-resistance rating of the wall or ceiling.

What Is Fire-Resistance Rating?

A building assembly's (walls, ceilings, partitions, gypsum, drywall, plaster, etc.) fire-resistance rating refers to the period of time the assembly will serve as a barrier to the spread of fire. It is an indication of how long it can hold back a fully developed blaze before it spreads to adjacent areas of the building and how long the assembly can function structurally after being exposed to a fire.

While undergoing specific tests, passage of flames and/or structural collapse are the determining factors for establishing fire-resistance ratings.

To be truly fire-resistance-rated, the construction and materials must conform to very rigid requirements, as set forth in the UL Standards discussed below.

Ratings of fire-resistance materials are expressed in hours. Terms such a 1-hour fire-resistance rating, 2-hour fire-resistance rating, and so on, are used.

UL Standard 263 *Fire Tests of Building Construction and Materials* and NFPA 251 cover fire-resistance ratings. In UL Standard 263, and in all building codes, you will find requirements such as: "the surface area of individual metallic outlet or switch boxes shall not exceed 16 square inches" (i.e., a 4-in. square box is 4 in. × 4 in. = 16 in.^{2}), "the aggregate surface area of the boxes shall not exceed 100 in.^{2} per 100 ft^2 of wall surface," "boxes located on opposite sides of walls or partitions shall be separated by a minimum horizontal distance of 24 in. (600 mm)," "the metallic outlet or switch boxes shall be securely fastened to the studs and the opening in the wallboard facing shall be cut so that the clearance between the box and the wallboard does not exceed ⅛ in. (3 mm)," and "the boxes shall be installed in compliance with the *NEC*.®"

The UL *Fire Resistance Directory* covers fire-resistant materials and assemblies and contains a rather detailed listing of *Outlet Boxes and Fittings Classified for Fire Resistance (CEYY)*, showing all manufacturers' product part numbers for *nonmetallic boxes* to be installed in walls, partitions, and ceilings that meet the fire-resistance standard. This category also covers special-purpose boxes for installation in floors.

▶When using nonmetallic boxes in fire-resistance rated walls, the restrictions are more stringent than for metallic boxes. Nonmetallic boxes shall be marked with:

- UL in a circle located in the base of the box.
- the hour rating (1 hr. or 2 hr.)
- the letters F, W, and/or C where F = floor, W = wall, and C = ceiling

Nonmetallic boxes are UL Classified for use in specific fire-resistant rated assemblies. The Classification data shows spacing restrictions and installation details.◀

Molded fiberglass outlet and device boxes have become available and are listed for use in fire-resistance-rated partitions without the use of putty pads, mineral wool batts, or fiberglass batts, provided a minimum horizontal distance of 3 in. (75 mm) is maintained between boxes and the boxes are not back-to-back. See Figure 2-31B.

If you are dealing with fire-resistance-rated construction, be sure to carefully read the box manufacturer's instructions and "Listing" details.

For both metallic and nonmetallic electric outlet boxes, the *minimum* distance between boxes on opposite sides of a fire-rated wall or partition is 24 in. (600 mm). There is an exception, which is discussed later.

For both metallic and nonmetallic electric outlet boxes, the maximum gap between the box and the wall material is ⅛ in. (3 mm). This holds true for fire-resistance-rated walls and non-fire-resistance-rated walls.

To maintain the hourly fire rating of a fire-rated wall that contains electrical outlet and switch boxes, the UL *Fire Resistance Directory* lists an *intumescent* (expands when heated) fire-resistant material that comes in "pads."

These "putty pads" are moldable and can be used to wrap metal electrical boxes or inserted on the inside back wall of metal electrical boxes. When exposed to fire, the material expands and chars, sealing off the opening to prevent the spread of flames and limit the heat transfer from the fire-resistance-rated side of the wall to the non-fire-resistance-rated side of the wall. It is not to be used on nonmetallic boxes.

The ⅛ in. (3 mm) thickness provides a 1-hour fire-resistance rating. A 2-hour rating is obtained with ¼ in. (6 mm) thickness.

When this material is properly installed, the 24-in. (600-mm) separation between boxes is not required. However, the electrical outlet boxes *must not* be installed back to back. Using this material meets the requirements of *NEC® 300.21* of the *NEC®* and other building codes.

The ICC *International Residential Code* states that "fireblocking" be provided to cut off all concealed draft openings (both vertical and horizontal) and to form an effective fire barrier between stories, and between a top story and the roof space. This includes openings around vents, pipes, ducts, chimneys, and fireplaces at ceiling and floor levels. Oxygen supports fire. Firestopping cuts off or significantly reduces the flow of oxygen. Most communities that have adopted the ICC code require firestopping around electrical conduits. In residential work, this is generally done by the insulation installer, before the drywall installer closes up the walls.

Be careful when roughing in wall boxes where wood paneling is to be installed. Some communities require that ½-in. (13-mm) gypsum board be installed on the studs behind finished wood paneling to establish a fire-resistance rating. Remember that where the finish wall or ceiling surface is combustible material such as wood paneling, the front edge of the box, plaster ring, domed cover, extension ring, or listed extender shall be set flush with the wall surface. Refer to *NEC® 314.20* and Figure 2-21.

The previous discussion makes it clear that the electrician must become familiar with certain building codes in addition to the *NEC*.® Knowing the *NEC®* is not enough!

It is extremely important to check with the electrical inspector and/or building official for complete clarification on the matter of fire-resistance requirements before you find yourself cited with serious violations and lawsuits regarding noncompliance with fire codes. Changes can be costly and will delay completion of the project. Improper wiring is hazardous. The *NEC®* addresses this issue in *300.21*.

Figure 2-29, Figure 2-30, Figure 2-31, and Figure 2-32 illustrate the basics for installing electrical outlet and switch boxes in fire-resistance-rated partitions. This is an extremely important issue. If in doubt, check with your local electrical inspector and/or building official.

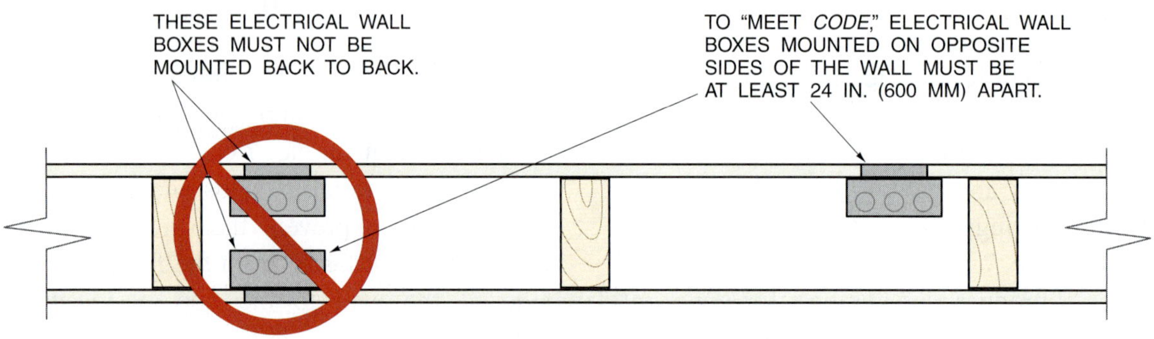

Figure 2-29 Building codes prohibit electrical wall boxes to be mounted back to back in fire-resistance-rated walls unless specific installation procedures, as illustrated in Figure 2-30, Figure 2-31, and Figure 2-32, are followed. One of these requirements is that electrical wall boxes must be kept at least 24 in. (600 mm) apart. This is to maintain the integrity of the fire-resistance rating of the wall.

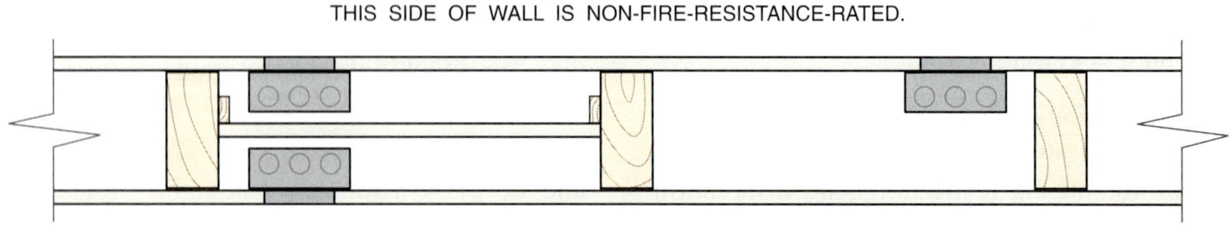

Figure 2-30 Building codes permit boxes to be mounted back to back or in the same wall cavity when the fire-resistance rating is maintained. In this detail, gypsum board has been installed in the wall cavity between the boxes, creating a new fire-resistance barrier. Verify if this is acceptable to the building authority in your area.

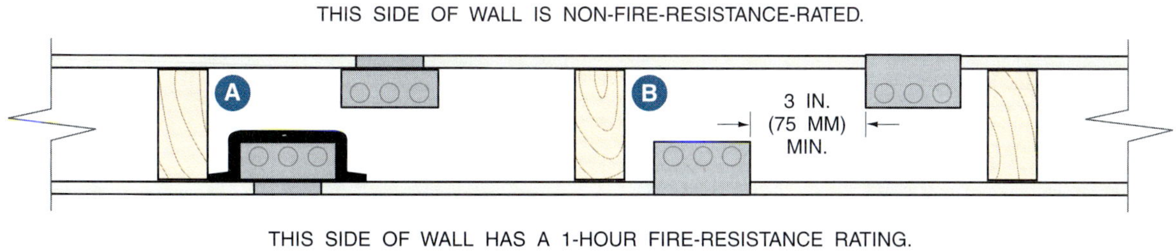

Figure 2-31 Building codes permit electrical outlet and device boxes to be mounted in the same stud space under certain conditions. (A) Here we see "Wall Opening Protective Material" packed around one outlet box. (B) Here we see molded fiberglass boxes in the same stud space with a minimum horizontal clearance of 3 in. (75 mm). These boxes are listed for this application. In both (A) and (B), the boxes are not permitted to be back-to-back.

Figure 2-32 This illustration shows an electrical outlet box that has been covered with "Listed" fire-resistance "putty pad" to retain the wall's fire-resistance rating per building codes.

BOXES FOR CONDUIT WIRING

Some local electrical ordinances require conduit rather than cable wiring. Conduit wiring is discussed in Chapter 18. Examples of conduit fill (how many wires are permitted in a given size conduit) are presented.

When conduit is installed in a residence, it is quite common to use 4-in. square boxes trimmed with suitable plaster covers, Figure 2-33(A). There are sufficient knockouts in the top, bottom, sides, and back of the box to permit a number of conduits to run to the box. Plenty of room is available for the conductors and wiring devices. Note how easily these 4-in. square outlet boxes can be mounted back to back by installing a small fitting between the boxes. This is illustrated in Figure 2-33(B) and Figure 2-33(C).

Four-inch square outlet boxes can be trimmed with one-gang or two-gang plaster rings where wiring devices will be installed. Where luminaires will be installed, a plaster ring having a round opening should be installed.

►Any and all unused openings in electrical equipment must be closed! This includes unused knockouts in boxes, spaces for circuit breakers in a panel, meter socket enclosures, and all other similar electrical equipment.◄ The closing material shall provide substantially the same protection as the wall of the equipment. See *110.12(A)*, *408.7*, and Figure 2-34.

►Openings that are intended for mounting purposes, for the operation of the equipment, or as part of the design of listed equipment do not have to be closed.◄

Close the Gap Around Boxes!

NEC® 314.21 requires that openings around electrical boxes shall be repaired so that "there will be no gaps or open space greater than ⅛ in. (3 mm) at the edge of the box or fitting." This is to minimize the spread of fire. The UL *Fire Resistance Directory* mirrors the *NEC®* rule by stating that "the outlet or switch boxes shall be securely fastened to the studs and the opening in the wallboard facing

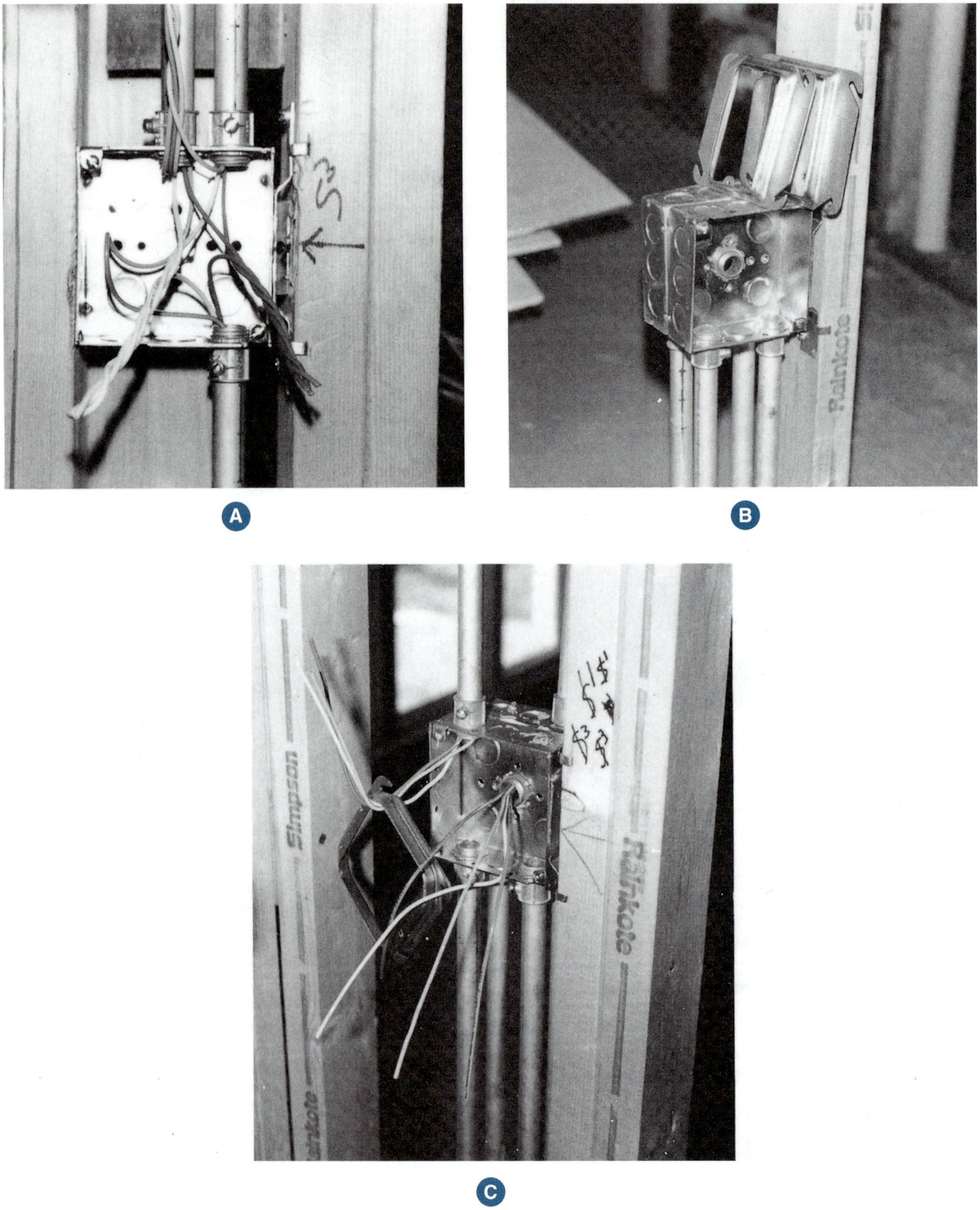

A B C

Figure 2-33 (A) shows electrical metallic tubing run to a 4-in. square box. (B) and (C) show 4-in. square boxes attached together for "back-to-back" installations. When mounting boxes back to back, be sure to consider possible transfer of sound between the rooms. IMPORTANT: See text ("Spread of Fire") for details of fire-resistance ratings and the restrictions related to installing electrical boxes back to back.

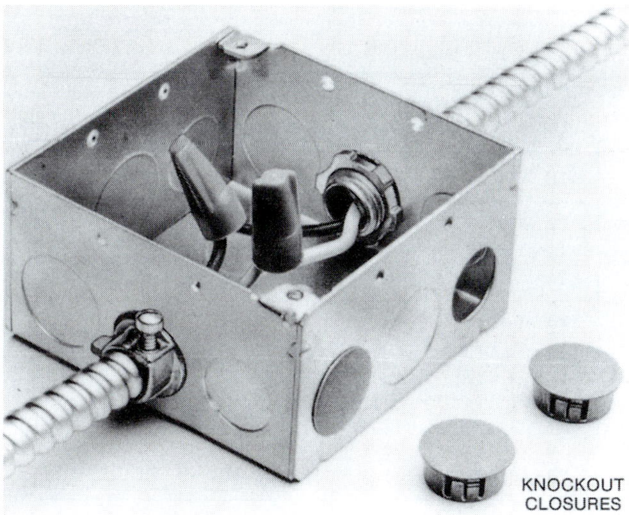

Figure 2-34 Unused openings in boxes must be closed according to *110.12(A)* and *408.7*. This is done to contain electrical short-circuit problems inside the box or panel and to keep rodents out. Note that the conductors *do not* meet the 3-in. (75-mm) and 6-in. (150-mm) conductor length requirements of *300.14*. This is a good example of a *Code* violation. See Figure 2-2 for proper installation regarding conductor length at boxes.

shall be cut so that the clearance between the box and the wallboard does not exceed ⅛ in." See Figure 2-21(B).

This is easier said than done. The electrician installs the wiring (rough-in), followed by an inspection by the electrical inspector. Next comes the drywall/plaster/panel installer, who many times cuts out the box openings much larger than the outlet or switch box. In most cases, the walls and ceilings are painted or wallpapered before the electrician returns to install the receptacles, switches, and luminaires. For gaps or openings greater than ⅛ in. (3 mm) around the electrical boxes, should the electrician repair the gap with patching plaster, possibly damaging or marring the finished wall? Whose responsibility is it? Is it the electrician's? Is it the drywall/plaster/panel installer's?

The electrician should check with the drywall/plaster/panel installer to clarify who is to be responsible for seeing to it that gaps or openings around electrical outlet and switch boxes do not exceed ⅛ in. (3 mm). *314.21* puts the responsibility on the electrician.

YOKE

We use the term "yoke." The *NEC*® uses the term "yoke." Yet, the *NEC*® does not define a "yoke." What is a "yoke"? It is the metal or polycarbonate mounting strap on which a wiring device or devices are attached. The yoke in turn is attached to a device box or device cover with No. 6-32 screws. One yoke may have one, two, or three wiring devices attached to it.

Visit an electrical distributor or home center. You will find many combination wiring devices on a single yoke or strap. Selecting one of these combination devices may eliminate the need to use combinations of interchangeable wiring devices.

SPECIAL-PURPOSE OUTLETS

Special-purpose outlets are usually indicated on the plans. These outlets are described by a notation and are usually detailed in the specifications. The plans indicate special-purpose outlets by a triangle inside a circle with subscript letters. In some cases, a subscript number is added to the letter.

When a special-purpose outlet is indicated on the plans or in the specifications, the electrician must check for special requirements. Such a requirement may be a separate circuit, a special 240-volt circuit, a special grounding or polarized receptacle, or other preparation.

A set of plans and specifications for this residence is found at the end of this text. The specifications include a *Schedule of Special Purpose Outlets*.

NUMBER OF CONDUCTORS IN BOX

NEC® *314.16* dictates that outlet boxes, switch boxes, and device boxes should be large enough to provide ample room for the wires in that box, without having to jam or crowd the wires into the box. Jamming the wires into the box can not only damage the insulation on the wires, but can result in heat buildup in the box that can further damage the insulation on the wires. The *Code* specifies the maximum number of conductors allowed in standard metal outlet, device, and junction boxes; see *Tables 314.16(A)* and *(B)*. Nonmetallic boxes are marked by the manufacturer with their cubic-inch capacity.

When conductors are the same size, the proper metal box size can be selected by referring to *Table 314.16(A)*. When conductors are of different sizes and nonmetallic boxes are installed, refer to *Table 314.16(B)* and use the cubic-inch volume for the particular size of wire being used.

Table 314.16(A) Metal Boxes

Box Trade Size			Minimum Volume		Maximum Number of Conductors* (arranged by AWG size)						
mm	in.		cm^3	$in.^3$	18	16	14	12	10	8	6
100 × 32	(4 × 1¼)	round/octagonal	205	12.5	8	7	6	5	5	5	2
100 × 38	(4 × 1½)	round/octagonal	254	15.5	10	8	7	6	6	5	3
100 × 54	(4 × 2⅛)	round/octagonal	353	21.5	14	12	10	9	8	7	4
100 × 32	(4 × 1¼)	square	295	18.0	12	10	9	8	7	6	3
100 × 38	(4 × 1½)	square	344	21.0	14	12	10	9	8	7	4
100 × 54	(4 × 2⅛)	square	497	30.3	20	17	15	13	12	10	6
120 × 32	(4 11/16 × 1¼)	square	418	25.5	17	14	12	11	10	8	5
120 × 38	(4 11/16 × 1½)	square	484	29.5	19	16	14	13	11	9	5
120 × 54	(4 11/16 × 2⅛)	square	689	42.0	28	24	21	18	16	14	8
75 × 50 × 38	(3 × 2 × 1½)	device	123	7.5	5	4	3	3	3	2	1
75 × 50 × 50	(3 × 2 × 2)	device	164	10.0	6	5	5	4	4	3	2
75 × 50 × 57	(3 × 2 × 2¼)	device	172	10.5	7	6	5	4	4	3	2
75 × 50 × 65	(3 × 2 × 2½)	device	205	12.5	8	7	6	5	5	4	2
75 × 50 × 70	(3 × 2 × 2¾)	device	230	14.0	9	8	7	6	5	4	2
75 × 50 × 90	(3 × 2 × 3½)	device	295	18.0	12	10	9	8	7	6	3
100 × 54 × 38	(4 × 2⅛ × 1½)	device	169	10.3	6	5	5	4	4	3	2
100 × 54 × 48	(4 × 2⅛ × 1⅞)	device	213	13.0	8	7	6	5	5	4	2
100 × 54 × 54	(4 × 2⅛ × 2⅛)	device	238	14.5	9	8	7	6	5	4	2
95 × 50 × 65	(3¾ × 2 × 2½)	masonry box/gang	230	14.0	9	8	7	6	5	4	2
95 × 50 × 90	(3¾ × 2 × 3½)	masonry box/gang	344	21.0	14	12	10	9	8	7	4
min. 44.5 depth	FS — single cover/gang (1¾)		221	13.5	9	7	6	6	5	4	2
min. 60.3 depth	FD — single cover/gang (2⅜)		295	18.0	12	10	9	8	7	6	3
min. 44.5 depth	FS — multiple cover/gang (1¾)		295	18.0	12	10	9	8	7	6	3
min. 60.3 depth	FD — multiple cover/gang (2⅜)		395	24.0	16	13	12	10	9	8	4

*Where no volume allowances are required by 314.16(B)(2) through (B)(5).

Table 314.16(B) Volume Allowance Required per Conductor

Size of Conductor (AWG)	Free Space Within Box for Each Conductor	
	cm^3	$in.^3$
18	24.6	1.50
16	28.7	1.75
14	32.8	2.00
12	36.9	2.25
10	41.0	2.50
8	49.2	3.00
6	81.9	5.00

Table 314.16(A) and *Table 314.16(B)* do not take into consideration the space taken by luminaire studs, cable clamps, hickeys, switches, pilot lights, or receptacles that may be in the box. These require additional space. Table 2-1 shows the additional allowances that must be considered for different situations.

SELECTING THE CORRECT SIZE BOX

Selecting the correct size box depends on the mix of conductors and wiring devices that will be contained in the particular box. Here are some examples.

When using a nonmetallic box where all conductors are the same size. A nonmetallic box is

• If box contains no fittings, devices, fixture studs, cable clamps, hickeys, switches, receptacles, or equipment grounding conductors:	• Refer directly to *Table 314.16(A)* or *Table 314.16(B)*.
• **Clamps.** If box contains one or more internal cable clamps:	• Add a single-volume based on the largest conductor in the box.
• **Support Fittings.** If box contains one or more luminaire studs or hickeys:	• Add a single-volume for each type based on the largest conductor in the box.
• **Device or Equipment.** If box contains one or more wiring devices on a yoke:	• Add a double-volume for each yoke based on the largest conductor connected to a device on that yoke. ►Some large wiring devices, such as a 30-ampere dryer receptacle, require a 2-gang box.◄
• **Equipment Grounding Conductors.** If a box contains one or more equipment grounding conductors:	• Add a single-volume based on the largest equipment grounding conductor in the box.
• **Isolated Equipment Grounding Conductor.** If a box contains one or more additional "isolated" (insulated) equipment grounding conductors as permitted by *250.146(D)* for "noise" reduction:	• Add a single-volume based on the largest equipment grounding conductor in the box.
• ►For conductors less than 12 in. (300 mm) long between the raceway entries for the conductor that is looped or coiled through the box without being spliced:◄	• ►Add a single-volume for each conductor that is looped or coiled through the box.◄
• ►For conductors 12 in. (300 mm) or longer between the raceway entries for the conductor that is looped or coiled through the box without being spliced:◄	• ►Add a double-volume for each conductor that is looped or coiled through the box.◄
• For conductors that originated outside of the box and terminate inside the box:	• Add a single-volume for each conductor that originates outside the box and terminates inside the box.
• If no part of the conductor leaves the box, as with a "jumper" wire used to connect three wiring devices on one yoke, or pigtails:	• Don't count this (these). No additional volume required.
• For small equipment grounding conductors or not more than four conductors smaller than 14 AWG that originate from a luminaire canopy or similar canopy (like a fan) and terminate in the box:	• Don't count this (these). No additional volume required.
• For small fittings, such as locknuts, bushings, and wire connectors:	• Don't count this (these). No additional volume required.

Table 2-1 Quick checklist for possibilities to be considered when determining proper size boxes. See *314.16(B)(1)* through *314.16(B)(5)*.

marked as having a volume of 22.8 in.^{3} The box contains no luminaire stud or cable clamps. How many 14 AWG conductors are permitted in this box?

From *Table 314.16(B)*, the volume requirement for a 14 AWG conductor is 2.00 in.^{3} Therefore, the maximum number of 14 AWG conductors permitted in this box is:

$$\frac{22.8}{2} = 11.4 \text{ (Round down to 11 conductors)}$$

When using a metal device box where all conductors are the same size. A box contains one luminaire stud and two internal cable clamps. The wiring method is two 12/2 NM w/ground cables.

four 12 AWG conductors	4
one luminaire stud	1
two cable clamps (only count one)	1
two 12 AWG equipment grounding conductors (only count one)	1
Total	7

Referring to *Table 314.16(A)* and *Table 314.16(B)*, a 3 × 2 × 3½ device box is suitable for this example.

When using a metal or nonmetallic box where the conductors are different sizes. What is the minimum cubic-inch volume required for a box that will contain one internal cable clamp, one switch, and one receptacle mounted on one yoke? One 14/2 Type AC and one 12/2 Type AC cable are used. There are no separate equipment grounding conductors involved as the bonding wire in the armored cables are laid back over the armor and do not take up any space within the box.

two 14 AWG conductors @ 2 in.^{3} per conductor	=	4.00 in.^{3}
two 12 AWG conductors @ 2.25 in.^{3} per conductor	=	4.50 in.^{3}
two cable clamp (only count one) @ 2.25 in.^{3}	=	2.25 in.^{3}
one switch and one receptacle on one yoke @ 2.25 in.^{3} × 2	=	4.50 in.^{3}
Total		15.25 in.^{3}

Select a box having a minimum volume of 15.25 in.^{3} of space. The cubic-inch volume might be marked on the box; otherwise refer to the second column of *Table 314.16(A)* entitled "Minimum Volume."

The *Code* in *314.16(A)(2)* requires that all boxes *other* than those listed in *Table 314.16(A)* be durably and legibly marked by the manufacturer with their cubic-inch capacity. Nonmetallic boxes have their cubic-inch volume marked on the box. When sectional boxes are ganged together, the calculated volume is the total cubic-inch volume of the assembled boxes.

When installing a box that will have a raised cover attached to it. When marked with their cubic-inch volume, the *additional* space provided by plaster rings, domed covers, raised covers, and extension rings is permitted to be used when determining the overall volume. This is illustrated in Figure 2-35.

How many 12 AWG conductors are permitted in this box and raised plaster ring? Refer to Figure 2-36 and *Table 314.16(A)* and *Table 314.16(B)*.

$$\frac{25.5 \text{ in.}^3 \text{ of total space}}{2.25 \text{ in.}^3 \text{ per 12 AWG conductor}} = \text{Eleven 12 AWG conductors}$$

This calculation actually resulted in 11.33. The conductor fill numbers in *Table 314.16(A)* were created by dropping any excess above the whole number after the calculations were made. Following the same procedure, this conductor fill calculation dropped off the excess.

Electricians and electrical inspectors have become very aware of the fact that GFCI receptacles, dimmers, and timers take up a lot more space than regular wiring devices. Therefore, it is a good practice to install boxes that will provide plenty of room for the wires, instead of pushing, jamming, and crowding the wires into the box.

Figure 2-37 shows that transformer leads 18 AWG or larger must be counted when selecting a proper size box.

The minimum required size of equipment grounding conductors is shown in *Table 250.122*. The equipment grounding conductors are the same size as the circuit conductors in cables having 14-AWG, 12-AWG, and 10-AWG circuit conductors. Thus, for normal house wiring, box sizes can be calculated using *Table 314.16(A)*. Refer to Figure 2-38.

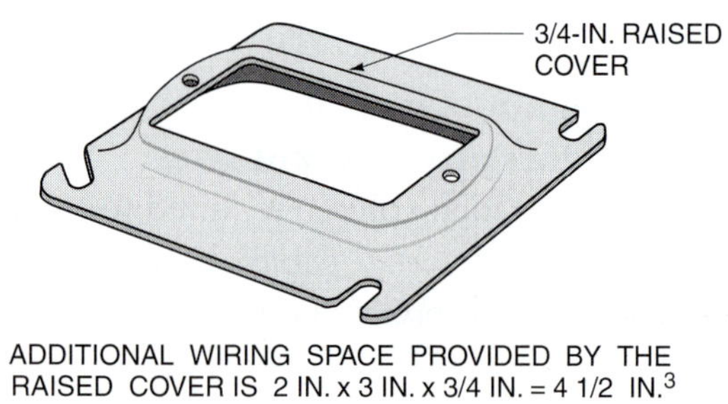

Figure 2-35 Raised cover. Raised covers are sometimes called plaster rings.

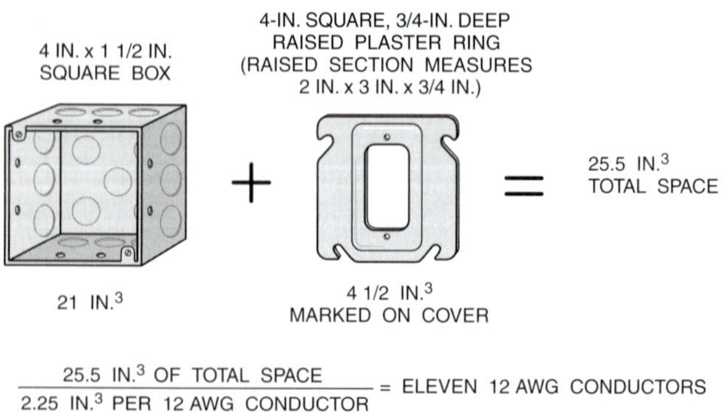

Figure 2-36 When marked with their cubic-inch volume, the volume of the cover may be added to the volume of the box to determine the total cubic-inch volume.

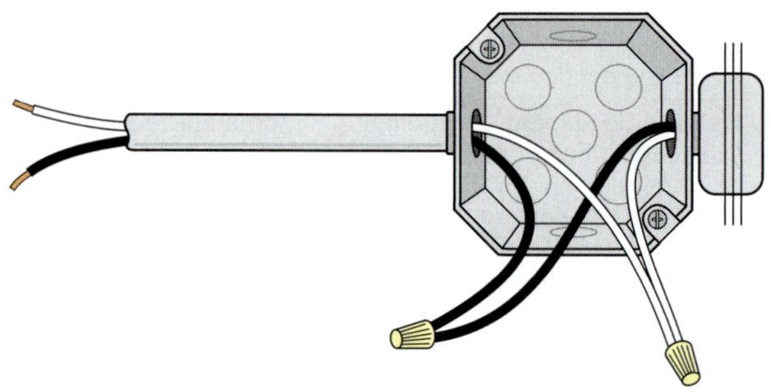

Figure 2-37 Transformer leads 18 AWG or larger must be counted when selecting the proper size box, *314.16(B)(1)*. In the example shown, the box contains four conductors.

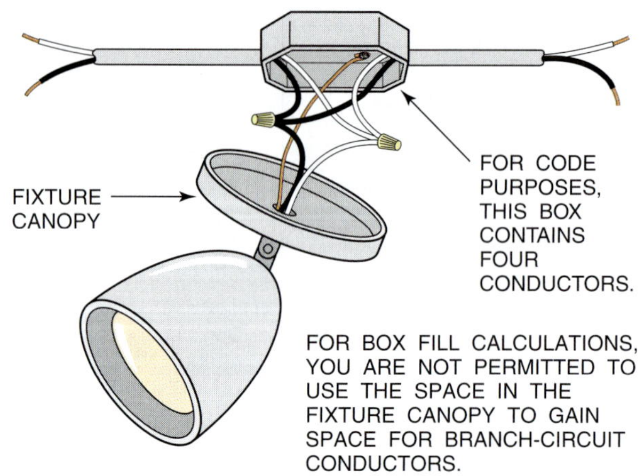

Figure 2-38 Four or fewer luminaire conductors, smaller than 14 AWG, and/or small equipment grounding conductors that originate in the luminaire and terminate in the box, need not be counted when calculating box fill, *314.16(B)(1), Exception*.

Figure 2-20, a quik-chek box selection guide, shows some of the most popular types of boxes used in residential wiring. This guide also shows the box's cubic-inch volume.

Figure 2-39 illustrates typical wiring using cable and conduit. Note in this figure how the conductor count is determined.

Using electrical metallic tubing (EMT) makes it possible to "loop" conductors through the box, which counts as one conductor only. Looping conductors through a box is not possible when using cable as the wiring method.

The basic rules for box fill are summarized in Table 2-1. Boxes that are intended to support ceiling fans are discussed in detail in Chapter 9.

Depth of Box—Watch Out!

►Determining the cubic volume of a box is not the end of the story. Outlet and device boxes shall be deep enough so that conductors will not be damaged when installing the wiring device or equipment into the box. Merely calculating and providing the proper volume of a box is not always enough. The

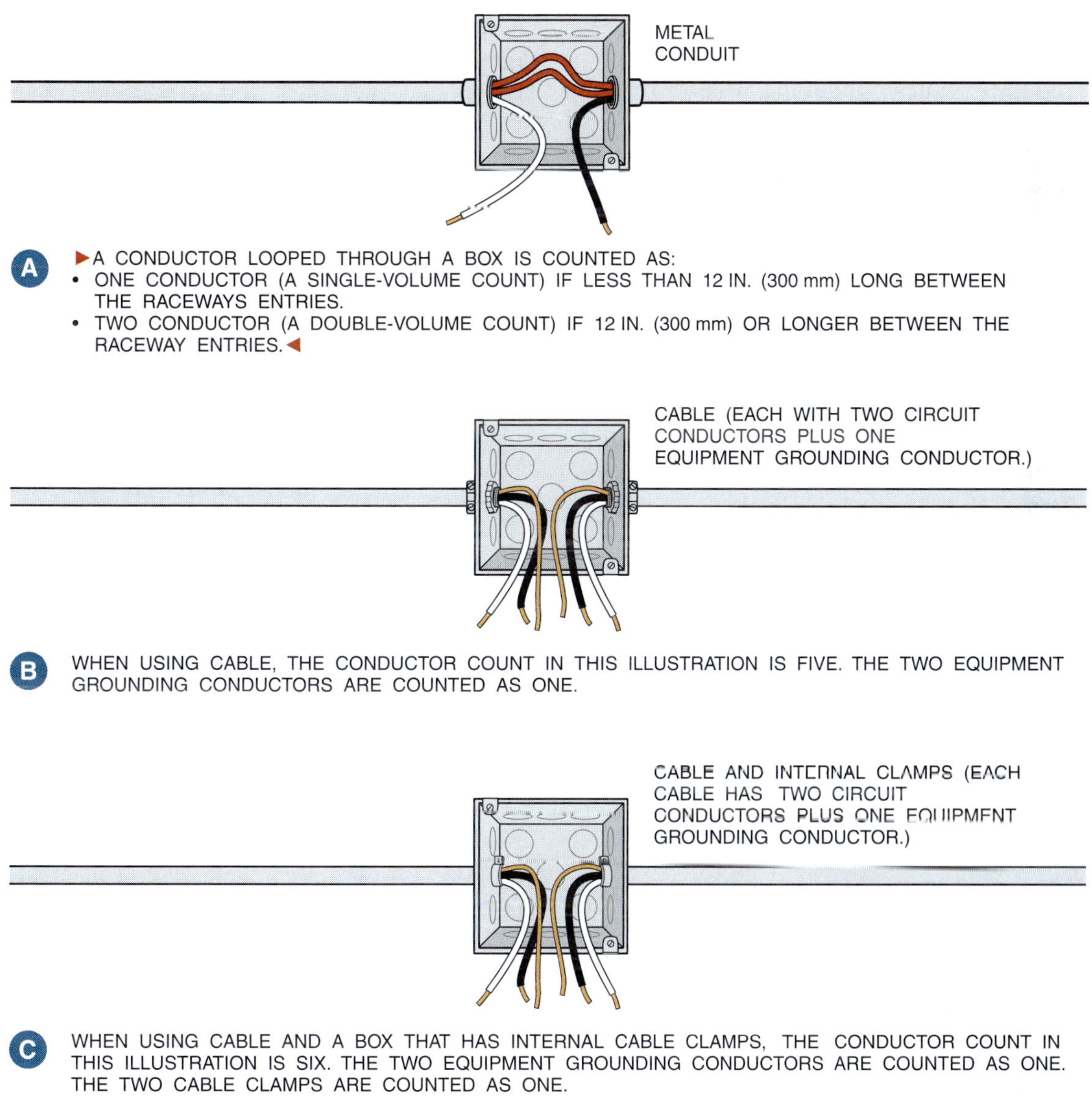

Figure 2-39 Example of conductor count for both metal conduit and cable installations.

volume calculation might prove adequate, yet the size (depth) of the wiring device or equipment might be such that conductors behind it may possibly be damaged. See *NEC® 314.24.*◄

Width of Box—Watch Out!

►Large wiring devices, such as a 30-ampere, three-pole, 4-wire dryer or 50-ampere range receptacle will not fit into a single-gang box that is 2 in. (50.8 mm) wide. These receptacles measure 2.10 in. (53.3 mm) in width. Likewise, a 50-ampere, three-pole, 4-wire receptacle measures 2.75 in. (69.9 mm) in width. Consider using a 4-in. (101.6-mm) square box with a two-gang plaster device ring for flush mounting or a two-gang raised cover for surface mounting, or use a two-gang device box. The center-to-center mounting holes of both the 30-ampere and the 50-ampere receptacles are 1.81 in. (46.0 mm) apart, exactly matching the center-to-center holes of a two-gang plaster ring, raised cover, or two-gang device box. See *NEC® 314.16(B)(4).*◄

Means for Connecting Equipment Grounding Conductors in a Box

►*NEC® 314.4* requires that all metal boxes be grounded and bonded. The specific requirements for specific applications are found in *Article 250, Parts I, IV, V, VI, VII*, and *X.*◄

NEC® 314.40(D) requires that *a means shall be provided in each metal box for the connection of **equipment grounding conductors***. Generally, these are tapped No. 10-32 holes in the box that are marked GR, GRN, GRND, or similar identification. The screws used for terminating the equipment grounding conductor must be hexagonal and must be green. Electrical distributors sell green, hexagonal No. 10-32 screws for this purpose.

HEIGHT OF RECEPTACLE OUTLETS

There are no hard-and-fast rules for locating most outlets. A number of conditions determine the proper height for a switch box. For example, the height of the kitchen counter backsplash determines where the switches and receptacle outlets are located between the kitchen countertop and the cabinets.

The residence featured in this text is electrically heated and is discussed in Chapter 23. The type of electric heat could be:

- electric furnace (as in this text).
- electric resistance heating buried in ceiling plaster or "sandwiched" between two layers of drywall material.
- electric baseboard heaters.
- heat pump.

Let us consider the electric baseboard heaters. In most cases, the height of these electric baseboard units from the top of the unit to the finished floor seldom exceeds 6 in. (150 mm). The important issue here is that the manufacturer's receptacle accessories may have to be used to conform to the receptacle spacing requirements, as covered in *210.52*.

Electrical receptacle outlets are not permitted to be located above an electric baseboard heating unit. Refer to the section "Location of Electric Baseboard Heaters in Relation to Receptacle Outlets," in Chapter 23.

It is common practice among electricians to consult the plans and specifications to determine the proper heights and clearances for the installation of electrical devices. The electrician then has these dimensions verified by the architect, electrical engineer, designer, or homeowner. This practice avoids unnecessary and costly changes in the locations of outlets and switches as the building progresses.

POSITIONING OF RECEPTACLES

Although no *NEC®* rules exist on positioning receptacles, there is always the possibility of a metal wall plate coming loose and falling downward onto the blades of an attachment plug cap that is loosely plugged into the receptacle. This can create sparks that could result in a fire, burns, and potential shock. Positioning the *equipment grounding* conductor slot or the *grounded* conductor slot on top will minimize these hazards.

The equipment grounding blade on a three-wire attachment plug cap is longer than the other blades. Thus, when inserted into a receptacle, in agreement with *250.124(A)*, the equipment grounding blade is first to make and last to break.

There is also the argument that with the equipment grounding slot to the bottom, if a plug cap comes loose and starts to fall out, the longer equipment grounding blade would be the last connection to be disconnected. See Figure 2-40, Figure 2-41, Figure 2-42, and Figure 2-43.

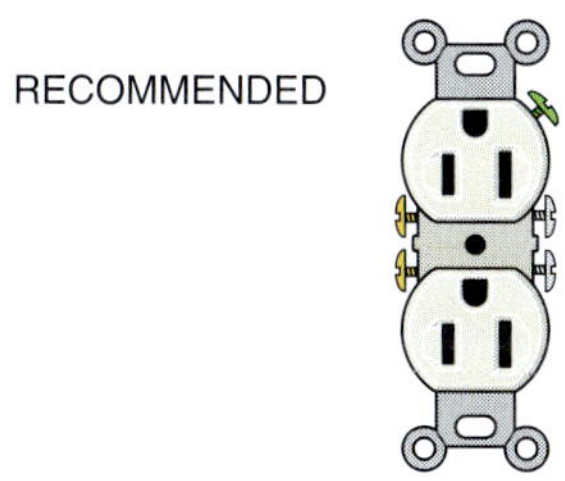

Figure 2-40 Grounding hole to the top. A loose metal faceplate could fall onto the grounding blade of the attachment plug cap, but no sparks would fly.

Figure 2-41 Grounding hole to the bottom. A loose metal faceplate could fall onto both the grounded neutral and "hot" blades. Sparks would fly.

Figure 2-42 Grounded neutral blades on top. A loose metal faceplate could fall onto these grounded neutral blades. No sparks would fly.

Figure 2-43 "Hot" terminal on top. A loose metal faceplate could fall onto these live blades. If this were a split-circuit receptacle fed by a three-wire, 120/240-volt circuit, the short would be across the 240-volt line. Sparks would fly.

TYPICAL HEIGHTS FOR SWITCHES AND OUTLETS

There are no hard-and-fast *Code* rules regarding the heights for switches and receptacles; local preferences prevail. Typical heights for switches and outlets are shown in Table 2-2. These dimensions usually are satisfactory. However, the electrician must check the blueprints, specifications, and details for measurements that may affect the location of a particular outlet or switch. The cabinet spacing, available space between the countertop and the cabinet, and the tile height may influence the location of the outlet or switch. For example, if the top of the wall tile is exactly 4 ft (1.2 m) from the finished floor line, a wall switch should not be mounted 4 ft (1.2 m) to center. This is considered poor workmanship. The switch should be located entirely within the tile area or entirely out of the tile area, as in Figure 2-44. This situation requires the full cooperation of all craftspersons involved in the construction job.

Faceplates

Faceplates for switches and receptacles shall be installed so as to completely cover the wall opening and seat against the wall surface, *404.9(A)* and *406.5*.

Faceplates should be level! No matter how good the wiring inside the wall is, no matter how good the connections and splices are, no matter how proper the equipment grounding is, the only thing the homeowner will see is the wiring devices and the faceplates. That establishes the impression the

SWITCHES	
Regular	46 in. (1.15 m). Some homeowners want wall switches mounted 30 in.–36 in. (750 mm–900 mm) so as to be easy for children to reach and easy for adults to reach when carrying something. The choice is yours!
Between counter and kitchen cabinets. Depends on backsplash.	44 in.–46 in. (1 m–1.15 m)
RECEPTACLE OUTLETS	
Regular	12 in. (300 mm)
Between counter and kitchen cabinets. Depends on backsplash.	44 in.–46 in. (1 m–1.15 m)
In garages	46 in. (1.15 m) Minimum 18 in. (450 mm)
In unfinished basements	46 in. (1.15 m)
In finished basements	12 in. (300 mm)
Outdoors (above grade or deck)	18 in. (450 mm)
WALL LUMINAIRE OUTLETS	
Outdoor entrance bracket luminaires	72 in. (1.8 m). If luminaire is "upward," mount wall box lower. If luminaire is "downward," mount wall box higher. A good appearance for typical outdoor wall lanterns is when the center of wall box is approximately 10 in. (0.254 m) below the top of the door. The final choice is yours.
Inside wall brackets	5 ft (1.5 m)
Side of medicine cabinet or mirror Above medicine cabinet or mirror	You need to know the measurement of the medicine cabinet. Check the rough-in opening of medicine cabinet measurement of mirror. Mount electrical wall box approx. 6 in. (150 mm) to center above rough-in opening or mirror. Medicine cabinets that come complete with luminaires have a wiring compartment with a conduit knockout(s) in which the supply cable or conduit is secured using the appropriate fitting. Many strip luminaires have a backplate with a conduit knockout in which the supply cable or conduit is secured using the appropriate fitting. Where to bring in the cable or conduit takes careful planning.

Note: All dimensions are from finished floor to center of the electrical box. If possible, try to mount wall boxes for luminaires based upon the type of luminaire to be installed. Verify all dimensions before "roughing in." If wiring for physically handicapped, the above heights may need to be lowered in the case of switches and raised in the case of receptacles.

Table 2-2 Typical heights for switches, receptacles, and wall luminaire outlets. Local height preferences prevail.

homeowner has of the overall wiring installation. Because of the elongated slots in the yoke of a wiring device, it is rather easy to level a wiring device and faceplate on a single-gang box even if the box is not level. This is not true for multi-gang boxes. It is extremely important to make sure multi-gang boxes are level. If a multi-gang box is not level, it will be virtually impossible to make the wiring devices and faceplate level.

Another nice detail that can improve the appearance is to align the slots in all of the faceplate mounting screws in the same direction, as in Figure 2-45. This is not a *Code* rule—just a nice little finishing touch.

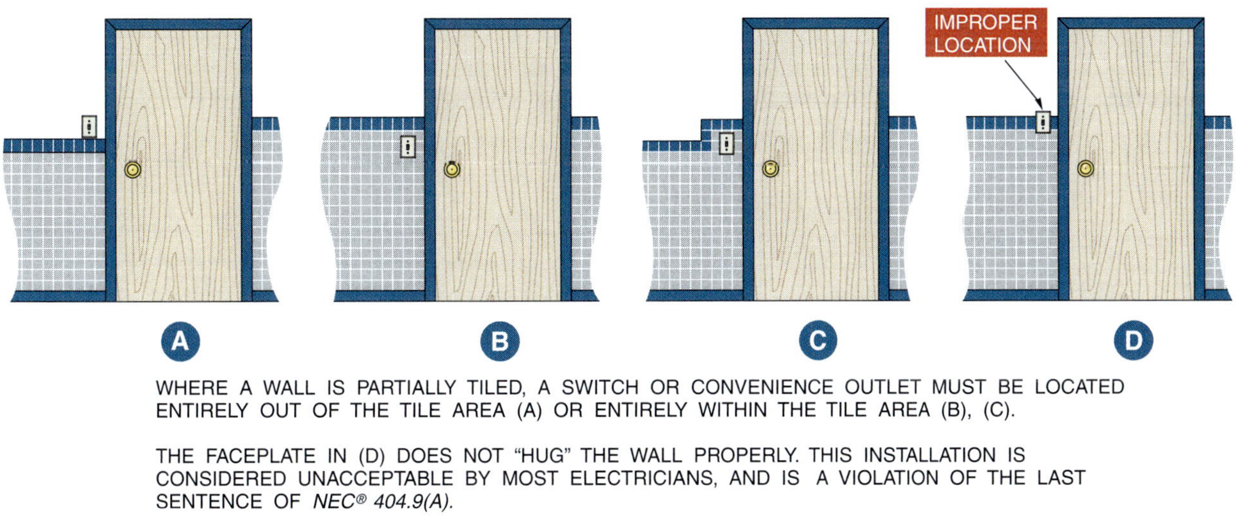

Figure 2-44 Locating an outlet on a tiled wall.

Figure 2-45 Aligning the slots of the faceplate. Mounting screws in the same direction makes the installation look neater. Make sure the faceplate is level.

REVIEW

Note: For assistance in finding the answers to these review questions, refer to the *NEC*,® the plans in the back of this text, and the specifications found in the Appendix.

PART 1—ELECTRICAL FEATURES

1. What does a plan show about electrical outlets? ______

2. What is an outlet? ______

3. Match the following switch types with the proper symbol.
   a. single-pole — S_p
   b. three-way — S_4
   c. four-way — S
   d. single-pole with pilot light — S_3

4. The plans show dashed lines running between switches and various outlets. What do these dashed lines indicate? ______

5. Why are dashed lines usually curved? ______

6. a. What are junction boxes used for? ______
   b. Are junction boxes normally used in wiring the first floor? Explain. ______
   c. Are junction boxes normally used to wire exposed portions of the basement? Explain. ______

7. How are standard sectional switch (device) boxes mounted? ______

8. a. What is an offset bar hanger? ______
   b. What types of boxes may be used with offset bar hangers? ______

9. What methods may be used to mount luminaires to an outlet box fastened to an offset bar hanger? ____

____

____

10. What advantage does a 4-in. octagon box have over a 3¼-in. octagon box?

____

____

11. What is the size of the opening of a switch (device) box for a single device? __________

____

12. The space between a door casing and a window casing is 3½ in. (88.9 mm). Two switches are to be installed at this location. What type of switches will be used?

____

____

13. Three switches are mounted in a three-gang switch (device) box. The wall plate for this assembly is called a ______________________________ plate.

14. The mounting holes in a device (switch) box are tapped for No. 6-32 screws. The mounting holes in an outlet box are tapped for No. 8-32 screws. The mounting holes in metal boxes for attaching equipment grounding conductors are tapped for ______________ screws.

15. a. How high above the finished floor in the living room are switches located?

____

b. How high above the garage floor are switches located?

____

16. a. How high above the finished floor in the living room are receptacles located?

____

b. How high above the garage floor are receptacles located?

____

17. Outdoor receptacle outlets in this dwelling are located ______________________________ ______________ in. above grade.

18. In the spaces provided, draw the correct symbol for each of the descriptions listed in (a) through (r).

a. __________ Lighting panel
b. __________ Clock outlet
c. __________ Duplex outlet
d. __________ Outside telephone
e. __________ Single-pole switch
f. __________ Motor
g. __________ Duplex outlet, split-circuit
h. __________ Lampholder with pull switch
i. __________ Weatherproof outlet
j. __________ Special-purpose outlet
k. __________ Fan outlet
l. __________ Range outlet
m. __________ Power panel
n. __________ Three-way switch
o. __________ Push button
p. __________ Thermostat
q. __________ Electric door opener
r. __________ Multi-outlet assembly

19. The front edge of a box installed in a combustible wall must be ________________ with the finished surface.

20. List the maximum number of 12 AWG conductors permitted in a
    a. 4 in. × 1½ in. octagon box. ________________
    b. 4^{11}⁄16 in. × 1½ in. square box. ________________
    c. 3 in. × 2 in. × 3½ in. device box. ________________

21. When a switch (device) box is nailed to a stud, and the nail runs through the box, the nails must not interfere with the wiring space. To accomplish this, keep the nail ____________ (Select a, b, or c.)
    a. halfway between the front and rear of the box.
    b. a maximum of ¼ in. (6 mm) from the front edge of the box.
    c. a maximum of ¼ in. (6 mm) from the rear of the box.

22. Hanging a ceiling luminaire directly from a plastic outlet box is permitted only if
    ____
    ____
    ____
    ____

23. It is necessary to count luminaire wires when counting the permitted number of conductors in a box according to *314.16*.

    (True) (False) Underline or circle the correct answer.

24. *Table 314.16(A)* allows a maximum of ten wires in a certain box. However, the box will have two cable clamps and one fixture stud in it. What is the maximum number of wires allowed in this box? ________________
    ____

25. When laying out a job, the electrician will usually make a layout of the circuit, taking into consideration the best way to run the cables and/or conduits and how to make up the electrical connections. Doing this ahead of time, the electrician determines exactly how many conductors will be fed into each box. With experience, the electrician will probably select two or three sizes and types of boxes that will provide adequate space to "meet Code." *Table 314.16(A)* of the *Code* shows the maximum number of conductors permitted in a given size box. In addition to counting the number of conductors that will be in the box, what is the additional volume that must be provided for the following items? Enter *single* or *double* volume allowance in the blank provided.
    a. one or more internal cable clamps: __________ volume allowance.
    b. for a fixture stud: __________ volume allowance.
    c. for one or more wiring devices on one yoke: __________ volume allowance.
    d. for one or more equipment grounding conductors: __________ volume allowance.

26. Is it permissible to install a receptacle outlet above an electric baseboard heater?

____

____

27. What is the maximum weight of a luminaire permitted to be hung directly from an outlet box in a ceiling? ______________ lb.

28. Two 12/2 and two 14/2 nonmetallic-sheathed AWG cables enter a box. Each cable has an equipment grounding conductor. The 12 AWG conductors are connected to a receptacle. Two of the 14 AWG conductors are connected to a toggle switch. The other two 14 AWG conductors are spliced together since they serve as a switch loop. The box contains two cable clamps. Calculate the minimum cubic-inch volume required for the box.

29. Using the same number and size of conductors as in question 28, but using electrical metallic tubing, calculate the minimum cubic-inch volume required for the box. There will be no separate equipment grounding conductors, nor will there be any clamps in the box.

30. To allow for adequate conductor length at electrical outlet and device boxes to make up connections, *300.14* requires that not less than [3 in. (75 mm), 6 in. (150 mm), 9 in. (225 mm)] of conductor length be provided. This length is measured from where the conductor emerges from the cable or raceway to the end of the conductor. For box openings having any dimension less than 8 in. (200 mm), the minimum length of conductor measured from the box opening in the wall to the end of the conductor is [3 in. (75 mm), 6 in. (150 mm), 9 in. (225 mm)]. Circle the correct answers.

31. When wiring a residence, what must be considered when installing wall boxes on both sides of a common partition that separates the garage and a habitable room? ________

____

____

32. Does the *NEC*® allow metal raceways to be used with nonmetallic boxes?

Yes ______________ No ______________, *NEC*® ______________

PART 2—STRUCTURAL FEATURES

1. To what scale is the basement plan drawn? ______
2. What is the size of the footing for the steel Lally columns in the basement? Refer to Plan 1 of 10. (Lally is the trademark used for a concrete-filled steel cylinder used as a supporting member for wood or steel girders and beams. The Lally column was named after John Lally, born in Ireland in 1859. The term "lolly" is also used.) ______
3. To what kind of material will the front porch lighting bracket luminaire be attached? ______
4. Give the size, spacing, and direction of the ceiling joists in the workshop. ______
5. What is the size of the lot on which this residence is located? ______
6. The front of the house is facing which compass direction? ______
7. How far is the front garage wall from the curb? ______
8. How far is the side garage wall from the property lot line? ______
9. How many steel Lally columns are in the basement and what size are they? ______
10. What is the purpose of the I-beams that rest on top of the steel Lally columns? ______
11. To make sure that switch boxes and outlet boxes are set properly in the garage walls and ceilings, we need to know the thickness of the gypsum wallboard used in these locations. In the garage, what is the thickness and type of the gypsum wallboard?
    a. on the "warm walls" of the garage? ______
    b. on the "cold walls" of the garage? ______
    c. on the ceiling of the garage? ______
12. Where is access to the attic provided? ______
13. Give the thickness of the outer basement walls. ______
14. What material is indicated for the foundation walls? ______
15. Where are the smoke detectors located in the basement? ______
16. What is the ceiling height in the basement workshop from the bottom of the joists to the floor? ______
17. Give the size and type of the front door. ______
18. What is the stud size for the partitions between the bathrooms in the bedroom area where substantial plumbing is to be installed? ______

19. Who is to furnish the range hood? ____

____

20. Who is to install the range hood? ____

CHAPTER 3

Determining the Required Number of Lighting Outlets, Receptacle Outlets, and Small-Appliance Branch Circuits

OBJECTIVES

After studying this chapter, you should be able to

- **understand the *NEC*® requirements for calculating branch-circuit sizing and loading.**
- **understand the term *volt-amperes per square foot*.**
- **calculate the occupied floor area of a residence.**
- **determine the minimum number of lighting and small-appliance branch circuits.**
- **know where receptacle outlets and lighting outlets are required.**

It is standard practice in the design and planning of dwelling units to permit the electrician to plan the circuits. Thus, the residence plans do not include layouts for the various branch circuits. The electrician may follow the general guidelines established by the architect. However, any wiring systems designed and installed by the electrician must conform to the *NEC*,® as well as local and state code requirements.

This chapter focuses on lighting branch circuits and small-appliance branch circuits. The circuits supplying the electric range, oven, clothes dryer, and other specific circuitry not considered to be a lighting branch circuit or a small-appliance branch circuit are covered later in this text. Refer to the index for the specific circuit being examined.

BASICS OF WIRE SIZING AND LOADING

The *NEC*® establishes some very important fundamentals that weave their way through the decision-making process for an electrical installation. They are presented here in brief form, and are covered in detail as required throughout this text.

The *NEC*® defines a **branch circuit** as: *the circuit conductors between the final overcurrent device protecting the circuit and the outlet(s)**. See Figure 3-1. In the residence discussed in this text, the wiring to wall outlets, the dryer, the range, and so on, are all examples of a branch circuit.

The *NEC*® defines a **feeder** as: *All circuit conductors between the service equipment, the source of a separately derived system, or other power supply source and the final branch-circuit overcurrent device.** In the residence discussed in this text, the wiring between Main Panel A and Subpanel B is a feeder.

The ampacity (current-carrying capacity) of a conductor must not be less than the rating of the

---

*Reprinted with permission from NFPA 70-2008.

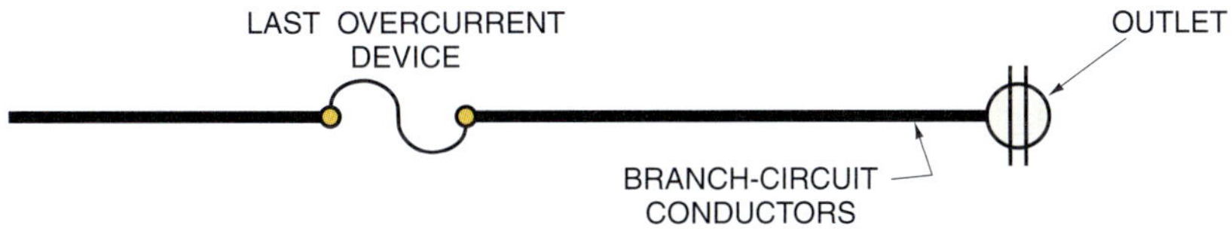

Figure 3-1 The branch circuit is that part of the wiring that runs from the final overcurrent device to the outlet. The rating of the overcurrent device, not the conductor size, determines the rating of the branch circuit.

overcurrent device protecting that conductor, *210.19* and *210.20*. A common exception to this is a motor branch circuit, where it is quite common to have overcurrent devices (fuses or breakers) sized larger than the ampacity of the conductor. Motors and motor circuits are covered specifically in *Article 430*. The **ampere** rating of the branch-circuit overcurrent protective device (fuse or circuit breaker) determines the rating of the branch circuit. For example, if a 20-ampere conductor is protected by a 15-ampere fuse, the circuit is considered to be a 15-ampere branch circuit, *210.3*.

Standard branch circuits that serve more than one receptacle outlet or more than one lighting outlet are rated 15, 20, 30, 40, and 50 amperes. A branch circuit that supplies an individual load can be of any ampere rating, *210.3*.

Where the ampacity of the conductor does not match up with a standard rating of a fuse or breaker, the next higher standard size overcurrent device may be used, provided the overcurrent device does not exceed 800 amperes, *240.4(B)*. This deviation is not permitted, however, if the circuit supplies receptacles where "plug-connected" appliances, and so on, could be used, because too many "plug-in" loads could result in an overload condition, *240.4(B)(1)*. You may go to the next standard size overcurrent device only when the circuit supplies other than receptacles for cord- and plug-connected portable loads.

For instance, when a conductor having an allowable ampacity of 25 amperes (see *Table 310.16*) 12 AWG Type TW is derated to 70%:

$$25 \times 0.70 = 17.5 \text{ amperes}$$

It is permitted to use a 20-ampere overcurrent device if the circuit supplies *only* fixed lighting outlets or other fixed loads.

If the previous example were to supply receptacle outlets, then the rating of the overcurrent device would have to be dropped to 15 amperes; otherwise it is possible to overload the conductors by plugging in more load than the conductors can safely carry.

The allowable ampacity of conductors commonly used in residential occupancies is found in *Table 310.16*. The ampacities in *Table 310.16* are subject to **correction factors** that must be applied if high ambient temperatures are encountered—for example, in attics. See the bottom of *Table 310.16*.

Conductor ampacities are also subject to a **factor** if more than three current-carrying conductors are installed in a single raceway or cable. See *Table 310.15(B)(2)(a)*. See Chapter 18 for complete coverage of correction and derating factors.

Most general-use receptacle outlets in a residence are included in the general lighting load calculations, *220.14(J)*.

Receptacle outlets connected to the 20-ampere small-appliance branch circuits in the kitchen, dining room, laundry, and workshop are not considered part of general lighting load. Additional load values must be added into the calculations for these receptacle outlets. This is discussed later in this text.

The minimum lighting load for dwellings is 3 **volt-amperes** per square foot. See *220.12* and *Table 220.12*.

Continuous Loads

The *NEC®* defines **continuous load** as: *a load where the maximum current is expected to continue for three hours or more. Continuous* loads shall not exceed 80% of the rating of the branch circuit. General lighting outlets and receptacle outlets in residences **are not** considered to be continuous loads.

Certain loads in homes are considered to be continuous and must be treated accordingly. Examples are electric water heaters (*422.13*), central electric heating [*424.3(B)*], snow-melting cables (*426.4*), and air-conditioning equipment (*440.32*). For these loads, the branch-circuit rating, the conductors, and the overcurrent device shall not be less than 125% of the rating of the equipment. Mathematically, sizing the conductors and overcurrent device at 125% of the load is the same as loading the conductors and overcurrent device to 80%.

For example, an electric furnace with a nameplate rating of 40 amperes would require the supply conductors and overcurrent protection to be not less than:

$$40 \times 1.25 = 50 \text{ amperes}$$

VOLTAGE

All calculations throughout this text use voltage values of 120 volts and 240 volts. This complies with the requirements of *220.5*, which lists the various voltage values to use for different electrical systems. This is repeated in the second paragraph of *Annex D* of the *NEC*.®

The word *nominal* means "in name only, not a fact." For example, in our calculations, we use 120 volts even though the actual voltage might be 110, 115, or 117 volts. This provides us with a uniformity that, without it, would lead to misleading and confusing results in our calculations.

Most public service commissions require that the voltage for residential services be held to ±5% of the nominal voltage as measured at the service point.

CALCULATING LOADS

When wiring a house, it is all but impossible to know which appliances, lighting, heating, and other loads will be turned on at the same time. Different families lead different lifestyles. There is tremendous diversity. There is a big difference between "connected load" and "actual load." Who knows what will be plugged into a wall receptacle, now or in the future? It's a guess at best. Over the years, the *NEC*® has developed procedures for calculating loads in typical one- and two-family homes.

The rules for doing the calculations are found in *Article 220*. For lighting and receptacles, the computations are based on volt-amperes per square foot. For the small-appliance circuits in kitchens and dining rooms, the basis is 1500 volt-amperes per circuit. For large appliances such as dryers, electric ranges, ovens, cooktops, water heaters, air conditioners, heat pumps, and so on, which are not all used continuously or at the same time, there are demand factors to be used in the calculations. Following the requirements in the *NEC*,® the various calculations roll together in steps that result in the proper sizing of branch circuits, feeders, and service equipment.

As you work your way through this text, examples are provided for just about every kind and type of load found in a typical residence.

Inch-pounds vs. Metrics When Calculating Loads

As discussed in Chapter 1, converting inch-pound measurements to metric measurements and vice versa results in odd fractional results. Adding further to this problem are the values rounded off when the *NEC*® Code-Making Panels did the metric conversions. When square feet is converted to square meters and the unit loads are calculated for each, the end results are different; close, but nevertheless different. To show both calculations would be confusing as well as space consuming. Many of the measurements in this text are shown in both inch-pound units and metric units. Load calculations throughout this text use inch-pound values only, which is in agreement with the *Examples* given in *Annex D* of the 2005 *NEC*.®

CALCULATING FLOOR AREA

The general lighting load for a dwelling is based on the square footage of the dwelling. Here is how this is done.

First Floor Area

To estimate the total load for a dwelling, the occupied floor area of the dwelling must be calculated. Note in the residence plans that the first floor area has an irregular shape. In this case, the simplest method of calculating the occupied floor area is to determine the total floor area using the outside dimensions of the dwelling. Then, the areas of the following spaces are subtracted from the total area: open porches, garages, or other unfinished or unused spaces if they are not adaptable for future use, *220.12*.

Many open porches, terraces, patios, and similar areas are commonly used as recreation and entertainment areas. Adequate lighting and receptacle outlets should be provided for these areas.

For practicality, the author has chosen to round up dimensions for the determining of total square footage and to round down dimensions for those areas (garage, porch, and portions of the inset at the front of the house) not to be included in the computation of the general lighting load. This produces a slightly larger result as opposed to being on the conservative side. Don't be miserly with your measurements; rather, be generous. Figure 3-2 shows the procedure for calculating the total square footage of this residence.

Basement Area

Although the *NEC*® in *220.12* tells us that *unused or unfinished spaces not adaptable for future use* do not have to be included in calculating the square footage of a dwelling, it makes sense to include some of these spaces.

Nearly all basements in homes today certainly could be considered as being adaptable for future use. A crawl space and most attics would not normally be considered as being adaptable for future use. This is a judgment call based upon a close examination of the Plans and Specifications. In this residence, more than half of the total basement area is finished off as a recreation room, which certainly is considered a living area. The workshop area also is intended to be used.

To simplify the calculation for this residence, we will consider the entire basement as usable space and figure the basement square footage area as being the same as the area of the first floor.

The combined occupied area of the dwelling is found by adding the first floor and basement areas together:

First Floor	1616 ft^2 (149 m^2)
Basement	1616 ft^2 (149 m^2)
Total	3232 ft^2 (298 m^2)

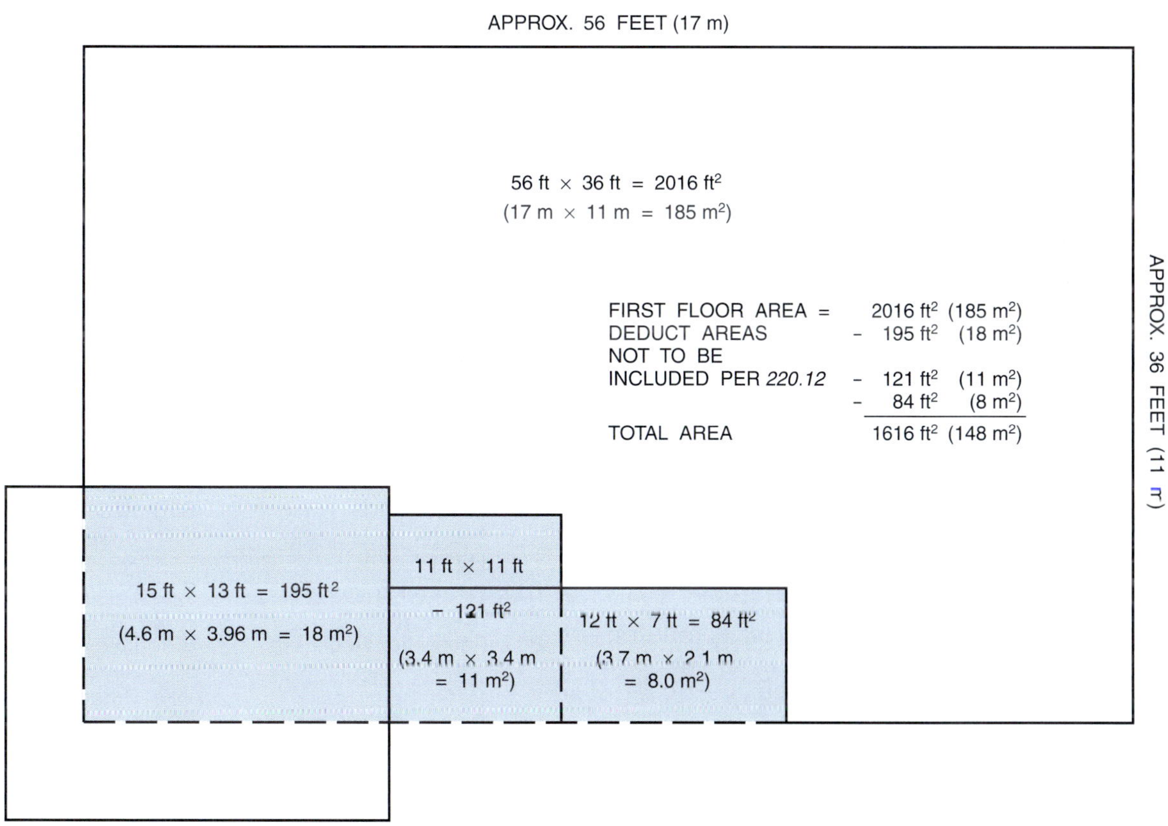

Figure 3-2 Determining the first floor square footage area. The basement area is the same as the first floor. See text for explanation of how the dimensions of the residence were rounded off to make the calculations much simpler and much more practical for the electrician and electrical inspector to calculate.

DETERMINING THE MINIMUM NUMBER OF LIGHTING BRANCH CIRCUITS

Table 220.12 of the *NEC*® tells us that the minimum load requirement for dwelling units is 3 volt-amperes (VA) per square ft (0.093 m^2) of occupied area.

To determine the minimum number of 15-ampere lighting branch circuits required for a residence, here are the simple steps.

$$\text{Step 1: } \frac{3 \text{ volt-amperes} \times \text{square ft}}{120 \text{ volts}} = \text{amperes}$$

$$\text{Step 2: } \frac{\text{amperes}}{15} = \text{minimum number of 15-ampere lighting branch circuits}$$

This equates to a minimum of:

- one 15-ampere lighting branch circuit for every 600 ft^2 (55.8 m^2).
- one 20-ampere lighting branch circuit for every 800 ft^2 (74.4 m^2).

Note: 20-ampere lighting branch circuits are rarely used in residential installations.

In this residence, let's calculate the load for the total occupied area of 3232 ft^2 (298 m^2):

$$3232 \times 3 = 9696 \text{ volt-amperes}$$

$$\text{Amperes} = \frac{\text{volt-amperes}}{\text{volts}} = \frac{9696}{120} = 80.8 \text{ amperes}$$

The minimum number of 15-ampere lighting branch circuits is:

$$\frac{80.0 \text{ amperes}}{15 \text{ amperes}} = \begin{array}{l}\text{5.39 branch circuits}\\ \text{(round up to 6)}\end{array}$$

Since we cannot have a fraction of a branch circuit, we rounded up to a minimum of six 15-ampere lighting branch circuits.

We get the same answer using 600 ft^2 (55.8 m^2) for each 15-ampere lighting branch circuit as follows:

$$\frac{3232 \text{ ft}^2}{600} = \begin{array}{l}\text{5.39 branch circuits}\\ \text{(round up to 6)}\end{array}$$

No matter which method we use, a minimum of six 15-ampere lighting branch circuits is required.

In *Annex D* of the *NEC*® we find many examples of load calculations. Here, we also find that *Except where the calculations result in a major fraction of an ampere (0.5 or larger), such fractions are permitted to be dropped.* **CAUTION: This permission is for load calculations such as in Step 1. This permission to drop fractions is *not* to be used in Step 2 because it is impossible to have a fraction of a branch circuit. That is why we rounded up from 5.39 to arrive at a minimum of six 15-ampere branch circuits.**

Load calculations for small-appliance branch circuits and other major appliance branch circuits are in addition to the general lighting loads. These calculations are discussed throughout this text as they appear.

The *NEC*® in *210.11(B)* states that the calculated load *shall be evenly proportioned among multioutlet branch circuits within the panelboard(s).*

Table 3-1 is the schedule of the 15-ampere lighting and 20-ampere small-appliance branch circuits in this residence.

SUMMARY OF 15-AMPERE LIGHTING AND 20-AMPERE RECEPTACLE CIRCUITS

15-Ampere Circuits		20-Ampere Circuits	
A14	Bathrooms, Hall Ltg.	A18	Workbench Receptacles
A15	Front Entry/Porch	A20	Workshop Receptacles, Window Wall
A16	Front Bedroom Ltg. & Outdoor Receptacle	A22	Master Bath Receptacle
A17	Workshop Ltg.	A23	Hall Bath Receptacle
A19	Master Bedroom Ltg. & Outdoor Receptacle		
A21	Study/Bedroom Ltg.		
B7	Kitchen Ltg.	B13	Kitchen North & East Wall Receptacles
B9	Wet Bar Ltg. & Receptacles	B15	Kitchen Receptacles, West Countertop
B10	Laundry, Rear Entry, Powder Room, Attic Ltg.	B16	Kitchen Receptacles, South Countertop, & Island
B11	Recreation Room Receptacles	B18	Washer Receptacle
B12	Recreation Room Ltg.	B20	Laundry Room Receptacles & Outdoor Receptacle
B14	Garage, Post Light	B21	Powder Room Receptacle
B17	Living Room & Outdoor Receptacle	B22	Refrigerator

Note: Panel "A" is the main panel located in the workshop. Panel "B" is the subpanel located in the corner of the recreation room.

Table 3-1

240.4(D) tells us that the maximum overcurrent protection is:

15 amperes for 14 AWG copper conductors

20 amperes for 12 AWG copper conductors

30 amperes for 10 AWG copper conductors

In conformance to *210.3*, a branch circuit is rated according to the rating or setting of the overcurrent device. For example, a lighting branch circuit is rated 15 amperes even if 12 AWG copper conductors are installed.

How Many Outlets per Circuit

This is covered in detail in Chapter 8, where you will find *Estimating Loads for Outlets, How Many Outlets per Circuit, Circuit Loading Rules of Thumb*, and the *80% Rule*.

TRACK LIGHTING LOADS

Track lighting loads are considered to be part of the general lighting load for residential installations, based upon the 3 volt-amperes per square foot as previously discussed. There is no need to add more wattage (volt-amperes) to the load calculations for track lighting in homes.

As required by *410.151(B)*, the connected load on a lighting track shall not exceed the rating of the track. Also, be sure that a lighting track is supplied by a branch circuit having a rating not more than that of the track. There is more on track lighting in Chapters 12 and 13.

DETERMINING THE NUMBER OF SMALL-APPLIANCE BRANCH CIRCUITS

NEC® 220.52(A) and *(B)* state that an additional load of not less than 1500 volt-amperes shall be included for each two-wire small-appliance circuit and each laundry circuit.

The receptacle for the refrigerator in the kitchen is permitted to be supplied by an individual 15- or 20-ampere branch circuit rather than connecting it to one of the two required 20-ampere small-appliance circuits. This permission is found in *210.52(B)(1), Exception No. 2*.

The *NEC®* defines an *individual branch circuit* as: *A branch circuit that supplies only one utilization equipment.*

Providing an individual branch circuit for the refrigerator diverts the refrigerator load from the receptacle branch circuits that serve the countertop areas. Because this individual branch circuit does not serve countertops, it is not considered a small-appliance branch circuit. An additional 1500 volt-amperes *does not* have to be added into the load calculations, *220-52(A), Exception No. 2*. There is nothing in the *Code* that prohibits adding another 1500 volt-amperes to the load calculations for this additional branch circuit, as this would result in more capacity in the electrical system.

NEC® 210.11(C)(1) requires that two or more 20-ampere small-appliance circuits must be provided for supplying receptacle outlets, as specified in *210.52(B)*.

NEC® 210.52(B)(1) states that the 20-ampere appliance circuits shall serve only the receptacle outlets in the kitchen, pantry, dining room, breakfast room, or similar rooms of dwelling units. *NEC® 210.52(B)(2)* also requires that these 20-ampere small-appliance circuits shall not supply other outlets.

Exceptions in *210.52(B)(2)* allow clock receptacles and receptacles that are installed to plug in the cords of gas-fired ranges, ovens, or counter-mounted cooking units in order to power up their timers and ignition systems, Figure 3-3.

NEC® 210.52(B)(3) requires that not less than two 20-ampere small-appliance circuits must supply the receptacle outlets serving the countertop areas in kitchens.

Food waste disposers and/or dishwashers shall not be connected to these required 20-ampere small-appliance circuits. They must be supplied by other circuits, as is discussed later. Generally, 12 AWG conductors are used to connect these applicances. The use of this larger conductor, rather than a 14 AWG conductor, helps improve appliance performance and lessens the danger of overloading the circuits.

A complete list of the branch circuits for this residence is found in Chapter 27. The circuit directories for Main Panel A and Subpanel B show clearly the number of lighting, appliance, and special-purpose circuits provided.

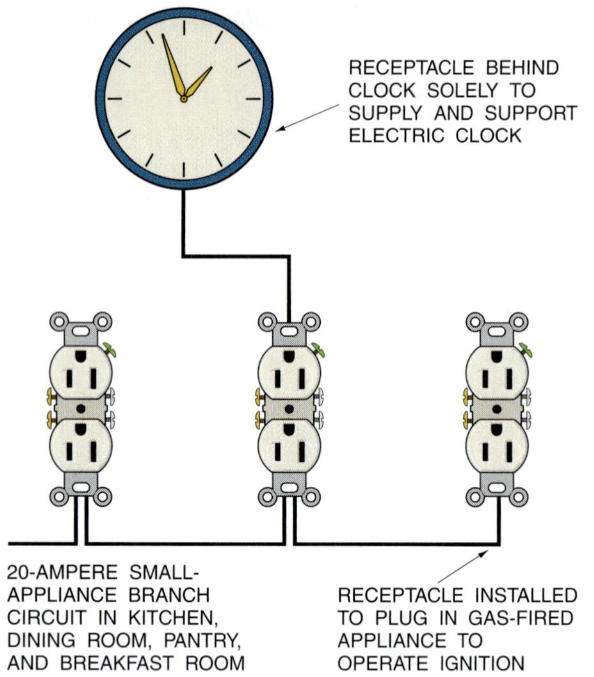

Figure 3-3 A receptacle installed solely to supply and support an electric clock, or a receptacle that supplies power for clocks, clock timers, and electric ignitions for gas ranges, ovens, and cooktops, may be connected to a 20-ampere small-appliance circuit or to a general-purpose lighting circuit, *210.52(B)(2), Exceptions.*

RECEPTACLE OUTLET BRANCH-CIRCUIT RATINGS

The receptacles in the kitchen, breakfast area, workshop, powder room, bathrooms, and laundry room are connected to 20-ampere branch circuits. All other receptacles are connected to 15-ampere branch circuits.

SUMMARY OF WHERE RECEPTACLE AND LIGHTING OUTLETS MUST BE INSTALLED IN RESIDENCES

The following is a recap of the *NEC*® requirements for receptacle and lighting outlets. We will look at these *Code* rules, room by room, later in this text.

Remember, the *NEC*® provides *minimum* requirements. There is nothing wrong with installing more receptacles than the *NEC*® *minimum*. You will never have enough receptacles! Think about it. A duplex receptacle can't handle computers, cable modems, small UPS devices, printers, stereos, VCRs, VDRs, CD players, CD burners, shredders, television sets, radios, fax machines, answering machines, typewriters, adding machines, pencil sharpeners, lamps, telephones, and others.

Consider spacing receptacles closer than the minimum. Consider quadplex receptacles or two duplex receptacles at each receptacle outlet location and consider surge suppression receptacles or surge protection multiple plug-in strips. See Chapter 6 for a discussion of surge protection.

TIP: Some electricians install a receptacle below the wall switch in bedrooms, living rooms, family rooms, and similar rooms. As is usually the case, the required receptacles will be behind furniture, making it difficult to reach for plugging in a vacuum cleaner or other temporarily used appliance. A receptacle below the wall switch will be very easy to get to. A real plus! See Figure 3-4 for an explanation of *receptacle* and *receptacle outlet*.

Receptacle Outlets (125 Volts, Single-Phase, 15 and 20 Amperes)

Ground-Fault Circuit-Interrupter (GFCI): GFCI protection is required in specific locations in a home. GFCIs are discussed in Chapter 6.

Arc-Fault Circuit-Interrupter (AFCI): AFCI protection is required in specific locations in a home. AFCIs are discussed in Chapter 6.

The following is a list of *Code* requirements where receptacles are required in new homes.

- ►Receptacles are located throughout a home for the convenience of plugging "things" in. The following required locations for receptacles are in addition to receptacles that are wall switch controlled, are part of a luminaire or appliance, or if located inside of a cabinet, or located more than 5½ ft (1.7 m) above the floor. A duplex receptacle that has one receptacle switched and one receptacle "hot" continuously meets the receptacle requirements of *210.52* and the switching requirements of *210.70*. See Figures 3-9, 3-10, and 8-10.◄
- Wall receptacles must be placed so that no point measured horizontally along the floor line in any wall space is more than 6 ft (1.8 m) from a receptacle outlet. Fixed room dividers and railings are considered to be walls for the purpose of this requirement. See *210.52(A)(1)*.

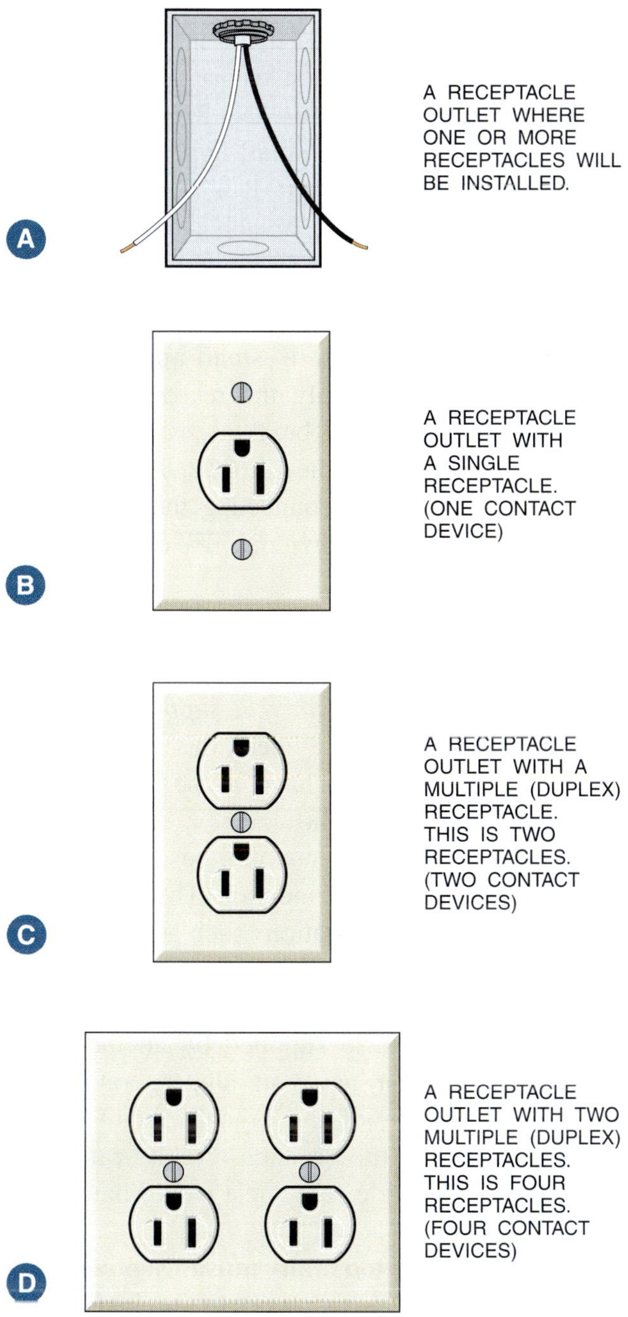

Figure 3-4 The branch-circuit wiring and the box where one or more receptacles will be installed is defined by the *Code* as a *receptacle outlet*. The receptacle itself, whether a single or multiple device (one, two, or three receptacles) on one strap (yoke) is defined as a *receptacle*. For house wiring, receptacle loads are considered to be part of the general lighting load calculations, *220.14(J)*.

- Any wall space 24 in. (600 mm) or more in width must have a receptacle outlet, *210.52(A)(2)(1)*.
- Nonsliding fixed glass panels on exterior walls are considered to be wall space and are to be figured in when applying the rule that no point along the floor line is more than 6 ft (1.8 m) from a receptacle. Sliding panels on exterior walls are not considered to be a wall, *210.52(A)(2)*.
- Receptacle outlets located in the floor more than 18 in. (450 mm) from the wall are not to be counted as meeting the required number of wall receptacle outlets, *210.52(A)(3)*. An example of this would be a floor receptacle installed under a dining room table for plugging in warming trays, coffee pots, or similar appliances.
- Hallways 10 ft (3.0 m) or longer in homes must have at least one receptacle outlet, *210.52(H)*. See Figure 3-5.
- Circuits supplying wall receptacle outlets for lighting loads are generally 15-ampere circuits but are permitted by the *Code* to be 20 amperes.

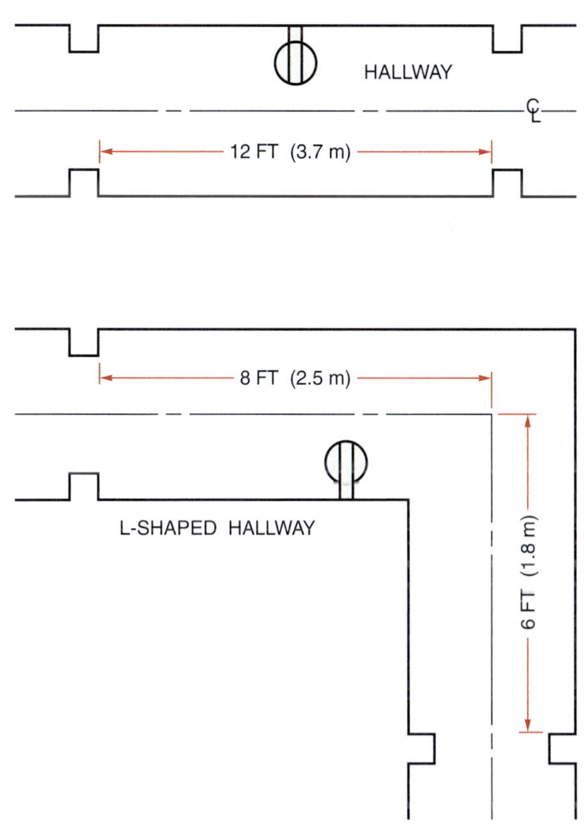

Figure 3-5 Determination of hallway length. Hallways 10 ft (3.0 m) or longer must have at least one receptacle outlet, *210.52(H)*.

- Outdoors: One receptacle is required in front and another in back, *210.52(E)*. This is discussed in detail later in this chapter.
- Receptacle(s) for HVAC equipment, *210.63*. This is discussed in detail later in this chapter.
- Outdoor receptacles are required to be GFCI protected, *210.8(A)(3)*. Exempt are receptacles that are not readily accessible, are supplied by a dedicated branch circuit, and serve snow-melting or deicing equipment. See *426.28*.

Basements

- At least one receptacle outlet must be installed in addition to the laundry outlet, *210.52(G)*.
- Connect to a 15- or 20-ampere circuit.
- In finished basements, the required number, spacing, and location of receptacles, lighting outlets, and switches shall be in conformance to *210.52(A)* and *210.70*.
- In finished basements, GFCI protection for receptacles is *not* required unless the receptacles are near a sink.
- ▶Any receptacle within 6 ft (1.8 m) from the outside edge of a laundry, utility, or wet bar sink shall be GFCI protected. There are no exceptions to this requirement. This is true even if the sink is in another room.◀
- Unfinished basements, or unfinished portions of basements that are not generally "lived in" such as work areas and storage areas, are not subject to the spacing requirements for receptacles as specified in *210.52(A)*.
- In each separate unfinished basement area that is not intended to be "lived in," such as storage areas or work areas, at least one 125-volt, single-phase, 15- or 20-ampere receptacle must be installed, *210.52(G)*. This receptacle(s) must be GFCI protected, *210.8(A)(5)*. This includes receptacles that are an integral part of porcelain or plastic pull chain or keyless lampholders.
- See the "Laundry Area" section in this chapter for receptacle outlet requirements in laundry areas.
- Refer to *210.8(A)*, *210.52(A)*, *210.52(G)*, and *210.70*.

Small-Appliance Receptacle Outlets

- At least two 20-ampere small-appliance circuits must supply the receptacles that serve the countertop surfaces in the kitchen, *210.11(C)(1)* and *210.52(B)(3)*. Two small-appliance branch circuits is the minimum. It is advisable to run additional 20-ampere branch circuits to these areas because of the heavy concentration of appliances.
- These two 20-ampere small-appliance circuits may also supply the receptacles in the dining area, pantry, breakfast room, and the refrigerator receptacle, *210.52(B)(1)*. *Exception No. 2* permits connecting the refrigerator receptacle to an individual 15- or 20-ampere circuit.

What is meant by the term *individual branch circuit*? The *NEC®* defines an *individual branch circuit* as: *A branch circuit that supplies only one utilization equipment.* To meet this definition, a single receptacle would have to be installed for the refrigerator. It's doubtful that a duplex receptacle behind a refrigerator would be used for anything other than the refrigerator. The same logic would apply in other situations such as a receptacle located behind a gas range. It's up to the electrical inspector.

A single receptacle supplied by an individual branch circuit must have an ampere rating not less than the rating of the branch circuit, *NEC® 210.21(B)(1)*. If the branch-circuit rating is 20 amperes, the single receptacle would have to be rated 20 amperes.

TIP: There are too many nuisance power outages when circuit breakers trip or fuses open because too many appliances are plugged in and used at the same time in the kitchen. Many large combination refrigerator/freezers today draw quite a bit of current. It is better to be safe than sorry. Connect the refrigerator receptacle to an individual 15- or 20-ampere branch circuit. Being behind the refrigerator, the receptacle does not have to be GFCI protected. Only receptacles that serve the countertops are required to be GFCI protected, *210.8(A)(6)*.

See Chapter 12 for more details about receptacles for refrigerators.

- Space countertop receptacles in kitchens according to *210.52(C)*.
- GFCI protection shall be provided for all receptacles in kitchens that serve countertop areas, *210.8(A)(6)*. GFCI protection may be GFCI receptacles or GFCI circuit breakers, as discussed in detail in Chapter 6.
- These two or more 20-ampere small-appliance circuits shall not supply other outlets, *210.52(B)(2)*. Exceptions to this are: (1) a clock receptacle and (2) a receptacle(s) for plugging in a gas-fired range, oven, or counter-mounted cooktop, which are permitted to be supplied by one of the 20-ampere small-appliance circuits.
- Allow 1500 volt-amperes for each 20-ampere small-appliance branch circuit when computing loads for determining the size of the service-entrance equipment, *220.52(A)*.
- Refer to *210.8(A)(6)*, *210.11(C)(1)*, *210.52(B)(1)*, *(2)*, and *(3)*, *210.52(C)*, and *220.52(A)*.

Countertops in Kitchens (See Figure 3-6)

▶The following requirements pertain to countertops in kitchens, pantries, breakfast rooms, dining rooms, and similar areas. See *210.52(C)*.◀

- Receptacles that serve countertops in kitchens must be GFCI protected. This includes a receptacle located inside an "appliance garage."
- Receptacles are not permitted to be installed "face up" in countertops.
- Receptacles shall be installed above all countertop spaces 12 in. (300 mm) or wider.
- Receptacles shall be installed not more than 20 in. (500 mm) above a countertop.

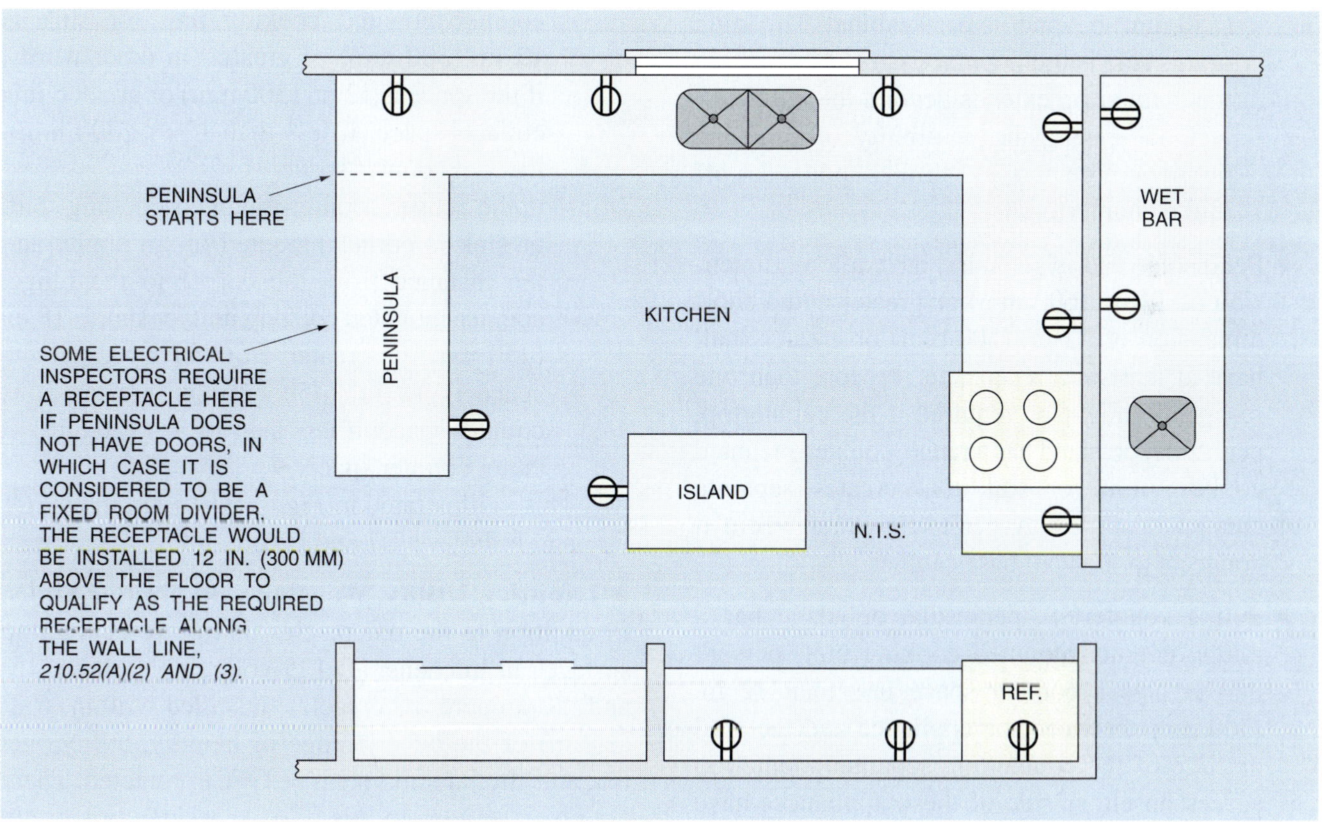

Figure 3-6 Floor plan showing placement of receptacles that serve countertop surfaces in kitchens and wet bar areas in conformance to *210.52(C)*. All 120-volt receptacles that serve countertops must be GFCI protected, *210.8(A)(6)* and *(7)*. Receptacles that are located behind the refrigerator, under the sink for plugging in a food waste disposer, or inside the cabinets for plugging in a microwave oven do not have to be GFCI protected because they do not serve the countertop surfaces. Drawing is not to scale. See text for detailed explanation.

- Receptacles above countertop spaces shall be positioned so that no point along the wall line is more than 24 in. (600 mm), measured horizontally, from a receptacle outlet in that space. Example: A section of a countertop measures 5 ft 3 in. (1.6 m) along the wall line. The minimum number of receptacles is 5 ft 3 in. ÷ 4 ft = 1+. Therefore, install two receptacles in this space.
- Receptacles may be installed below countertops only:
  - where the construction is for the physically impaired, or
  - on islands and peninsulas where there is no way to mount a receptacle within 20 in. (500 mm) above the countertop.

  For either of these two conditions:
  - Receptacles shall be mounted not more than 12 in. (300 mm) below the countertop.
  - No receptacles shall be installed below a countertop that extends more than 6 in. (150 mm) beyond its base cabinet. The logic to this rule is the popular use of stools where the countertop extends beyond the base cabinet, increasing the possibility of someone pulling coffee pots and similar appliances off of the countertop.
- Peninsulas and islands that have a long dimension of 24 in. (600 mm) or greater and a short dimension of 12 in. (300 mm) or greater shall have at least one receptacle. ▶More than one receptacle might be required if the countertop, peninsula, or island has a range, counter-mounted cooking unit, or sink that creates separate counter spaces.◀ A peninsula starts where it connects to the wall base cabinet.
- ▶If a countertop, peninsula, or island has a range, counter-mounted cooking unit, or sink that creates a counter space less than 12 in. (300 mm) between the appliance and the wall or edge of the countertop, separate countertop spaces on either side of these appliances have been created. Receptacles shall be installed to comply with the required number of receptacles in these spaces.◀
- Receptacles that do not serve countertops, such as behind a refrigerator, under the sink for plugging in a food waste disposer or dishwasher, or behind or above an appliance that is fastened in place, are not considered part of the receptacle outlet requirement for serving countertops. These receptacles are not required to be GFCI protected.
- Receptacles inside an "appliance garage" are *in addition* to the receptacles required to serve countertops. They must be GFCI protected. Although permitted to be connected to one of the two required 20-ampere small-appliance circuits, consider running a separate 20-ampere branch circuit.
- A receptacle located inside an upper cabinet that serves a "hang below cabinet" microwave oven should be connected to an individual branch circuit. This is discussed in Chapter 20.
- ▶Receptacles are generally not required on the wall behind a range, counter-mounted cooking unit, or sink. However, a receptacle is required:
  - if the distance from the wall to the range, counter-mounted cooking unit, or sink is 12 in. (300 mm) or greater. In other words, if the space is 12 in. (300 mm) or greater, it is counter space; if less than 12 in. (300 mm), it is not counter space.
  - if the range, counter-mounted cooking unit, or sink is corner mounted on an angle, and the distance from the corner to the range, counter-mounted cooking unit, or sink is 18 in. (450 mm) or greater. In other words, if the space is 18 in. (450 mm) or greater, it is counter space; if less than 18 in. (450 mm), it is not counter space.◀

  This is illustrated in *Figure 210.52* in the *NEC*® and in Figure 3-7 and Figure 3-8.

▶**Laundry, Utility, Wet Bar, and Similar Sinks:** In addition to the receptacles that serve countertop surfaces in kitchens, all 125-volt, single-phase, 15- and 20-ampere receptacles installed within 6 ft (1.8 m) of the outside edge of laundry, utility, wet bar, and similar sinks shall be GFCI protected. There are no exceptions to this rule. As written, it's pretty clear that this requirement includes receptacles that might be in a different area, around the corner in another room or hallway. Just take a tape measure and draw a 6-ft (1.8-m) arc from the outside edge of the sink.◀

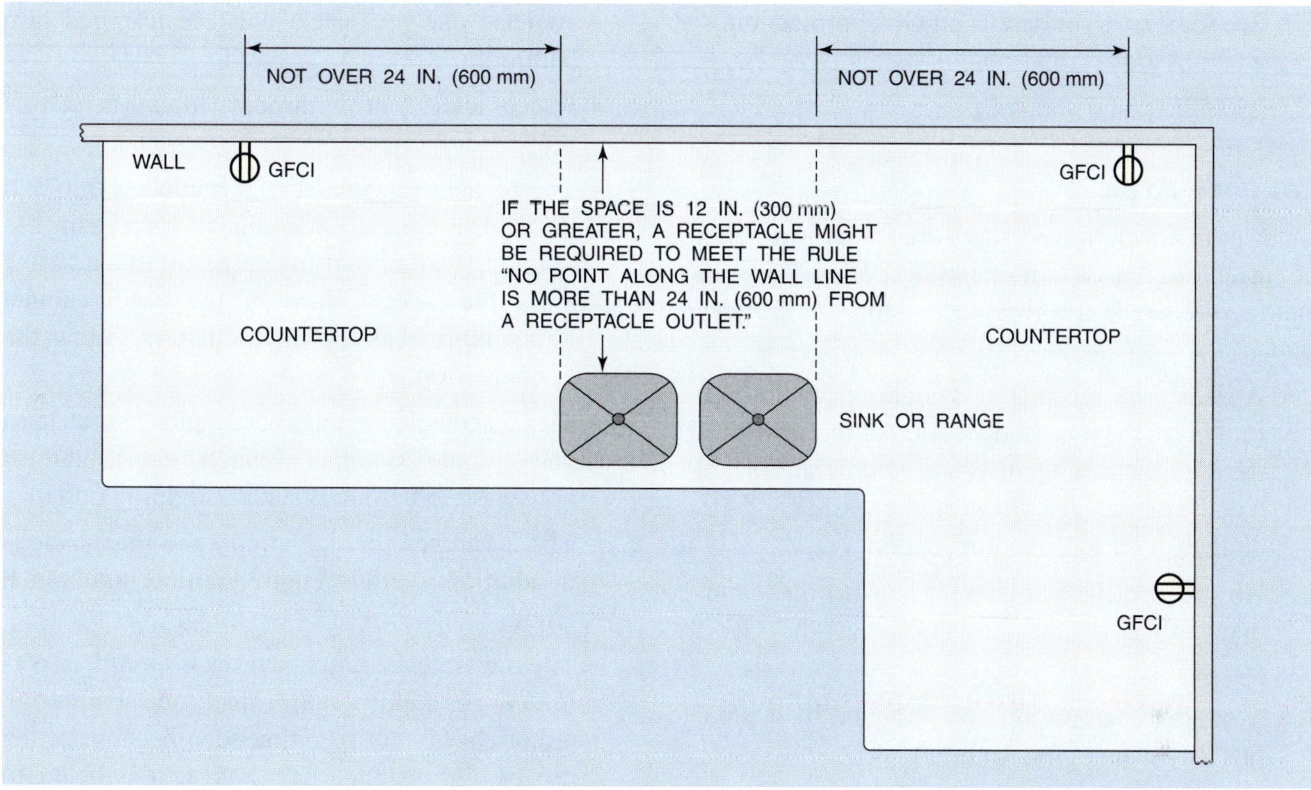

Figure 3-7 ►A receptacle might be required in the space behind a range, counter-mounted cooking unit, or sink.◄ This illustration shows a conventionally installed sink. See *210.52(C)(1)*.

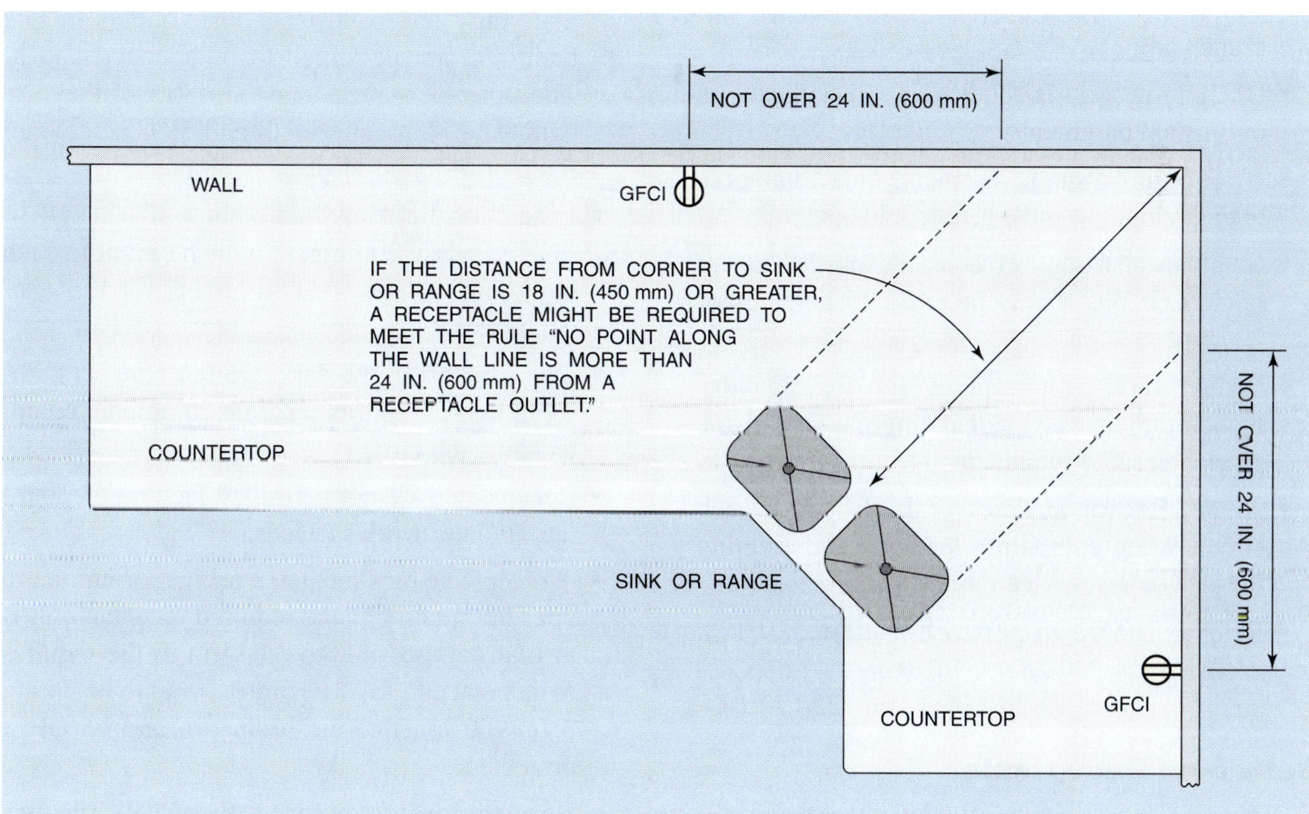

Figure 3-8 A receptacle might be required in the space behind a range, counter-mounted cooking unit, or sink. This illustration shows a corner installed sink. See *210.52(C)(1)*.

- See Chapter 6 for details on GFCI protection.
- See *210.8(A)(6)* and *(7)*, *210.11(C)*, *210.52(C)*, *220.52(A)*, and *406.4(E)*.

Laundry Area

Automatic clothes washers draw a large amount of current during certain operating cycles. Here are the requirements for receptacles for the laundry area:

- At least one receptacle is required within 6 ft (1.8 m) of the intended location of the washer in the laundry area. Quite often, electricians install a duplex receptacle between the washer and gas clothes dryer to serve both appliances.
- Any receptacle within 6 ft (1 .8 m) of a laundry, utility, or wet bar sink must be GFCI protected.
- This receptacle(s) must be supplied by a separate 20-ampere branch circuit.
- This branch circuit shall not supply any other outlets outside the laundry area.
- This branch circuit and receptacle(s) are in addition to other required receptacles and branch circuits.
- GFCI protection is required for receptacles in unfinished basements.
- If you install a single receptacle on a 20-ampere branch circuit, it must be rated 20 amperes.
- If you install a duplex receptacle on a 20-ampere branch circuit, it may be rated 15 amperes or 20 amperes.
- Figure 1500 volt-amperes for this laundry branch circuit when calculating the size of the service-entrance conductors.
- Allow 1500 volt-amperes for this laundry branch circuit when computing loads for determining the size of the service-entrance equipment.
- Refer to *210.8(A)(5)*, *210.8(A)(7)*, *210.11(C)(2)*, *210.21(B)(1)*, *210.21(B)(3)*, *210.50(C)*, *210.52(F)* and *(G)*, *220.14(J)*, *220.16(B)*, and *220.52(B)*.

Bathroom Receptacles

Here is a recap of the *NEC*® requirements for receptacles in bathrooms:

- At least one receptacle must be installed in a bathroom.
- Receptacle(s) in bathrooms must be GFCI protected.
- The receptacle(s) must be installed within 3 ft (900 mm) of the outside edge of each basin:
  - on the wall or partition adjacent to the basin.
  - on the side or face of the basin cabinet not more than 12 in. (300 mm) below the countertop.
- The receptacle(s) must be supplied by at least one separate 20-ampere branch circuit and must not supply other loads such as lighting outlets.
- The 20-ampere branch circuit and receptacle is in addition to other required outlets and branch circuits.
- The separate 20-ampere branch circuit is permitted to supply more than one bathroom, although it is not recommended because of the use of high-wattage hair dryers. It is better to run a separate 20-ampere branch circuit to each bathroom.
- If the separate 20-ampere branch circuit supplies only one bathroom, other outlets in that bathroom are permitted to be connected to it. The other permitted loads are 80% if they are cord- and plug-connected, and 50% if they are fixed or fastened-in-place equipment.
- Instead of the "only one bathroom" exception, run a separate 20-ampere branch circuit to each bathroom. That's what the plans for the residence call for.
- Don't be left in the dark. Do not connect bathroom lighting to this separate 20-ampere receptacle branch circuit.
- Receptacles are not permitted face up on counters or other work surfaces.
- A receptacle on a medicine cabinet or luminaire does not qualify as the required receptacle. It is virtually impossible to conform to the requirements that call for a separate circuit to be within 3 ft (900 mm) of the basin rim and be GFCI protected.
- No additional load need be added for this separate 20-ampere branch circuit. The sep-

arate branch-circuit requirement merely redirects the receptacle load off the lighting branch circuit.

- See *210.8(A)(1)*, *210.11(C)(3)*, *210.23(A)(1)* and *(2)*, *210.52(D)*, *220.14(J)*, and *406.4(E)*.

Outdoors

- ►At least one receptacle shall be installed in the front and another in the back of a one-family dwelling, *210.52(E)(1)*. These receptacles shall be accessible while standing at grade level and not more than 6½ ft (2.0 m) above grade. See Figure 3-9. The same is true for each unit of a multifamily dwelling where the entrance/egress is at grade level, *210.52(E)(2)*◄

  Grade level could be grass, sidewalk, or driveway. It is possible that a concrete or brick patio might be built at grade level.

  In addition to the "front and back" receptacle requirement, let's take a look at receptacle requirements for balconies, decks, and porches.

- ►**Balconies, decks, and porches:** We don't want people running extension cords through doors or window openings and pinching the cord. In *210.52(E)(3)* we find these requirements for balconies, decks, and porches that are accessible from inside the dwelling:
  - At least one receptacle shall be installed within the perimeter of the balcony, deck, or porch.
  - The receptacle shall not be more than 6½ ft (2.0 m) above the surface of the balcony, deck, or porch.
  - A receptacle is not required for a balcony, deck, or porch that has a usable area of less than 20 ft^2.◄

Roughing-in receptacle(s) on the front of the house is usually a no-brainer. Plans clearly show the construction of the porch. In the residence in this text, there is one switched receptacle on the front porch, and another non-switched receptacle on the outside of the Front Bedroom wall.

A rear deck/patio/porch is another story. They are generally built after the house is completed. It is easier said than done to figure out where to rough-in the required receptacle.

The electrician must consider: Where will the deck/patio be built? Is the deck/patio poured

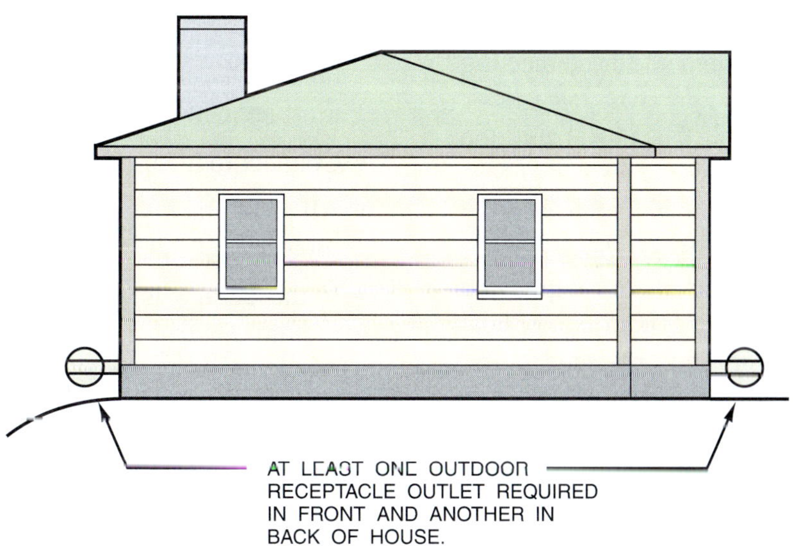

Figure 3-9 Outdoor receptacle requirements for residences, *210.52(E)*, require that for one-family dwellings, and each unit of a two-family dwelling that is at grade level, at least one receptacle outlet must be installed in the front and another in the back. These receptacles must not be mounted more than 6½ ft (2.0 m) above grade.

concrete or decorative brick/stone at grade level? What is the height if built above grade? Does it have rails or walls? Is it screened in? Sometimes the surest thing to do is:

- rough-in the one receptacle on the rear of the house *close* to the means of entrance/egress such as a sliding door not over 6½ ft (2.0 m) above grade.
- rough-in a second receptacle somewhere else on the rear of the house outside the footprint of the intended deck/patio/porch.

For the more elaborate deck/patio/porch, consider installing a few additional receptacles around the perimeter of the deck/patio/porch. These would be wired in after the deck/patio is completed.

- Additional receptacles may be installed higher, such as receptacles used for plugging in ice and snow-melting heating cables and/or decorative outdoor lighting.
- For servicing HVAC equipment, *210.63* requires that a 125-volt, single-phase, 15- or 20-ampere-rated receptacle be installed as follows:
  - Be at an accessible location.
  - Be on the same level as the HVAC equipment.
  - Be within 25 ft (7.5 m) of the HVAC equipment.
  - The receptacle shall not be connected to the load side of the equipment disconnecting means.
  - Evaporative coolers are exempt from the above requirements.*

*Why are evaporative coolers, often referred to as *swamp coolers*, exempt? Because they do not contain anywhere near as much complicated internal parts as a typical air conditioner or heat pump. There is less need for maintenance on this type of equipment. Less expensive than an air conditioner or a heat pump, they contain one motor that pumps water to the top of the unit. The water "falls" downward over porous filter pads where the water is cooled by evaporation A second motor (fan) pulls in outside air and blows the air over the cooled water into the room. Evaporative coolers work great in hot, dry climates. The higher the humidity, the less efficient is an evaporative cooler.

- The outdoor receptacles required by *210.52(E)* (one in the front, one in the back) might or might not meet the requirements of *210.63*. If the HVAC equipment is located on a roof, in an attic, in a crawl space, or in a similar location, a receptacle must be installed in that location so as to be on the same level as the equipment.
- All outdoor receptacles must be GFCI protected, *210.8(A)(3)*. Exempt from this requirement are GFCI outdoor receptacle(s) that are not readily accessible and are supplied by a dedicated branch circuit installed for snow- and ice-melting equipment (e.g., heating cables).
- Ground-fault protection of equipment (GFPE) must be provided for "fixed" outdoor deicing and snow-melting equipment. GFPE can be a circuit breaker, a receptacle, or be self-contained in the equipment. GFPE devices for equipment protection trip at approximately 30 milliamperes. See *426.28*.

  When used for deicing and snow melting, mineral-insulated metal-sheathed cable embedded in noncombustible material such as concrete does not require ground-fault protection.
- See *210.8(A)(3)*, *210.52(E)*, *210.63*, and *426.28*.

Garages

- At least one receptacle outlet in addition to receptacles installed for specific equipment must be provided. ◀
- Connect to a 15- or 20-ampere circuit.
- All receptacles in garages must be GFCI protected.
- If the garage is detached, the *Code* does not require electric power, but if electric power is provided, then at least one GFCI receptacle outlet must be installed.

  Receptacles are not required in a storage shed (accessory building), but if installed, they must be GFCI protected if the floor is at or below grade level.
- See *210.8(A)(2)* and *210.52(G)*.

Receptacles in Other Locations. All of the required receptacles discussed previously are *in addition* to any receptacles that are part of luminaires or appliances, are located inside cabinets, or are located more than 5½ ft (1.7 m) above the floor, *210.52*.

GFCI Exemptions

The 2008 *NEC*® deleted most of the exceptions for GFCI protection that were in previous editions. These have been discussed earlier and are covered in detail in Chapter 6.

Specific Loads. Appliances such as electric ranges, ovens, air conditioners, electric heat, heat pumps, water heaters, and similar loads are discussed later in this text. See the Index for their location.

Receptacle Definitions. The *NEC*® in *Article 100* defines the following:

- receptacle: *A receptacle is a contact device installed at the outlet for the connection of an attachment plug.*
- single receptacle: *A single receptacle is a single contact device with no other contact device on the same yoke.*
- multiple receptacle: *A multiple receptacle is two or more contact devices on the same yoke.*

See Figure 3-4 for an illustration of these definitions.

Receptacle and Branch-Circuit Ratings

Table 3-2 shows the requirements of *210.21(B)* and *Table 210.21(B)(3)* where the branch circuit supplies two or more receptacles or outlets in homes. The table also points out that where the branch circuit supplies a single receptacle, the receptacle must have a rating not less than the ampere rating of the branch circuit.

Arc-Fault Circuit Interrupters (AFCIs). See Chapter 6 for complete information about AFCI requirements in bedrooms.

Replacing Existing Receptacles. See Chapter 6 for detailed discussion and illustrations about replacing existing receptacles in older homes.

Lighting Outlets *(Section 210.70)*

The *NEC*® contains minimum requirements for providing lighting for dwellings.

Switched Lighting Outlets. Per *210.70*, lighting outlets in dwellings must be installed as shown in Figure 3-10. Here is a summary of these requirements.

Habitable Rooms. In every habitable room and in every bathroom, at least one wall-switch-controlled lighting outlet must be installed. Switched receptacles meet the intent of this requirement except in kitchens and bathrooms. Quite often, ceiling luminaires are omitted in bedrooms, living rooms, and similar rooms. Instead, the room lighting is dependent upon cord- and plug-connected table, floor, wall, and/or swag lamps.

The NFPA defines a habitable room as: *A room in a residential occupancy used for living, sleeping, cooking, and eating, but excluding bath, storage and service area, and corridors.*

As illustrated in Figure 3-11, swag lamps are not hardwired. They are connected by weaving the cord through the chain.

▶Wiring split-circuit receptacles is the key to providing convenient control of cord- and plug-connected lighting. The required minimum spacing of receptacles is found in *210.52*, already discussed

BRANCH-CIRCUIT RATING	RECEPTACLE RATING
15-ampere lighting branch circuit: circuit has two or more receptacles or outlets.	15-ampere maximum
20-ampere small-appliance branch circuit: circuit has two or more receptacles.	15 or 20 amperes
Individual 15-ampere branch circuit: circuit has only a single receptacle connected.	15 or 20 amperes
Individual 20-ampere branch circuit: circuit has only a single receptacle connected.	20 amperes

Table 3-2 This table shows the ampere rating for receptacles connected to 15- and 20-ampere branch circuits. See *210.21(B)* and *Table 210.21(B)(3)*.

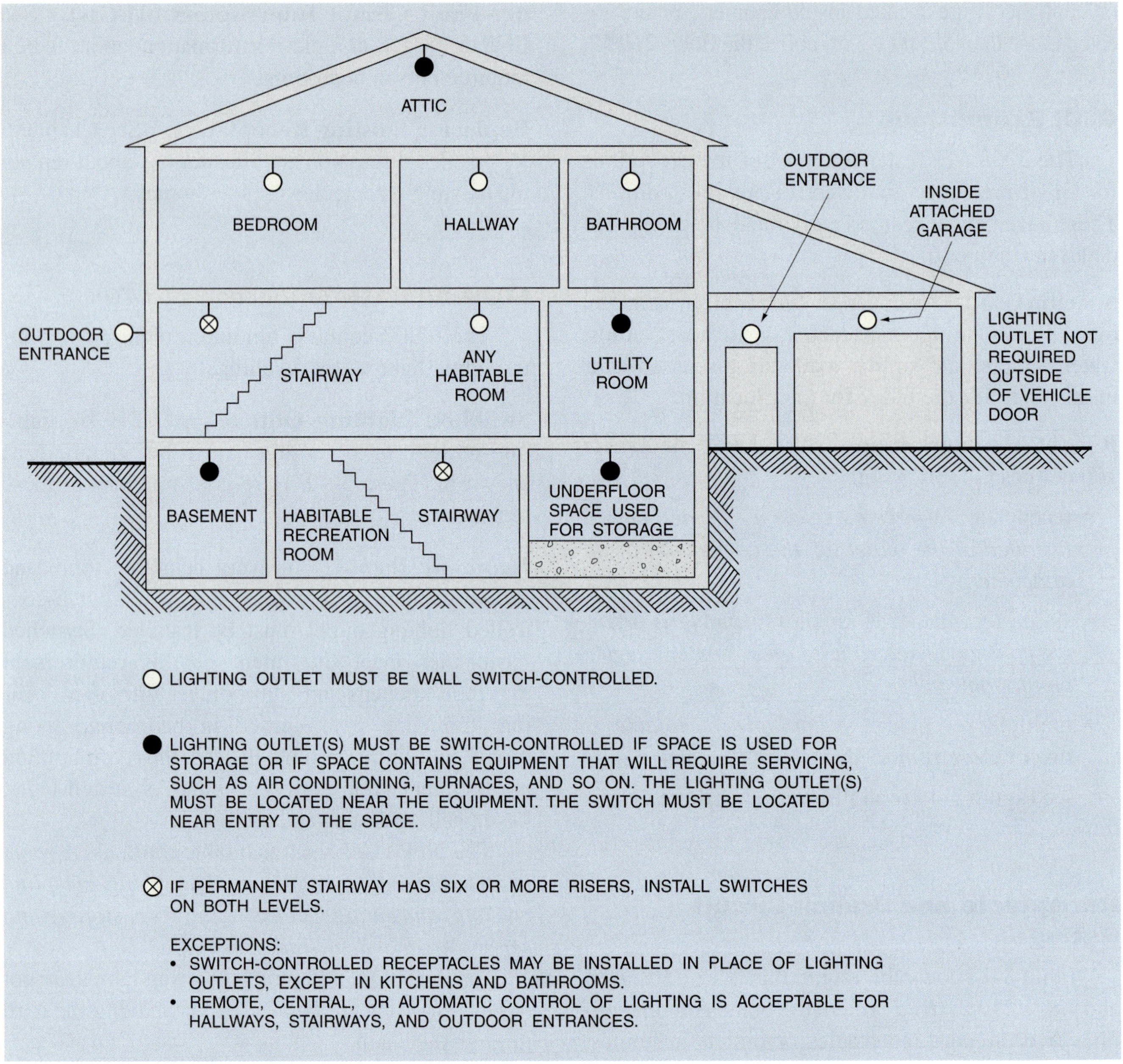

Figure 3-10 Lighting outlets required in a typical dwelling unit.

in this chapter. When laying out and roughing in the wiring for split-circuit receptacles, remember that:

- The "always hot" portion of a split-circuit receptacle qualifies for the required receptacle.
- The "switched" portion of a split-circuit receptacle is not considered to be one of the required receptacles but, rather, is considered to be "in addition."◀

If plug-in swag lighting as illustrated in Figure 3-11 is used in a dining room, a switched receptacle connected to a general lighting branch circuit must be installed. In other words, you still must install the receptacles supplied by the required 20-ampere small-appliance branch circuits, *210.52(B)(1), Exception No. 1*, Figure 3-12.

Where Do I Learn More about Split-Circuit Receptacles? In this residence, split-circuit receptacles are used in the living room and the bedrooms. The wiring of split-circuit receptacles is covered in Chapters 8, 12, 13, 14, and on Plan 9 or 10.

Occupancy motion sensors may be used if: (1) they are in addition to the required wall switch, or (2) they have a manual override and are located

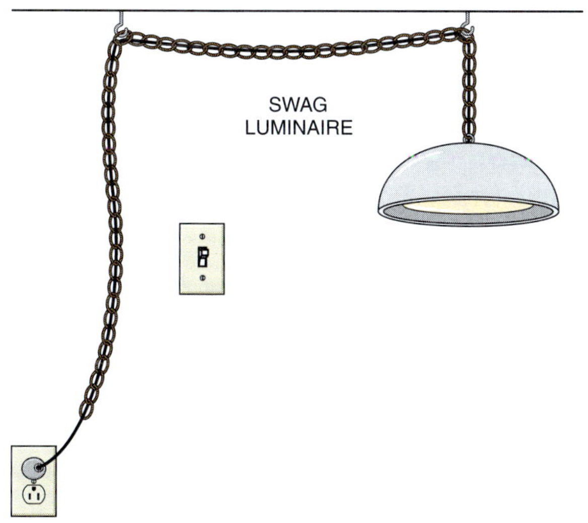

Figure 3-11 **A receptacle controlled by a wall switch is acceptable as the required lighting outlet in rooms other than a kitchen or bathroom, *210.70(A)(1), Exception.***

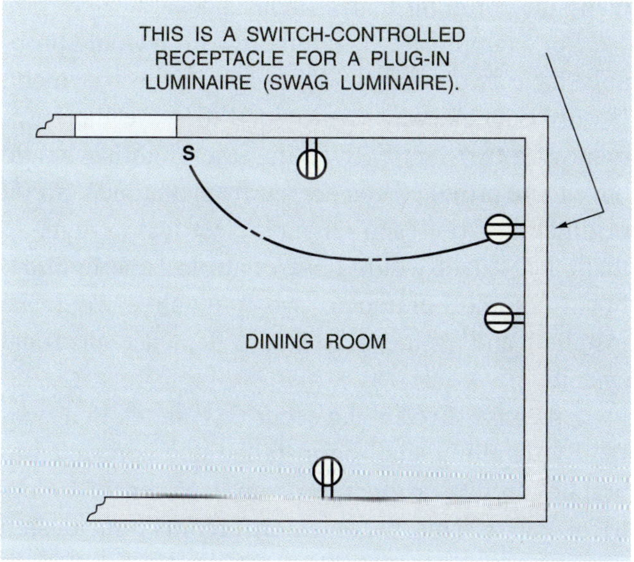

Figure 3-12 **When a switch-controlled receptacle outlet is installed in rooms where the receptacle outlets normally would be 20-ampere small-appliance circuits (breakfast room, dining room, and so on), it must be in addition to the required small-appliance receptacle outlets, *210.52(B)(1), Exception No. 1.***

where the wall switch would normally be located.

Additional Locations. At least one wall switch-controlled lighting outlet must be installed in hallways, stairways, attached garages, and detached garages with electric power, *210.70(A)(2)(a)*.

The *NEC*® does *not* require that a detached garage have electric power, but if it does have electric power, then it must have at least one GFCI receptacle, and it must have wall switch-controlled lighting.

Some electrical inspectors consider a tool shed or other similar accessory building to be a storage or utility room that comes under the requirements of *210.70(A)(3)*, thus requiring a wall switch-controlled lighting outlet.

At least one wall switch-controlled lighting outlet must be installed to provide illumination on the exterior side of outdoor entrances or exits that have grade-level access to dwelling units, attached garages, and detached garages if they have electric power. A sliding glass door is considered to be an outdoor entrance. A vehicle door is not considered to be an outdoor entrance. See *210.70(A)(2)(b)*.

Although not necessarily good design practice,

- One switch could control the required outdoor lighting at more than one entrance.
- One switch could control both the required outdoor and indoor lighting of a garage.
- One outdoor luminaire, properly located, could meet the required outdoor lighting for both the house entrance and the garage entrance.

Stairways. Where there are six stair risers or more on an interior stairway, the *NEC*® requires that wall switch-control led stairway lighting must be provided on each floor level and any landing level that has an entryway, *210.70(A)(2)(c)*.

This switching requirement includes permanent stairways to basements and attics but does not include fold-down storable ladders commonly installed for access to residential attics.

The *NEC*® does not tell us how to illuminate the stairway.

The *International Residential Code* is more specific about stairway lighting. It requires indoor stairways to have lighting that will illuminate the landings and treads, and that the lighting shall be located in the immediate vicinity of each landing at the top and bottom of the stairs. This *Code* also requires that the switching must be accessible at the top and bottom of the stairway without using any step to reach a switch.

If You Don't Install Switches, What Else Is Acceptable? Remote control, central control, motion sensors, photocells, and other automatic devices may be installed instead of wall switches for the control of lighting in hallways, stairways, and at outdoor entrances. For example, an outdoor post light controlled by a photocell does not require a separate switch.

This is permitted by the *Exception* to *210.70(A)(2)(a)*, *(b)*, and *(c)*.

Clothes Closet Lighting. The *NEC*® does not require lighting in clothes closets, but some local codes do. Check this out in your locality. Lighting in clothes closets is particularly hazardous because of the possibility of broken light bulbs. See Chapter 8 for a detailed explanation of *Code* requirements for clothes closet lighting. ▶The *NEC*® defines a clothes closet as: *A non-habitable room or space intended primarily for storage of garments and apparel.*◀ A utility closet, broom closet, china closet, or "game" closet would not come under the stringent clothes closet requirements found in *410.16* unless it is obvious that the room or area is primarily for storage of garments and apparel.

Basements, Attics, Storage, and Other Equipment Spaces. At least one switch-controlled lighting outlet must be installed in spaces that are used for storage or contain equipment that requires servicing, such as attics, underfloor spaces, utility rooms, and basements. Examples of equipment that may need servicing are furnaces, air conditioners, heat pumps, sump pumps, and so on. The control is permitted to be a wall switch or a lighting outlet that has an integral switch such as a pull chain switch. The lighting outlet must be at or near the equipment that may require servicing. The control must be at the usual point of entrance to the space.

The Number of Branch Circuits Required, and How to Determine the Number of Lighting and Receptacle Outlets to Be Connected to One Branch Circuit

This chapter explains the *NEC*® rules on where receptacle and lighting outlets are to be installed. The question of *how many* receptacle outlets and lighting outlets should be connected to each branch circuit is covered in detail in Chapter 8, where we begin the actual layout of the wiring for the residence discussed throughout this text.

Common Areas in Two-Family or Multifamily Dwellings

NEC® *210.25* contains specific requirements for circuits that serve common areas of two-family or multifamily dwellings. Be careful when wiring a two-family or multifamily dwelling. For areas such as a common entrance, common basement, or common laundry area, the branch circuits for lighting, central fire/smoke/security alarms, communication systems, or any other electrical requirements that serve the common area *shall not* be served by circuits from any individual dwelling unit's power service. Common areas will require separate circuits, associated panels, and metering equipment. The reasoning for this requirement is that power could be lost in one occupant's electrical system, resulting in no lights or alarms for the other tenant(s) using the common shared area.

For example, a two-family dwelling would probably have two separate stairways to the basement. If only one stairway is provided to serve the basement of a two-family dwelling, then lighting would have to be provided and served from a branch circuit originating from each tenant's electrical system, so that each tenant would have control of the lighting. For a common entrance, two luminaires would be installed and connected to each tenant's electrical system.

Likewise, fire/smoke/security systems in a two-family dwelling shall be installed and connected to branch circuits originating from each tenant's electrical panel. This becomes an architectural design issue. This is not generally a problem in two-family dwellings but can become a problem in dwellings having more than two tenants. Rather than having to install a third watt-hour meter and associated electrical equipment on a two-family dwelling, the design of the structure can be such that there are no common areas, Figure 3-13. A fourplex will probably require a fifth watt-hour meter, four watt-hour meters for the tenants and one watt-hour meter to serve common area lighting and the fire/smoke/security systems.

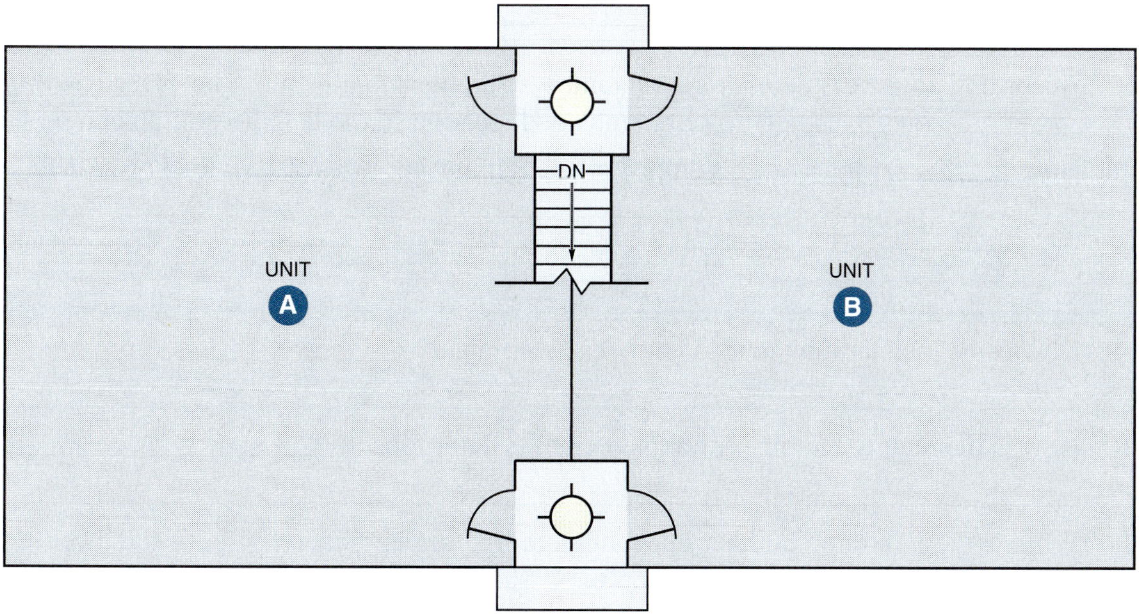

Figure 3-13 This outline of a two-family dwelling shows a common rear entry, a common stairway to the basement, and a common front entry. Note that each entry has one luminaire. These common area luminaires are not permitted to be connected to either of the tenants' electrical systems in the individual dwelling units, *210.25*. The choices are: (1) architect/designer must redo the layout of the building to eliminate the common entrances, (2) provide two luminaires in each entry, with each luminaire connected to the respective individual tenant's electrical circuit, or (3) install a third meter and panel to supply the electrical loads in the common areas.

REVIEW

Note: In the following questions the student may refer to the *NEC*® to obtain the answers. To help the student find these answers, references to *Code* sections are included after some of the questions. These references are not given in later reviews, where it is assumed that you are becoming familiar with the *Code*.

1. What is the meaning of calculated load? ____________________

2. How are branch circuits rated? See *NEC*® *210.3*. ____________________

3. How is the rating of the branch-circuit protective device affected when the conductors used are of a larger size than called for by the *Code*? See *NEC*® *210.3*. ____________

4. What dimensions are used when measuring the area of a building? See *NEC*® *220.12*.

5. What spaces are not included in the floor area when computing the load in volt-amperes per square foot? See *NEC*® *220.12*. ____________________

6. What is the unit load per square foot for dwelling units? See *Table 220.12*. ________

____

7. According to *NEC® 210.50(C)*, a laundry equipment outlet must be placed within ________ ft (________ m) of the intended location of the laundry equipment.

8. How is the total load in volt-amperes for lighting purposes determined? See *NEC® 220.12*. ____

____

____

9. How is the total lighting load in amperes determined? ________________

____

10. How is the required number of branch circuits determined? ________________

____

11. What is the minimum number of 15-ampere lighting circuits required if the dwelling has an occupied area of 4000 ft^2 (368 m^2)? Show all calculations.

12. How many lighting branch circuits are provided in this dwelling? ________________

13. a. What is the minimum load allowance for small-appliance circuits for dwellings? See *NEC® 220.52(A)*. ____

    b. An individual 15-ampere branch circuit is run to the receptacle outlet behind the refrigerator instead of connecting it to one of the two 20-ampere small-appliance branch circuits that are required in kitchens. For this separate circuit, an additional 1500 volt-amperes (shall) (does not have to) be added to the load calculations for dwellings. Circle the correct answer.

14. What is the smallest size wire that can be used in a branch circuit rated at 20 amperes?

____

15. How is the load determined for outlets supplying specific appliances? See *NEC® 220.14*. ____

____

16. What type of circuits must be provided for receptacle outlets in the kitchen, pantry, dining room, and breakfast room? See *NEC® 210.11(C)(1)*. ________________

____

17. How is the minimum number of receptacle outlets determined for most occupied rooms? See *NEC® 210.52(A)*. ______________________________

____

____

____

____

____

____

____

18. In a single-family dwelling, what types of overload protection for circuits are used? See *NEC® 240.6*. ______________________________

____

____

____

____

19. The *NEC®* in *Article 100* defines a *continuous load* as *a load where the maximum current is expected to continue for three hours or more.* According to *210.19(A)* and *210.20(A)*, the branch-circuit conductors and overcurrent protection for a continuous load shall be sized at not less than (100%) (125%) (150%) of the continuous load. Circle the correct answer.

20. The minimum number of outdoor receptacles for a residence is ______________, *NEC®* ______________. State the location. ______________

21. The *Code* indicates the rooms in a dwelling that are required to have switched lighting outlets or switched receptacles. Write yes (switch required) or no (switch not required) for the following areas: See *NEC® 210.70(A)*.
    a. attic ______________
    b. stairway ______________
    c. crawl space (where used for storage) ______________
    d. hallway ______________
    e. bathroom ______________
    f. clothes closet ______________

22. Is a receptacle required in a bedroom on a 3-ft (900-mm) wall space behind the door? The door is normally left open.______________

23. The *Code* requires that at least one 20-ampere circuit feeding a receptacle outlet must be provided for the laundry. May this circuit supply other outlets?______________

24. In a basement, at least one receptacle outlet must be installed in addition to the receptacle outlet installed for the laundry equipment. This additional receptacle outlet and any other receptacle outlets in unfinished areas must be ______________ protected.

25. *NEC® 210.8(A)(2)* requires that *all* receptacles installed in garages must have GFCI protection, but there are certain exceptions. What are these exceptions?

____

____

____

____

26. Define a branch circuit. ____

____

27. Although the *Code* contains many exceptions to the basic overcurrent protection requirements for conductors, in general, the rating of the branch-circuit overcurrent device must (not be less than) (not be more than) the ampacity of a conductor. Circle the correct answer.

28. The rating of a branch circuit is based upon (circle the correct answer)
    a. the rating of the overcurrent device.
    b. the length of the circuit.
    c. the branch-circuit wire size.

29. a. A 25-ampere branch-circuit conductor is derated to 70%. It is important to provide proper overcurrent protection for these conductors. The derated conductor ampacity is ____

    ____.

    b. If the connected load is a "fixed" nonmotor, noncontinuous load, the branch-circuit overcurrent device may be sized at (20) (25) amperes. Circle the correct answer.

    c. If the above circuits supply receptacle outlets, the branch-circuit overcurrent device must be sized at not over (15) (20) (25) amperes. Circle the correct answer.

30. Small-appliance receptacle outlets are (included) (not included) in the 3 volt-ampere per square foot calculations. Circle the correct answer.

31. If a homeowner wishes to have a switched receptacle outlet for a swag lamp in a dining room, may this switched receptacle outlet be considered to be one of the receptacle outlets required for the 20-ampere small-appliance circuits? _______________

32. How many receptacle outlets are required on a 13-ft (4.0-m) wall space between two doors? Refer to *NEC® 210.52(H)*. Draw the outlets in on the diagram.

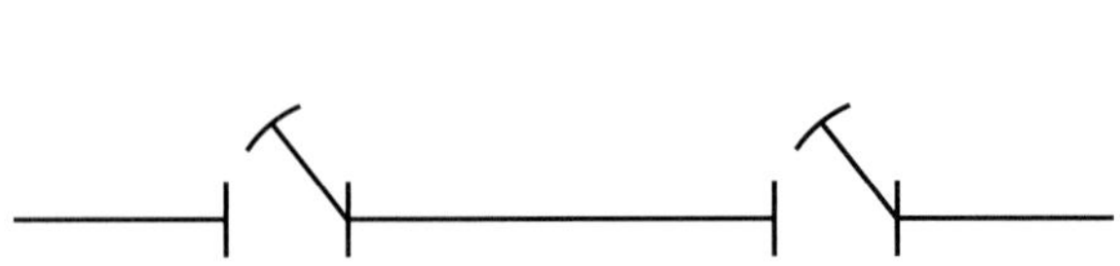

33. Is a receptacle required in a hallway in a home when the hallway is 8 ft (2.5 m) long?

____

34. A split-level home has one stairway that has six risers between two levels of the home. Which of the following choices meets *Code*? Choose the correct answer.
    a. Two three-way switches must be installed (one switch at the top of the stairs, one switch at the bottom of the stairs) to control the lighting for the stairway.
    b. One single-pole switch is permitted on either level to control the lighting for the stairway.
    c. No switches are necessary for the stairway lighting because the lighting on the upper level and the lower level provides enough illumination on the stairway.

35. A sliding glass door is installed in a family room that leads to an outdoor deck. The sliding door has one 4-ft (1.22-m) sliding section and one 4-ft (1.22-m) permanently mounted glass section. Inside the recreation room, what does the *Code* say about wall receptacle outlets relative to the receptacle's position near the sliding glass door?

36. The *Code* permits certain other receptacles to be connected to a 20-ampere small-appliance circuit. What are they? Which section of the *NEC*® supports your answer?

37. What is the minimum number of 20-ampere small-appliance circuits required by the *Code* to supply the receptacle outlets that serve the countertop surfaces in the kitchen? In which section of the *Code* is this requirement found? ______

38. Does the *Code* allow a 120-volt receptacle located behind a gas range to be supplied by a small-appliance circuit? (Yes) (No) Circle the correct answer.

39. When determining the location and number of receptacles required, fixed room dividers and railings (shall be) (need not be) considered to be wall space. Circle the correct answer.

40. No point along the wall line shall be more than 6 ft (1.8 m) from a receptacle outlet. This requirement (does apply) (does not apply) to unfinished residential basements. Circle the correct answer.

41. Receptacle outlets that serve countertop surfaces in kitchens are required to be __________ protected and shall be installed so that no point along the wall line above the base cabinets is more than [18 in. (450 mm)] [24 in. (600 mm)] [36 in. (900 mm)] from a receptacle. Circle the correct answer.

42. In kitchens, the *Code* requires that at least (one) (two) receptacle(s) be installed to serve the countertop surfaces on an island or peninsula. Circle the correct answer. Where in the *Code* is this requirement found? *NEC*® __________________________

43. In the past, it was common practice to connect the lighting and receptacle(s) in a bathroom to the same circuit. Because of overloads caused by high-wattage grooming appliances, the *Code* now requires that these receptacle(s) be supplied by a separate 20-ampere branch circuit. Where in the *Code* is this requirement found? *NEC*® ______

44. If a residence has two bathrooms, the *Code* states:
    a. The receptacles in each bathroom must be connected to a separate 20-ampere branch circuit. For two bathrooms, this would mean two circuits. (True) (False) Circle the correct answer.
    b. The receptacles in both bathrooms are permitted to be served by the same 20-ampere branch circuit. (True) (False) Circle the correct answer.

45. In your own words, explain the GFCI exemptions for receptacle outlets installed in unfinished basements and garages. Give some examples.

____

____

____

____

46. *NEC*® ______________ of the *Code* prohibits connecting lighting and/or fire/smoke/security systems to an individual tenant's electrical source where common (shared) areas are present, in which case the lighting provided for both tenants is connected on one tenant's electrical source.

47. When installing weatherproof outdoor receptacles high up under the eaves of a house intended to be used for plugging in deicing and snow-melting cable for the rain gutters, must these receptacles be GFCI protected for personnel protection? (Yes) (No) Circle the correct answer.

48. An individual 20-ampere branch circuit supplies a receptacle for a refrigerator. The receptacle shall be (circle the correct answer)
    a. a duplex receptacle.
    b. a single receptacle

    Explain why you chose your answer. ______________________________

    ____

    ____

    ____

49. A balcony on the second floor of a new residence measures 4 ft (1.22 m) × 10 ft (3.05 m). The balcony is accessed by a sliding door. Is a receptacle required for this balcony? Circle the correct answer. Give the *NEC*® section where the answer is found.

    YES   NO   *NEC*® *Section* ________________

CHAPTER 4

Conductor Sizes and Types, Wiring Methods, Wire Connections, Voltage Drop, Neutral Conductor Sizing for Services

OBJECTIVES

After studying this chapter, you should be able to

- **determine the current-carrying capacity (ampacity) of conductors.**
- **understand overcurrent protection for conductors and maximum loading of branch circuits.**
- **understand aluminum conductors and the possible fire hazards if they are not properly installed.**
- **know the *NEC*® installation requirements for all types of cables and raceways.**
- **understand the special ampacity ratings of service-entrance conductors.**
- **make voltage-drop calculations.**
- **learn an alternate cost and time-saving method permitted to bring nonmetallic-sheathed cables into the top of a surface-mounted panel.**

CONDUCTORS

Throughout this text, all references to conductors are for copper conductors, unless otherwise stated.

Wire Size

The copper wire used in electrical installations is graded for size according to the American Wire Gauge (AWG) Standard. The wire diameter in the AWG standard is expressed as a whole number. The higher the AWG number, the smaller the wire. AWG sizes vary from fine, hairlike wire used in coils and small transformers to very large diameter wire required in industrial wiring to handle heavy loads.

The wire may be a single strand (solid conductor), or it may consist of many strands. Each strand of wire acts as a separate conducting unit. The wire size used for a circuit depends on the maximum current to be carried. The *NEC*® in *Table 210.24* shows that the minimum conductor size for branch-circuit wiring is 14 AWG. Smaller size conductors are permitted for bell wiring, thermostat wiring, communications wiring, intercom wiring, luminaire wires, and similar low-energy circuits.

Don't Get Confused!

In the past, conductor size was shown as, for example, "No. 12 AWG." This same conductor now appears in the *NEC*® as "12 AWG." The "12" is a size, not a quantity.

Table 4-1 shows typical applications for different size conductors.

Solid and Stranded Conductors

For residential wiring, sizes 14, 12, and 10 AWG conductors are generally solid when the wiring method is nonmetallic-sheathed cable or armored cable.

In a raceway, the preference is to use stranded 10 AWG conductors because of the flexibility and ease of handling and pulling in the conductors.

NEC® *310.3* requires that conductors 8 AWG and larger must be stranded where installed in a raceway.

Ampacity

Ampacity means "the current, in amperes, that a conductor can carry continuously under the conditions of use without exceeding its temperature rating." This value depends upon the conductor's cross-sectional area, whether the conductor is copper or aluminum, and the type of insulation around the conductor. Ampacity values, also referred to as current-carrying capacity, are found in *Article 310*. The most commonly used conductor ampacities are found in *Table 310.16*.

The allowable ampacity values in the tables are valid where there are no more than three current-carrying conductors in a raceway or cable, and where the temperature does not exceed 86°F (30°C).

When there are more than three current-carrying conductors in a raceway or cable, the allowable ampacity values are adjusted according to the factors in *Table 310.15(B)(2)(a)*.

When the ambient temperature exceeds 86°F (30°C), the allowable ampacity values are corrected according to the factors found below the tables.

If both conditions are present, then both penalties (adjustment and correction factors) must be applied. More on conductor ampacities, derating, adjusting, and correction factors is presented in Chapter 18.

Conductors must have an ampacity not less than the maximum load that they are supplying, as shown in Figure 4-1. All conductors of a specific branch circuit must have an ampacity of the branch circuit's

CONDUCTOR APPLICATIONS CHART		
Conductor Size	**Overcurrent Protection**	**Typical Applications** (Check wattage and/or ampere rating of load to select the correct size conductors based on *Table 310.16*.)
20 AWG	Class 2 circuit transformers provide overcurrent protection. See *Article 725*.	Telephone wiring is usually 20 or 22 AWG.
18 AWG	Class 2 circuit transformers provide overcurrent protection. See *Article 725*. For motor control circuits, 7 amperes, see *Table 430.72(B)*.	Low-voltage wiring for thermostats, chimes, security, remote control, home automation systems, etc. For these types of installations, 18 or 20 AWG conductors can be used depending on the connected load and length of circuit.
16 AWG	Class 2 circuit transformers provide overcurrent protection. See *Article 725*. For motor control circuits, 10 amperes, see *Table 430.72(B)*.	Same applications as above. Good for long runs to minimize voltage drop.
14 AWG	15 amperes	Typical lighting branch circuits.
12 AWG	20 amperes	Small-appliance branch circuits for the receptacles in kitchens and dining rooms. Also laundry receptacles and workshop receptacles. Often used as the "home run" for lighting branch circuits. Some water heaters.
10 AWG	30 amperes	Most clothes dryers, built-in ovens, cooktops, central air conditioners, some water heaters, heat pumps.
8 AWG	40 amperes	Ranges, ovens, heat pumps, some large clothes dryers, large central air conditioners, heat pumps.
6 AWG	50 amperes	Electric furnaces, heat pumps.
4 AWG	70 amperes	Electric furnaces, feeders to subpanels.
3 AWG and larger	100 amperes	Main service-entrance conductors, feeders to subpanels, electric furnaces.

Table 4-1 Conductor Applications Chart

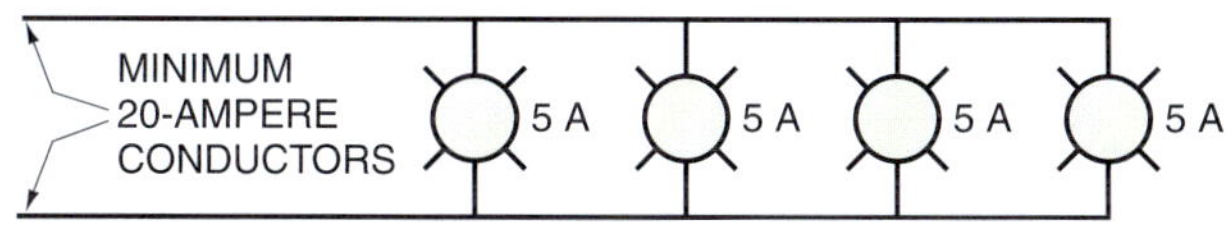

Figure 4-1 Branch-circuit conductors shall have an ampacity not less than the maximum load to be served, *210.19(A)*. See *210.23* for permissible loads.

rating, as shown in Figure 4-2. There are exceptions to this rule, such as taps for electric ranges (see Chapter 20.)

Ampacity of Flexible Cords

Table 4-2 shows the allowable ampacities for some sizes of flexible cords. Refer to *Table 400.5(A)* in the *NEC®* for other specific types and sizes of flexible cords.

Overcurrent protection requirements for extension cords are found in *240.5*.

Conductor Sizing

The diameter of wire is usually given in a unit called a "mil." A *mil* is defined as one-thousandth of an inch (0.001 inch). Mils squared are known as "circular mils."

Table 8 in *Chapter 9* of the *NEC®* clearly shows that conductors are expressed in AWG numbers from 18 (1620 circular mils) through 4/0 (211,600 circular mils). Wire sizes larger than 4/0 are expressed in circular mils.

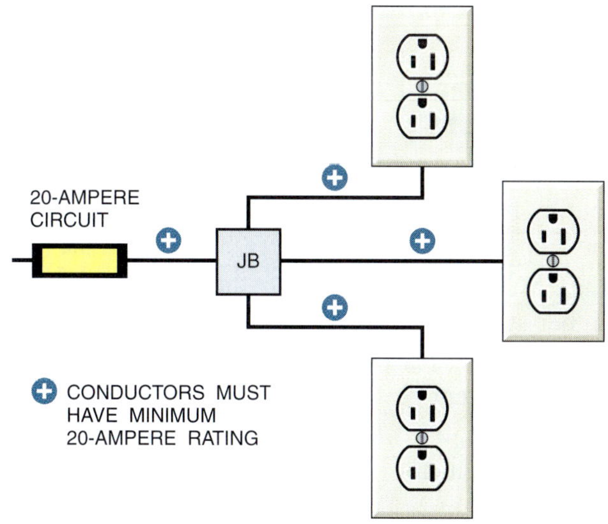

Figure 4-2 All conductors in this circuit supplying receptacles shall have an ampacity of not less than the rating of the branch circuit. In this example, 20-ampere conductors must be used, *210.19(A)(2)* and *Table 210.24*.

Large conductors, such as 500,000 circular mils, are generally expressed as 500 kcmil. Since the letter *k* designates 1000, the term *kcmil* means "thousand circular mils." This is much easier to express in both written and verbal terms.

Older texts used the term *MCM*, which also means "thousand circular mils." The first letter *M* refers to the Roman numeral that represents 1000. Thus, 500 MCM means the same as 500 kcmil.

ALLOWABLE AMPACITIES FOR FLEXIBLE CORDS

Conductor Size AWG Copper	Cords in Which Three Conductors Carry Current Example: black, white, red, plus equipment grounding conductor	Cords in Which Two Conductors Carry Current Example: black, white, plus equipment grounding conductor
18	7	10
16	10	13
14	15	18
12	20	25
10	25	30
8	35	40
6	45	55
4	60	70

Table 4-2 Allowable ampacities for some of the more common flexible cords used for residential applications. These values were taken from *Table 400.5(A), NEC®*. Refer to the *NEC®* table for other specific types and sizes.

Roman numerals are no longer used in the electrical industry for expressing conductor sizes.

Overcurrent Protection for Conductors

Conductors must be protected against overcurrent by fuses or circuit breakers rated not more than the ampacity of the conductors, *Section 240.4*.

NEC® 240.4(B) permits the use of the next higher standard overcurrent device rating as shown in *240.6(A)*. This permission is granted *only* when the overcurrent device is rated 800 amperes or less. For example, from *Table 310.16*, a 6 Type TW 140°F (60°C) conductor has an allowable ampacity of 55 amperes. In *240.6(A)*, we find that the next higher standard size overcurrent device is 60 amperes. Nonstandard ampere ratings of fuses and breakers are also permitted.

NEC® 240.4(D) spells out the maximum overcurrent protection for small branch-circuit conductors. Table 4-3 illustrates the requirements of *240.4(D)*.

There are exceptions for motor branch circuits and HVAC equipment. Motor circuits are discussed in Chapter 19 and Chapter 22. HVAC circuits are discussed in Chapter 23.

Branch-Circuit Rating

The rating of the overcurrent device (OCD) determines the rating of a branch circuit, as shown in Figure 4-3.

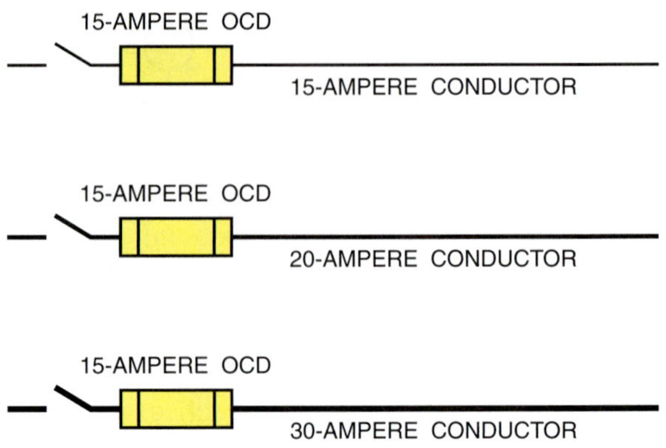

Figure 4-3 All three of these branch circuits are rated as 15-ampere circuits, even though larger conductors were used for some other reason, such as solving a voltage-drop problem. The rating of the overcurrent device (OCD) determines the rating of a branch circuit, *210.3*.

PERMISSIBLE LOADS ON BRANCH CIRCUITS *(210.23)*

The *NEC®* is very specific about the loads permitted on branch circuits. Here is a recap of these requirements.

- The load shall not exceed the branch-circuit rating.
- The branch circuit must be rated 15, 20, 30, 40, or 50 amperes when serving two or more outlets.
- An individual branch circuit may supply any size load.
- 15- and 20-ampere branch circuits:
  a. May supply lighting, other equipment, or both types of loads.
  b. Cord- and plug-connected equipment shall not exceed 80% of the branch-circuit rating.
  c. Equipment fastened in place shall not exceed 50% of the branch-circuit rating if the branch circuit also supplies lighting, other cord- and plug-connected equipment, or both types of loads.
- The 20-ampere small-appliance circuits in homes shall not supply other loads, *210.11(C)(1)*.
- 30-ampere branch circuits may supply equipment such as dryers, cooktops, etc. Cord- and plug-connected equipment shall not exceed 80 percent of the branch-circuit rating.
- 40- and 50-ampere branch circuits may supply cooking equipment that is fastened in place, such as an electric range.
- Over 50-ampere-rated branch circuits are for electric furnaces, large heat pumps, air-conditioning equipment, large double-ovens, and similar large loads.

CONDUCTOR SIZE	MAXIMUM OVERCURRENT PROTECTION
14 AWG copper	15 amperes
12 AWG copper	20 amperes
10 AWG copper	30 amperes

Table 4-3 Maximum overcurrent protection for 14, 12, and 10 AWG copper conductors.

ALUMINUM CONDUCTORS

The conductivity of aluminum is not as great as that of copper for a given size. For example, checking *Table 310.16*, an 8 AWG Type THHN copper conductor has an allowable ampacity of 55 amperes. An 8 AWG Type THHN aluminum or copper-clad aluminum conductor has an ampacity of 45 amperes.

In *240.4(D)*, the maximum overcurrent protection for a 12 AWG copper conductor is 20 amperes but only 15 amperes for a 12 AWG aluminum or copper-clad aluminum conductor.

Aluminum conductors have a higher resistance compared to a copper conductor of the same size. When considering voltage drop, a conductor's resistance is a key ingredient. Voltage-drop calculations are discussed later on in this chapter.

Common Connection Problems

Some common problems associated with aluminum conductors when not properly connected may be summarized as follows:

- A corrosive action is set up when dissimilar wires come in contact with one another when moisture is present.
- The surface of aluminum oxidizes as soon as it is exposed to air. If this oxidized surface is not penetrated, a poor connection results. When installing aluminum conductors, particularly in large sizes, an inhibitor (antioxidant) is brushed onto the aluminum conductor, then the conductor is scraped with a stiff brush where the connection is to be made. The process of scraping the conductor breaks through the oxidation, and the inhibitor keeps the air from coming into contact with the conductor. Thus, further oxidation is prevented. Aluminum connectors of the compression type usually have an inhibitor paste already factory-installed inside of the connector.
- Aluminum wire expands and contracts to a greater degree than does copper wire for an equal load. This is referred to as *creep* or *cold flow*. This factor is another possible cause of a poor connection. Crimp connectors for aluminum conductors are usually longer than those for comparable copper conductors, thus resulting in greater contact surface of the conductor in the connector.
- Older technology aluminum such as Alloy 1350 experienced the above problems. The newer technology aluminum such as AA-8000 has much better conductivity, creep resistance, and strength. Still, extreme care must be taken when terminating aluminum conductors. The manufacturer of the aluminum conductor will provide detailed installation instructions.

Proper Installation Procedures

Proper, trouble-free connections for aluminum conductors require terminals, lugs, and/or connectors that are suitable for the type of conductor being installed.

Terminals on receptacles and switches must be suitable for the conductors being attached. Table 4-4 shows how the electrician can identify these terminals. Listed connectors provide proper connection when properly installed.

See *110.14*, *404.14(C)*, and *406.2(C)*.

TYPE OF DEVICE	MARKING ON TERMINAL OR CONDUCTOR	CONNECTOR PERMITTED
15- or 20-ampere receptacles and switches	CO/ALR	aluminum, copper, copper-clad aluminum
15- and 20-ampere receptacles and switches	NONE	copper, copper-clad aluminum
30-ampere and greater receptacles and switches	AL/CU	aluminum, copper, copper-clad aluminum
30-ampere and greater receptacles and switches	NONE	copper only
Screwless pressure terminal connectors of the push-in type	NONE	copper or copper-clad aluminum
Wire connectors	AL	aluminum
Wire connectors	AL/CU or CU/AL	aluminum, copper, copper-clad aluminum
Wire connectors	CC	copper-clad aluminum only
Wire connectors	CC/CU or CU/CC	copper or copper-clad aluminum
Wire connectors	CU or CC/CU	copper only
Any of the above devices	COPPER OR CU ONLY	copper only

Table 4-4 Terminal identification markings and the acceptable types of conductors permitted to be connected to a specific type of terminal.

Electrical Fires Caused by Improper Connections of Aluminum Conductors

Many electrical fires have been caused by improper connections and terminations of aluminum conductors. The problem is not the aluminum conductors. The problem is with the connections and terminations.

Many of these problems occurred in the meter base and at the main panel where aluminum service-entrance conductors were installed years ago. In the course of time, the connections failed. Troubles also happened where aluminum conductors were terminated on receptacles and switches.

The Consumer Product Safety Commission (CPSC) (Washington, D.C. 20207) publishes an excellent free booklet (#516) entitled *Repairing Aluminum Wiring* that explains what you can do with connections and terminations for the small aluminum wires that were installed years ago for the branch-circuit wiring of receptacles and switches.

The CPSC states that older homes wired with aluminum conductors are 55 times more likely to have one or more connections that will reach "Fire Hazard Conditions" than are homes wired with copper.

Although the *NEC*,® notably in *110.5*, *110.14*, *240.4(D)*, *310.2(B)*, *310.14*, *Table 310.16* and other sections, recognizes aluminum conductors in sizes 12 AWG and larger, there are some local electrical codes that do not allow aluminum conductors to be used. Check this out before using aluminum conductors.

Some of the signs of potential problems might be:

- Wall switches and receptacles that feel warm to the touch.
- Smell of burning plastic or rubber at switches, receptacle, main panel, or meter.
- Flickering lights.
- Lights getting bright or dim.
- Circuits that don't work; some circuits are on, others are off.
- TV shifts to another channel for no apparent reason.
- Appliances with electronic controls shut off or change settings for no apparent reason.
- Security system sounds off for no apparent reason.

Wire Connections

Wire connectors are known in the trade by such names as *screw terminal, pressure terminal connector, wire connector, Wing-Nut,® Wire-Nut,® Scotchlok,® Twister, split-bolt connector, pressure cable connector, solderless lug, soldering lug, solder lug*, and others.

All cartons and manufacturers' literature show the size, number, and types of conductors permitted.

Solder-type lugs and connectors are rarely, if ever, used today. In fact, connections that depend upon solder are *not* permitted for connecting service-entrance conductors to service equipment, *230.81*. Nor is solder permitted for grounding and bonding connections, *250.8*. The labor costs and time spent make the use of the solder-type connections prohibitive.

Solderless connectors designed to establish *Code*-compliant electrical connections are shown in Figure 4-4.

As with the terminals on wiring devices (switches and receptacles), wire connectors must be marked AL when they are to be used with aluminum conductors. This marking is found on the connector itself, or it appears on or in the shipping carton.

Connectors marked **AL/CU** are suitable for use with aluminum, copper, or copper-clad aluminum conductors. This marking is found on the connector itself, or it appears on or in the shipping carton.

Connectors not marked *AL* or *AL/CU* are for use with copper conductors only.

Unless specially stated on or in the shipping carton, or on the connector itself, conductors made of copper, aluminum, or copper-clad aluminum *may not* be used in combination in the same connector.

When combinations are permitted, the connector will be identified for the purpose and for the conditions when and where they may be used. The conditions usually are limited to dry locations only. There are some "twist-on" wire connectors that have recently been listed for use with combinations of copper and aluminum conductors.

The preceding data are found in *110.14* and in the Underwriters Laboratories (UL) Standards. When terminating large conductors such as service-entrance conductors, be sure to read any instructions that might be included with the equipment where these conductors will be terminated. Terminations for all electrical connections to devices and equipment shall be torqued as required by the manufacturer of such electrical device or equipment, *110.12(D)*.

CRIMP CONNECTORS USED TO SPLICE AND TERMINATE 20 AWG TO 500 KCMIL ALUMINUM-TO-ALUMINUM, ALUMINUM-TO-COPPER, OR COPPER-TO-COPPER CONDUCTORS.

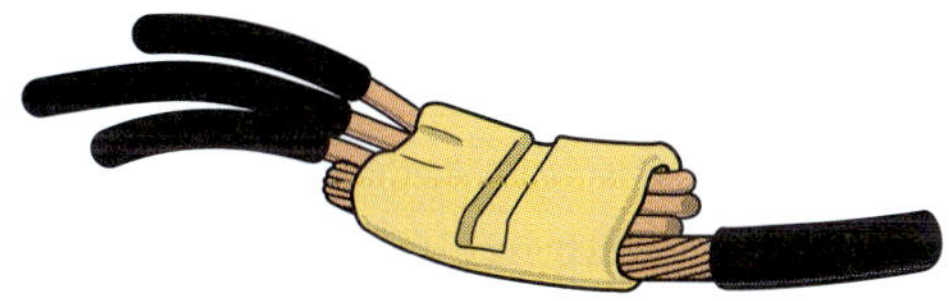

PROPERLY CRIMP THEN TAPE

CONNECTORS USED TO CONNECT WIRES TOGETHER ON COMBINATIONS OF 18 AWG THROUGH 6 AWG CONDUCTORS. THEY ARE TWIST-ON, SOLDERLESS, AND TAPELESS.

*WIRE-NUT,® WING-NUT,® and TWISTER® are registered trademarks of IDEAL INDUSTRIES, INC. Scotchlok® is a registered trademark of 3M.

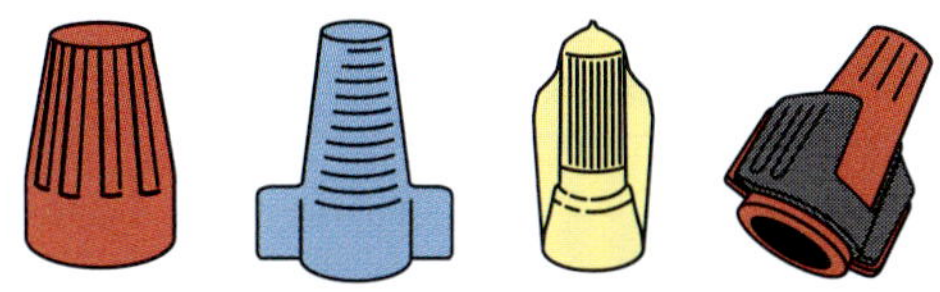

WIRE CONNECTORS VARIOUSLY KNOWN AS WIRE-NUT,® WING-NUT,® TWISTER,® AND SCOTCHLOK®

CONNECTORS USED TO CONNECT WIRES TOGETHER IN COMBINATIONS OF 16, 14, AND 12 AWG CONDUCTORS. THEY ARE CRIMPED ON WITH A SPECIAL TOOL, THEN COVERED WITH A SNAP-ON INSULATING CAP.

CRIMP-TYPE WIRE CONNECTOR AND INSULATING CAP

SOLDERLESS CONNECTORS ARE AVAILABLE IN SIZES 14 AWG THROUGH 500 KCMIL CONDUCTORS. THEY ARE USED FOR ONE SOLID OR ONE STRANDED CONDUCTOR ONLY, UNLESS OTHERWISE NOTED ON THE CONNECTOR OR ON ITS SHIPPING CARTON. THE SCREW MAY BE OF THE STANDARD SCREWDRIVER SLOT TYPE, OR IT MAY BE FOR USE WITH AN ALLEN WRENCH OR SOCKET WRENCH.

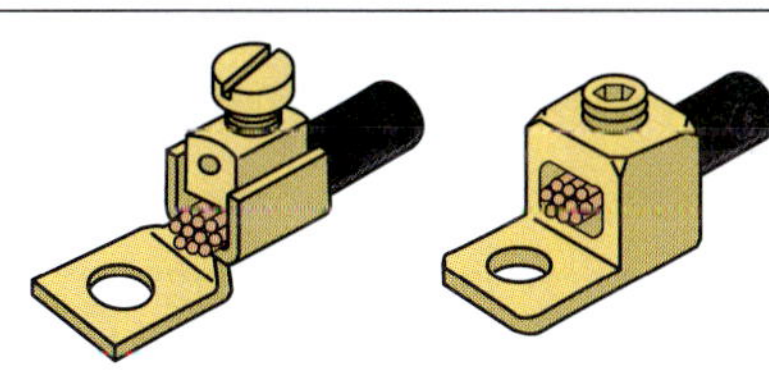

SOLDERLESS CONNECTORS

COMPRESSION CONNECTORS ARE USED FOR 8 AWG THROUGH 1000 KCMIL CONDUCTORS. THE WIRE IS INSERTED INTO THE END OF THE CONNECTOR, THEN CRIMPED ON WITH A SPECIAL COMPRESSION TOOL.

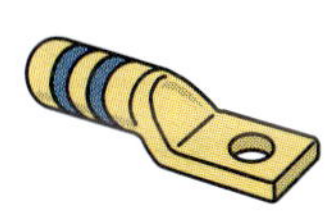

COMPRESSION CONNECTOR

SPLIT-BOLT CONNECTORS ARE USED FOR CONNECTING TWO CONDUCTORS TOGETHER, OR FOR TAPPING ONE CONDUCTOR TO ANOTHER. THEY ARE AVAILABLE IN SIZES 10 AWG THROUGH 1000 KCMIL. THEY ARE USED FOR TWO SOLID AND/OR TWO STRANDED CONDUCTORS ONLY, UNLESS OTHERWISE NOTED ON THE CONNECTOR OR ON ITS SHIPPING CARTON.

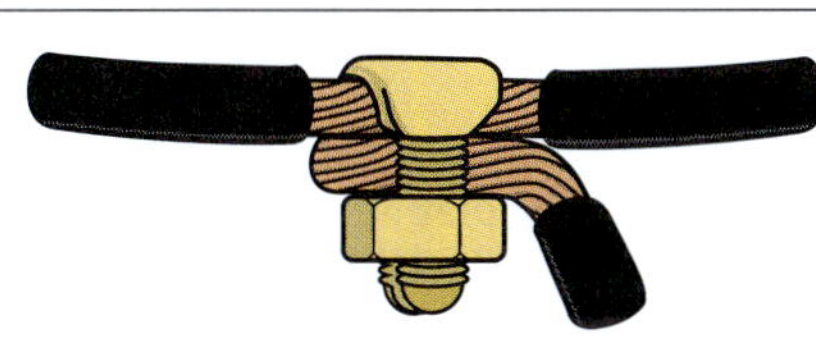

SPLIT-BOLT CONNECTOR

Figure 4-4 Types of wire connectors.

Old Houses Wired with Aluminum Conductors

If you come across a house wired with aluminum conductors, it was probably wired back in the mid sixties or early seventies. You will very likely find problems where the conductors are terminated on switches and receptacles. Take special care when changing out switches and receptacles or making splices. Use wiring devices that bear the AL/CU marking. You can also use special "pigtails" designed to make the connection between aluminum and copper conductors and terminals. One such connector is COPALUM®—a compression (crimp) connector. Apply an antioxidant to the splice or connection as recommended by the manufacturer of the connector.

CONDUCTOR INSULATION

The *NEC*® requires that all conductors be insulated, *310.2(A)*. There are a few exceptions, such as the permission to use a bare neutral conductor for services, and bare equipment grounding conductors.

NEC® *Table 310.13* shows many types of conductors, their applications, and insulations. The conductors most commonly used fall in the thermoplastic and thermoset categories.

What Is Thermoplastic Insulation?

Thermoplastic insulation is the most common. It is like chocolate. It will soften and melt if heated above its rated temperature. It can be heated, melted, and reshaped. Thermoplastic insulation will stiffen at temperatures colder than 14°F (minus 10°C). Typical examples of thermoplastic insulation are Types THHN, THHW, THW, THWN, and TW.

What Is Thermoset Insulation?

Thermoset insulation can withstand higher and lower temperatures. It is like baking a cake. Once the ingredients have been mixed, heated, and formed, it can never be reheated and reshaped. If heated above its rated temperature, it will char and crack. Typical examples of thermoset insulation are Types RHH, RHW, XHH, and XHHW.

Table 310.13 lists the various conductor insulations and their applications.

The allowable ampacities of copper conductors are given in *Table 310.16* for various types of insulation. *Table 310.15(B)(6)* is a table of conductor ampacities that are greater than the ampacities found in *Table 310.16*. This table is permitted to be used *only* for dwelling unit 120/240-volt, three-wire, single-phase service-entrance conductors, service-lateral conductors, and feeder conductors that serve as the main power feeder to a dwelling unit. This table is based upon the tremendous known load diversity found in homes. These special ampacities must not be used for feeder conductors that do not serve as the main power feeder to a dwelling. An example of this would be the feeder from the Main Panel A to Panel B in the residence discussed later on in this text.

Table 4-5 shows the special ampacities discussed previously. This table is a mirror image of *Table 310.15(B)(6)* in the *NEC*.®

The insulation covering wires and cables used in house wiring is usually rated at 600 volts or less. Exceptions to this statement are low-voltage wiring and luminaire wiring.

SPECIAL AMPACITY RATINGS FOR RESIDENTIAL 120/240-VOLT, 3-WIRE, SINGLE-PHASE SERVICE-ENTRANCE CONDUCTORS, SERVICE-LATERAL CONDUCTORS, AND FEEDER CONDUCTORS THAT SERVE AS THE MAIN POWER FEEDER TO A DWELLING UNIT. CONDUCTOR TYPES RHH, RHW, RHW-2, THHN, THHW, THW, THW-2, THWN, THWN-2, XHHW, XHHW-2, SE, USE, USE-2.

Copper Conductor AWG for Insulation of RH-RHH-RHW-THW-THWN-THHW-THHN-XHHW USE	Aluminum or Copper-Clad Aluminum Conductors (AWG)	Allowable Special Ampacity
4	2	100
3	1	110
2	1/0	125
1	2/0	150
1/0	3/0	175
2/0	4/0	200
3/0	250 kcmil	225
4/0	300 kcmil	250
250 kcmil	350 kcmil	300
350 kcmil	500 kcmil	350
400 kcmil	600 kcmil	400

Note: Where the conductors will be exposed to temperatures in excess of 86°F (30°C), apply the correction factors found at the bottom of *Table 310.16*. **Note:** Conductors having a suffix "2," such as THWN-2, are permitted for continuous use at 194°F (90°C) in wet or dry locations.

Table 4-5

Older Types of Conductor Insulation

Although Type THHN/THWN is the most common building wire used today, older types of conductor insulation might still be found, such as Types A, RH, RHH, RHW, RU, RUH, RUW, T, TW, and THW. Some of these are still shown in the *NEC*® but may no longer be manufactured. Some are still manufactured but are difficult, if not impossible, to find at an electrical supply house. Others are available only as a special-order product.

WET, DAMP, DRY, AND SUNLIGHT LOCATIONS

Conductors are listed for specific locations. Be sure that the conductor you use is suitable for the location. Table 4-6 shows some of the more typical conductors used in house wiring. Here are some definitions taken directly from the *NEC*.®

- **Damp Location.** Locations protected from weather and not subject to saturation with water or other liquids but subject to moderate degrees of moisture. Examples of such locations include partially protected locations under canopies, marquees, roofed open porches, and like locations; and interior locations subject to moderate degrees of moisture, such as some basements, some barns, and some cold-storage warehouses. (See Figure 11-4.)
- **Dry Location.** A location not normally subject to dampness or wetness. A location classified as dry may be temporarily subject to dampness or wetness, as in the case of a building under construction.

TRADE NAME	TYPE LETTER	MAXIMUM OPERATING TEMP.	APPLICATION PROVISIONS	INSULATION	AWG	OUTER COVERING
Heat-resistant thermoplastic	THHN	194°F (90°C)	Dry and damp locations	Flame-retardant, heat-resistant thermoplastic	14 through 1000 kcmil	Nylon jacket or equivalent
Moisture- and heat-resistant thermoplastic	THHW	167°F (75°C) 194°F (90°C)	Wet location Dry location	Flame-retardant, moisture- and heat-resistant thermoplastic	14 through 1000 kcmil	None
Moisture- and heat-resistant thermoplastic	THWN Note: If marked THWN-2, OK for 194°F (90°C) in dry or wet locations	167°F (75°C)	Dry and wet locations	Flame-retardant, moisture- and heat-resistant thermoplastic	14 through 1000 kcmil	Nylon jacket or equivalent
Moisture- and heat-resistant thermoplastic	THW Note: If marked THW-2, OK for 194°F (90°C) in dry or wet locations	167°F (75°C)	Dry and wet locations	Flame-retardant, moisture- and heat-resistant thermoplastic	14 through 2000 kcmil	None
Underground feeder and branch-circuit single conductor or multiconductor cable. See *Article 339*	UF	140°F (60°C) 167°F (75°C)	See *Article 339* See *Article 339*	Moisture-resistant Moisture-resistant	14 through 4/0	Integral with insulation

Table 4-6 Typical conductors used for residential wiring.

- ▶**Wet Location.** Installations underground or in concrete slabs or masonry in direct contact with the earth; locations subject to saturation with water or other liquids, such as vehicle washing areas; locations exposed to weather and unprotected. The interior of raceways installed in wet locations is considered a wet location. Insulated conductors and cables in these locations shall be listed for wet locations. See *300.5(B)*, *300.9*, and *310.8(C)*. Also see Figure 11-4.◀
- **Locations Exposed to Direct Sunlight.** Insulated conductors and cables used where exposed to direct rays of the sun shall be listed, or listed and marked as being "sunlight resistant."

See *NEC*® *310.8*, *310.10*, *310.13*, and *Table 310.13* for additional information.

Conductor Temperature Ratings

Conductors are also rated as to the temperature they can withstand. For example:

	Celsius	Fahrenheit
Type TW	60°	140°
Type THWN	75°	167°
Type THHN	90°	194°

Without question, conductors with Type THHN insulation are the most popular and most commonly used, particularly in the smaller sizes, because of their small diameter (easy to handle; more conductors of a given size permitted in a given size raceway) and their suitability for installation where high temperatures are encountered, such as attics, buried in insulation, and supplying recessed fixtures.

The temperature rating of nonmetallic-sheathed cable is 194°F (90°C). However, *334.80* states that the allowable ampacity is that of the 140°F (60°C) column in *Table 310.16*.

Multiple-Type Designations

Some conductors are listed for more than one application. For example, a conductor marked THHN/THWN is rated 600 volts, 90°C (194°F) when used in dry locations, *and* 600 volts, 75°C (167°F) when used in wet locations. As always, read the surface marking on the conductor insulation, on the tag, on the reel, or on the carton. The *NEC*® covers *Conductors for General Wiring* in *Article 310*.

The Weakest Link of the Chain

A conductor has two ends!

Selecting a conductor ampacity based solely on the allowable ampacity values found in *Table 310.16* is a very common mistake that can prove costly.

In any given circuit, we have an assortment of electrical components that have different maximum temperature ratings. Our job is to find out which component is the "weakest link" in the system and do our circuit design based on the lowest rated component in the circuit. Maximum temperature ratings are found in the *NEC*® and in the UL Standards.

- **Circuit breakers:** UL 489. Generally marked "75°C Only" or "60°C/75°C" (140°F/167°F).
- **Conductors:** *Table 310.13*, *Table 310.16*, and UL 83.
- **Disconnect switches:** UL 98. Generally marked "75°C Only" or "60°C/75°C" (140°F/167°F).
- **Panelboards:** UL 67. Panelboards are generally marked 167°F (75°C). The temperature rating of a panelboard has been established as an assembly with circuit breakers in place. Do not use the circuit breakers' temperature marking by itself. It is the panelboard temperature marking that counts.
- **Receptacles and attachment-plug caps:** UL 498. Most 15- and 20-ampere branch circuits have receptacles that have a maximum temperature rating of 140°F (60°C). Some 30-ampere receptacles are rated 140°F (60°C) and some are rated for 167°F (75°C). Larger 50-ampere receptacles are rated 167°F (75°C).
- **Snap switches:** UL 20. Most 15- and 20-ampere branch circuits have snap switches with a maximum temperature rating of 140°F (60°C).
- **Wire splicing devices and connectors:** Wire-Nuts®, Wing-Nuts®, Twisters®, and Scotchloks® for copper conductors (UL 486) and for aluminum conductors (UL 486B). These types of connectors are rated 221°F (105°C).

Table 4-7 indicates the correct applications for conductors and terminations.

Another key *NEC*® requirement is found in *110.14(C)*, "Termination Limitations," where we find the following:

For circuits rated 100 amperes or less, or marked for conductor sizes 14 through 1 AWG, unless other-

TERMINATION RATING	CONDUCTOR INSULATION RATING		
	60°C	75°C	90°C
60°C	OK	OK (at 60°C ampacity)	OK (at 60°C ampacity)
75°C	NO	OK	OK (at 75°C ampacity)
60/75°C	OK	OK (at 60°C or 75°C ampacity)	OK (at 60°C or 75°C ampacity)
90°C	NO	NO	OK (Only if equipment has a 90°C rating.)

Table 4-7 Types of conductor temperature ratings permitted for various terminal temperature ratings in conformance to the *NEC*® and the UL Standards.

wise identified, the terminals on wiring devices, switches, breakers, motor controllers, and other electrical equipment are based upon the ampacity of 140°F (60°C) conductors. It is acceptable to install conductors having a higher temperature rating, such as 90°C (194°F) THHN, but you must use the 140°F (60°C) ampacity values.

For circuits rated over 100 amperes, or marked for conductors larger than 1 AWG, the conductors installed must have a minimum 167°F (75°C) rating. The ampacity of the conductors is based on the 167°F (75°C) values. It is acceptable to install conductors having a higher temperature rating, such as 194°F (90°C) THHN, but you must use the 167°F (75°C) ampacity values.

When using high-temperature insulated conductors where adjustment factors are to be applied, such as *derating* for more than three current-carrying conductors in a raceway or cable, or *correcting* where high temperatures are encountered, the final results of these adjustments (in amperes) must comply with the requirements of *110.14(C)*. Similar requirements are found in the UL Standards.

Examples of applying *derating factors* and *correcting factors* are found in Chapter 18.

Temperature ratings of conductors and cables are discussed later in this chapter.

In *240.4(D)*, there is a built-in code compliance limitation for applying small branch-circuit conductors. Here we find that the maximum overcurrent protection is 15 amperes for 14 AWG, 20 amperes for 12 AWG, and 30 amperes for 10 AWG.

From *Table 310.16* we find that:

- 14 AWG copper conductors' allowable ampacity is:
  20 amperes in the 60°C (140°F) column
  20 amperes in the 75°C (167°F) column
  25 amperes in the 90°C (194°F) column
- 12 AWG copper conductors' allowable ampacity is:
  25 amperes in the 60°C (140°F) column
  25 amperes in the 75°C (167°F) column
  30 amperes in the 90°C (194°F) column
- 10 AWG copper conductors' allowable ampacity is:
  30 amperes in the 60°C (140°F) column
  35 amperes in the 75°C (167°F) column
  40 amperes in the 90°C (194°F) column

There are exceptions to this maximum overcurrent protection rule for motor, air-conditioner, and heat pump branch circuits. These exceptions are covered elsewhere in this text.

In summary, we cannot arbitrarily use the ampacity values for conductors as found in *Table 310.16*. Conductor ampacity is not a "stand-alone" issue. We must also consider the temperature limitations of the equipment, such as panelboards, receptacles, snap switches, receptacles, connectors, and so on. The lowest maximum temperature-rated device in an electrical system is the weakest link, and it is the weakest link that we must base our ultimate conductor ampacity and conductor insulation decision on.

Knob-and-Tube Wiring

Older homes were wired with open, individual, insulated conductors supported by porcelain *knobs* and *tubes*. In its day, knob-and-tube wiring served its purpose well. This text does not cover knob-and-tube wiring because this method is no longer used in new construction. On occasion, it is necessary to make some modifications to knob-and-tube wiring when doing remodel work. The *NEC*® covers this wiring method in *Article 394*.

Watch out when working on old knob-and-tube wiring. You will possibly find the old rubber insulation on the conductors dried out and brittle from the many years of heat generated by luminaires and from the extreme heat in attics, particularly when the conductors are completely buried in thermal insulation. The conductor insulation might fall apart when touched or moved. This is a potential fire hazard!

If you do find this situation, one fix is to slide insulation (heat shrink) tubing (available from electrical distributors) over the conductors to reinsulate them.

Figure 4-5 is a photo of typical knob-and-tube wiring from the 1930s.

Neutral Conductor Size

Figure 4-6 shows how *line-to-line* loads and *line-to-neutral* loads are connected. The grounded neutral (white) conductor Ⓝ for residential services and feeders is permitted to be smaller than the "hot" ungrounded phase (black, red) conductors L1 and L2 only when the neutral conductor is properly and adequately sized to carry the maximum unbalance loads calculated according to *215.2*, *220.61*, and *230.42*.

NEC® 215.2 relates to feeders and refers us to *Article 220* for calculation requirements.

NEC® 230.42 relates to services and refers us to *Article 220* for calculation requirements.

Focusing on the neutral conductor, *220.61* states that *the feeder or service neutral load shall be the maximum unbalance of the load determined by this Article.*

NEC® 220.61 further states that *the maximum unbalanced load shall be the maximum net calculated load between the neutral and any one ungrounded conductor.*

In a typical residence, we find a number of loads that carry little or no neutral current, such as an elec-

Figure 4-5 Photograph of a typical knob-and-tube wiring from the 1930s.

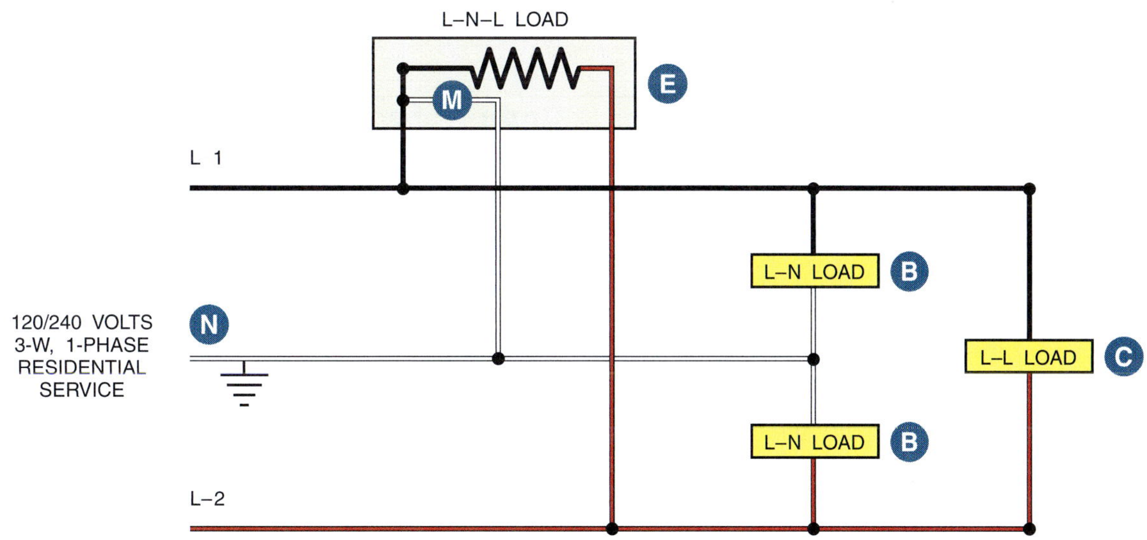

Figure 4-6 Diagram showing line-to-line and line-to-neutral loads.

tric water heater, electric clothes dryer, electric oven and range, electric furnace, and air conditioner. Checking Figure 4-6, you can readily see that load (C) is connected to a straight 240-volt, 2-wire circuit and has no neutral current. Note that load (E) is connected to a 120/240-volt 3-wire circuit, and in this hookup the120-volt motor (M) will result in current flowing in the neutral conductor. Loads (B) are 120-volt loads that are connected line to neutral.

Thus we find logic in the *NEC*,® which permits reducing the neutral conductor size on services and feeders where the calculations prove that the neutral conductor will be carrying less current than the "hot" phase conductors.

See Chapter 20 for sizing neutral conductors for electric range branch circuits and Chapter 29 for sizing neutral service-entrance conductors.

VOLTAGE DROP

Low voltage can cause lights to dim, some television pictures to "shrink," motors to run hot, electric heaters to not produce their rated heat output, and appliances to not operate properly.

Low voltage in a home can be caused by:

- wire that is too small for the load being served
- a circuit that is too long
- poor connections at the terminals
- conductors operating at high temperatures having higher resistance than when operating at lower temperatures

A simple formula for calculating voltage drop on single-phase systems considers only the dc resistance of the conductors and the temperature of the conductor. See *Table 8, Chapter 9* in the *NEC®* for the dc resistance values. The more accurate formulas consider ac resistance, reactance, temperature, spacing, in metal conduit and in nonmetallic conduit, *NEC® Table 9, Chapter 9*. Voltage drop is covered in great detail in *Electrical Wiring—Commercial* (Delmar/Cengage Learning). The simple voltage-drop formula is more accurate with smaller conductors and gets less and less accurate as conductor size increases. It is sufficiently accurate for voltage-drop calculations necessary for residential wiring.

To Find Voltage Drop in a Single-Phase Circuit:

$$E_d = \frac{K \times I \times L \times 2}{CMA}$$

To Find Conductor Size for a Single-Phase Circuit:

$$CMA = \frac{K \times I \times L \times 2}{E_d}$$

In the above formulae:

E_d = allowable voltage drop in volts.

K = approximate resistance in ohms per circular-mil foot at 167°F (75°C).

- for uncoated copper wire, use 12 ohms.*
- for aluminum wire, use 20 ohms.*

I = current in amperes flowing through the conductors.

L = length in feet from beginning of circuit to the load.

CMA = cross-sectional area of the conductors in circular mils.**

We use the factor of 2 for single-phase circuits because there is voltage drop in both conductors to and from the connected load.

To Find Voltage Drop and Conductor Size for a Three-Phase Circuit

Although residential wiring does not use three-phase systems, commercial and industrial systems do. To make voltage-drop and conductor sizing calculations for a three-phase system, substitute the factor of 1.73 (the square root of 3) in place of the factor 2 in the voltage-drop formulae.

Code References to Voltage Drop

For branch circuits, refer to *210.19(A), FPN No. 4*. The recommended maximum voltage drop is 3%, as shown in Figure 4-7.

For feeders, refer to *215.2(A), FPN No. 2*. The recommended maximum voltage drop is 3%. See Figure 4-8.

When both branch circuits and feeders are involved, the total voltage drop should not exceed 5%. This is shown in Figure 4-8.

According to *90.5(C)*, *FPNs* are explanatory only and are not to be enforced as *Code* requirement.

There is nothing in the *NEC®* that dictates what the incoming voltage to a home must be. Incoming voltage is really determined by the electric utility and is affected by the type, size, and length of the service conductors, transformer(s), and primary lines. Electric utilities come under the jurisdiction of the *National Electrical Safety Code® (NESC®)*. A local public service commission, usually at the state level, mandates maximum over- and undervoltages. This is generally within the 5 percent range of nominal voltage.

---

*Derived values from *Tables 8* and *9, Chapter 9, NEC®*

**From Table 4-8 in this text or from *Table 8, Chapter 9, NEC®*

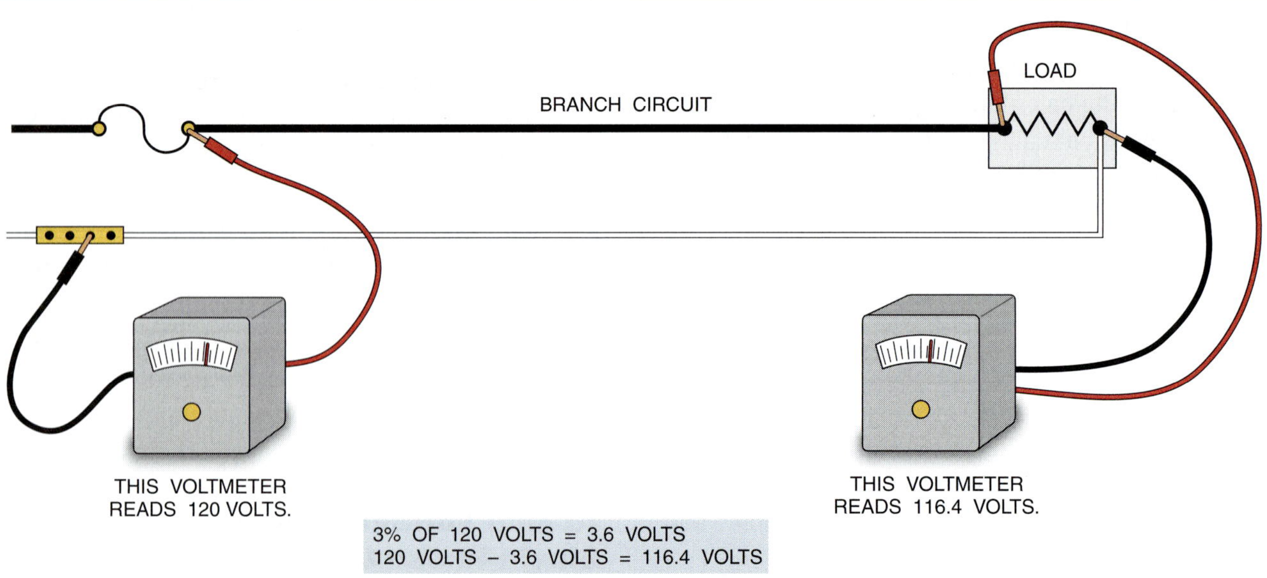

Figure 4-7 Maximum recommended voltage drop on a branch circuit is 3%, *210.19(A), FPN No. 4*.

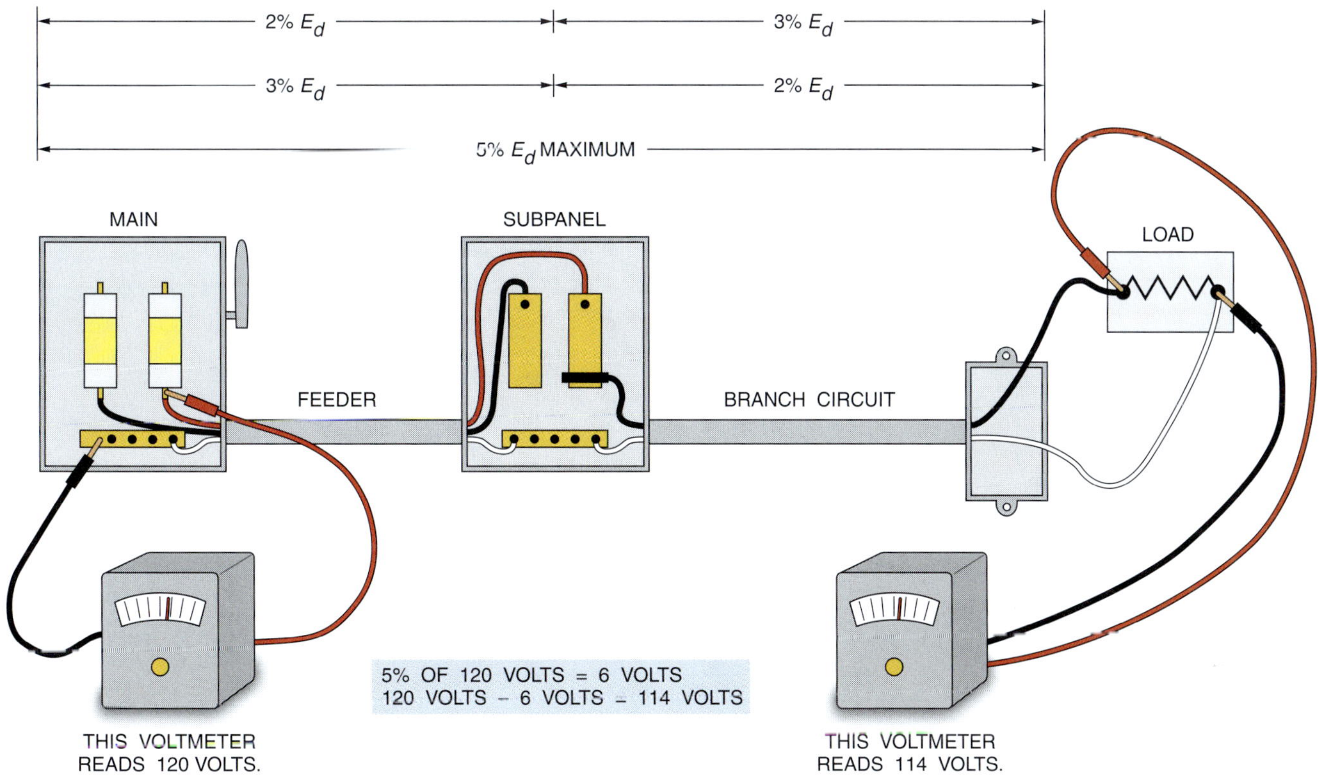

Figure 4-8 ***210.19(A), FPN No. 4*** **and** ***215.2(A), FPN No. 2*** **of the** ***Code*** **state that the total voltage drop from the beginning of a feeder to the farthest outlet on a branch circuit should not exceed 5 percent. In this figure, if the voltage drop in the feeder is 3%, then do not exceed 2 percent voltage drop in the branch circuit. If the voltage drop in the feeder is 2 percent, then do not exceed 3 percent voltage drop in the branch circuit.**

Examples of Voltage-Drop Calculations

EXAMPLE 1: What is the approximate voltage drop on a 120-volt, single-phase circuit consisting of 14 AWG copper conductors where the load is 11 amperes and the distance of the circuit from the panel to actual load is 85 ft (25.91 m)?

SOLUTION:

$$E_d = \frac{K \times I \times L \times 2}{CMA}$$

$$E_d = \frac{12 \times 11 \times 85 \times 2}{4110}$$

$$E_d = 5.46 \text{ volts drop}$$

Note: Refer to Table 4-8 for the CMA value.

CONDUCTOR SIZE, AWG	CROSS-SECTIONAL AREA IN CIRCULAR MILS
18	1620
16	2580
14	4110
12	6530
10	10,380
8	16,510
6	26,240
4	41,740
3	52,620
2	66,360
1	83,690
0	105,600
00	133,100
000	167,800
0000	211,600

Table 4-8 Circular mil cross-sectional area for many of the more common conductors.

Table 310.16 Allowable Ampacities of Insulated Conductors Rated 0 Through 2000 Volts, 60°C Through 90°C (140°F Through 194°F), Not More Than Three Current-Carrying Conductors in Raceway, Cable, or Earth (Directly Buried), Based on Ambient Temperature of 30°C (86°F)

	Temperature Rating of Conductor [See Table 310.13(A).]						
	60°C (140°F)	75°C (167°F)	90°C (194°F)	60°C (140°F)	75°C (167°F)	90°C (194°F)	
Size AWG or kcmil	Types TW, UF	Types RHW, THHW, THW, THWN, XHHW, USE, ZW	Types TBS, SA, SIS, FEP, FEPB, MI, RHH, RHW-2, THHN, THHW, THW-2, THWN-2, USE-2, XHH, XHHW, XHHW-2, ZW-2	Types TW, UF	Types RHW, THHW, THW, THWN, XHHW, USE	Types TBS, SA, SIS, THHN, THHW, THW-2, THWN-2, RHH, RHW-2, USE-2, XHH, XHHW, XHHW-2, ZW-2	
	COPPER			ALUMINUM OR COPPER-CLAD ALUMINUM			Size AWG or kcmil
18	—	—	14	—	—	—	—
16	—	—	18	—	—	—	—
14*	20	20	25	—	—	—	—
12*	25	25	30	20	20	25	12*
10*	30	35	40	25	30	35	10*
8	40	50	55	30	40	45	8
6	55	65	75	40	50	60	6
4	70	85	95	55	65	75	4
3	85	100	110	65	75	85	3
2	95	115	130	75	90	100	2
1	110	130	150	85	100	115	1
1/0	125	150	170	100	120	135	1/0
2/0	145	175	195	115	135	150	2/0
3/0	165	200	225	130	155	175	3/0
4/0	195	230	260	150	180	205	4/0
250	215	255	290	170	205	230	250
300	240	285	320	190	230	255	300
350	260	310	350	210	250	280	350
400	280	335	380	225	270	305	400
500	320	380	430	260	310	350	500
600	355	420	475	285	340	385	600
700	385	460	520	310	375	420	700
750	400	475	535	320	385	435	750
800	410	490	555	330	395	450	800
900	435	520	585	355	425	480	900
1000	455	545	615	375	445	500	1000
1250	495	590	665	405	485	545	1250
1500	520	625	705	435	520	585	1500
1750	545	650	735	455	545	615	1750
2000	560	665	750	470	560	630	2000
	CORRECTION FACTORS						
Ambient Temp. (°C)	For ambient temperatures other than 30°C (86°F), multiply the allowable ampacities shown above by the appropriate factor shown below.						Ambient Temp. (°F)
21–25	1.08	1.05	1.04	1.08	1.05	1.04	70–77
26–30	1.00	1.00	1.00	1.00	1.00	1.00	78–86
31–35	0.91	0.94	0.96	0.91	0.94	0.96	87–95
36–40	0.82	0.88	0.91	0.82	0.88	0.91	96–104
41–45	0.71	0.82	0.87	0.71	0.82	0.87	105–113
46–50	0.58	0.75	0.82	0.58	0.75	0.82	114–122
51–55	0.41	0.67	0.76	0.41	0.67	0.76	123–131
56–60	—	0.58	0.71	—	0.58	0.71	132–140
61–70	—	0.33	0.58	—	0.33	0.58	141–158
71–80	—	—	0.41	—	—	0.41	159–176

* See 240.4(D).

This exceeds the voltage drop recommended by the *Code*, which is:

$$3\% \text{ of } 120 \text{ volts} = 3.6 \text{ volts}$$

Let's try it again using 12 AWG conductors:

$$E_d = \frac{12 \times 11 \times 85 \times 2}{6530}$$

$$E_d = 3.44 \text{ volts drop}$$

This "meets the intent of the *Code*."

EXAMPLE 2: Find the wire size needed to keep the voltage drop to no more than 3% on a single-phase, 240-volt, air-conditioner circuit. The nameplate reads: "Minimum Circuit Ampacity 40 Amperes." The circuit originates at the main panel located approximately 65 ft (19.81 m) from the air-conditioner unit. No neutral conductor is required.

SOLUTION: Checking *Table 310.16*, the conductors could be 6 AWG Type TW copper or 8 AWG Type THHN copper.

The permitted voltage drop is:

$$E_d = 240 \times 0.03 = 7.2 \text{ volts}$$

Let's see what voltage drop we might experience if we installed the 8 AWG Type THHN conductors.

$$E_d = \frac{12 \times 40 \times 65 \times 2}{16{,}510}$$

$$= 3.78 \text{ volts drop}$$

This is well below the recommended 7.2 volts drop and would make an acceptable installation.

A Word of Caution When Using High-Temperature Conductors

Note in *Table 310.16* that conductors fall into three classes of temperature ratings—60°C, 75°C, and 90°C. For a given conductor size, we find that the allowable ampacity of a 90°C insulated conductor is greater than that of a 60°C insulated conductor. Therefore, be careful when selecting conductors based on their ability to withstand high temperatures. For example:

- 8 AWG THHN (90°C) copper has an allowable ampacity of 55 amperes.
- 8 AWG THW (75°C) copper has an allowable ampacity of 50 amperes.
- 8 AWG TW (60°C) copper has an allowable ampacity of 40 amperes.

We learned earlier in this chapter that according to *110.14(C)*, we use the 60°C column of *Table 310.16* for circuits rated 100 amperes or less, and the 75°C column for circuits rated over 100 amperes. However, when the equipment is marked as being suitable for 75°C, we can take advantage of the higher ampacity of 75°C conductors. This oftentimes results in a smaller size conductor and a correspondingly smaller raceway.

But installing smaller conductors might result in excessive voltage drop.

Therefore, after selecting the proper size conductor for a given load, it is always a good idea to run a voltage-drop calculation to make sure the voltage drop is not excessive.

What Is the Advantage of High-Temperature Conductors?

They can withstand the high temperatures found in attics and high-temperature climates.

Another big advantage of the higher ampacities of high-temperature insulation is that the *NEC*® permits the higher ampacity values to be used as the starting point when applying derating and correcting factors. Example calculations of this are found in Chapter 18.

Effect of Voltage Variation

Chapter 19 has more information on the effect voltage differences have on wattage output of appliances and on electric motors.

APPROXIMATE CONDUCTOR SIZE RELATIONSHIP

There is a definite relationship between the circular mil area and the resistance of conductors. The following rules explain this relationship.

Rule One: For wire sizes up through 0000, every third size doubles or halves in circular mil area.

Thus, a 1 AWG conductor is 2 times larger than a 4 AWG conductor (83,690 versus 41,470). Thus, a "0" wire is one-half the size of "0000" wire (105,600 versus 211,600).

Rule Two: For wire sizes up through 0000, every consecutive wire size is approximately 1.26 times larger or smaller than the preceding wire size.

Thus, a 3 AWG conductor is approximately 1.26 times larger than a 4 AWG conductor (41,740 × 1.26 = 52,592). A 2 AWG conductor is approximately 1.26 times smaller than a 1 AWG conductor (83,690 ÷ 1.26 = 66,420).

Try to fix in your mind that a 10 AWG conductor has a cross-sectional area of 10,380 circular mils, and that it has a resistance of 1.2 ohms per 1000 ft (300 m). The resistance of aluminum wire is approximately 2 ohms per 1000 ft (300 m). By remembering these numbers, you will be able to perform voltage-drop calculations without having the wire tables readily available.

EXAMPLE: What is the approximate cross-sectional area, in circular mils, and resistance of a 6 AWG copper conductor?

SOLUTION: Note in Table 4-9 that when the CMA of a wire is doubled, then its resistance is cut in half. Inversely, when a given wire size is reduced to one-half, its resistance doubles.

WIRE SIZE (AWG)	CMA (In Circular Mils)	OHMS PER 1000 FT
10	10,380	1.2
9		
8		
7	20,760	0.6
6	26,158	0.476

Table 4-9 "Every third size" and the 1.26 relationship between the circular-mil area (CMA) and the resistance in ohms per 1000 ft of copper conductors sizes 10 AWG through 6 AWG.

NONMETALLIC-SHEATHED CABLE *(ARTICLE 334)*

The *NEC*® and UL Standard 719 describe the construction details of nonmetallic-sheathed cable. The following is a summary of these details.

Description

Most electricians still refer to nonmetallic-sheathed cable as *Romex*, a name chosen years ago by the Rome Wire and Cable Company. Romex® is now a registered trademark of Southwire Company.

Nonmetallic-sheathed cable is a factory assembly of two or more insulated conductors having an outer sheath of moisture-resistant, flame-retardant, nonmetallic material. This cable is available with two or three current-carrying conductors. The conductors range in size from 14 AWG through 2 AWG for copper conductors, and from 12 AWG through 2 AWG for aluminum or copper-clad aluminum conductors. Two-wire cables contain one black conductor, one white conductor, and one bare equipment grounding conductor. Three-wire cables contain one black, one white, one red, and one bare equipment grounding conductor. Equipment grounding conductors are permitted to have green insulation, but bare equipment grounding conductors are the most common.

NEC® 334.108 requires that nonmetallic-sheathed cable have an insulated or a bare equipment grounding conductor.

Figure 4-9 clearly shows a bare equipment grounding conductor. Sometimes the bare equipment grounding conductor is wrapped with paper or fiberglass, which acts as a filler. The equipment grounding conductor is *not* permitted to be used as a current-carrying conductor.

Types of Nonmetallic-Sheathed Cable

UL 719 lists two types of nonmetallic-sheathed cable. The *NEC*® shows three types of nonmetallic-sheathed cable.

- **Type NM-B** is the most common type of nonmetallic-sheathed cable in use today. Type NM-B cable has a flame-retardant, moisture-resistant, nonmetallic outer jacket. The conductors are rated 194°F (90°C). The ampacity is based on the 140°F (60°C) column in *NEC® Table 310.16*. The conductors in Type NM-B meet all of the requirements of THHN but do not have the identifying marking along the entire length of the individual conductors. In the past, Type NM cable contained TW-style conductors.
- **Type NMC-B** cable has a flame-retardant, moisture-resistant, fungus-resistant, and corrosion-resistant, nonmetallic outer jacket. The conductors are rated 194°F (90°C). The ampacity is based on the 140°F (60°C) column in *NEC® Table 310.16*. Type NMC-B cable is not commercially available. Underground feeder Type UF-B cable can be used as a substitute for NMC.
- **Type NMS-B** cable is a hybrid cable that contains the conventional insulated power conductors as well as telephone, coaxial, home entertainment, and signaling conductors all in one cable. This type of cable is used for home automation systems using the latest in digital technology.

►Prior to the 2008 *NEC®, Article 780* recognized this wiring method for closed loop and programmed power distribution. In the 2008 *NEC®, Article 780* was deleted. The Type NMS-B cable had a moisture-resistant, flame-retardant, nonmetallic outer jacket. Type NMS-B cable is not commercially available. This type of home automation never did

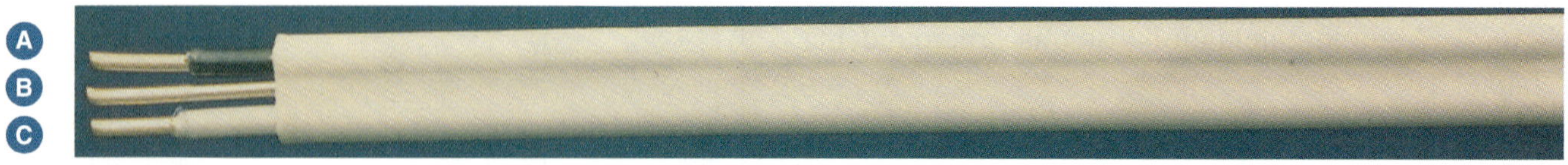

Figure 4-9 A nonmetallic-sheathed Type NM-B cable showing (A) black "ungrounded" (hot) conductor, (B) bare equipment "grounding" conductor, and (C) white "grounded" conductor. *Courtesy of* Southwire Company.

take off. It fell by the wayside. Today, we are seeing a tremendous amount of wireless home automation systems. ◀

Although somewhat confusing, the UL standards use the suffix B, whereas the *NEC*® refers to nonmetallic-sheathed cables as Type NM, NMC, and NMS. The conductors in these cables are rated 194°F (90°C). Types NM, NMC, and NMS cable, identified by the markings NM-B, NMC-B, and NMS-B, meet this 194°F (90°C) requirement. See *334.112*.

As of the writing of this edition of *Electrical Wiring—Residential*, there are no UL listings for Type NMS and NMS-B cables.

Why the Suffix *B*?

The suffix "B" means that the conductors have 194°F (90°C) insulation.

Older nonmetallic-sheathed cable contained 140°F (60°C) rated conductors. There were many problems with the insulation becoming brittle and breaking off due to the extremely high temperatures associated with recessed and surface-mounted luminaires: fires resulted. In hot attics, after applying correction factors, the adjusted allowable ampacity of the conductors could very well be zero. To solve this dilemma, since December 17, 1984, UL has required that the conductors be rated 194°F (90°C), and that the cable be identified with the suffix *B*. This suffix makes it easy to differentiate the newer 194°F (90°C) from the old 140°F (60°C) cable.

The ampacity of the conductors in nonmetallic-sheathed cable is based on that of 140°F (60°C) conductors. The 194°F (90°C) ampacity is permitted to be used for derating purposes, such as might be necessary in attics. The final derated ampacity must not exceed the ampacity for 140°F (60°C) conductors. More specifics can be found in *334.80*.

Table 310.16 shows the allowable ampacities for conductors.

Overcurrent Protection for Small Conductors

Overcurrent protection for small copper conductors, in conformance to *240.4(D)*, is:

- 14 AWG 15 amperes
- 12 AWG 20 amperes
- 10 AWG 30 amperes

A typical nonmetallic-sheathed cable is illustrated in Figure 4-9.

Color Coding of Type NM-B Jacket

To make installations easier for the electrician and the electrical inspector to identify the conductor size, color-coded nonmetallic-sheathed cable is available.

Conductor Size	Color of Jacket
14 AWG	White
12 AWG	Yellow
10 AWG	Orange
8 and 6 AWG	Black

New Types of NM-B Cable

At least one manufacturer offers a four-conductor Type NM-B that can be used for two branch circuits. This cable is used where sharing of the neutral is *not wanted*, as in a multiwire branch circuit, or for branch circuits supplying GFCIs and AFCIs, where sharing the neutral is *not permitted*.

This cable contains:

One bare equipment grounding conductor

Pair 1: one black and one white

Pair 2: one black and one white (with a red stripe)

Because all four conductors in this cable are current-carrying conductors, the ampacity of the conductors must be adjusted (derated) according to *310.15(B)(2)*.

Where Nonmetallic-Sheathed Cable May Be Used

Table 4-10 shows the uses permitted for Types NM B, NMC-B and NMS-B.

Equipment Grounding Conductors (*250.122*)

Equipment grounding conductor (EGC) sizing is based on the rating or setting of the overcurrent device protecting a given branch circuit or feeder. See *Table 250.122*.

The EGC in a nonmetallic-sheathed cable is sized according to *Table 250.122* and is usually bare. Table 4-11 is a short version of *Table 250.122*.

▶An EGC does not have to be larger than the ungrounded conductors of a given circuit. Why? Because in the event of a ground fault, the amount of

	TYPE NM-B	TYPE NMC-B	TYPE NMS-B
May be used on circuits of 600 volts or less.	Yes	Yes	Yes
May be run exposed or concealed in dry locations.	Yes	Yes	Yes
May be installed exposed or concealed in damp and moist locations.	No	Yes	No
Has flame-retardant and moisture-resistant outer covering.	Yes	Yes	Yes
Has fungus-resistant and corrosion-resistant outer covering.	No	Yes	No
May be used to wire one- and two-family dwellings or multifamily dwellings. See *334.10*.	Yes	Yes	Yes
May be embedded in masonry, concrete, plaster, adobe, fill.	No	No	No
May be installed or fished in the hollow voids of masonry blocks or tile walls where not exposed to excessive moisture or dampness.	Yes	Yes	Yes
May be installed or fished in the hollow voids of masonry blocks or tile walls where exposed to excessive moisture.	No	Yes	No
In outside walls of masonry block or tile.	No	Yes	No
In inside wall of masonry block or tile.	Yes	Yes	Yes
May be used as service-entrance cable.	No	No	No
Must be protected against physical damage.	Yes	Yes	Yes
May be run in shallow chase of masonry, concrete, or adobe if protected by a steel plate(s) at least 1⁄16 in. (1.6 mm) thick, then covered with plaster, adobe, or similar finish.	No	Yes	No

Table 4-10 Uses permitted for nonmetallic-sheathed cable.

ground-fault current returning on the EGC can never be more than the ground-fault current flowing on the ungrounded conductor of that circuit that caused the problem. It's a simple series circuit. What goes out—comes back! See *250.122(A)*.◀

Rating or Setting of Overcurrent Device	MINIMUM SIZE (AWG) EQUIPMENT GROUNDING CONDUCTOR: Copper	MINIMUM SIZE (AWG) EQUIPMENT GROUNDING CONDUCTOR: Aluminum or Copper-Clad Aluminum
15	14	12
20	12	10
30	10	8
40	10	8
60	10	8
100	8	6
200	6	4

Table 4-11 Minimum size equipment grounding conductors is based on the rating or setting of the overcurrent device protecting that particular branch circuit. This table is based on *Table 250.122* of the *NEC*.®

Installation

Nonmetallic-sheathed cable is probably the least expensive of the various wiring methods. It is relatively lightweight and easy to install. It is widely used for dwelling unit installations on circuits of 600 volts or less. Figure 4-10 shows an example of a stripper used for stripping nonmetallic-sheathed cable. A knife also works fine with care. The instal-

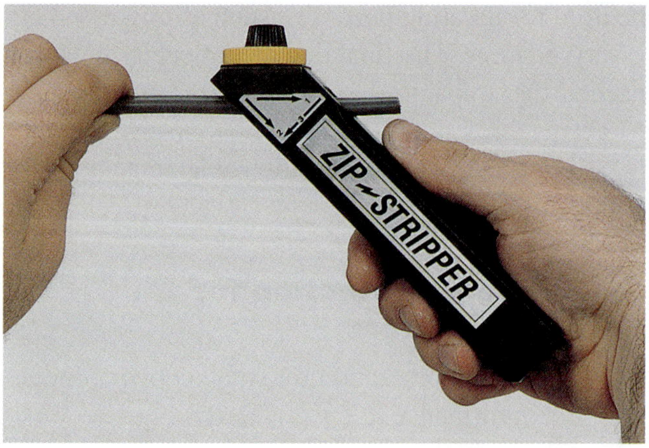

Figure 4-10 This stripper is used to remove the outer jacket from nonmetallic-sheathed cable. *Courtesy of Seatek Co., Inc.*

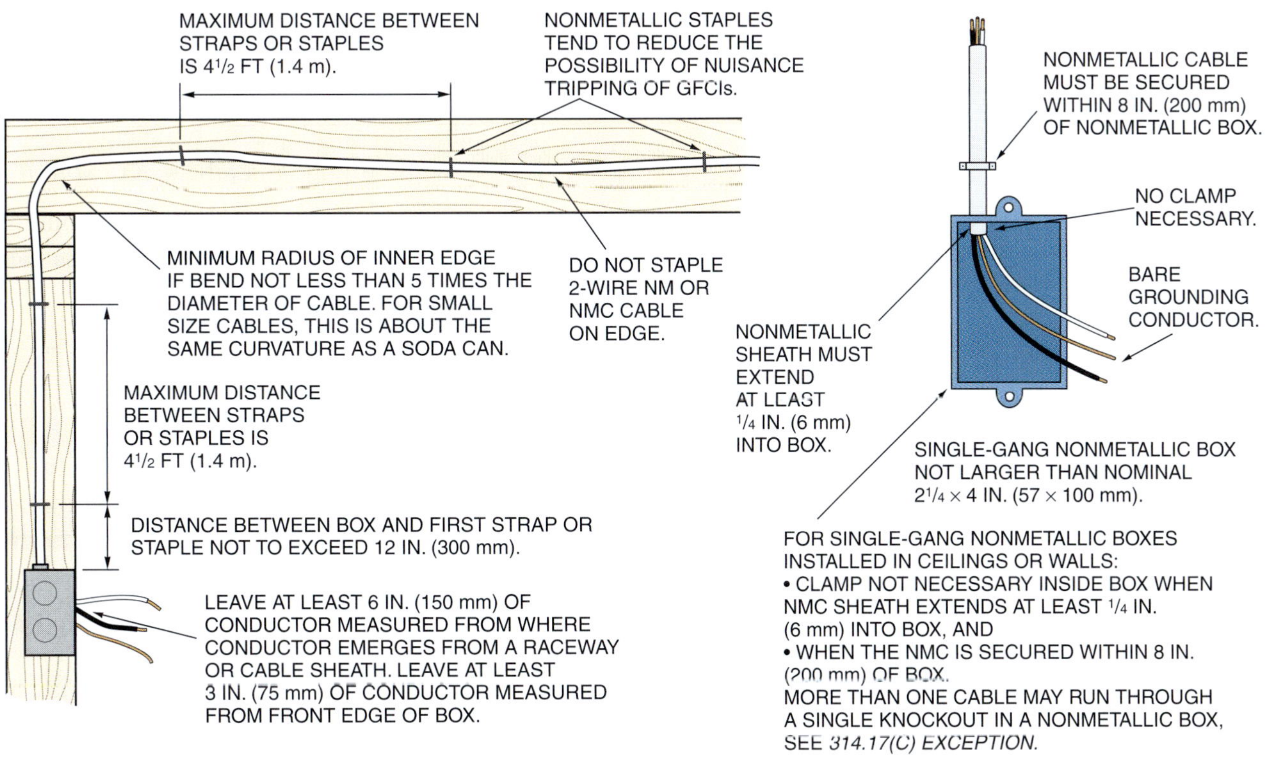

Figure 4-11 Installation of nonmetallic-sheathed cable.

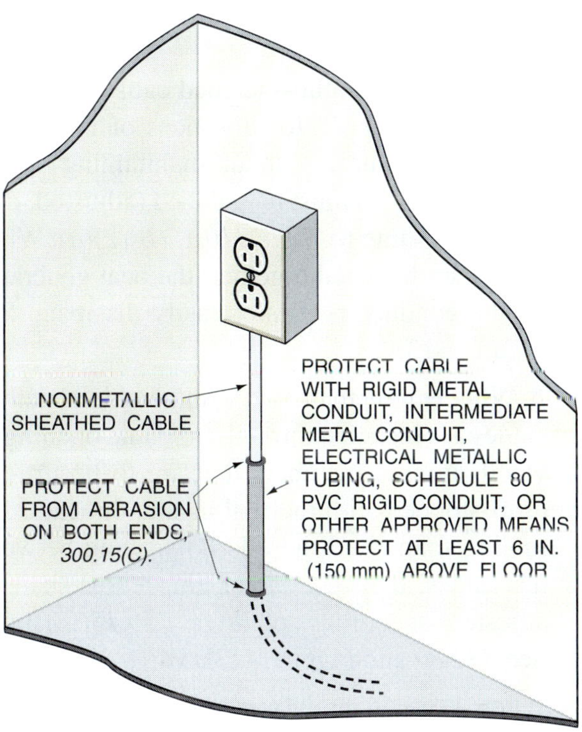

Figure 4-12 Installation of exposed nonmetallic-sheathed cable where passing through a floor. See *334.15(B)*.

lation of nonmetallic-sheathed cable must conform to the requirements of *Article 334*. Refer to Figure 4-11, Figure 4-12, Figure 4-13, Figure 4-14, Figure 4-15, and Figure 4-16.

- The cable must be strapped or stapled not more than 12 in. (300 mm) from a box or fitting.
- Do not staple flat nonmetallic-sheathed cables on edge, Figure 4-15.
- The intervals between straps or staples must not exceed 4½ ft (1.4 m).
- Exposed runs of cables can be subjected to lots of abuse. A child may pull or stand on the cables and adults may use the cables to hang things on. *NEC® 334.15* requires that cables be protected against physical damage where necessary. For example, where exposed in a garage with open studs, run the cables on the sides of the studs. Where cables are run horizontally from/through stud to stud, protection is required. Some inspectors require protective boards over exposed horizontal cable runs, or sheet rock, or other wall finish up to the ceiling, or at least 7 ft (2.13 m) up. For protection of cables in attics, see Chapter 15.

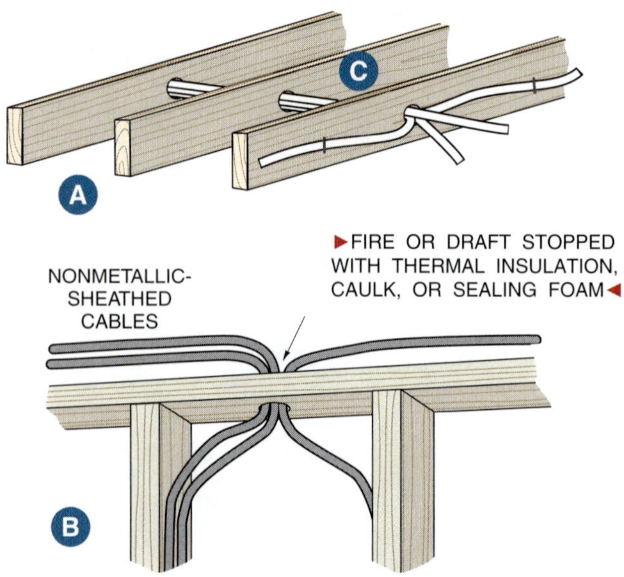

Figure 4-13 ►**The conductor ampacity in NM cables shall be adjusted according to *Table 310.15(B)(2)(a)*: (A) when NM cables are "bundled" or "stacked" for distances more than 24 in. (600 mm) without maintaining spacing; or (B) when more than two NM cables pass through wood framing members where fire-stopping material is used, and there is no spacing between the cables; or (C) when more than two NM cables are installed in contact with thermal insulation◄ See *310.15(2)* and *334.80*.**

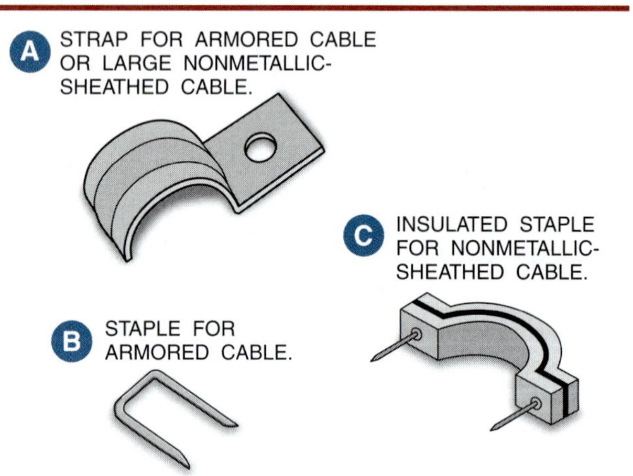

Figure 4-14 (A) One-hole strap used for conduit, EMT, large nonmetallic-sheathed cable and armored cable. (B) Metal staple for armored cable and nonmetallic-sheathed cable. (C) Insulated staple for nonmetallic-sheathed cable. Certain types of insulated and noninsulated staples can be applied with a staple gun.

- The 4½ ft (1.4 m) securing requirement is not needed where nonmetallic-sheathed cable is run *horizontally* through holes in wood or metal framing members (studs, joists, rafters, etc.). The cable is considered to be adequately supported by the framing members, *334.30(A)*.
- The inner edge of the bend shall have a minimum radius not less than 5 times the cable diameter, *334.24*.
- The cable must not be used in circuits of more than 600 volts.
- **CAUTION: Be very careful when installing staples. Driving them too hard can squeeze and damage the insulation on the conductors, causing short circuits and/or ground faults.**
- See Figure 4-11 for special conditions when using single-gang nonmetallic device boxes.
- Nonmetallic-sheathed cable must be protected where passing through a floor by at least 6 in. (150 mm) of rigid metal conduit, intermediate metal conduit, electrical metallic tubing, Schedule 80 rigid PVC conduit, or other approved means, *334.15(B)*. A fitting (bushing or connector) must be used at both ends of the conduit to protect the cable from abrasion, Figure 4-12.
- ►When nonmetallic-sheathed cables are "bundled" or "stacked" for distances of more than 24 in. (600 mm) without maintaining space, their ampacities must be reduced (adjusted, derated) according to *Table 310.15(B)(2)(a)*. When cables are bunched together, the heat generated by the conductors cannot easily dissipate. See Figure 4-13A.◄
- ►When more than two nonmetallic-sheathed cables are installed through the same opening in wood framing members that are to be fire- or draft-stopped with thermal insulation, caulk, or sealing foam, and there is no spacing between the cables, their conductor ampacities shall be adjusted according to *Table 310.15(B)(2)(a)*. See *334.80* and Figure 4-13B.◄
- When Type AC and Type MC cables are "bundled" or "stacked," derating is not necessary if the following is true:
  - the conductors are 12 AWG copper

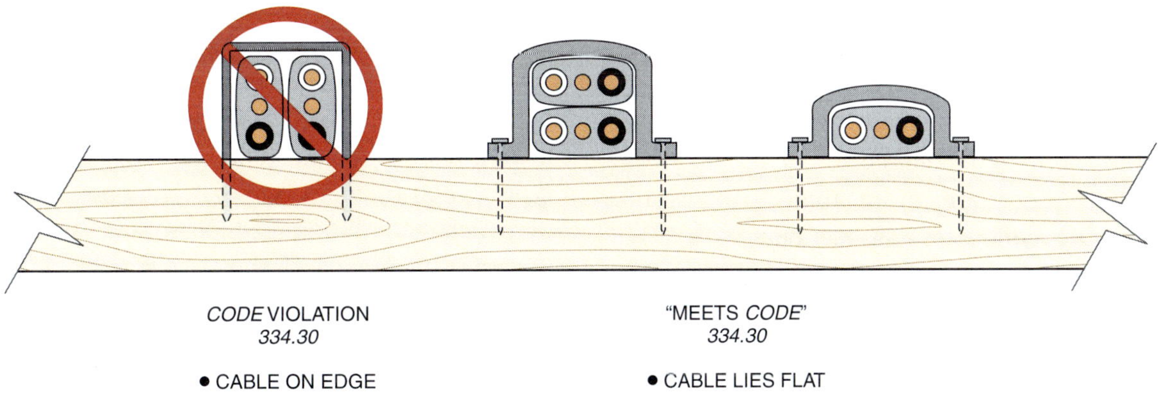

Figure 4-15 It is a *Code* violation to staple flat nonmetallic-sheathed cables on edge, *334.30.*

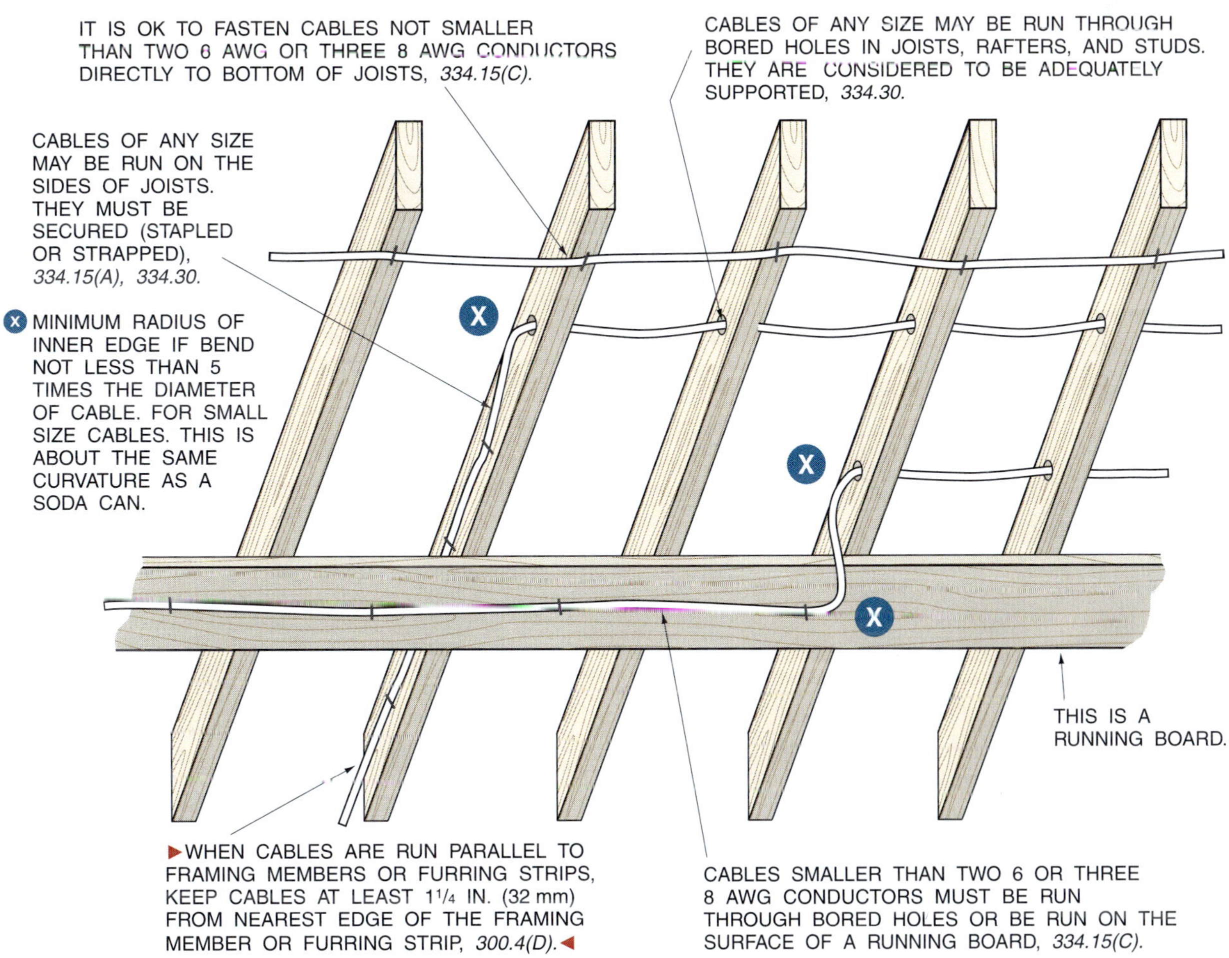

Figure 4-16 The requirements for running nonmetallic-sheathed cable in unfinished basements and crawl spaces.

- if the bundling or stacking is not more than 24 in. (600 mm)
- there are no more than three current-carrying conductors in each cable
- there are no more than 20 current-carrying conductors in the bundle
- When there are more than 20 current-carrying conductors in the bundle, a 60% adjustment factor shall be applied. See *310.15(B)(2), Exception No. 5.*

- The cable may be run in unsupported lengths of not more than 4½ ft (1.4 m) between the last point of support of the cable and a luminaire or other equipment within an accessible ceiling. For this last 4½ ft (1.4 m), the 12-in. (300-mm) and 4½-ft (1.4-m) securing requirements mentioned above are not necessary if the nonmetallic-sheathed cable is used as a luminaire (fixture) whip to connect luminaires of other equipment. See *334.30*. Luminaire (fixture) whips are discussed in Chapter 7 and Chapter 17.

Figure 4-16 shows the installation of nonmetallic-sheathed cable in unfinished basements, *334.15(C)*.

See Chapter 15 and Figures 15-13 and Figure 15-14 for additional text and diagrams covering the installation of cables in attics.

Figure 4-17 Gang-type switch (device) box.

Figure 4-11 shows the *Code* requirements for securing nonmetallic-sheathed cable when using nonmetallic boxes.

The *Code* in *314.40(D)* requires that all metal boxes have provisions for the attachment of an equipment grounding conductor. Figure 4-17 shows a gang-type switch (device) box that is tapped for a screw by which the grounding conductor may be connected underneath. Figure 4-18 shows an outlet box, also with provisions for attaching grounding conductors. Figure 4-19 illustrates the use of a small grounding clip.

NEC® 410.44 requires that there be a provision whereby the equipment grounding conductor can be attached to the exposed metal parts of luminaires.

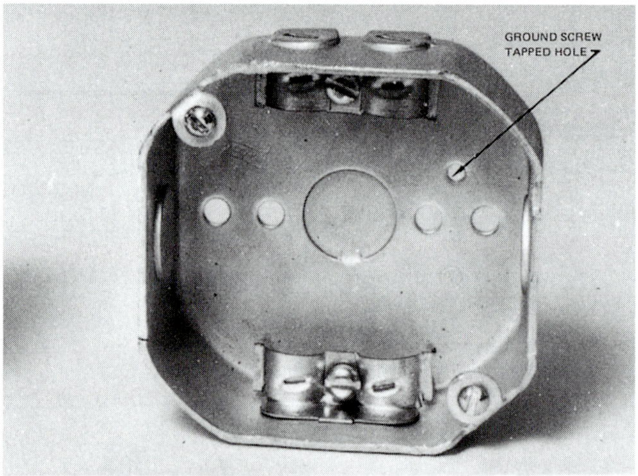

Figure 4-18 Outlet box.

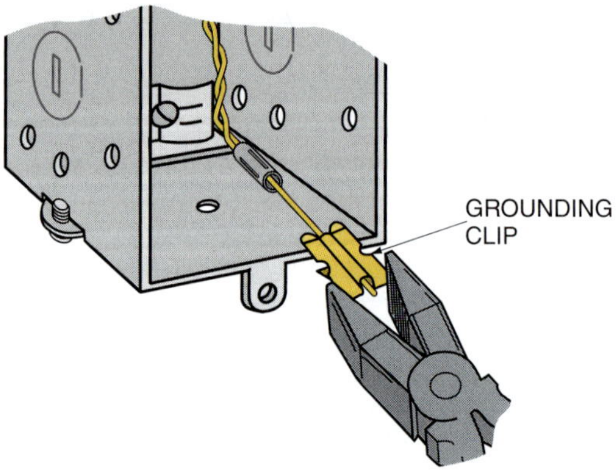

Figure 4-19 Method of attaching ground clip to a metal switch (device) box. See *250.148*.

Are Cables Permitted in Raceways?

Yes, but only if certain conditions are met.

NEC® 300.15(C) permits using a listed conduit or tubing without a box where the conduit or tubing is used to protect a nonmetallic-sheathed cable against physical damage. Figure 4-20 shows an example of this in a basement where the wiring method in the ceiling is NM cable and a switch or

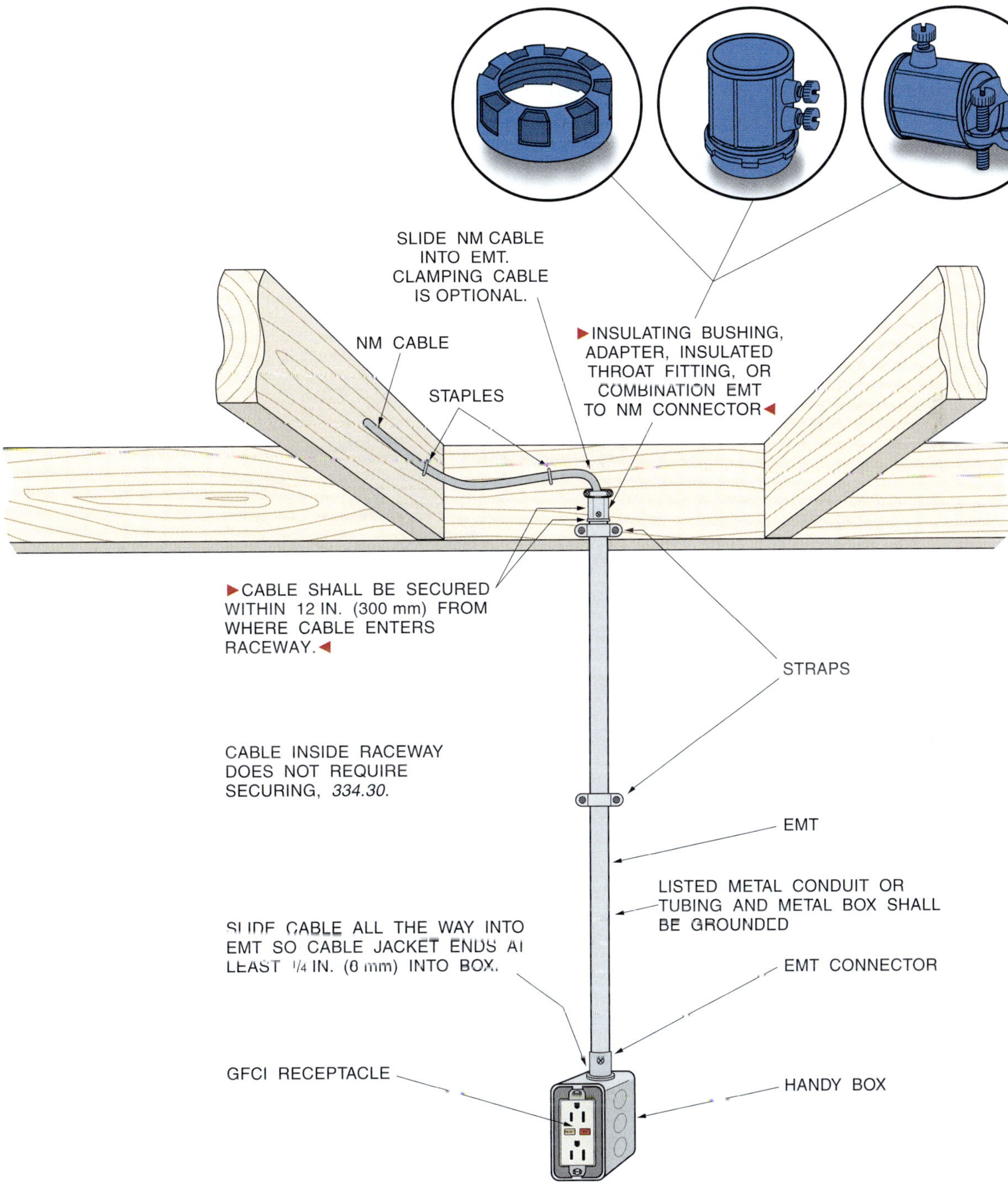

Figure 4-20 An example of EMT protecting a nonmetallic-sheathed cable from physical damage where the cable is run down the wall of an unfinished basement. This also makes a neat installation. The EMT and the metal box must be grounded. Physical protection and grounding are required by *334.15(C)*. *NEC® 300.18(A), Exception* also recognizes this type of installation.

receptacle is in a box mounted on the wall. An EMT is installed from the box to a point above the ceiling joists, where the EMT is secured to the side of the joists. The NM cable is then run inside the EMT, and an insulating fitting is installed on the upper end of the tubing to protect the cable against abrasion. The cable does not require securing inside the raceway, *334.30*. The finished job is neat.

The conductors inside a nonmetallic-sheathed cable meet all of the UL requirements for Type THHN conductors but are not surface marked in any manner.

NEC® 334.15(B) requires protection of nonmetallic-sheathed cable from physical damage where necessary. This section lists different types of raceways permitted to be used for protection of the cable.

The raceway fill for a cable in a conduit or tubing is based on the allowable percentage fill values specified in *Table 1, Chapter 9*.

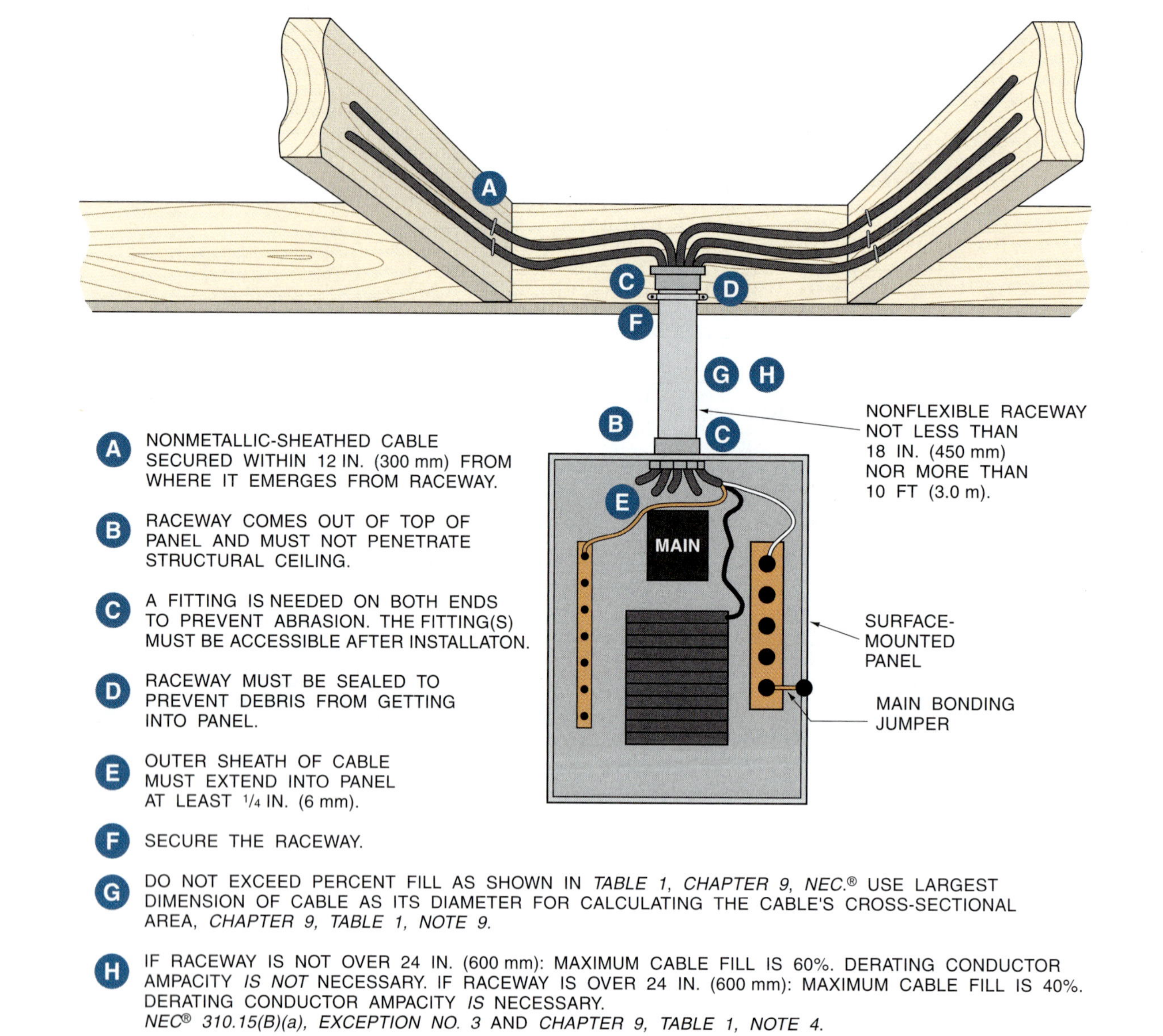

Figure 4-21 An alternate method for running nonmetallic-sheathed cables into a surface-mounted panel. This is permitted for surface-mounted panels only, *312.5(C), Exception*.

Alternate Method of Installing NM Above Panel

Nonmetallic-sheathed cables are usually secured to a panel, box, or cabinet, with a cable clamp or connector. For surface-mounted enclosures only, *312.5(C), Exception* provides an alternate method for running nonmetallic-sheathed cables as illustrated in Figure 4-21.

Identifying Nonmetallic-Sheathed Cables

One nice thing about nonmetallic-sheathed cable, particularly that with a white outer jacket, is that at panelboards and device and outlet boxes, you can use a permanent marking pen to mark the outer jacket with a few words indicating what the cable is for. Examples: ***FEED TO ATTIC; FEED TO L.R.; FEED TO DINING ROOM RECEPTACLES; FEED TO PANEL; BC#6; TO OTHER 3-WAY SWITCH; SWITCH LEG TO CEILING LIGHT; TO OUTSIDE LIGHT; ETC.***

By marking the cables when they are installed, confusion when making the connections is reduced considerably.

Another great idea is to make a sleeve by cutting off a short 2 in. length of NM cable, pull out the conductors, then mark an identifying statement on the sleeve. Slide the sleeve over the specific conductors inside the panel or box.

Multifamily Dwellings

Nonmetallic-sheathed cable is permitted to be installed in one- and two-family dwellings and in multifamily dwellings where the building construction is Type III, Type IV, or Type V. See *334.12(A)*. Definitions of construction types are found in building codes, the glossary of this text, and in *Annex E* of the *NEC*®

For years, the *NEC*® restricted nonmetallic-sheathed cable to a maximum of three floors above finished grade. This limitation was removed in the *2002 NEC*®

ARMORED CABLE (TYPE AC) AND METAL-CLAD CABLE (TYPE MC)

Type AC and Type MC cables look very much the same (Figure 4-22), yet there are significant differences. Table 4-12 compares some of these differences.

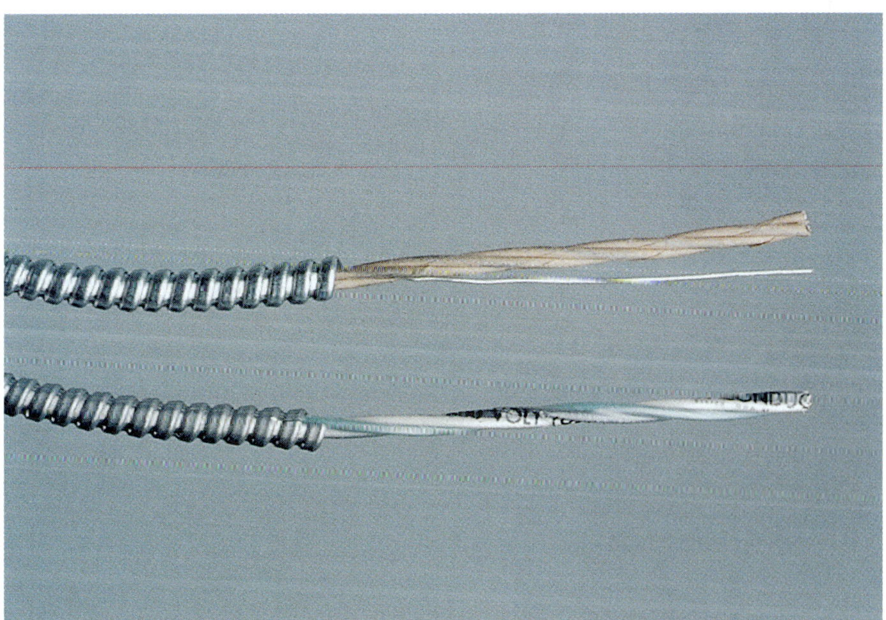

Figure 4-22 Flexible Type AC armored cable. *Courtesy of* AFC Cable Systems, Inc., New Bedford, MA.

TYPE AC (*ARTICLE 320*)	TYPE MC (*ARTICLE 330*)
Article 320: This article contains all of the installation requirements for the installation of Type AC armored cable.	***Article 330:*** This article contains all of the installation requirements for the installation of Type MC metal-clad cable.
320-1. **Definition:** Type AC cable is a fabricated assembly of insulated conductors in a flexible metallic enclosure.	***330.1.*** **Definition:** Type MC cable is a factory assembly of one or more insulated circuit conductors with or without optical fiber members and enclosed in an armor of interlocking metal tape or a smooth or corrugated metallic sheath.
Number of Conductors: Two to four current-carrying conductors plus bonding wire. It may also have a separate equipment grounding conductor.	**Number of Conductors:** Any number of current-carrying conductors. At least one manufacturer has a "Home Run Cable" that has conductors for more than one branch circuit, plus the equipment grounding conductors.
Conductor Size and Type: 14 AWG thru 1 AWG for copper conductors. 12 AWG thru 1 AWG for aluminum conductors will be marked "AL" on a tag on the carton or reel. 12 AWG thru 1 AWG for copper-clad aluminum conductors will be marked "*AL (CU-CLAD)*" or "*Cu-Clad Al*" on a tag on the carton or reel.	**Conductor Size and Type:** 18 AWG thru 2000 kcmil for copper conductors. 12 AWG thru 2000 kcmil for aluminum or copper-clad aluminum conductors. 12 AWG thru 2000 kcmil for copper-clad aluminum conductors will be marked "*AL (CU-CLAD)*" or "*Cu-Clad Al*" on a tag on the carton or reel.
Color Coding: Two-conductor: one black, one white. Three-conductor: one black, one white, one red. Four-conductor: one black, one white, one red, one blue. These are in addition to any equipment grounding and bonding conductors.	**Color Coding:** Two-conductor: one black, one white. Three-conductor: one black, one white, one red. Four-conductor: one black, one white, one red, one blue. These are in addition to any equipment grounding and bonding conductors.
Bonding & Grounding: ►Type AC cable shall provide an adequate path for fault current.◄ Type AC cable has a bonding wire or strip. Bonding wire is in continuous direct contact with the metal armor. The bonding wire and armor act together to serve as the acceptable equipment ground. The bonding wire does not have to be terminated, just folded back over the armor. Figure 4-23 shows how the bonding strip is folded back over the armor. Never use the bonding strip as a grounded neutral conductor or as a separate equipment grounding conductor. It is an internal bonding strip—nothing more!	**Bonding & Grounding:** Has a separate green insulated equipment grounding conductor. May have two equipment grounding conductors for isolated ground requirements, such as for computer wiring. Unless specifically listed for grounding, the jacket of MC cable is not to be used as an equipment grounding conductor. The sheath of smooth or corrugated tube Type MC is listed as acceptable as the required equipment grounding conductor. Some MC cables have a full size bare aluminum conductor in continuous, direct contact with the metal armor. This bare conductor and the metal act together to serve as the acceptable equipment ground. Cut off the bare conductor at the armor.
Insulation: Type ACTHH has 194°F (90°C) thermoplastic insulation, by far the most common. Type ACTH has 167°F (75°C) thermoplastic insulation. Type AC has thermoset insulation. Type ACHH has 194°F (90°C) thermoset insulation.	**Insulation:** Type MC has 194°F (90°C) thermoplastic insulation. Some Type MC has thermoset insulation. Type MC cable is available with a PVC outer jacket suitable for direct burial.
Conductors are individually wrapped with a flame-retardant fibrous cover: light brown Kraft paper. *Author's comment:* This is an easy way to distinguish Type AC from Type MC.	No individual wrap. Has a polyester (Mylar) tape over all conductors. Has no bare bond wire. *Author's comment:* These are easy ways to distinguish Type AC from Type MC.
Armor: Galvanized steel or aluminum. Armored cable with aluminum armor is marked *Aluminum Armor*.	**Armor:** Galvanized steel, aluminum, or copper. Three types: *Interlocked* (*most common*). Requires a separate equipment grounding conductor. The armor by itself is not an acceptable equipment grounding conductor. Steel or aluminum. *Smooth tube*. Does not require a separate equipment grounding conductor. Aluminum only. *Corrugated tube*. Does not require a separate equipment grounding conductor. Copper or aluminum.

(continues)

Table 4-12 Comparisons of Type AC and Type MC cables.

<table>
<tr><th>TYPE AC (ARTICLE 320)</th><th>TYPE MC (ARTICLE 330)</th></tr>
<tr><td>Covering over armor: None</td><td>Covering over armor: Available with PVC outer covering.</td></tr>
<tr><td>Locations:
OK for dry locations.
Not OK for damp or wet locations.
Not OK for direct burial.</td><td>Locations:
OK for wet locations if so listed.
OK for direct burial is so listed.
OK to be installed in a raceway.</td></tr>
<tr><td>Insulating bushings: Required to protect conductor insulation from damage. Referred to as "antishorts," these keep any sharp metal edges of the armor from cutting the conductor insulation. Usually supplied in a bag with cable.
Figure 4-23(A) shows an antishort being inserted.
Figure 4-23(B) shows the recommended way of bending the bonding strip over the antishort to hold the antishort in place.</td><td>Insulating bushings: Recommended but not required to protect conductor insulation from damage. Usually in a bag supplied with cable.</td></tr>
<tr><td>Minimum radius of bends: 5× diameter of cable. For small size cables, this is about the same curvature as a soda can.</td><td>Minimum radius of bends:
Smooth Sheath:
• 10× for sizes not over ¾ in. (19 mm) in diameter.
• 12× for sizes over ¾ in. (19 mm) and not over 1½ in. (38 mm) in diameter.
• 15× for sizes over 1½ in. (38 mm) in diameter.
Corrugated or interlocked:
• 7× diameter of cable.</td></tr>
<tr><td>Not available with "super neutral conductor."</td><td>Available with "super neutral conductor" when required for computer branch-circuit wiring. For example, three 12 AWG and one 10 AWG neutral conductor.</td></tr>
<tr><td>Not available with fiber-optic cables.</td><td>Available with power conductors and fiber-optic cables in one cable.</td></tr>
<tr><td>Support: Not more than 4½ ft (1.4 m) apart.
Not more than 12 in. (300 mm) from box or fitting.
Support not needed where cable is fished through walls and ceilings.
Cables run horizontally through holes in studs, joists, rafters, etc., are considered supported by the framing members.
Support not needed when used as a fixture whip within an accessible ceiling for lengths not over 6 ft (1.8 m) from last point of support.</td><td>Support:
Not more than 6 ft (1.8 m) apart.
Not more than 12 in. (300 mm) from box or fitting for cables having four or fewer 10 AWG or smaller conductors.
Support not needed where cable is fished through walls and ceilings.
Cables run horizontally through holes in studs, joists, rafters, etc., are considered supported by the framing members.
Support not needed when used as a fixture whip within an accessible ceiling for lengths not over 6 ft (1.8 m) from last point of support.</td></tr>
<tr><td>Voltage: 600 volts or less</td><td>Voltage: 600 volts or less. Some MC has a voltage rating not to exceed 2000 volts.</td></tr>
<tr><td>Ampacity: Use the 60°C column of Table 310.16.</td><td>Ampacity: Use the 60°C column of Table 310.16. For 1/0 and larger conductors, OK to use the 75°C column.</td></tr>
<tr><td>Thermal insulation: If buried in thermal insulation, the conductors must be rated 194°F (90°C).</td><td>Thermal insulation: No mention in NEC.®
Type MC has 194°F (90°C) thermoplastic insulation.</td></tr>
<tr><td>Connectors: Set screw-type connectors not permitted with aluminum armor. Listed connectors are suitable for grounding purposes.</td><td>Connectors: Set screw-type connectors not permitted with aluminum armor. Listed connectors are suitable for grounding purposes.</td></tr>
<tr><td>UL Standard 4. Because UL standards have evolved in numerical order, it is apparent that the armored cable standard is one of the first standards to be developed.</td><td>UL Standard 1569.</td></tr>
</table>

Table 4-12 (*continued*)

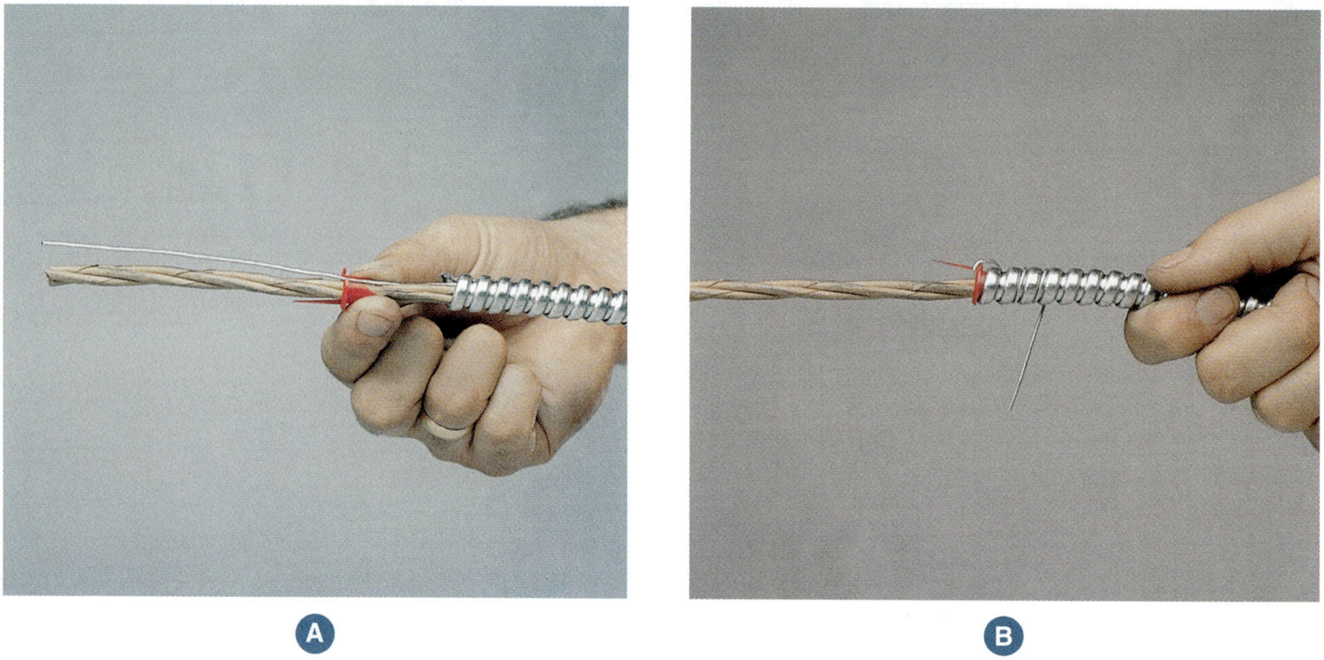

Figure 4-23 **Antishort bushing prevents cutting of the conductor insulation by the sharp metal armor.** ***Courtesy of*** **AFC Cable Systems, Inc., New Bedford, MA.**

To remove the outer metal armor, a tool like that shown in Figure 4-24 may be used.

If a hacksaw is used, make an angle cut on one of the armor's convolutions as long as the conductors need to be, perhaps 10–12 in. Be careful not to cut too deep or you might cut into the conductor insulation. Bend the armor at the cut and snap it off. Then slide the 10–12 in. of armor off the end of the cable. See Figure 4-25.

Most electricians, when using armored cable, will make three cuts with their hacksaw. The middle cut is where the cable and conductors will be cut off

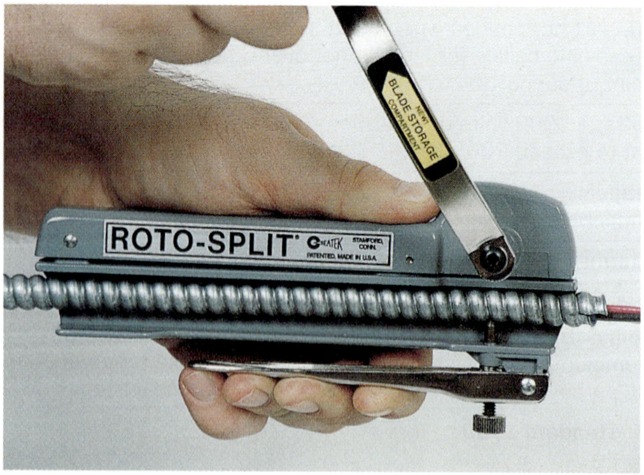

Figure 4-24 **This is an example of a tool that precisely cuts the outer armor of armored cable, making it easy to remove the armor with a few turns of the handle.** ***Courtesy of*** **Seatek Co., Inc.**

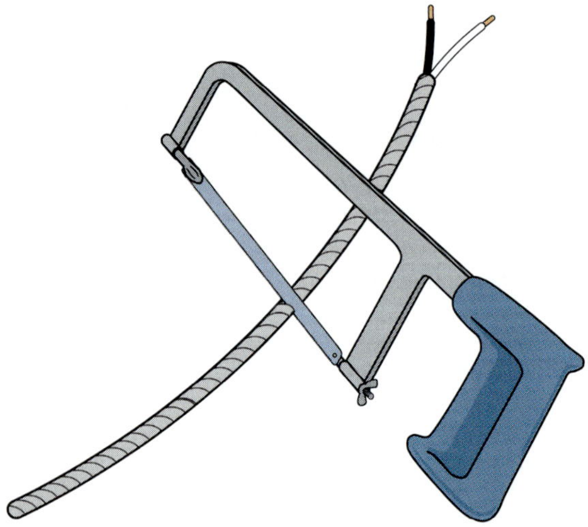

Figure 4-25 **Using a hacksaw to cut through a raised convolution of the cable armor. Don't cut too deep into the armor or you will damage the conductors.**

completely. The first and third cuts are where the armor will be snapped off. This saves time because it actually prepares two ends of the cable.

Most electricians still refer to armored cable as BX, supposedly derived from an abbreviation of the Bronx in New York City, where armored cable was once manufactured. BX was a trademark owned by the General Electric Company, but over the years it has become a generic term.

Figure 4-22 shows armored cable with the armor removed to show the conductors that are wrapped with paper and the bare bonding wire.

Table 4-13 shows the uses and installation requirements for Type AC and Type MC cables for residential wiring.

INSTALLING CABLES THROUGH WOOD AND METAL FRAMING MEMBERS *(300.4)*

Wood Construction

When wiring a house, nonmetallic-sheathed cables are run through holes drilled in studs, joists, and other framing members. Typically, holes are drilled in the approximate centers of wood framing members. To avoid possible damage to the cables, make sure that the edge of the hole is at least 1¼ in. (32 mm) from the nearest edge of the framing member, *300.4(A)(1)*. Refer to Figure 4-26.

You have probably noticed that a 2 × 4 measures 1½ in. × 3½ in., and that a 2 × 3 measures 1½ in. × 2½ in. This can present a real problem!

USES & INSTALLATION IN DWELLINGS	Type AC	Type MC
a) Branch circuits & feeders	Yes	Yes
b) Services	No	Yes
c) Exposed & concealed work in:		
Dry locations	Yes	Yes
Wet locations	No	Yes (See *300.10(A)(12)* for specifics)
d) Where subject to physical damage	No	No
e) May be embedded in plaster finish on masonry walls or run through the hollow spaces of such walls if these locations are not considered damp or wet.	Yes	Yes
f) Run or fished in air voids of masonry block or tile walls where not exposed to excessive moisture or dampness. Masonry in direct contact with earth is considered to be a wet location.	Yes	Yes
g) In any raceway	No	Yes
h) Direct burial, embedded in concrete, or in cinder fill.	No	Yes, if identified for such use
i) In accessible attics or roof spaces, must be protected by guard strips at least as high as the cable when run across top of floor joists, or within 7 ft (2.1 m) of the floor or floor joists when the cable is run across the face of studs or rafters. If there is no permanent stairway or ladder, protection is needed only within 6 ft (1.8 m) from edge of scuttle hole or entrance to attic. No guard strips or running boards are necessary for cables run parallel to the sides of joists, rafters, or studs. See Chapter 15 for additional discussion and diagrams regarding physical protection of cables in attics.	Yes	Yes

Table 4-13 Uses and installation in dwellings (Type AC and Type MC).

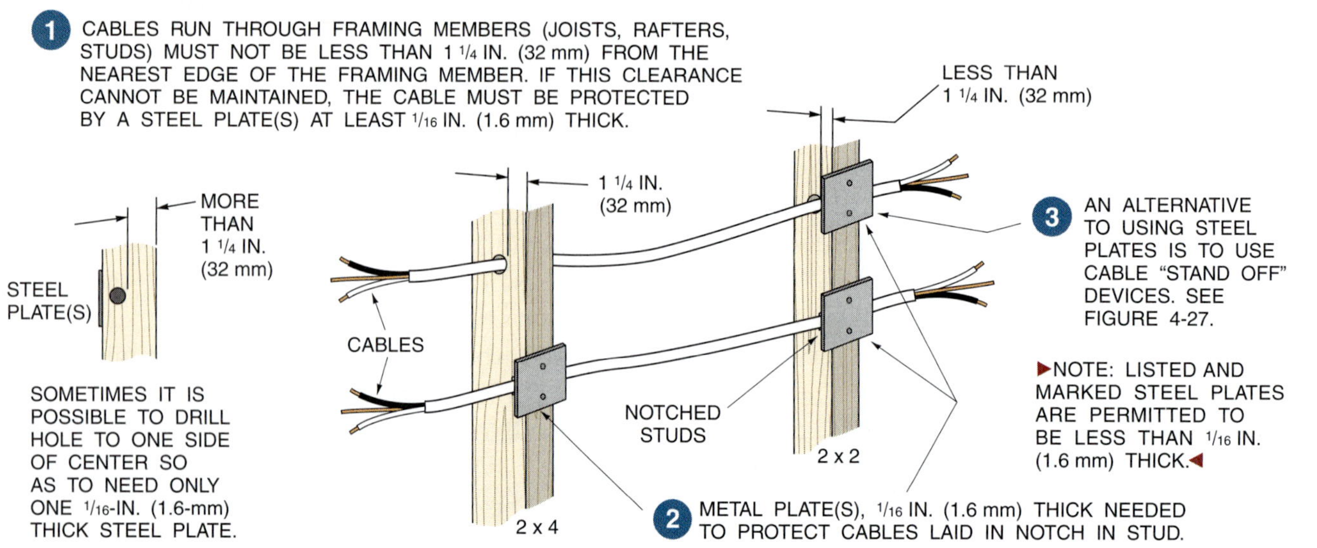

Figure 4-26 Methods of protecting nonmetallic and armored cables so nails and screws that "miss" the studs will not damage the cables, *300.4(A)(1)* and *(2)*. Because of their strength, intermediate and rigid metal conduit, PVC rigid conduit, and electrical metallic tubing are exempt from this rule per the *Exceptions* found in *300.4*. See Figure 4-28 for alternative methods of protecting cables.

Steel Plates

If the 1¼ in. (32 mm) from the edge of hole to the edge of framing member cannot be maintained, or if the cable is laid in a notch, a steel plate(s) at least 1⁄16 in. (1.6 mm) thick must be used to protect the cable from errant nails or drywall screws, *300.4(A)(1)*. In all cases where the *NEC*® requires 1⁄16-in. (1.6-mm) steel plates, listed and marked steel plates are permitted to be less than 1⁄16 in. (1.6 mm) because they have passed tough mechanical tests. This permission is found in *300.4(A)(1) Exception 2, 300.4(A)(2) Exception 2, 300.4(B)(2) Exception, 300.4(D) Exception 3*, and *300.4(E) Exception 2*. See Figure 4-26.

Instead of using steel plates, Figure 4-27 illustrates devices that can be used to *stand off* the cables from a framing member.

Cables Installed Parallel to Framing Members or Furring Strips

►To protect nonmetallic-sheathed cables, armored cables, or nonmetallic raceways that are run parallel to framing members or furring strips from being damaged by drywall screws and nails, you have two choices: (1) keep them more than 1¼ in. (32 mm) from the nearest edge of the framing member or furring strip, or (2) use steel plates. Refer to *300.4(D)*, *320.17*, and *334.17*. See Figures 4-16, 4-26, 4-27, and 4-28.◄

Metal Construction

Metal studs are being used more and more. They don't burn and termites don't eat them. They are stronger than wood and can be set 20 in. (500 mm) on center instead of the usual 16-in. (400-mm) spacing. Metal studs are 10 times more conductive than wood, so treatment of insulation must be addressed.

Where nonmetallic-sheathed cables pass through holes or slots in metal framing members, the cable must be protected by a listed bushing or listed grommet securely fastened in place prior to installing the cable. The bushing or grommet shall:

- remain in place during the wall finishing process,
- cover the complete opening, and
- be listed for the purpose of cable protection.

This information is found in *300.4(B)(1)* and *334.17*. See Figure 4-29.

Bushings that snap into a hole sized for the specific size bushing (½ in., ¾ in., etc.), or a two-piece snap-in bushing that fits just about any size precut

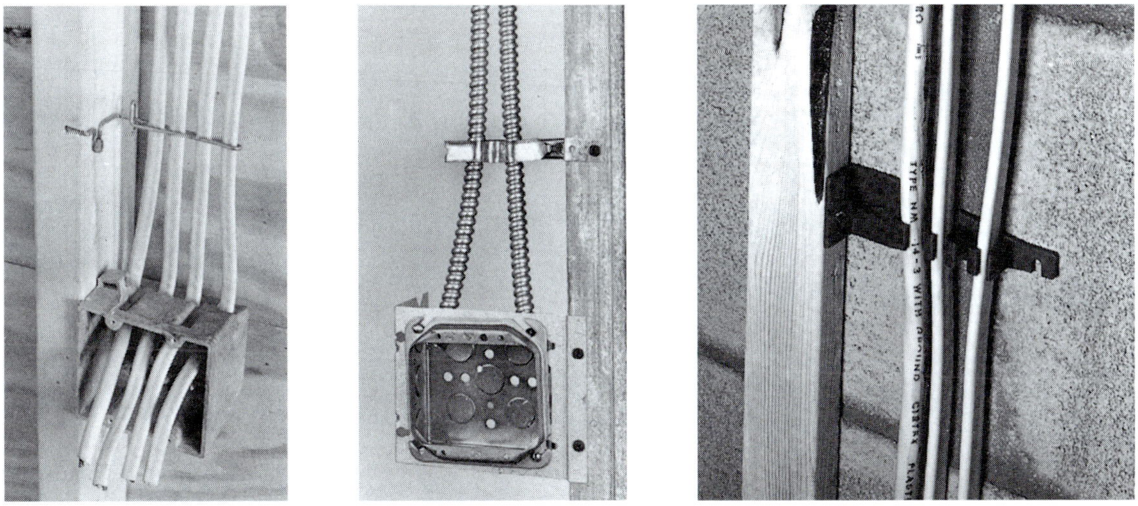

Figure 4-27 Devices that can be used to meet the *Code* requirement to maintain a 1¼-in. (32-mm) clearance from framing members.

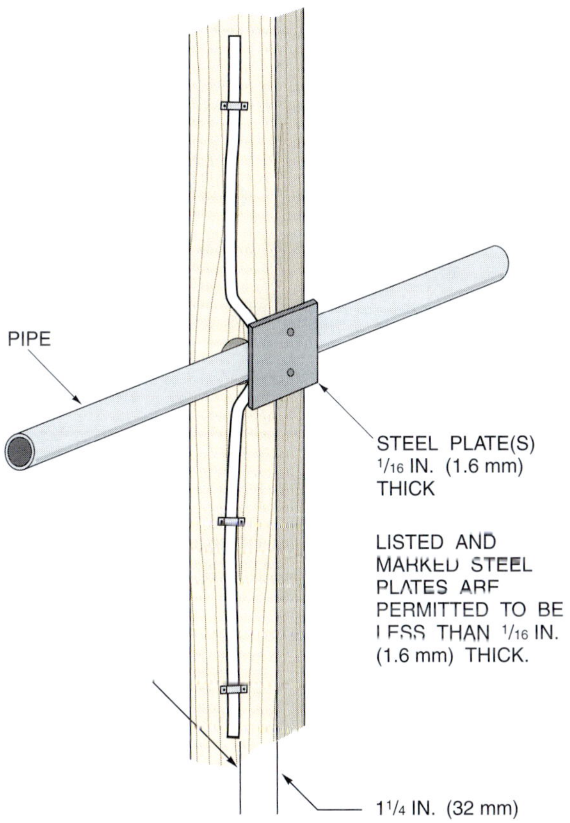

Figure 4-28 Where it is necessary to cross pipes or other similar obstructions, making it impossible to maintain at least 1¼-in. (32-mm) clearance from the framing member to the cable, install a steel plate(s) at least 1⁄16 in. (1.6 mm) thick to protect the cable from possible damage from nails or screws. See *300.4(A)(1)* and *(A)(2)*.

hole in the metal framing members are acceptable to use, as shown in Figure 4-29. These types of bushings (insulators) are not required in metal framing members when the wiring method is armored cable, EMT, FMC, or electrical nonmetallic tubing.

When running nonmetallic-sheathed cable or electrical nonmetallic tubing through metal framing members where there is a likelihood that nails or screws could be driven into the cables or tubing, a steel plate, steel sleeve, or steel clip at least 1⁄16 in. (1.6 mm) thick must be installed to protect the cables and/or tubing. This is spelled out in *300.4(B)(2)*. See Figure 4-28 and Figure 4-29.

►CABLES IN SHALLOW GROOVES AND CHASES◄

NEC® 300.4(E) addresses the wiring problems associated with cutting grooves into building material because there is no hollow space for the wiring. Nonmetallic-sheathed cable and some raceways must be protected when laid in a groove. Protection must be provided with a 1⁄16-in. (1.6-mm) steel plate(s), sleeve, or equivalent, or the groove must be deep enough to allow not less than 1¼-in. (32-mm) free space for the entire length of the groove. This situation can be encountered where styrofoam insulation building blocks are grooved to receive the electrical cables, then covered with wallboard, wood paneling, or other finished wall material. Another typical example is where solid wood planking is

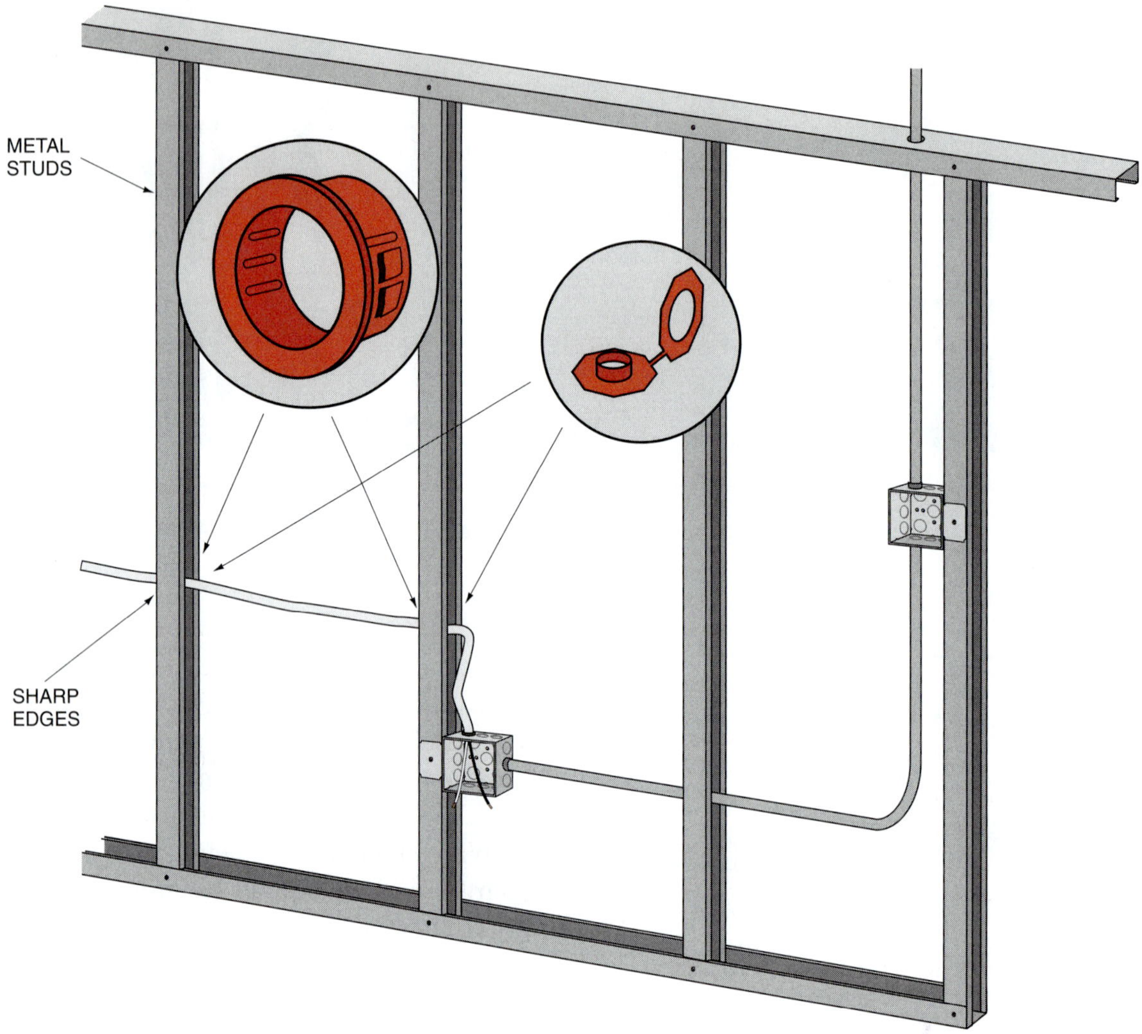

Figure 4-29 ***NEC® 300.4(B)*** **and** ***334.17*** **require protection of nonmetallic-sheathed cable where it runs through holes in metal framing members. Shown are two types of listed bushings (grommets) that can be installed to protect nonmetallic-sheathed cable from abrasion. Electricians generally avoid using nonmetallic-sheathed cable through metal studs and joists. They use electrical metallic tubing, flexible metal conduit, armored cable (Type AC or MC), or electrical nonmetallic tubing. Where there is a likelihood that nails or screws might penetrate the nonmetallic-sheathed cable, ⅛-in. (1.6-mm) thick steel plates, sleeves, or clips must be installed to protect the cable or electrical nonmetallic tubing.**

installed on top of wood beams. The top side of the planking is covered with roofing material, and the bottom side is exposed and serves as the finished ceiling. The only way to install wiring for ceiling luminaires and fans is to groove the planking in some manner, as shown in Figure 4-30.

This additional protection is not required when the raceway is intermediate metal conduit *(Article 342)*, rigid metal conduit *(Article 344)*, rigid PVC conduit *(Article 352)*, or electrical metallic tubing *(Article 358)* (see Figure 4-29).

NEC® 334.30(B)(1), and *300.4(D), Exception 2* allow cables to be "fished" between outlet boxes or other access points without additional protection.

In the recreation room of the residence plans, precautions must be taken so that there is adequate

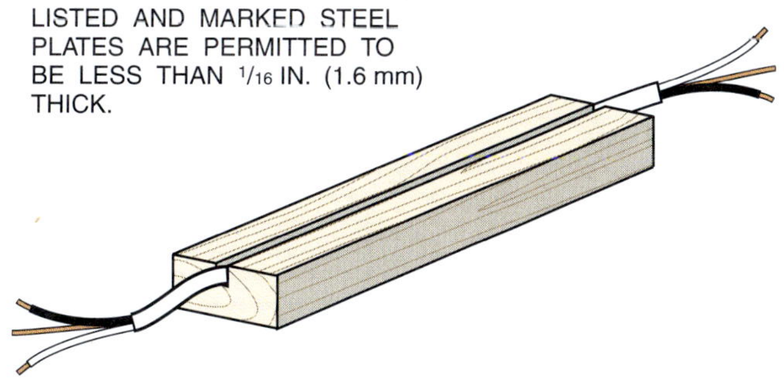

Figure 4-30 Example of how a solid wood framing member or Styrofoam insulating block might be grooved to receive the nonmetallic-sheathed cable. After the cable is laid in the groove, a steel plate(s) not less than 1⁄8 in. (1.6 mm) thick must be installed over the groove to protect the cable from damage, such as from driven nails or screws. See *300.4(E)* and *334.15(B)*.

protection for the wiring. The walls in the recreation room are to be paneled. Therefore, if the carpenter uses 1 × 2 or 2 × 2 furring strips, as in Figure 4-31, nonmetallic-sheathed cable would require the additional 1⁄16-in. (1.6-mm) steel plate(s) protection or the use of *stand off* devices similar to those illustrated in Figure 4-27.

Some building contractors attach 1-in. insulation to the walls, then construct a 2 × 4 wall in front of the basement structural foundation wall, leaving 1-in. spacing between the insulation and the back side of the 2 × 4 studs. This makes it easy to run cables or conduits behind the 2 × 4 studs and eliminates the need for the additional mechanical protection, as shown in Figure 4-32.

Watch out for any wall partitions where 2 × 4 studs are installed "flat," as in Figure 4-33. In this case, the choice is to provide the required mechanical protection as required by *300.4*, or to install the wiring in EMT.

See Chapter 15 concerning the installation of cables in attics.

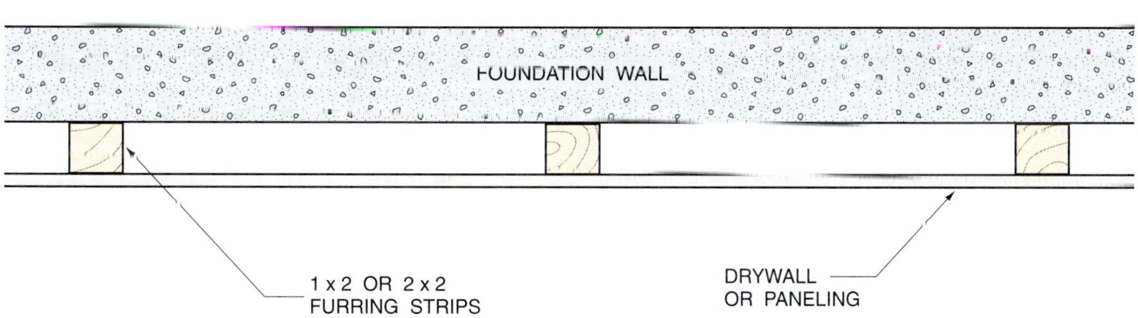

Figure 4-31 When 1 × 2 or 2 × 2 furring strips are installed on the surface of a basement wall, additional protection, as shown in Figure 4-26, Figure 4-27, Figure 4-29, and Figure 4-30, must be provided. It is impossible to maintain the minimum distance of 1¼ in. (32 mm) from the nearest edge of the framing member, in which case protection is required the entire length of the cable run, *300.4(D)*.

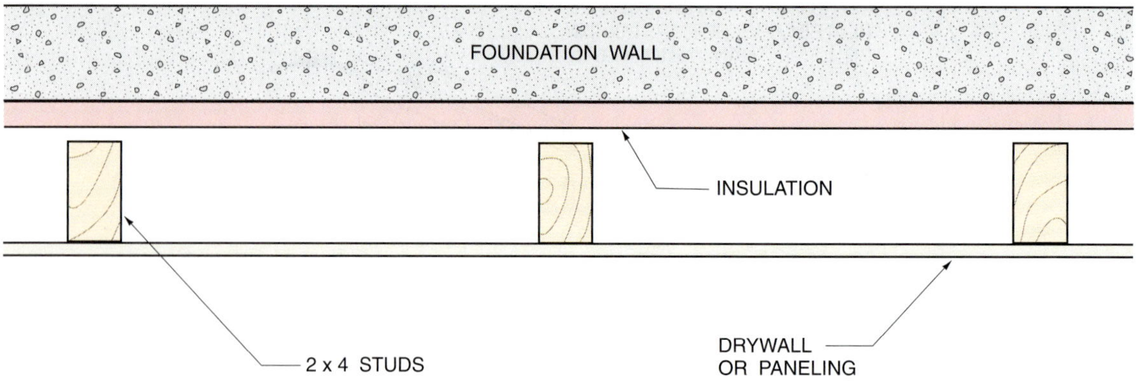

Figure 4-32 This sketch shows how to insulate a foundation wall and how to construct a wall that provides a space to run cables and/or raceways that will not require the additional protection as shown in Figure 4-26, Figure 4-27, Figure 4-29, and Figure 4-30.

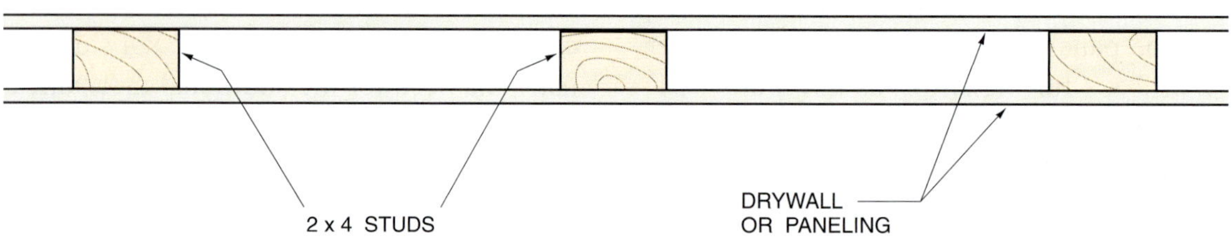

Figure 4-33 When 2 × 4 studs are installed "flat," such as might be found in nonbearing partitions, cables running parallel to or through the studs must be protected against the possibility of having nails or screws driven through the cables. This means protecting the cable with 1⁄16-in. (1.6-mm) steel plates or equivalent for the entire length of the cable, or installing the wiring using intermediate metal conduit, rigid metal conduit, rigid PVC conduit, or EMT. See Figure 4-26, Figure 4-27, Figure 4-28, and Figure 4-29.

Building Codes

When complying with the *NEC*,® be sure to also comply with the building code. Building codes are concerned with the weakening of framing members when drilled or notched. Meeting the requirements of the *NEC*® can be in conflict with building codes and vice versa. Here is a recap of some of the key building code requirements found in the ICC *International Residential Code*.

Studs:

- Cuts or notches in exterior or bearing partitions shall not exceed 25% of the stud's width.
- Cuts or notches in nonbearing partitions shall not exceed 40% of the stud's width.
- Bored or drilled holes in any stud:
  - shall not be greater than 40% of the stud's width,
  - shall not be closer than 5⁄8 in. (15.9 mm) to the edge of the stud, and
  - shall not be located in the same section as a cut or notch.

Joists:

- Notches on the top or bottom of joists shall not exceed one-sixth the depth of the joist, shall not be longer than one-third the width of the joists, and shall not be in the middle third of the joist.

- Holes bored in joists shall not be within 2 in. (50 mm) of the top or bottom of the joist or any other hole, and the diameter of any such hole shall not exceed one-third the depth of the joist. If the joist is also notched, the hole shall not be closer than 2 in. (50 mm) to the notch.

Engineered Wood Products

Today, we find many homes constructed with engineered wood I-joists and beams. The strength of these factory-manufactured framing members conform to various building codes. It is critical that certain precautions be taken relative to drilling and cutting these products so as not to weaken them. In general,

- Do not cut, notch, or drill holes in trusses, laminated veneer lumber, glue-laminated members, or I-joists unless specifically permitted by the manufacturer.
- Do not cut, drill, or notch flanges. Flanges are the top and bottom pieces.
- Do not cut holes too close to supports or to other holes.
- For multiple holes, the amount of web to be left between holes must be at least twice the diameter of the largest adjacent hole. The web is the piece between the flanges.
- Holes not over 1½ in. (38 mm) usually can be drilled anywhere in the web.
- Do not hammer on the web except to remove knockout prescored holes.
- Check and follow the manufacturer's instructions!

INSTALLATION OF CABLES THROUGH DUCTS

NEC® 300.22 is extremely strict as to what types of wiring methods are permitted for installation of cables through ducts or plenum chambers. These stringent rules are for fire safety.

The *Code* requirements are somewhat relaxed by *300.22(C), Exception*. In this exception, permission is given to run nonmetallic-sheathed and armored cables in joist and stud spaces (i.e., cold air returns), but only if they are run perpendicular to the long dimensions of such spaces, as illustrated in Figure 4-34.

CONNECTORS FOR INSTALLING NONMETALLIC-SHEATHED AND ARMORED CABLE

The connectors shown in Figure 4-35 are used to fasten nonmetallic-sheathed cable and armored cable to the boxes and panels in which they terminate. These connectors clamp the cable securely to each outlet box. Many boxes have built-in clamps and do not require separate connectors.

The question continues to be asked: May more than one cable be inserted in one connector? Unless the UL listing of a specific cable connector indicates that the connector has been tested for use with more than one cable, the rule is *one cable, one connector*. This will be marked on the carton.

INTERMEDIATE METAL CONDUIT *(ARTICLE 342)*, RIGID METAL CONDUIT *(ARTICLE 344)*, RIGID PVC CONDUIT *(ARTICLE 352)*, AND ELECTRICAL METALLIC TUBING *(ARTICLE 358)*

Some communities do not permit cable wiring. They require that the wiring method be a raceway—metallic or nonmetallic. You will have to check this out before starting a project.

The following comparison chart provides the highlights of the *NEC®* requirements for different types of raceways that might be used in a residence. For more detailed information, refer to the manufacturer's installation instructions, the specific *NEC®* article, and the UL White Book.

Grounding: All listed fittings for listed metallic raceways and listed metal jacketed cables are tested to carry a specified amount of fault current for a specified length of time, making the fittings acceptable for grounding when properly installed.

In this residence, the wiring method for all of the exposed wiring in the workshop is to be electrical metallic tubing (EMT). Wiring with EMT is covered in detail in Chapter 18.

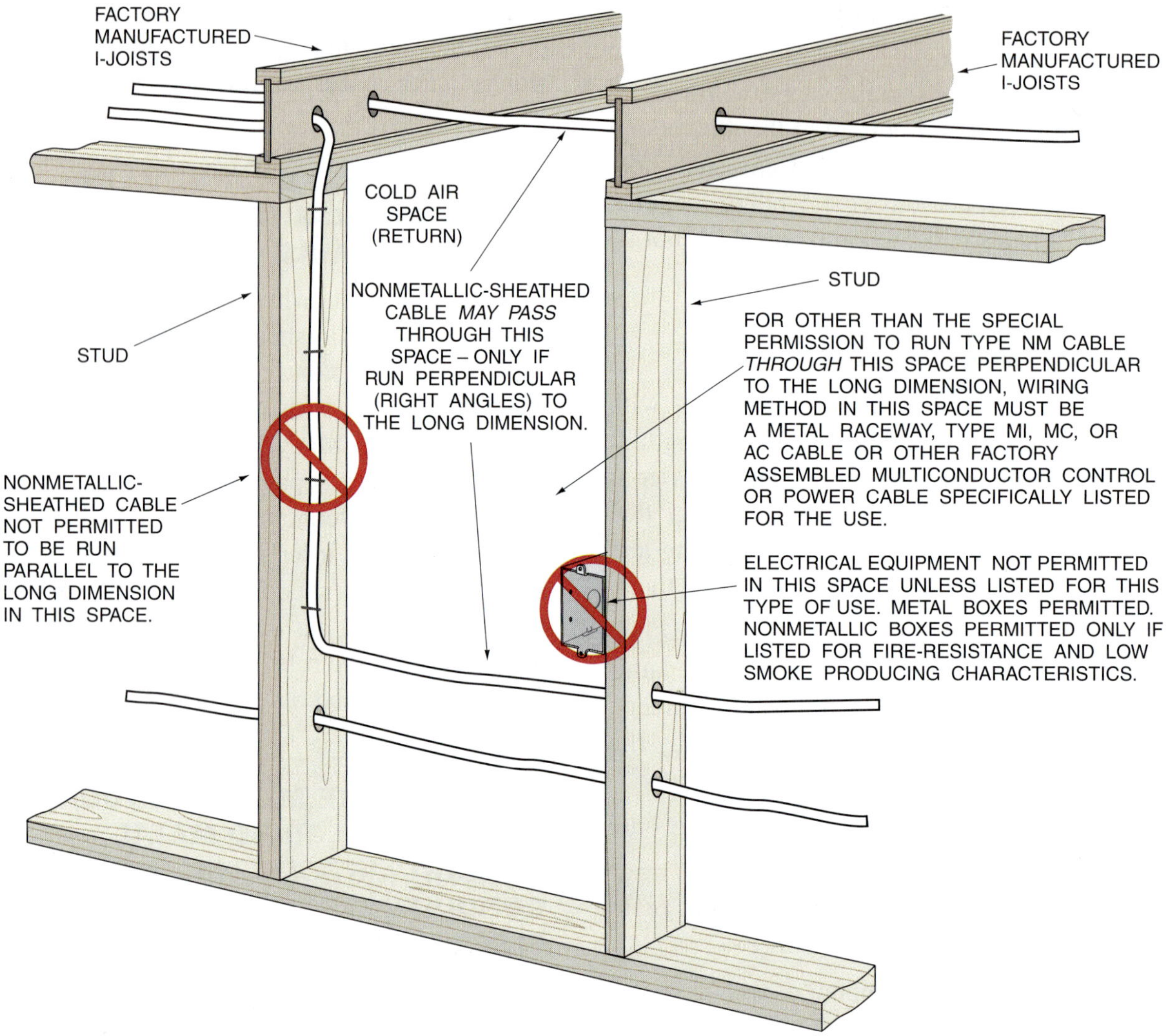

Figure 4-34 Nonmetallic-sheathed cable may pass through cold air return, joist, or stud spaces in dwellings, but only if it is run at right angles to the long dimension of the space, *300.22(C), Exception*.

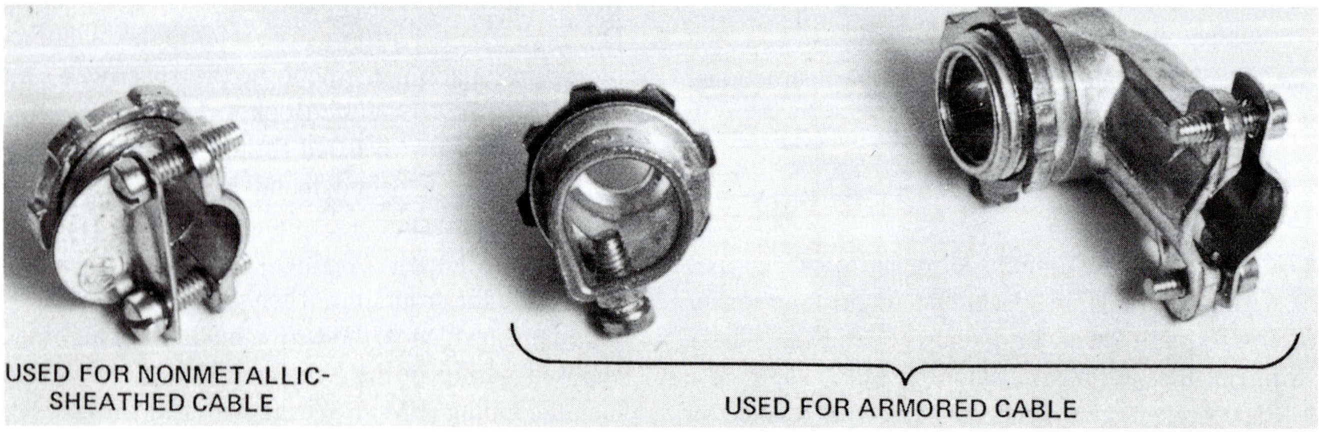

Figure 4-35 Cable connectors.

CONDUIT AND TUBING				
	INTERMEDIATE METAL CONDUIT IMC *Article 342*	**RIGID METAL CONDUIT RMC *Article 344***	**RIGID PVC CONDUIT *Article 352***	**ELECTRICAL METALLIC TUBING EMT *Article 358***
Bends	Not more than the equivalent of four quarter bends between pull points. 360° total. Manufactured bends available. Field bends made with benders.	Not more than the equivalent of four quarter bends between pull points. 360° total. Manufactured bends available. Field bends made with benders.	Not more than the equivalent of four quarter bends between pull points. 360° total. Manufactured bends available. Field bends made with benders that electrically heat the PVC to just the right temperature.	Not more than the equivalent of four quarter bends between pull points. 360° total. Manufactured bends available. Field bends made with benders.
Bend radius	See *Table 2, Chapter 9, NEC.®*	See *Table 2, Chapter 9, NEC.®*	See *Table 2, Chapter 9, NEC.®*	See *Table 2, Chapter 9, NEC.®*
Bushings	►Where 4 AWG or larger ungrounded conductors are installed, smoothly rounded insulating fittings or the equivalent must be used, *300.4(F)* and *312.6(C)*. See Figure 27-30 and Figure 27-31.◄ Not required where the IMC terminates in a hub or boss. See Figure 27-16.	►Where 4 AWG or larger ungrounded conductors are installed, smoothly rounded insulating fittings or the equivalent must be used, *300.4(F)* and *312.6(C)*. See Figure 27-30 and Figure 27-31.◄ Not required where the RMC terminates in a hub or boss. See Figure 27-16.	►Where 4 AWG or larger ungrounded conductors are installed, smoothly rounded insulating fittings or the equivalent must be used, *300.4(F)* and *312.6(C)*. See Figure 27-30 and Figure 27-31.◄ Not required where the PVC terminates in a hub or boss. See Figure 27-16.	►Where 4 AWG or larger ungrounded conductors are installed, smoothly rounded insulating fittings or the equivalent must be used, *300.4(F)* and *312.6(C)*. See Figure 27-30 and Figure 27-31.◄ Not required where the EMT terminates in a hub or boss. See Figure 27-16.
Cable permitted inside	Yes, if permitted by the specific cable *Code* article.	Yes, if permitted by the specific cable *Code* article.	Yes, if permitted by the specific cable *Code* article.	Yes, if permitted by the specific cable *Code* article.
Cinder fill	Yes, where subject to permanent moisture if protected on all sides by noncinder concrete not less than 2 in. (50 mm), or if at least 18 in. (450 mm) under the fill, or if it has corrosion protection.	Yes, where subject to permanent moisture if protected on all sides by noncinder concrete not less than 2 in. (50 mm), or if at least 18 in. (450 mm) under the fill, or if it has corrosion protection.	Yes.	Yes, where subject to permanent moisture if protected on all sides by noncinder concrete not less than 2 in. (50 mm), or if at least 18 in. (450 mm) under the fill, or if it has corrosion protection.
Concealed in walls, ceilings, and floors	Yes.	Yes.	Yes.	Yes.
Concrete above grade	Yes.	Steel: Yes. Aluminum: Yes.	Yes.	Steel: Yes. Aluminum: Yes, if it has supplemental corrosion protection.
Concrete on grade	Yes.	Steel: Yes for galvanized. Steel: No for non-galvanized. Aluminum: Needs supple-mental corrosion protection.	Yes.	Steel: Yes Aluminum: Yes, if it has supplemental corrosion protection.
Concrete below grade	Yes.	Steel: Yes for galvanized. Steel: No for non-galvanized. Aluminum: Needs supplemental corrosion protection.		Steel: Yes, if it has supplemental corrosion protection. Aluminum: Yes, if it has supplemental corrosion protection.

(continues)

(continued)

	INTERMEDIATE METAL CONDUIT IMC ***Article 342***	**RIGID METAL CONDUIT RMC** ***Article 344***	**RIGID PVC CONDUIT** ***Article 352***	**ELECTRICAL METALLIC TUBING EMT** ***Article 358***
Conductor fill	As determined by *Table 1, Chapter 9, NEC.®* Inside interior diameter greater than RMC of same trade size. More room for conductors. See Chapter 18 for examples of conductor fill calculations.	As determined by *Table 1, Chapter 9, NEC.®* See Chapter 18 for examples of conductor fill calculations.	As determined by *Table 1, Chapter 9, NEC.®* See Chapter 18 for examples of conductor fill calculations.	As determined by *Table 1, Chapter 9, NEC.®* See Chapter 18 for examples of conductor fill calculations.
Conductors, when to install?	After complete raceway system is installed, *300.18(A).*	After complete raceway system is installed, *300.18(A).*	After complete raceway system is installed, *300.18(A).*	After complete raceway system is installed, *300.18(A).*
Corrosive conditions	Yes, if protected by corrosion protection and judged suitable for the condition. Listing will indicate this.	Yes, if protected by corrosion protection and judged suitable for the condition. Listing will indicate this. Aluminum resists most corrosive atmospheres.	Yes. Like those found around swimming pool areas.	Yes, if protected by corrosion protection and judged suitable for the condition. Listing will indicate this.
Dry and damp locations	Yes.	Yes.	Yes.	Yes.
Expansion fittings for thermal expansion	Not required.	Not required.	Yes. Refer to *Table 352.44(A)* and *(B).* Without expansion fittings, RNC in direct sunlight will pull out of hubs of boxes, or will pull the boxes off the wall.	Not required.
Exposed	Yes.	Yes.	Yes.	Yes.
Fittings	Threaded and threadless.	Threaded and threadless compression. For aluminum conduit, aluminum threaded fittings recommended, but cadmium plated or galvanized fittings are satisfactory in most installations.	Attached with solvent-type cement.	Set screw and threadless compression.
Grounding	Is considered to be an equipment grounding conductor.	Is considered to be an equipment grounding conductor.	Where required, a separate equipment grounding conductor must be installed.	Is considered to be an equipment grounding conductor.
Joints	Use listed couplings, connectors, and fittings.	Use listed couplings, connectors, and fittings.	Use proper cement.	Use listed couplings, connectors, and fittings.
Length	10 ft	10 ft	10 ft	10 ft
Listed	Yes.	Yes.	Yes.	Yes.
Material	Steel—galvanized. Is as strong as same trade size RMC.	Steel—galvanized. Also aluminum.	Polyvinyl chloride (PVC). Schedule 40 (heavy wall thickness). Schedule 80 (extra-heavy wall thickness). O.D. same for both. I.D. of Schedule 40 is greater than that of Schedule 80.	Steel—galvanized. Also aluminum.

(continues)

continued

	INTERMEDIATE METAL CONDUIT IMC *Article 342*	RIGID METAL CONDUIT RMC *Article 344*	RIGID PVC CONDUIT *Article 352*	ELECTRICAL METALLIC TUBING EMT *Article 358*
Rough edges	Must be properly reamed to remove rough edges.	Must be properly reamed to remove rough edges.	Must be properly reamed to remove rough edges.	Must be properly reamed to remove rough edges.
Support of conduit bodies	Yes.	Yes.	Yes. Conduit bodies not to contain device or support luminaires or other equipment.	Yes.
Securing	Maximum 3 ft (900 mm) from box, panel, cabinet, conduit body, etc.	Maximum 3 ft (900 mm) from box, panel, cabinet, conduit body, etc.	Maximum 3 ft (900 mm) from box, panel, cabinet, conduit body, etc.	Maximum 3 ft (900 mm) from box, panel, cabinet, conduit body, etc.
Supporting	At least every 10 ft (3 m.). ▶No support needed between outlet and device boxes, panels, cabinets, or other terminations if: • not longer than 18 in. (450 mm), and • there are no couplings, and • there are no concentric or eccentric knockouts.◀ See *Table 344.30(B)(2)*. See Figure 4-36.	At least every 10 ft (3 m.). ▶No support needed between outlet and device boxes, panels, cabinets, or other terminations if: • not longer than 18 in. (450 mm), and • there are no couplings, and • there are no concentric or eccentric knockouts.◀ See *Table 344.30(B)(2)*. See Figure 4-36.	See Table *352.30* for distance between supports. ▶No support needed between outlet and device boxes, panels, cabinets, or other terminations if: • not longer than 18 in. (450 mm), and • there are no couplings, and • there are no concentric or eccentric knockouts.◀ See Table 4-14 and Figure 4-36.	At least every 10 ft (3 m). ▶No support needed between outlet and device boxes, panels, cabinets, or other terminations if: • not longer than 18 in. (450 mm), and • there are no couplings, and • there are no concentric or eccentric knockouts.◀ See Figure 4-36.
Sizes	Trade sizes ½ thru 4.	Trade sizes ½ thru 6.	Trade sizes ½ thru 6.	Steel: Trade sizes ½ thru 4. Aluminum: Trade sizes 2 thru 4.
Threaded	Yes. Same threads as RMC. Field cut threads shall be coated with an approved electrically conductive corrosion-resistant compound.	Yes. Field cut threads shall be coated with an approved electrically conductive corrosion-resistant compound.	No.	No.
Underground in soil.	Yes.	Steel: Yes for galvanized. Steel: No for non-galvanized. Aluminum: Needs supplemental corrosion protection.	Yes.	Steel: Yes, if it has supplemental corrosion protection. Aluminum: Yes, if it has supplemental corrosion protection.
Weight	Medium. For example, trade size ½: 100 ft (30.5 m) approx. 62 lb (28.1 kg).	Heavy. For example, trade size ½: 100 ft (30.5 m) approx. 82 lb. (37.2 kg). Aluminum is approx. ⅓ as heavy as steel. For example, trade size ½: 100 ft (30.5 m) approx. 28 lb. (12.7 kg).	Very light. For example, trade size ½ Schedule 40: 100 ft (30.5 m) approx. 17 lb. (7.7 kg); Schedule 80 approx. 21 lb. (9.53 kg).	Light. For example, trade size ½: 100 ft (30.5 m) approx. 30 lb. (13.5 kg).
Wet locations	Yes, if raceway, fittings, bolts, screws, straps, etc., are of corrosion-resistant material.	Yes. if raceway, fittings, bolts, screws, straps, etc., are of corrosion-resistant material.	Yes, if raceway, fittings, bolts, screws, straps, etc., are of corrosion-resistant material.	Yes, if raceway, fittings, bolts, screws, straps, etc., are of corrosion-resistant material.

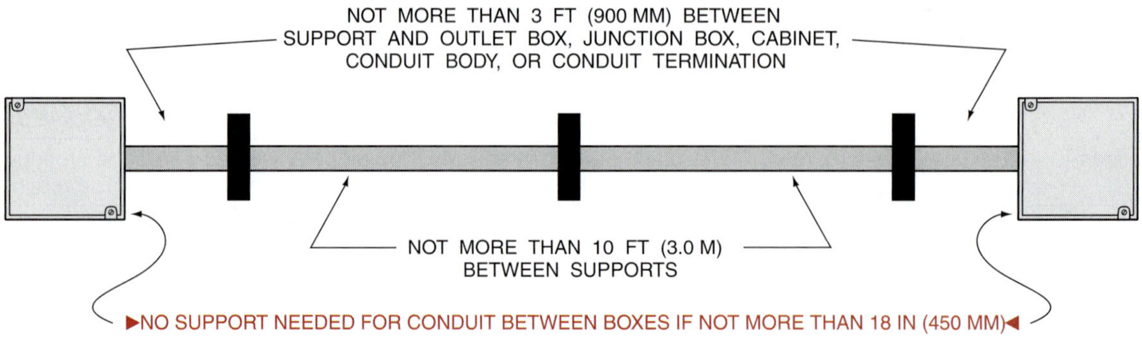

Figure 4-36 ***Code*** **requirements for securing and supporting raceways are found in *342.30* (intermediate metal conduit), *344.30* (rigid metal conduit, *352.30* (rigid PVC conduit), and *358.30* (electrical metallic tubing).**

RIGID PVC CONDUIT TRADE SIZE	MAXIMUM SPACING BETWEEN SUPPORTS
1/2, 3/4, 1	3 ft (900 mm)
1 1/4, 1 1/2, 2	5 ft (1.5 m)

Table 4-14 Maximum distance between supports for rigid PVC conduit.

FLEXIBLE CONNECTIONS

The installation of some equipment requires flexible connections, both to simplify the installation and to stop the transfer of vibrations. In residential wiring, flexible connections are used to connect such equipment such as attic fans, food waste disposers, dishwashers, air conditioners, heat pumps, and recessed luminaires.

The following chart shows the *NEC*® requirements for three types of commonly used flexible conduit.

FLEXIBLE CONNECTIONS			
	FLEXIBLE METAL CONDUIT FMC *Article 348*	**LIQUIDTIGHT FLEXIBLE METAL CONDUIT LFMC *Article 350***	**LIQUIDTIGHT FLEXIBLE NONMETALLLIC CONDUIT LFNC *Article 356***
	See Figure 4-38(A).	See Figure 4-38(B).	See Figure 4-38(C).
Bends	Not more than the equivalent of four quarter bends between pull points. 360° total.	Not more than the equivalent of four quarter bends between pull points. 360° total.	Not more than the equivalent of four quarter bends between pull points. 360° total.
Bend radius	See *Table 2, Chapter 9, NEC.*®	See *Table 2, Chapter 9, NEC.*®	See *Table 2, Chapter 9, NEC.*®
Bushings	▶Where 4 AWG or larger ungrounded conductors are installed, smoothly rounded insulating fittings or the equivalent must be used, *300.4(F)* and *312.6(C)*.◀	▶Where 4 AWG or larger ungrounded conductors are installed, smoothly rounded insulating fittings or the equivalent must be used, *300.4(F)* and *312.6(C)*.◀	▶Where 4 AWG or larger ungrounded conductors are installed, smoothly rounded insulating fittings or the equivalent must be used, *300.4(F)* and *312.6(C)*.◀
Cable permitted inside	Yes, if permitted by the specific cable *Code* article.	Yes, if permitted by the specific cable *Code* article.	Yes, if permitted by the specific cable *Code* article.
Concealed in walls, ceilings, and floors	Yes.	Yes.	Yes.
Concrete above grade	No.	Yes, if marked "Direct Burial."	Yes, if marked "Direct Burial."
Concrete on grade	No.	Yes, if marked "Direct Burial."	Yes, if marked "Direct Burial."

(continues)

(continued)

	FLEXIBLE METAL CONDUIT FMC *Article 348*	**LIQUIDTIGHT FLEXIBLE METAL CONDUIT LFMC *Article 350***	**LIQUIDTIGHT FLEXIBLE NONMETALLLIC CONDUIT LFNC *Article 356***
Concrete	No.	Yes, if marked "Direct Burial."	Yes, if marked "Direct Burial."
Conductor fill	As determined by *Tables 1* and *4*, *Chapter 9, NEC.®* For trade size 3/8, use *Table 348.22.*	As determined by *Table 1*, *Chapter 9, NEC.®* For trade size 3/8, use *Table 348.22.*	As determined by *Table 1*, *Chapter 9, NEC.®* For trade size 3/8, use *Table 348.22.*
Conductors, when to install?	After complete raceway system is installed, *300.18(A).*	After complete raceway system is installed, *300.18(A).*	After complete raceway system is installed, *300.18(A).*
Corrosive conditions	Yes, if protected by corrosion protection and judged suitable for the condition. Listing will indicate this.	Yes, if protected by corrosion protection and judged suitable for the condition. Listing will indicate this. Aluminum resists most corrosive atmospheres.	Yes. Like those found around swimming pool areas.
Dry and damp locations	Yes.	Yes.	Yes.
Exposed	Yes.	Yes.	Yes.
Fittings	Must be listed. Sizes larger than trade size 3/4 will be marked GRND if acceptable for grounding. Do not conceal angle-type fittings. See Figure 4-37.	Must be listed. Sizes larger than trade size 3/4 will be marked GRND if acceptable for grounding. Do not conceal angle-type fittings. See Figure 4-37.	Must be listed. Do not conceal angle-type fittings. See Figure 4-37.
Grounding	When terminated with listed fittings, it is considered to be an EGC: • not over 6 ft (1.8 m) and the overcurrent device does not exceed 20 amperes. See Figure 4-40 and Figure 4-41. Longer than 6 ft (1.8 m), not acceptable as a grounding means. Install a separate equipment grounding conductor sized per *Table 250.122.* ▶Where flexibility is needed after installation, install an equipment grounding conductor sized per *250.122.*◀ ▶Where flexibility is not needed after installation, the FMC is acceptable as the equipment grounding conductor.◀ For grounding, install per *250.134(B).* For bonding, install per *250.102.* See *250.118(5).*	When terminated with listed fittings, it is considered to be an EGC: • in trade sizes 3/8 and 1/2 not over 6 ft (1.8 m) and the overcurrent device does not exceed 20 amperes. • in trade sizes 3/4, 1, and 1-1/4 not over 6 ft (1.8 m) and the overcurrent device does not exceed 60 amperes. Trade size 1-1/2 and larger, not acceptable for grounding. See Figure 4-40, Figure 4-41, Figure 4-42, and Figure 4-43. Longer than 6 ft (1.8 m), LFMC is not acceptable as a grounding means. Install a separate equipment grounding conductor sized per *Table 250.122.* ▶Where flexibility is needed after installation, install an equipment grounding conductor sized per *250.122.*◀ ▶Where flexibility is not needed after installation, the LFMC is acceptable as the equipment grounding conductor.◀ For grounding, install per *250.134(B).* For bonding, install per *250.102.* See *250.118(6).*	Where flexibility is required, install an equipment grounding conductor sized per *250.122.* For grounding, install per *250.134(B).* For bonding, install per *250.102.* See Figure 4-42.

(continues)

(continued)

	FLEXIBLE METAL CONDUIT FMC ***Article 348***	**LIQUIDTIGHT FLEXIBLE METAL CONDUIT LFMC** ***Article 350***	**LIQUIDTIGHT FLEXIBLE NONMETALLLIC CONDUIT LFNC** ***Article 356***
Length	No limit.	No limit.	Not longer than 6 ft (1.8 m) unless secured per *356.30.*
Listed	Must be listed. See UL 1.	Must be listed. See UL 360.	Must be listed. See UL 1660.
Material	Steel and aluminum. Must not be used where subject to physical damage.	Steel with nonmetallic outer jacket. Must not be used where subject to physical damage.	Nonmetallic. Three types. See *356.2* and UL White Book. Must not be used where subject to physical damage.
Rough edges	Must be properly trimmed to remove rough edges.	Must be properly trimmed to remove rough edges.	Must be properly trimmed to remove rough edges.
Securing and supporting	Maximum 12 in. (300 mm) from box, cabinet, or fitting. Maximum 4½ ft (1.4 m) between supports. Waived if fished through walls and ceilings—where flexibility is needed and the flex is not more than 3 ft (900 mm) from where it is terminated, or as a whip not over 6 ft (1.8 m). See Figure 4-39, Figure 7-2, Figure 7-6, and Figure 7-10. Also waived when supported horizontally through framing members not more than 4½ ft (1.4 m) apart and secured within 12 in. (300 mm) of box, cabinet, or fitting.	Maximum 12 in. (300 mm) from box, cabinet, or fitting. Maximum 4½ ft (1.4 m) between supports. Waived if fished through walls and ceilings—where flexibility is needed and the flex is not more than 3 ft (900 mm) from where it is terminated, or as a whip not over 6 ft (1.8 m). See Figure 4-39, Figure 7-2, Figure 7-6, and Figure 7-10. Also waived when supported horizontally through framing members not more than 4½ ft (1.4 m) apart and secured within 12 in. (300 mm) of box, cabinet, or fitting.	Maximum 12 in. (300 mm) from box, cabinet, or fitting. Maximum 4½ ft (1.4 m) between supports. Waived if fished through walls and ceilings—where flexibility is needed and the flex is not more than 3 ft (900 mm) from where it is terminated, or as a whip not over 6 ft (1.8 m). See Figure 4-39, Figure 7-2, Figure 7-6, and Figure 7-10. Also waived when supported horizontally through framing members not more than 3 ft (900 mm) apart and secured within 12 in. (300 mm) of box, cabinet, or fitting.

(continues)

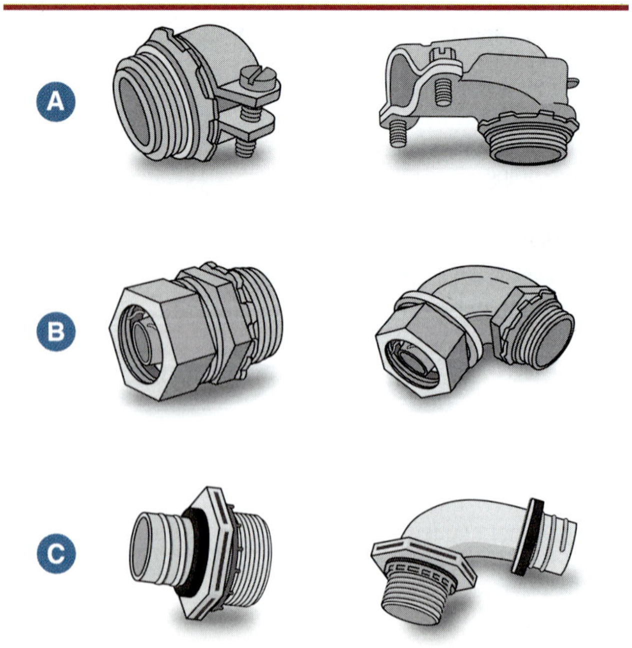

Figure 4-37 Various fittings for (A) flexible metal conduit, (B) liquidtight flexible metal conduit, and (C) liquidtight flexible nonmetallic conduit.

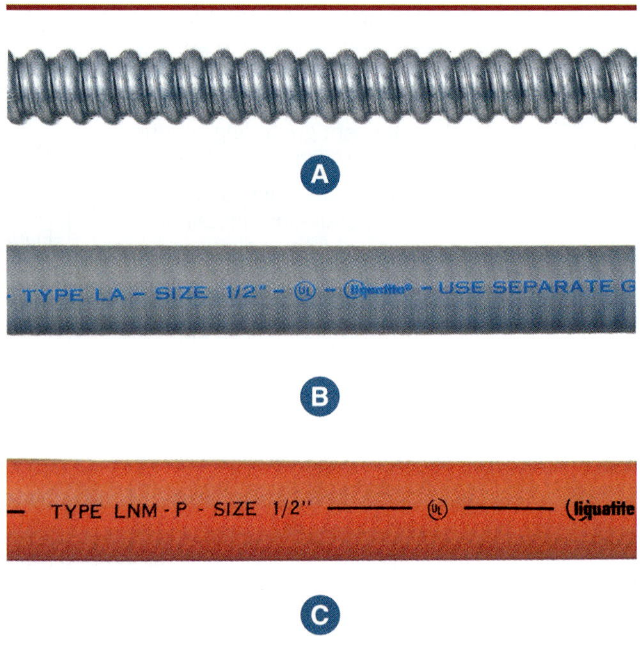

Figure 4-38 (A) Flexible metal conduit. (B) Flexible liquidtight metal conduit. (C) Flexible liquidtight nonmetallic conduit. ***Courtesy of*** **Electri-Flex Co.**

(continued)

	FLEXIBLE METAL CONDUIT FMC *Article 348*	LIQUIDTIGHT FLEXIBLE METAL CONDUIT LFMC *Article 350*	LIQUIDTIGHT FLEXIBLE NONMETALLLIC CONDUIT LFNC *Article 356*
Sizes	Steel: Trade sizes ½ thru 4. Aluminum: Trade sizes ½ thru 3. Trade size ⅜ OK for enclosing leads to a motor or as a luminaire (fixture) whip not longer than 6 ft (1.8 m).	Trade sizes ½ thru 4. Trade size ⅜ OK for enclosing leads to a motor or as a luminaire (fixture) whip not longer than 6 ft (1.8 m).	Trade sizes ½ thru 4. Trade size ⅜ OK for enclosing leads to a motor or as a luminaire (fixture) whip not longer than 6 ft (1.8 m).
In sunlight	Yes.	Yes.	Yes, if listed and marked "Outdoor."
Temperature	Limited to the temperature rating of the conductors.	Limited to 60°C (140°F) unless marked otherwise. Also limited to temperature rating of the conductors.	Limited to 60°C (140°F) unless marked otherwise. Also limited to temperature rating of the conductors. Can become brittle in extreme cold.
Underground in soil.	No.	Yes, if marked "Direct Burial."	Yes, if marked "Direct Burial."
Uses	Where flexibility is required. Do not use where subject to physical damage.	Where flexibility is required. Do not use where subject to physical damage.	Where flexibility is required. Do not use where subject to physical damage.
Wet locations	►No.◄	Yes.	Yes.

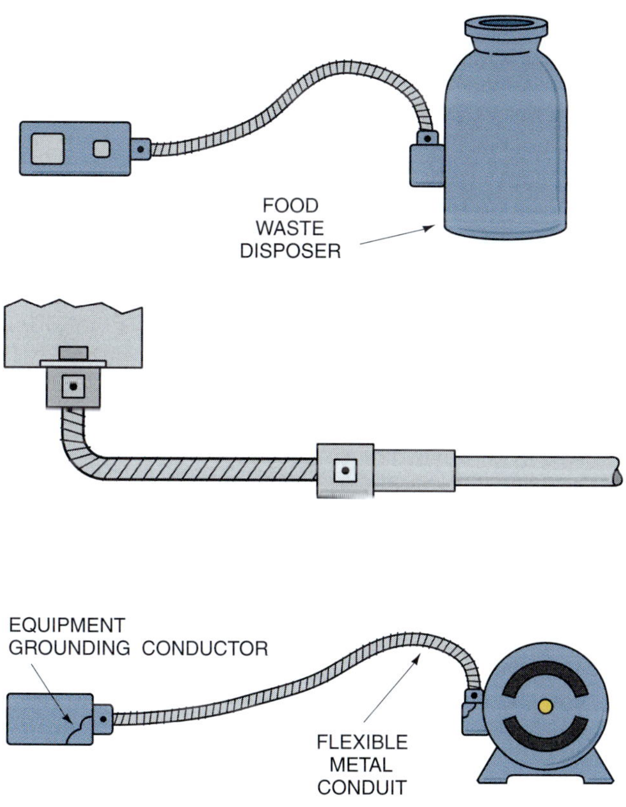

Figure 4-39 Some of the more common places where flexible connections could be used.

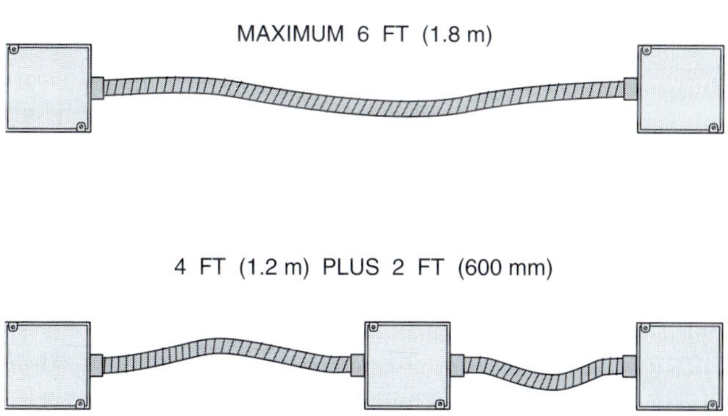

Figure 4-40 If a flexible metal conduit is serving as an equipment ground return path, the total length shall not exceed 6 ft (1.8 m). Refer to *250.118(5)c*, and *250.118(6)d*.

ELECTRICAL NONMETALLIC TUBING (ENT) *(ARTICLE 362)*

Electrical nonmetallic tubing (ENT) is covered in *Article 362* of the *NEC*.® It is a pliable, lightweight, corrugated raceway made of PVC. It requires

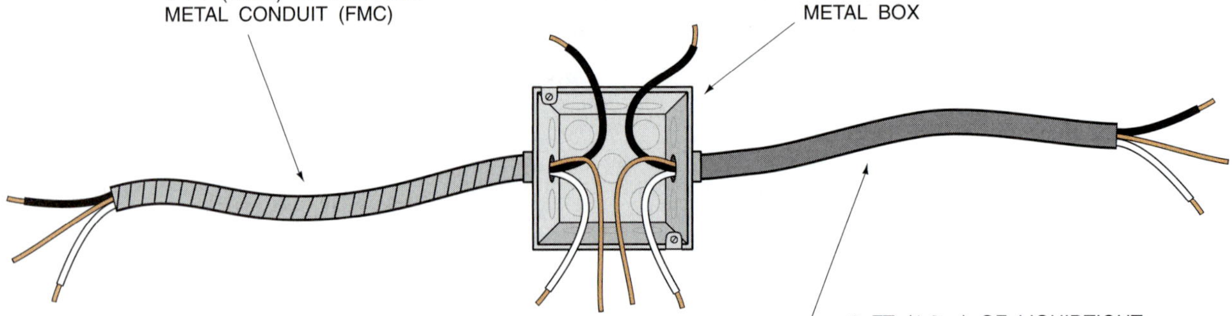

Figure 4-41 The "combined" length of flexible metal conduit and liquidtight flexible metal conduit shall not exceed 6 ft (1.8 m) if it is to serve as the same ground return path, *250.118(5)c*, and *250.118(6)d*. In the above illustration, a separate equipment grounding conductor would have to be provided.

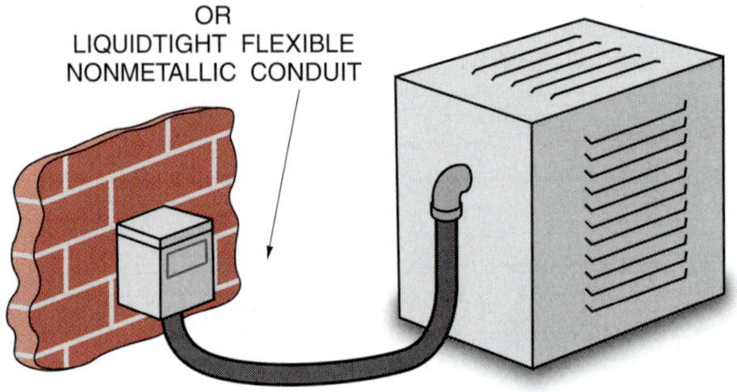

Figure 4-42 Use of liquidtight flexible metal conduit or flexible liquidtight nonmetallic conduit.

fittings made specifically for the ENT. Figure 4-44 shows color-coded ENT and some fittings. Color-coded ENT can be used to differentiate power, communication, and fire protection signaling system.

Although not often used in typical house wiring, some electricians find ENT very practical for providing a raceway system for installing structured wiring conductors and cables. Structured wiring is discussed in Chapter 31.

SERVICE-ENTRANCE CABLE *(ARTICLE 338)*

Service-entrance cable is covered in *Article 338* of the *NEC*.®

Service-entrance cable is defined as: *a single conductor or multi-conductor assembly provided with or without an overall covering, primarily used for services.*

Where permitted by local electrical codes, service-entrance cable is most often run from the utility's **service point** to the meter base, then from the meter base to the main panel.

It is also permitted as a branch circuit to connect major electrical appliances and as a feeder to a subpanel. For these situations, the choice of whether to use Type SE cable or nonmetallic-sheathed cable becomes a matter of choice, the major issue being the cost of the cable. Some Type SE cable with aluminum conductors may cost less than that for nonmetallic-sheathed cable with copper conductors. The labor for the installation of either type is the same.

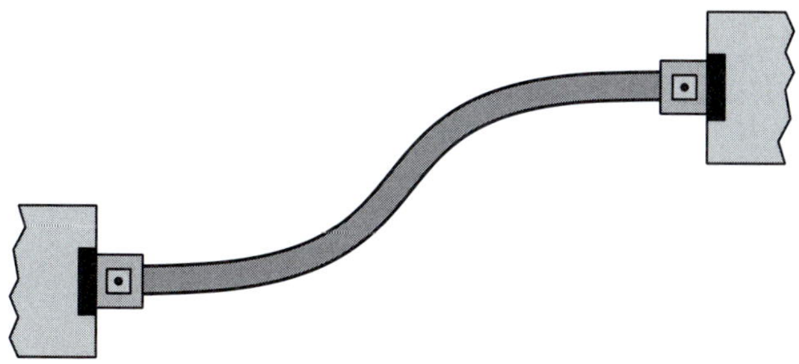

A PERMITTED AS A GROUNDING MEANS IF IT IS NOT OVER TRADE SIZE 1¼, IS NOT OVER 6 FT (1.8 m) LONG, AND IS CONNECTED BY FITTINGS LISTED FOR GROUNDING. THE 6 FT (1.8 m) LENGTH INCLUDES THE TOTAL LENGTH OF ANY AND ALL FLEXIBLE CONNECTIONS IN THE RUN. SEE FIGURE 4-41.

B MINIMUM TRADE SIZE ½. TRADE SIZE ⅜ PERMITTED AS A LUMINAIRE (FIXTURE) WHIP NOT OVER 6 FT (1.8 m) LONG.

C WHEN USED AS THE GROUNDING MEANS, THE MAXIMUM OVERCURRENT DEVICE IS 20 AMPERES FOR TRADE SIZES ⅜ AND ½, AND 60 AMPERES FOR TRADE SIZES ¾, 1, AND 1¼.

D NOT SUITABLE AS A GROUNDING MEANS UNDER ANY OF THE FOLLOWING CONDITIONS:

- TRADE SIZES 1½ AND LARGER
- TRADE SIZES ⅜ AND ½ WHEN OVERCURRENT DEVICE IS GREATER THAN 20 AMPERES
- TRADE SIZES ⅜ AND ½ WHEN LONGER THAN 6 FT (1.8 m)
- TRADE SIZES ¾, 1 AND 1¼ WHEN OVERCURRENT DEVICE IS GREATER THAN 60 AMPERES
- TRADE SIZES ¾, 1 AND 1¼ WHEN LONGER THAN 6 FT (1.8 m)

FOR THESE CONDITIONS, INSTALL A SEPARATE EQUIPMENT GROUNDING CONDUCTOR SIZED PER *TABLE 250.122.*

Figure 4-43 Grounding capabilities of liquidtight flexible metal conduit (LFMC). See *Article 350.*

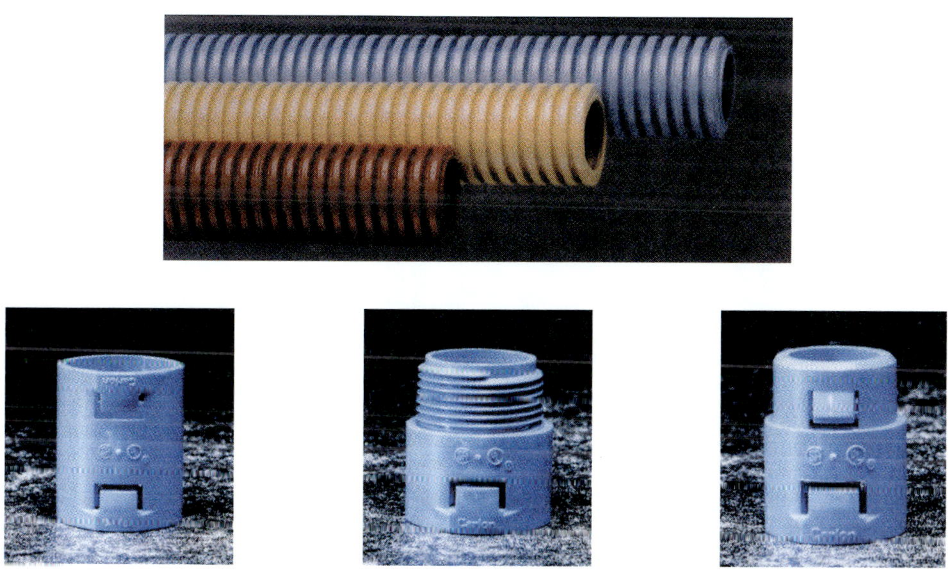

Figure 4-44 Color-coded ENT, a coupling, a threaded connector, and a snap-in connector.

There are two styles of Type SE cable: SER and SEU. Table 4-15 shows the *NEC*® installation requirements and the key differences in construction of these cables. See Table 4-15 and Figure 4-45.

Type UF Cable *(Article 340)*

Type UF is an underground feeder and branch-circuit cable. Type UF cable is discussed in Chapter 16.

SERVICE-ENTRANCE CABLES TYPE SE, SER, SEU, AND USE COMPARISONS					
TYPE	**COVERING**	**INSULATION**	**USES PERMITTED**	**BENDS**	**AMPACITY**
SE Service-Entrance Cable Conforms to UL Standard 854: Service-Entrance Cables. See Figure 4-45. m	Flame-retardant, moisture- and sunlight-resistant covering.	Type RHW, XHHW, or THWN insulation. Sizes 12 AWG and larger for copper. Sizes 10 AWG and larger for aluminum or copper-clad aluminum. If aluminum conductors, jacket will be marked "AL." If copper-clad aluminum conductors, jacket will be marked "AL (CU-CLAD)" or "Cu-Clad AL". If letter "H" on insulation, temperature rating 167°F (75°C), wet or dry locations. If letter "HH" on insulation, temperature rating 167°F (75°C) wet/194°F (90°C) dry locations. If marked with a "-2", suitable for wet or dry locations as high as 194°F (90°C). May have one conductor uninsulated. May have reduced neutral conductor as permitted by *220.61* and *310.15(B)(6)*.	600 volts or less. Above ground. Suitable for use where exposed to sun. Use "sill plate" where cable is bent to pass through a wall. See Figure 27-3. Permitted for interior wiring (feeder to a subpanel, ranges, dryers, cooktops, ovens) where all conductors are insulated. Must be installed according to the requirement in *Article 334* (Nonmetallic-sheathed cable). A bare, uninsulated conductor is permitted: • as the neutral conductor when used as service-entrance cable. • as an equipment grounding conductor when used for interior wiring. ▶For existing installations only, may have a bare neutral conductor. Must originate at service panel, *338.10(B)(2), Exception*. Also see *250.140*. Not permitted for new work.◀ Shall not be used where subject to physical damage unless protected. ▶Shall not be used underground whether in or not in a raceway.◀	Internal radius of bend not to exceed 5 times the diameter of the cable.	See *Table 310.16*. Refer to the 75°C and 90°C columns. For single-phase dwelling services, see *310.15(B)(6)*.
SER Conforms to UL Standard 854: Service-Entrance Cables. Subject to the same rules as Type SE.	Same as above.	Same as above. Available with two insulated phase conductors and one insulated neutral conductor. Also available with two insulated phase conductors, one insulated neutral conductor, and one bare equipment grounding conductor. Available with reduced neutral conductor as permitted by *220.61* and *310.15(B)(6)*. Type XHHW-2 conductors. Rated 194°F (90°C), wet or dry.	Same as above.	Same as above.	Refer to the 75°C and 90°C columns. For single-phase dwelling services, see *310.15(B)(6)*.

Table 4-15

SERVICE-ENTRANCE CABLES TYPE SE, SER, SEU, AND USE COMPARISONS (*continued*)

TYPE	COVERING	INSULATION	USES PERMITTED	BENDS	AMPACITY
SEU Conforms to UL Standard 854: Service-Entrance Cables. Subject to the same rules as Type SE.	Same as above.	Type XHHW-2 conductors. Rated 194°F (90°C), wet or dry. Type THHN/THWN Rated 90°C, dry; 75°C, wet. Easily identified by the bare wraparound neutral conductor. Available with two and three insulated conductors plus the bare wraparound neutral conductor. Available with reduced neutral conductor as permitted by *220.61* and *310.15(B)(6)*.	Same as above.	Same as above.	Refer to the 75°C and 90°C columns. For single-phase dwelling services, see *310.15(B)(6)*.
USE Service-Entrance Conductor. Individual conductors may be bundled in an assembly. Conforms to UL Standard 854: Service-Entrance Cables. USE cable is shown in Figure 4-46.	Moisture-resistant covering. Not required to have flame-retardant covering.	Insulation equivalent to Type RHW or XHHW. The temperature rating of the cable is the same as the temperature rating of the individual conductors. If this is not marked on the outer jacket, then the cable is rated 167°F (75°C). If Type USE-2, insulation equivalent to Type RHW-2 or XHHW-2. Rated 194°F (90°C), wet or dry. Cabled single conductor may have bare copper conductor with the assembly. May have reduced neutral conductor if multiple conductor assembly, as permitted by *220.61* and *310.15(B)(6)*.	Same as above except USE is also permitted for underground, direct burial. Permitted to emerge above ground in meter bases and similar enclosures. Where cable emerges from the ground, protect according to the requirement found in *300.5(D)*. Not permitted for interior wiring.	Same as above.	Refer to the 75°C and 90°C columns. For single-phase dwelling services, see *310.15(B)(6)*.

Table 4-15 (*continued*)

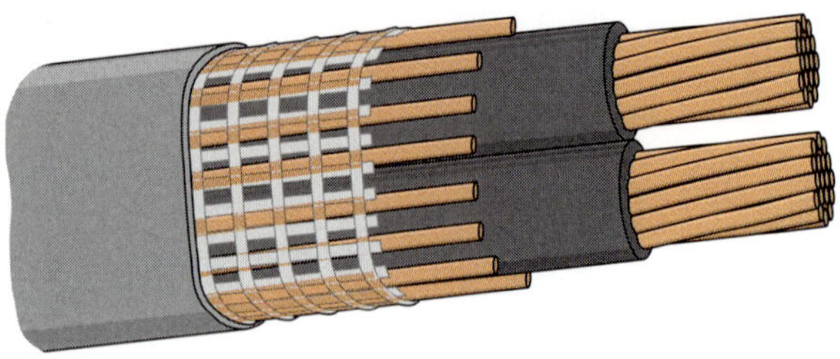

Figure 4-45 Type SEU service-entrance cable. The major characteristic is the uninsulated wraparound neutral conductor. See Table 4-15 for *NEC*® requirements for the permitted uses of Type SE cables.

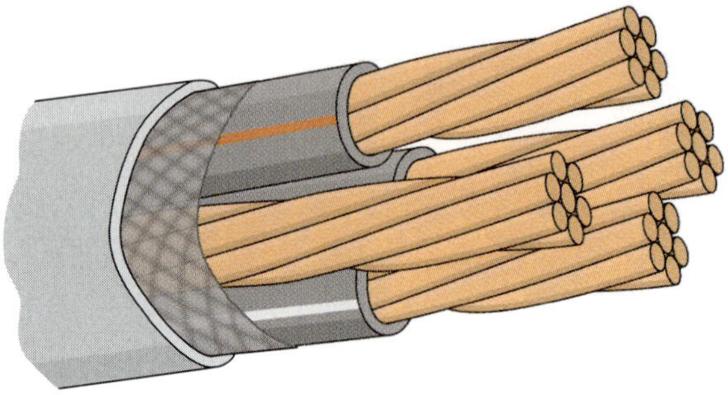

Figure 4-46 Type SER service-entrance cable. The major characteristics are the insulated neutral conductor and bare equipment grounding conductor. See Table 4-15 for *NEC*® requirements for the permitted uses of Type SE cables.

REVIEW

Note: Refer to the *Code* or the plans where necessary.

1. The largest size solid conductor permitted to be installed in a raceway is (10 AWG) (8 AWG) (6 AWG). Circle the correct answer.
2. What is the minimum branch-circuit wire size that may be installed in a dwelling?

   ____

3. What exceptions, if any, are there to the answer for question 2? ________________

4. What determines the ampacity of a wire? ________________

5. What unit of measurement is used for the diameter of wires? ________________
6. What unit of measurement is used for the cross-sectional area of wires? ________________

7. What is the voltage rating of the conductors in Type NMC cable? ________________

8. Indicate the allowable ampacity of the following Type THHN (copper) conductors. Refer to *Table 310.16*.

   a. 14 AWG ________ amperes
   b. 12 AWG ________ amperes
   c. 10 AWG ________ amperes
   d. 8 AWG ________ amperes
   e. 6 AWG ________ amperes
   f. 4 AWG ________ amperes

9. What is the maximum operating temperature of the following conductors? Give the answer in degrees Fahrenheit and in degrees Celsius.

   a. Type XHHW ________________
   b. Type THWN ________________
   c. Type THHN ________________
   d. Type TW ________________

10. What are the colors of the conductors in nonmetallic-sheathed cable for

    a. two-wire cable? ______________, ______________
    b. three-wire cable? ______________, ______________, ______________

11. For nonmetallic-sheathed cable, may the uninsulated conductor be used for purposes other than grounding? ________________

12. What size equipment grounding conductor is used with the following sizes of nonmetallic-sheathed cable?

    a. 14 AWG ________________
    b. 12 AWG ________________
    c. 10 AWG ________________
    d. 8 AWG ________________

13. Under what condition may nonmetallic-sheathed cable (Type NM) be fished in the hollow voids of masonry block walls? ________________

    ____

    ____

14. a. What is the maximum distance permitted between straps on a cable installation?

    ____

    b. What is the maximum distance permitted between a box and the first strap in a cable installation? ________________

    c. Does the *NEC*® permit two-wire Romex stapled on edge? ________________

    d. When Type NMC cable is run through holes in studs and joists, must additional support be provided? ________________

15. What is the difference between Type AC and Type ACT armored cables? ________________

    ____

    ____

    ____

    ____

    ____

    ____

    ____

16. Type ACT armored cable may be bent to a radius of not less than ______________ times the diameter of the cable.

17. When armored cable is used, what protection is provided at the cable ends?

 ____

 ____

 ____

 ____

18. What protection must be provided when installing a cable in a notched stud or joist, or when a cable is run through bored holes in a stud or joist where the distance is less than 1¼ in. (32 mm) from the edge of the framing member to the cable, or where the cable is run parallel to a stud or joist and the distance is less than 1¼ in. (32 mm) from the edge of the framing member to the cable? ______________________________

 ____

 ____

 ____

 ____

19. For installing directly in a concrete slab, (armored cable) (nonmetallic-sheathed cable) (conduit) may be used. Circle the correct method of installation.

20. Circle the correct answer to the following statements:

a. Type SE service-entrance cable is for aboveground use.	True	False
b. Type USE service-entrance cable is suitable for direct burial in the ground.	True	False
c. Type SE cable with an uninsulated neutral conductor is permitted for hooking up an electric range.	True	False
d. Type SE cable with an insulated neutral conductor is permitted for hooking up an electric range.	True	False
e. Are Types SE and USE service-entrance cables used in your area?	Yes	No

21. When running NMC through a bored hole in a stud, the nearest edge of the bored hole shall not be less than ____________ in. from the face of the stud unless the cable is protected by a 1⁄16 in. (1.6 mm) metal steel plate(s).

22. Where is the main service-entrance panel located in this residence? ______________

 ____

23. a. Is nonmetallic-sheathed cable permitted in your area for residential wiring?

 ____

 b. From what source is this information obtained? ____________________________

24. Is it permitted to use flexible metal conduit over 6 ft (1.8 m) in length as a grounding means? (Yes) (No) Circle the correct answer.

25. Liquidtight flexible metal conduit may serve as a grounding means in sizes up to and including ____________ in. where used with listed fittings.

26. The allowable current-carrying capacity (ampacity) of aluminum wire, or the maximum overcurrent protection in the case of 14 AWG, 12 AWG, and 10 AWG conductors, is less than that of copper wire for a given size, insulation, and temperature of 86°F (30°C). Refer to *Table 310.16* and *240.4(D)* and complete the following table. Important: where the ampacity of the conductor does not match the rating of a standard fuse or circuit breaker as listed in *240.6(A)*, *240.4(B)* permits the selection of the next "higher" standard rating of fuse or circuit breaker if the next higher standard rating does not exceed 800 amperes. Nonstandard ampere ratings are also permitted.

WIRE (AWG-KCMIL)	COPPER		ALUMINUM	
	Ampacity	**Overcurrent Protection**	**Ampacity**	**Overcurrent Protection**
12 AWG THHN				
10 AWG THHN				
3 AWG THW				
0000 THWN				
500 KCMIL THWN				

27. It is permissible for an electrician to connect aluminum, copper, or copper-clad aluminum conductors together in the same connector. (True) (False) Circle the correct answer.

28. Terminals of switches and receptacles marked CO/ALR are suitable for use with ______________, ______________, and ______________ conductors.

29. Wire connectors marked AL/CU are suitable for use with ____________________, ____________________, and ____________________ conductors.

30. A wire connector bearing no marking or reference to AL, CU, or ALR is suitable for use with (copper) (aluminum) conductors only. Circle the correct answer.

31. When Type NM or NMC cable is run through a floor, it must be protected by at least __________ in. (__________ mm) of ____

____

____

32. When nonmetallic-sheathed cables are bunched or bundled together for distances longer than 24 in. (600 mm), what happens to their current-carrying ability?

____

33. In diagrams A and B, nonmetallic-sheathed cable is run through the cold air return. Which diagram "meets Code"? A ________ B ________ Check one.

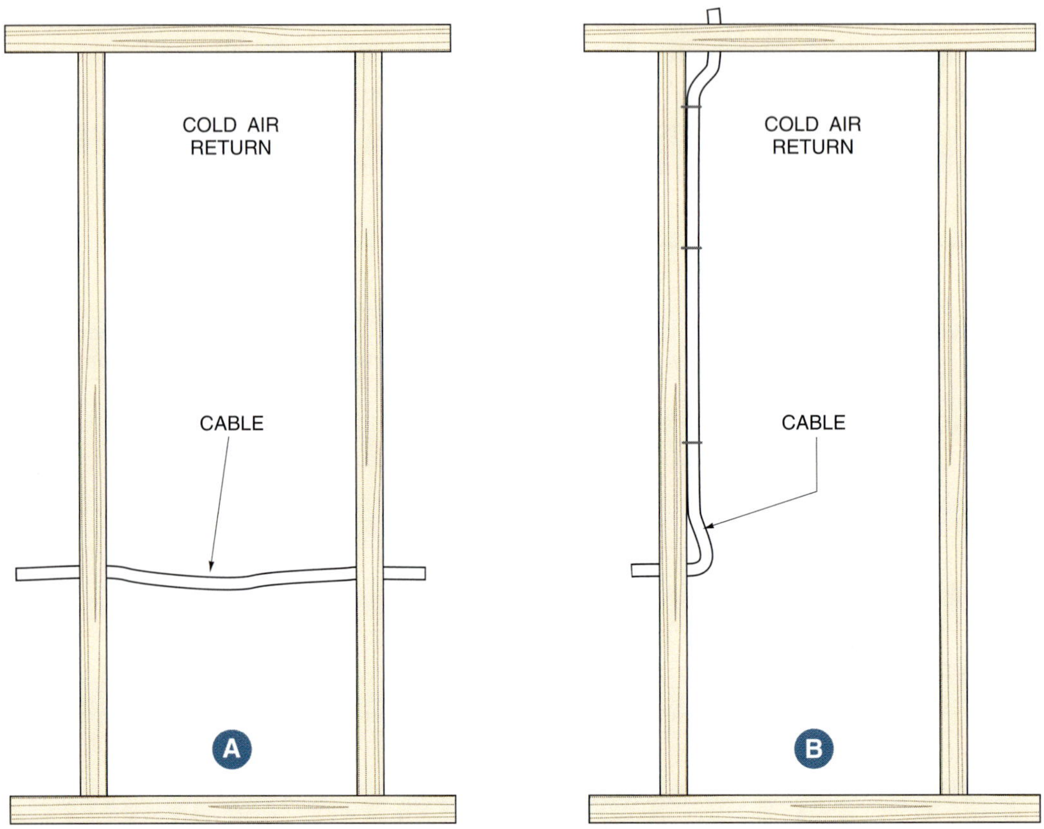

34. The marking on the outer jacket of a nonmetallic-sheathed cable indicates the letters NMC-B. What does the letter **B** signify?____

____

____

35. A 120-volt branch circuit supplies a resistive heating load of 10 amperes. The distance from the panel to the heater is approximately 140 ft. Calculate the voltage drop using (a) 14 AWG, (b) 12 AWG, (c) 10 AWG, (d) 8 AWG copper conductors. See *210.19(A), FPN No. 4* and *215.2(A)(3), FPN No. 2.*

36. In question 35, it is desired to keep the voltage drop to 3% maximum. What minimum size wire would be installed to accomplish this 3% maximum voltage drop? See *210.19(A), FPN No. 4* and *215.2(A)(3), FPN No. 2*.

____

____

____

____

____

37. *NEC® 215.2, 220.61, 230.42,* and *310.15(B)(6)* state that the neutral conductor of a residential service or feeder can be smaller than the phase conductors, but only:

____

____

____

38. The allowable ampacity of a 4 AWG THHN from *Table 310.16* is 95 amperes. What is this conductor's ampacity if connected to a terminal listed for use with 60°C wire?

____

39. If, because of some obstruction in a wall space, it is impossible to keep an NMC cable at least 1¼ in. (32 mm) from the edge of the stud, then it shall be protected by a metal plate at least ______________ in. thick.

40. The recessed fluorescent luminaires installed in the ceiling of the recreation room of this residence are connected with trade size ⅜ flexible metal conduit. These flexible connections are commonly referred to as fixture whips. Does the flexible metal conduit provide adequate grounding for the luminaires, or must a separate equipment grounding conductor be installed? ______________________________

____

____

____

____

41. Flexible liquidtight metal conduit will be used to connect the air-conditioner unit. It will be trade size ¾. Must a separate equipment grounding conductor be installed in this FLMC to ground the air conditioner properly? ______________________________

____

____

____

____

42. What size overcurrent device protects the air-conditioning unit? ______________________________

____

43. May the 20-ampere small-appliance branch circuits in the kitchen of a residence also supply the lighting above the kitchen sink and under-cabinet lighting? Check the correct answer. Yes __________ No __________

44. A 30-ampere branch circuit is installed for an electric clothes dryer. What is the maximum ampere rating of a dryer permitted by the *NEC*® to be cord- and plug-connected to this circuit? Check the correct answer.

    a. __________ 30 amperes

    b. __________ 24 amperes

    c. __________ 15 amperes

45. In many areas, metal framing members are being used in residential construction. When using nonmetallic-sheathed cable, what must be used where the cable is run through the metal framing members?__________

46. Are set-screw-type connectors permitted to be used with armored cable that has an aluminum armor? __________

47. Most armored cable today has 90°C conductors. What is the correct designation for this type of armored cable?__________

48. If you saw two different types of SE cables, how would you distinguish them?

    ____

    ____

    ____

    ____

49. Circle the correct answer defining the type of location:

    a. A raceway installed underground. (Dry) (Wet)

    b. A raceway installed in a concrete slab that is in direct contact with the earth. (Dry) (Wet)

    c. A raceway installed in a concrete slab between the first and second floor. (Dry) (Wet)

    d. A raceway installed on the outside of a building exposed to the weather. (Dry) (Wet)

    e. The interior of a raceway installed on the outside of a building exposed to the weather. (Dry) (Wet)

CHAPTER 5

Conductor Identification, Switch Control of Lighting Circuits, Bonding/Grounding of Wiring Devices, Induction Heating

OBJECTIVES

After studying this chapter, you should be able to

- **identify the grounded and ungrounded conductors in cable or conduit (color coding).**
- **identify the various types of toggle switches for lighting circuit control.**
- **select a switch with the proper rating for the specific installation conditions.**
- **describe the operation that each type of toggle switch performs in typical lighting circuit installations.**
- **demonstrate the correct wiring connections for each type of switch per *Code* requirements.**
- **understand the various ways to bond wiring devices to the outlet box.**
- **understand how to design circuits to avoid heating by induction.**

WARNING! Improper wiring can result in fires, personal injuries, and electrocutions! All wiring must be done in conformance to the *NEC*.® Anything less is unacceptable!

CONDUCTOR IDENTIFICATION (*ARTICLES 200* AND *210*)

Before making any electrical connections, an electrician must understand conductor color coding.

Grounded Conductor: For alternating-current circuits, the *NEC*® requires that the grounded (identified) conductor have an outer finish that is either continuous white or gray, or have an outer finish (not green) that has three continuous white stripes along the conductor's entire length. In multiwire circuits, the grounded conductor is also called a *neutral* conductor.

Ungrounded Conductor: An ungrounded conductor must have an outer finish that is a color other than green, white, gray, or three continuous white stripes. This conductor is commonly called the "hot" conductor. You will get a shock if this "hot" conductor and a grounded conductor or grounded surface such as a metal water pipe are touched at the same time.

Popular colors are black, white, red, blue, green, yellow, brown, orange, and gray. Conductors 1 AWG and larger are generally available in black only.

Three Continuous White Stripes: In house wiring, you will probably never run across a conductor that has three continuous white stripes. This method of identifying conductors is done by the cable manufacturer, and would be found on larger size conductors and some service-entrance cables such as those used for a mobile home feeder (two black, one black that has three white stripes, one green).

Grounded Neutral Conductor

For residential wiring, the white grounded conductor is commonly referred to as the *neutral*. However, this conductor is not always a neutral conductor as you will learn.

For branch circuits and feeders, the grounded neutral conductor must be insulated, *310.2(A)*.

For residential services, the grounded neutral conductor is permitted to be insulated or bare, *230.41*.

For residential wiring, the 120/240-volt electrical system is grounded by the electric utility at their transformer, and again by the electrician at the main service. This is in accordance with *250.20(B)(1)* requiring that the system be grounded so the maximum voltage to ground on the ungrounded conductors does not exceed 150 volts. *250.26(2)* requires that the neutral conductor be grounded for single-phase, 3-wire systems.

Electricians often use the term "neutral" whenever they refer to a white grounded circuit conductor. The correct definition is found in the *NEC*®

▶**Neutral Conductor.** "The conductor connected to the neutral point of a system that is intended to carry current under normal conditions." See Figure 5-1.◀

▶**Neutral Point.** "The common point on a wye-connection in a polyphase system or midpoint on a single-phase, 3-wire system, or midpoint of a single-phase portion of a 3-phase delta system, or a midpoint of a 3-wire, direct current system." See Figure 5-1.◀

By these definitions, the white grounded conductor in a 2-wire circuit is a neutral conductor. In a multiwire 3-wire branch circuit, the white grounded conductor is a neutral conductor. See Figure 5-1.

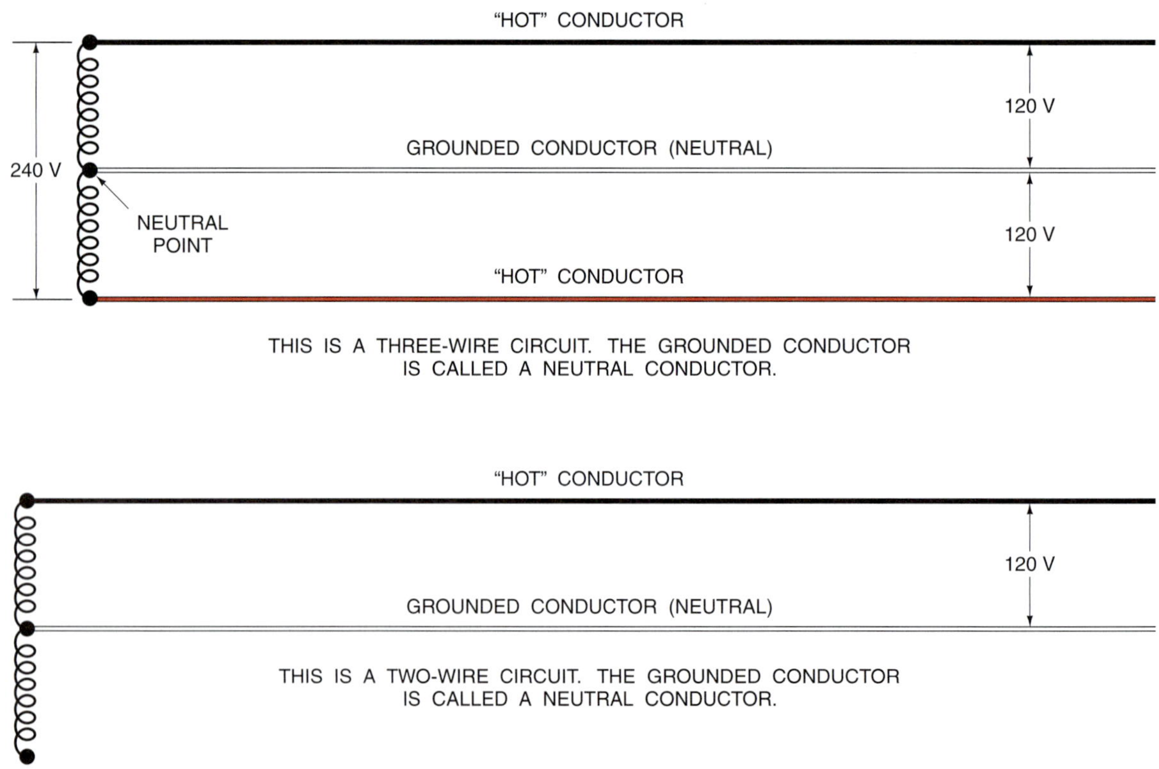

Figure 5-1 Definition of a neutral conductor.

For those of you who will broaden your training into commercial and industrial wiring, you will find that there are electrical systems such as a 3-phase Delta corner grounded system where the grounded conductor is a phase conductor and is not a neutral conductor. This is covered in detail in the *Electrical Wiring—Commercial* text.

A neutral conductor in residential wiring is always a grounded conductor—but a grounded conductor is not always a neutral conductor.

▶Although it may seem obvious to trained electricians, *250.14* prohibits using a metal enclosure, a metal raceway, or metal cable armor to be part of a grounded conductor's path.◀

Multiwire Branch-Circuit

The *Code* defines a *multiwire branch circuit* as: *A branch circuit consisting of two or more ungrounded conductors having a voltage between them, and a grounded conductor having equal voltage between it and each ungrounded conductor of the circuit and that is connected to the neutral or grounded conductor of the system.**

For additional information relative to the hazards involved with multiwire circuits, refer to Figure 17-5, Figure 17-6, Figure 17-7, Figure 17-8, and Figure 17-9 in Chapter 17.

Color Coding (Cable Wiring)

The conductors in nonmetallic-sheathed cable (Romex) are color coded as follows.

2-wire: one black ("hot" phase conductor)
one white (grounded "identified" conductor)
one bare (equipment grounding conductor)

3-wire: one black ("hot" phase conductor)
one white (grounded "identified" conductor)
one red ("hot" phase conductor)
one bare (equipment grounding conductor)

4-wire: one black ("hot" phase conductor)
one white (grounded "identified" conductor)
one red ("hot" phase conductor)
one blue ("hot" phase conductor)
one bare (equipment grounding conductor)

Four-wire nonmetallic-sheathed cable and armored cable are not commonly used for house wiring. In fact, it may be impossible to find this type of cable in stock at electrical supply houses, hardware stores, or home centers. It may need to be ordered special. The cost is very high when compared to 2-wire and 3-wire cables. It is generally easier and more economical to lay out the wiring using two-conductor and three-conductor cables.

Color Coding (Raceway Wiring)

When the wiring method is a raceway such as EMT, the choice of colors for the ungrounded "hot" conductors is virtually unlimited, with the following restrictions:

Green or green with yellow stripe(s): Reserved for use as an equipment grounding conductor only. Not permitted to be used as a grounded or ungrounded conductor. See *250.119* and *310.12(B)*.

White or gray: Reserved for use only as a grounded circuit conductor (neutral). See Table 5-1 for more information about identifying conductors.

What about Conductors with Gray Insulation?

The *NEC*® recognizes a conductor with gray insulation to be used as a grounded conductor. See *200.6(A)* and *(B)*.

The *NEC*® prohibits a conductor with gray insulation to be used as an ungrounded "hot" conductor. See *200.6(A)* and *(B)*.

For years, conductors with gray insulation were used in commercial and industrial installations as both grounded conductors and ungrounded conductors. Past editions of the *NEC*® used the term *natural gray*, but no one really knew what it was. Was it "dirty white"? Was it "light gray"? Was it "dark gray"? Confusion was the end result. To bring an end to the confusion, all references to the term *natural gray* have been deleted in the *NEC*.®

You might be saying to yourself "no cable that I use for house wiring has a gray conductor in it." Right! But in commercial and industrial work, there

*Reprinted with permission from NFPA 70-2008.

TO CHANGE FROM THIS	TO THIS	DO THIS
red, black, blue, etc.	an *equipment grounding* conductor	**Conductors 6 AWG or smaller:** No reidentification permitted for conductors 6 AWG and smaller. An equipment grounding conductor must be bare, covered, or insulated. If covered or insulated, the outer finish must be green or green with yellow stripes. The outer finish color must run the entire length of the conductor. **Conductors larger than 6 AWG:** Insulation on large conductors is usually black. Therefore, at time of installation, at both ends, and at every place where the conductor is accessible except in a conduit body where there are no splices, do any one of the following: • strip off the insulation for the entire exposed length, or • ▶at the termination, encircle the insulation with green color, or◀ • ▶at the termination, encircle the insulation with a few wraps of green tape, green adhesive labels, or green heat shrink tubing◀ See *210.5(B)*, *250.119*, and *310.12(B)*.
red, black, blue, etc.	a *grounded* conductor	**Conductors 6 AWG or smaller:** For the conductor's entire length, the insulation must be white, gray, or have three continuous white stripes on other than green insulation. Reidentification in the field is not permitted when the wiring method is a raceway. **Conductors larger than 6 AWG:** For the conductor's entire length, the insulation must be white, gray, or have three continuous white stripes on other than green insulation. At terminations, reidentification may be white paint, white tape, or white heat shrink tubing. This marking must encircle the conductor or insulation. Do this marking at time of installation.Identification must encircle the conductor. See *200.2*, *200.6(A)* and *(B)*, *200.7(A)*, *(B)*, and *(C)*, *210.5(A)*, and *310.12(A)*.
white, gray	an *ungrounded* (hot) conductor	**No change permitted:** Insulated conductors that are white, gray, or have three continuous white stripes are to be used as grounded conductors only. There is no provision in the *NEC*® for reidentifying white or gray conductors for use as ungrounded conductors in raceways. The only exception to use white or gray insulated conductors as ungrounded conductors is for cable wiring. See *200.7(A)*, *(B)*, and *(C)*, and *310.12(C)*.

Table 5-1 Changing colors of conductor insulation in a raceway or cable.

are situations where two systems are installed in the same raceway, such as a 120/208-volt and a 277/480-volt circuit. This is an example of where you might want to use a white insulated conductor for the 120/208-volt system neutral conductor, and a gray insulated conductor for the 277/480-volt system neutral conductor.

Changing Colors When Conductors Are in a Cable

The basic rule in *200.7* is that grounded conductors must be white, gray, or have three continuous white stripes on other than green insulation.

For cable wiring such as nonmetallic-sheathed cable or armored cable, *200.7(C)(1)* and *(2)* permits the white or gray conductor to be used for single-pole, three-way, or four-way switch loops. These sections require that when used for a switch "loop," the conductor that is white, gray, or marked with three continuous white stripes is to be used for the supply to the switch, and not as the return conductor from the switch to the switched outlet. Also, the conductor must be permanently reidentified to indicate its use by painting or other effective means, at its terminations, and at each location where the conductor is visible and accessible. See Figure 5-2.

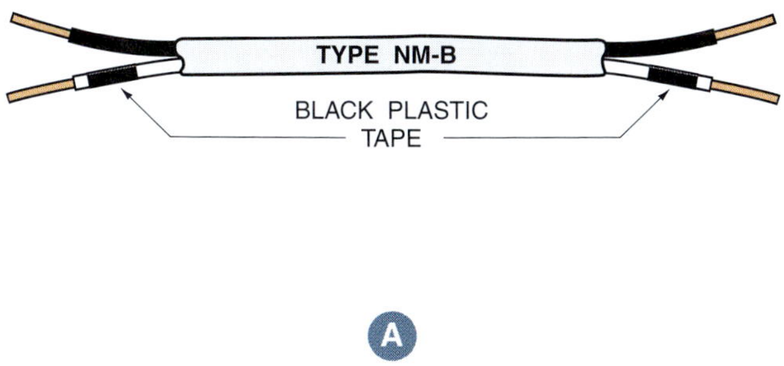

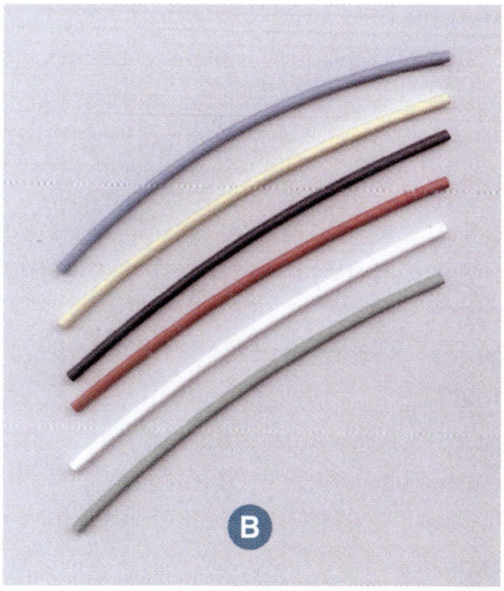

Figure 5-2 (A) Shows a white conductor reidentified with black plastic electrical tape. (B) Shows an assortment of easy-to-use, 6-in. long heat shrink tubing that is slid over the conductor to be reidentified, then shrunk tightly over the conductor by applying heat as specified in the instructions.

How to Reidentify Conductor Insulation

Small conductors are available with insulation colors of black, blue, brown, gray, green, orange, pink, purple, red, tan, white, and yellow. Conductor 1 AWG and larger, unless special ordered, are available in black only.

There are a number of ways to reidentify a conductor's insulation. Plastic electrical tape, heat shrink tubing, permanent felt tip marking pens, and fast-drying "touch-up" paint are generally considered acceptable ways to permanently reidentify conductor insulation. You might want to test the paint on a conductor to make sure that it does not have a harmful effect on the insulation, *NEC*® *310.9*. Whichever method you choose to reidentify a conductor, be sure it encircles the insulation.

More and more electricians are finding that permanent marking pens are a great way to reidentify conductor insulation. These pens are readily available with a wide felt tip (5/8 inch). Cut a notch or drill a small hole in the felt tip. Slide the notched marker up and down the conductor insulation, or slide the marker with the small hole over the conductor and slide it up and down. This makes the job of reidentifying a conductor very easy—and fast. Inspectors like this method.

Heat shrink tubing (UL recognized) with a shrink ratio of 2:1 is available at electrical distributors in packages of assorted colors and sizes, for example, 6 in. (150 mm) long. See Figure 5-2B. This method is more labor intensive than using permanent marking pens or tape.

Some electrical inspectors have very strong feelings about what they will accept for reidentifying conductors. They might not consider plastic tape as being a "permanent" material. Check it out!

It is pretty obvious that the intent of the *Code* is to permanently reidentify a white conductor when it is used as a "hot" conductor. If not properly reidentified, someone someday will get a surprise. An accident waiting to happen—such "surprises" can prove to be fatal!

The wiring diagrams that follow are good examples of where permanent reidentification of the white conductor is necessary.

Changing Colors When Conductors Are in a Raceway

Because of the availability of so many insulation colors, it is rarely necessary to reidentify a conductor. If, however, it becomes necessary to change the actual color of a conductor's insulation, refer to Table 5-1.

CONNECTING WIRING DEVICES

Terminating and splicing conductors is a skill. The connections must be tight so as not to overheat under load.

NEC® 110.3(B) requires us to follow the manufacturers' instructions regarding the listing and labeling of all electrical products. *NEC® 110.14* provides clear requirements for making electrical connections.

Table 4-4 shows in detail the terminal identification markings found on wiring devices (switches and receptacles) indicating the types of conductors permitted to be connected to them.

Most commonly used wiring devices have screw terminals.

Some wiring devices have back-wiring holes only. For these, the conductor insulation is stripped off for the desired length, inserted into the hole, and held in place by the device's internal spring pressure mechanism. These wiring devices are referred to as having *push-in* terminals.

For convenience, some wiring devices have both screw terminals and back-wiring holes, as illustrated in Figure 5-3 and Figure 5-4. These can be connected or hooked up in different ways. One way is if the conductor insulation is stripped off for the desired length and inserted into the back hole, then the screw terminal is properly tightened. In another way, the conductor insulation is stripped off for the desired length and terminated under the screw terminal, in which case the back-wiring holes are not used.

Using both the back-wiring terminals and the screw terminals, it would be possible to terminate as many as four conductors to the white terminal, and four conductors to the brass terminal. This is a violation of *110.3(B)*. UL does not test receptacles with so many conductors connected to the device. A much better way is shown in Figure 5-5 where all of the necessary splicing is done independent of the receptacle. Short lengths of wire called *pigtails* are included in the splice, and these pigtails in turn connect to the receptacle. Removal of the receptacle would not have any effect on the splice.

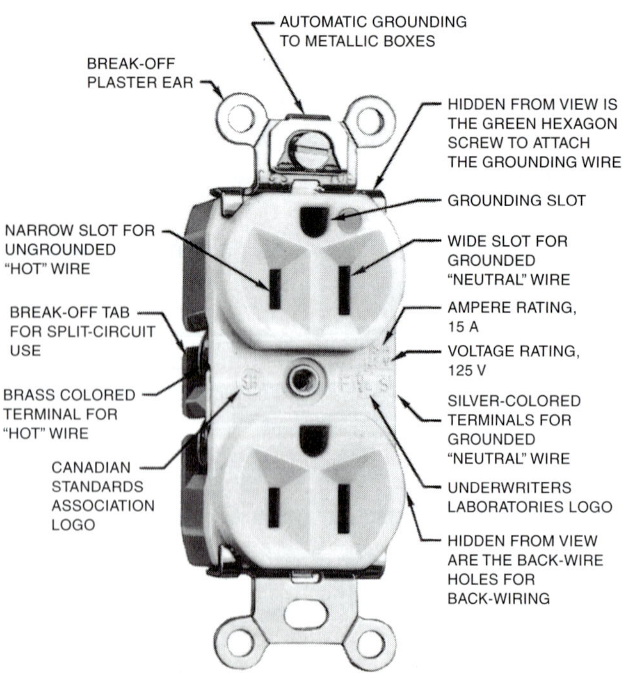

Figure 5-3 Grounding-type receptacle detailing various parts of the receptacle.

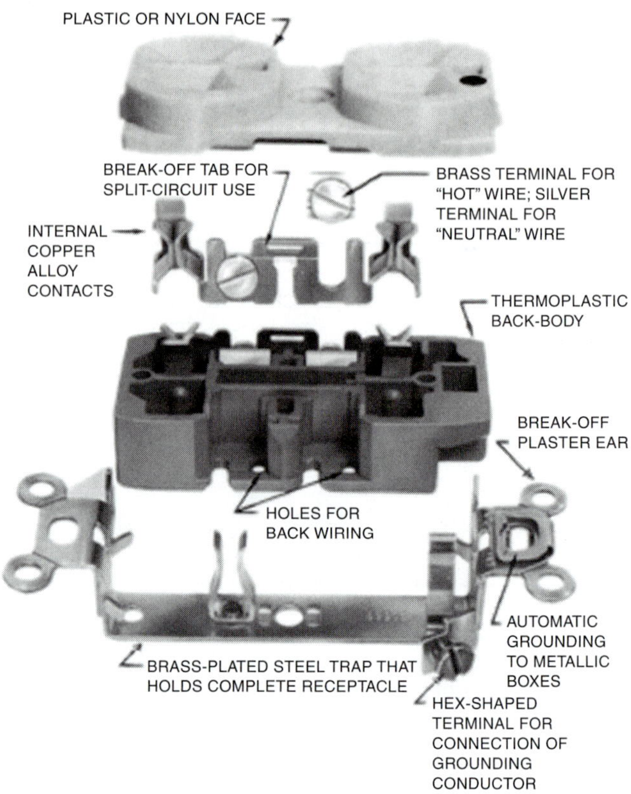

Figure 5-4 Exploded view of a grounding-type receptacle, showing all internal parts. *200.10(B)* requires that terminals on receptacles, plugs, and connectors that are intended for the ground-circuit conductor be substantially white (usually silver colored), or marked with the word "white" or the letter "W" adjacent to the terminal. The terminal for the ungrounded "hot" conductor is usually brass colored.

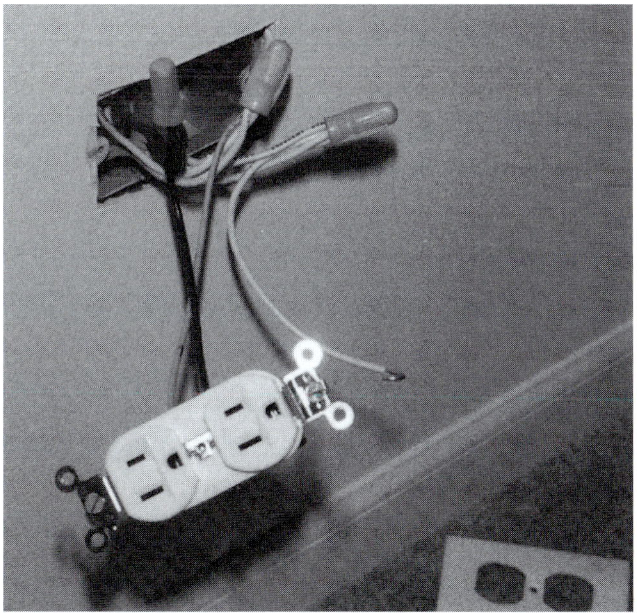

Figure 5-5 A receptacle connected with pigtails. This particular installation has one outlet switched and one outlet on continuously. Six conductors enter the box because the wiring runs from receptacle to receptacle around the room. A 4-in. square outlet box trimmed with a single-gang plaster (dry-wall) cover is used. Removal of the receptacle does not affect the circuit to the other receptacles.

Installing Switches and Receptacles

Always make sure that the yokes of switches and receptacles are rigidly held in place so they do not twist. Not tightly securing wiring devices is unsafe as well as being an example of sloppy workmanship, *406.4(A)*.

Receptacle Configuration

Figure 5-6 illustrates some of the common receptacle configurations used in homes in conformance to *Table 210.21(B)(3)*. Range and dryer receptacles are discussed in Chapter 20.

▶Tamper-Resistant Receptacles

A major step to reduce the number of injuries (burns), particularly to small children who always seem to find a way to insert "things" into the slots of a receptacle, was enacted for the *2008 National Electrical Code*.® The new requirement for receptacles in dwellings is:

***406.11* Tamper Resistant Receptacles in Dwelling Units.** In all areas specified in *210.52*, all 125-volt, 15- and 20-ampere receptacles shall be listed tamper-resistant receptacles.

	A 15-ampere, 125-volt, NEMA 5-15R receptacle. **Short slot:** "hot" conductor. **Long slot:** grounded conductor. **Horseshoe slot:** equipment grounding conductor.
	A 20-ampere, 125-volt, NEMA 5-20R receptacle. Accepts a 125-volt, 15- or 20-ampere attachment plug. **Short slot:** "hot" conductor. **Long "T" slot:** grounded conductor. **Horseshoe slot:** equipment grounding conductor.
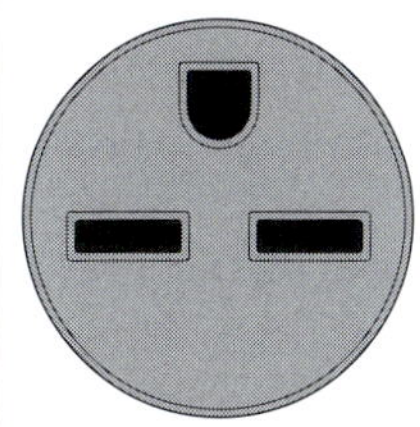	A 15-ampere, 250-volt, NEMA 6-15R receptacle. Slot arrangement will not accept standard 125-volt attachment plug cap; could be used for a 240-volt window air conditioner. **Short slots:** "hot" conductors. **Horseshoe slot:** equipment grounding conductor.
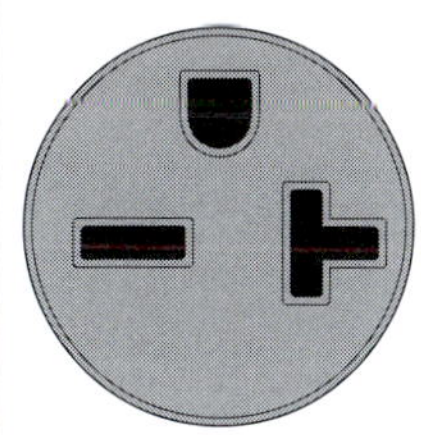	A 20-ampere, 250-volt, NEMA 6-20R receptacle. Slot arrangement will not accept standard 125-volt attachment plug cap; could be used for a 240-volt window air conditioner. Accepts a 250-volt, 15- or 20-ampere attachment plug. **Short slot:** "hot" conductor. **"T" slot:** "hot" conductor. **Horseshoe slot:** equipment grounding conductor.

Figure 5-6 Slot configuration of receptacles. Receptacles have the suffix "R" and plug caps have the suffix "P."

Recall that *210.52* lists the rooms, areas, and other locations inside and outside of a new home where receptacles have to be installed, the spacing, and the number or receptacles required.

Tamper-resistant receptacles have a unique internal interlocking mechanism that energizes the blade contacts of the receptacle ONLY when a male attachment plug cap is inserted. If a paper clip or similar object is inserted into any one slot of the receptacle, no power is supplied to any of the blade contacts of the receptacle. Both slot shutters remain closed. Figure 5-7 is a typical tamper-resistant receptacle. Tamper-resistant receptacles have been required for many years in pediatric (children) areas of health care facilities, *517.18(C)*.◀

Figure 5-7 A typical duplex tamper-resistant receptacle. *Courtesy of* Pass & Seymour Legrand.

PUSH-IN TERMINATIONS

Be careful when using screwless push-in terminals.

Screwless push-in terminals on receptacles are listed by Underwriters Laboratories (UL) for use *only* with solid 14 AWG copper conductors. They *are not* to be used with:

- aluminum or copper-clad aluminum conductors.
- stranded conductors.
- 12 AWG conductors. By design, the holes are large enough to take only a 14 AWG solid conductor.

Push-in terminals for 12 AWG solid copper conductors are still permitted on snap switches.

TOGGLE SWITCHES *(ARTICLE 404)*

UL refers to them as snap switches. Manufacturers and electricians refer to them as toggle switches. They are one and the same.

The most frequently used switch in lighting circuits is the toggle flush switch, Figure 5-8. When mounted in a flush switch box, the switch is concealed in the wall with only the insulated handle or toggle protruding.

Figure 5-9 shows how switches are weatherproofed.

Toggle Switch Ratings

UL lists toggle switches used for lighting circuits as *general-use snap switches*. The UL requirements are the same as *404.14(A)* and *(B)* of the *NEC*.®

AC/DC General-Use Snap Switches *[404.14(B)]*

The requirements for general-use snap switches include the following:

- Alternating-current (ac) or direct-current (dc) circuits.

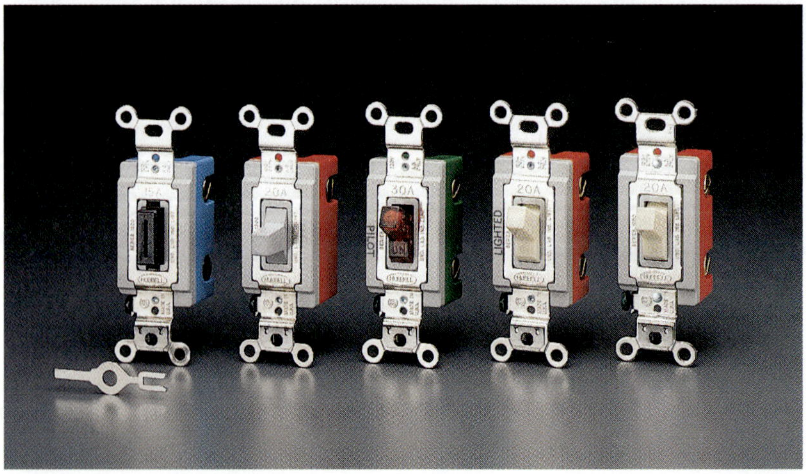

Figure 5-8 Toggle flush switches. *Courtesy of* Hubbell, Incorporated.

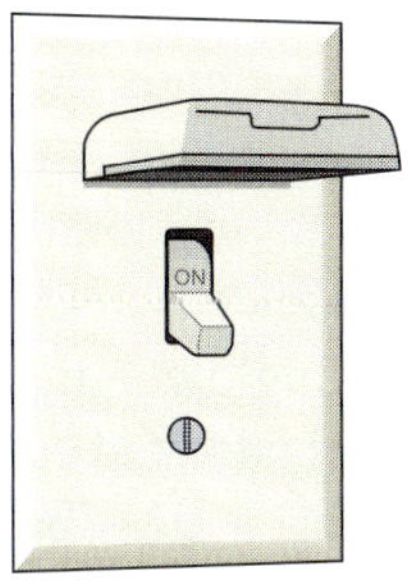

Figure 5-9 Switch is protected by a weatherproof cover.

- Resistive loads not to exceed the ampere rating of the switch at applied voltage.
- Inductive loads not to exceed one-half the ampere rating of the switch at applied voltage.
- Motor loads not to exceed the ampere rating of the switch at applied voltage only if the switch is marked in horsepower.
- Tungsten filament lamp loads not to exceed the ampere rating of the switch at applied voltage when marked with the letter "T."
- For switches marked with a horsepower rating, a motor load shall not exceed the rating of the switch at rated voltage.

Why "T" Rating?

A tungsten filament lamp draws a very high momentary inrush current at the instant the circuit is energized. This is because the *cold resistance* of tungsten is very low. For instance, the cold resistance of a typical 100-watt lamp is approximately 9.5 ohms. This same lamp has a *hot resistance* of 144 ohms when operating at 100% of its rated voltage.

Normal operating current would be

$$I = \frac{E}{R} = \frac{120}{144} = 0.83 \text{ ampere}$$

The instantaneous inrush current could be as high as

$$I = \frac{E}{R} = \frac{170 \text{ (peak voltage)}}{9.5} = 17.9 \text{ amperes}$$

This instantaneous inrush current drops off to normal operating current in about 6 cycles (0.10 second). The contacts of T-rated switches are designed to handle these momentary high inrush currents. See Chapter 13 for more information pertaining to inrush currents.

The ac/dc general-use snap switch normally is not marked ac/dc. However, it is always marked with the current and voltage rating, such as 10A-125V or 5A-250V-T.

AC General-Use Snap Switches *[404.14(A)]*

This is the type most commonly used for house wiring projects. Alternating-current general-use snap switches are marked "ac only," in addition to identifying their current and voltage ratings. A typical switch marking is 15A, 120-277V ac. The 277-volt rating is required on 277/480-volt systems. Other requirements include:

- Alternating-current (ac) circuits only.
- Resistive and inductive loads not to exceed the ampere rating of the switch at the voltage involved. This includes electric-discharge lamps that involve ballasts, such as fluorescent lamps.
- Tungsten-filament lamp loads not to exceed the ampere rating of the switch at 120 volts.
- Motor loads not to exceed 80% of the ampere rating of the switch at rated voltage. A UL requirement is that the load shall not exceed 2 horsepower.

What Are the Switching Conductors Called?

In *200.7(C)(2)*, we find a few unique words that need to be explained. There are also local and regional expressions for these words. It is always best to use the terms found in the *NEC*.®

- *Switch loop:* The conductors that run between (to and from) a switched outlet and the switch controlling that outlet.
- *Supply:* The conductor that runs from the source to the switch. It might also be referred to as the *feed*, *hot*, *hot leg*, or *supply leg*.

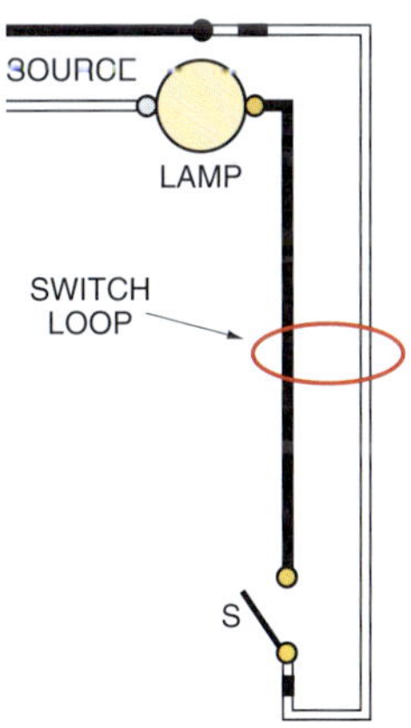

- *Return:* The conductor that runs from the switch back to the switched outlet. It might also be referred to as the *switch leg* or *switched leg*.

Conductor Color Coding for Switch Connections

The insulated conductors in nonmetallic-sheathed cable or armored cable are black-white, black-white-red, or, in some cases, black-white-red-blue. We usually think of the black insulated conductor as the supply to a switch and a red insulated conductor as the return. However, when wiring with nonmetallic-sheathed cable or armored cable, we are "stuck" with the colors found in the cables. We must not use a white conductor as the return conductor from a switch, *200.7(C)(2)*. A color-coding scheme needs to be established for the supplies and returns. In the case of three-way and four-way switches, we also have "travelers"—the conductors that connect between three-way and four-way switches. The wiring diagrams in Figures 5-12 through 5-23 show the recommended color schemes when wiring with cable.

When the wiring method is a raceway or electrical metallic tubing (EMT), the choices of insulation colors are virtually unlimited.

Always connect a white wire to the white (silverish) terminal or to the white wire of a lampholder or receptacle, *200.9* and *200.10*. Always connect the black switch leg conductor (or red in some cases) to the black wire (or dark brassy terminal) of a lampholder or receptacle.

In cables, always reidentify white conductors when they are used as ungrounded (hot) conductors. This reidentification must be done wherever the conductors are visible and accessible. These requirements are found in *200.7(C)(2)*. See Table 5-1.

Never use a green-colored insulation for a grounded or ungrounded conductor. Green is reserved for equipment grounding conductors. See *210.5* and *250.119*. See Table 5-1.

Induction Heating

Excessive heat damages conductor insulation. Care must be taken to avoid induction heating when running branch circuits, connecting switches, receptacles, and lighting outlets.

A conductor carrying an alternating current produces a magnetic field (flux) around the conductor. This magnetic field extends outside of the conductor. The greater the current, the stronger the magnetic field. In a 60-Hz (pronounced 60-hertz) circuit, the current and magnetic field reverses 120 times each cycle. If this single conductor is run through a steel raceway, a steel jacketed cable (i.e., Type AC or MC), a steel locknut, a steel bushing, or through a knockout in a steel box, the alternating magnetic field "induces" heat in the steel. Heat in the steel, in turn, can harm the insulation on the conductor. When all conductors of the same circuit are run through the same raceway, the magnetic fields around the conductors are equal and opposite, thereby canceling one another out.

To prevent induction heating and to keep the impedance of a circuit as low as possible where conductors are run in metal raceways, metal jacketed cables, and in metal enclosures, the installation must follow certain *NEC®* requirements.

NEC® 300.3(B) requires that *all conductors of the same circuit and, where used, the grounded conductor, all equipment grounding conductors, and bonding conductors shall be contained within the same raceway, auxiliary gutter, cable tray, trench, cable, or cord, unless otherwise permitted.** There are four exceptions: for paralleled installations, for grounding conductors, for nonferrous wiring methods, and certain enclosures.

▶*NEC® 300.20(A)* requires that *Where conductors carrying alternating current are installed in ferrous metal enclosures or metal raceways, they shall be so arranged as to avoid heating the surrounding metal by induction. To accomplish this, all phase conductors and, where used, the grounded conductor and all equipment grounding conductors shall be grouped together.*◀

Similar requirements are found in *300.3(B)* and *300.5*.

NEC® 404.2(A) requires that *Three-way and four-way switches shall be so wired that all switching is done only in the ungrounded circuit conductor. Where in metal raceways or metal-armored cables, wiring between switches and outlets shall be in accordance with 300.20(A).** Switch loops do not require a grounded conductor.

---

*Reprinted with permission from NFPA 70-2008.

Figure 5-10 and Figure 5-11 illustrate the intent of the *NEC*® to prevent induction heating.

Don't Do It!

Unusual switch connections may or may not conform to the *NEC*,® depending upon how the circuitry is run. Some electricians have found that they can save substantial lengths of 3-wire cable when hooking up three-way and four-way switches by using 2-wire cable.

Connections as shown in Figure 5-12 are in violation of *300.3(B)*, *300.20(A)*, and *404.2(A)* when metal boxes and/or steel jacketed Types AC and MC are used. If nonmetallic-sheathed cable and plastic boxes are used, this connection is not a *Code* violation because there would be no induction heating. If the framing members are steel, we have a *Code* violation because of the induction heating issue. The circuitry in Figure 5-12 results in greater impedance and greater voltage drop than if wired in a conventional manner. High impedance will cause the tripping time of a breaker or opening time of a fuse to increase. Another possible problem would be that of picking up "noise" from the magnetic field surrounding the conductor. This could affect the operation of a computer or telephone located in the vicinity, particularly if non-twisted telephone cables are used. The circuitry is very confusing and is certainly an odd way to do a simple job.

Because of possible adverse interference created by magnetic fields, and confusion for someone who at some later date may be involved with that circuit for troubleshooting, repair, replacement, or remodel, the circuitry in Figure 5-12 is strongly discouraged. **Don't do it**.

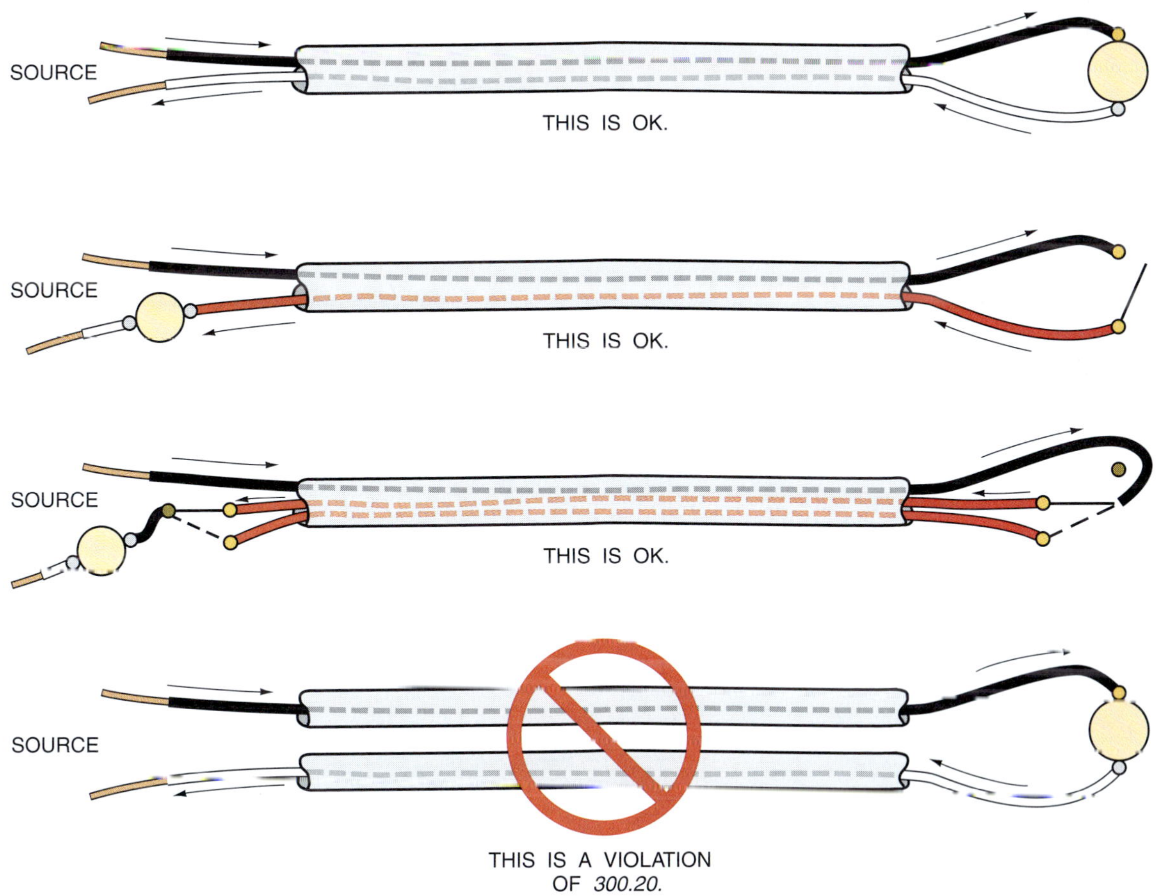

Figure 5-10 **A few examples of arranging circuitry to avoid induction heating according to *300.20* when metal raceway or metal cables (BX) are used. Always ask yourself, "Is the same amount of current flowing in both directions in the metal raceway?" If the answer is "no," there will be induction heating of the metal that can damage the insulation on the conductors.**

Figure 5-11 Arrangement of conductors in trenches. Refer to Chapter 16 for complete information pertaining to underground wiring.

Is It a Light, a Lamp, a Fixture?

Let's not get hung up on words! We say things such as "Turn on the light."

Light is "The radiant energy that is capable of exciting the retina and producing a visual sensation."

A **lamp** is "A generic term for a man-made source of light."

A bulb is "A glass envelope—the glass component part used in a bulb assembly.

►A **luminaire** is "A complete lighting unit consisting of a light source such as a lamp or lamps, together with the parts designed to position the light source and connect it to the power supply."◄ The *NEC*® uses the term *luminaire* as the internationally used term for *lighting fixture*.

Use whatever term that you feel comfortable with. Most of us will continue to say "Turn on the light."

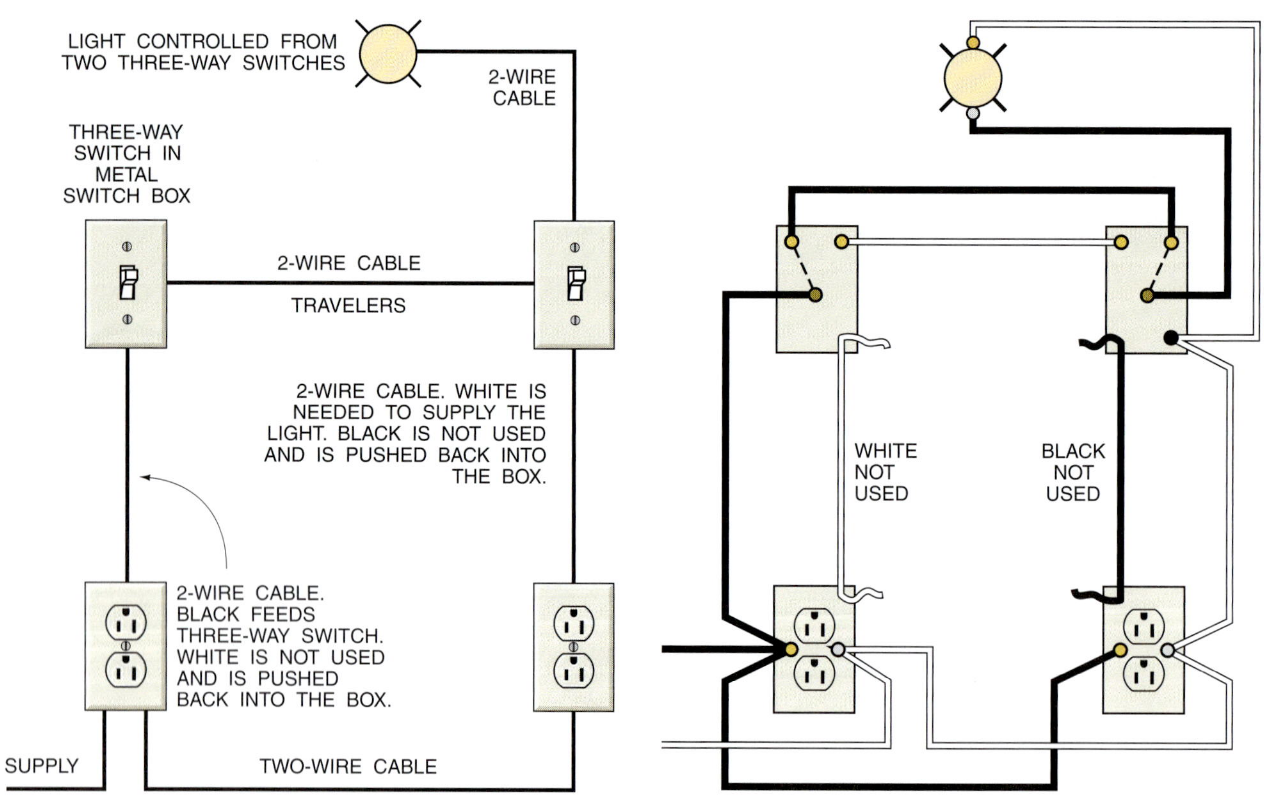

Figure 5-12 This connection is a violation of *300.3(B)*, *300.20(A)*, and *404.2(A)* when using steel jacketed cables, steel raceways, or steel outlet and device boxes. See text for a full explanation. This is not a recommended way of connecting three-way and four-way switches.

Switch Types

Switches are available in single-pole, three-way, four-way, double-pole, dimmer, and speed control types. They are available in snap (toggle), push, rocker, slider, rotary, electronic, and with or without pilot lights. Faceplates are commonly available in white, brown, and ivory plastic, stainless steel, brass, chrome, and wood.

In all of the following wiring diagrams, the equipment grounding conductors are not shown as this is a separate issue covered elsewhere in this text.

Single-Pole Switches. A single-pole switch is marked with "ON" and "OFF" positions. Used when the load is to be controlled from one switching point, a single-pole switch is connected in series with the ungrounded (hot) conductor.

Single-Pole Switch, Feed at Switch. In Figure 5-13, the 120-volt source enters the switch box where the white grounded conductor is spliced directly through to the lamp. The black conductor from the supply circuit connects to one terminal on the switch. The black conductor in the cable coming from the outlet box at the lamp is connected to the other terminal on the switch. Because a single-pole switch connection is simply a series circuit, it makes no difference which terminal is the supply and which terminal is the load.

This layout needs no reidentification of the white conductor. That is why many electricians prefer to run the feed to the switch then up to the light.

Single-Pole Switch, Feed at Light. In Figure 5-14, the 120-volt source enters the outlet box at the lamp. The switch loop is a 2-wire cable. The white wire of a cable is permitted in *200.7(C)(2)* to be used as the supply (feed) to the switch. When so used, *200.7(C)(2)* requires that the white conductor be permanently reidentified in the ceiling outlet box and in the device box. The white conductor is not permitted to be used as the return (switch leg) from the switch to the switched outlet. Color plastic tape is most often used to reidentify a conductor. For this diagram, black tape would be suitable.

Single-Pole Switch, Feed at Switch, Receptacle "On" Continuously. Figure 5-15 shows the 120-volt source entering the switch box where the switch is located. The switch controls the lamp. The receptacle remains "hot" at all times. The white conductor in the switch box is spliced straight through to the outlet box. The black conductor in the switch box is spliced through to the outlet box and also feeds the switch. The red conductor in the 3-wire cable is the switch leg, connecting to the switch and to the lamp. A 2-wire cable from the outlet box carries the circuit to the receptacle. The circuitry is such that no reidentification of the white conductor is necessary.

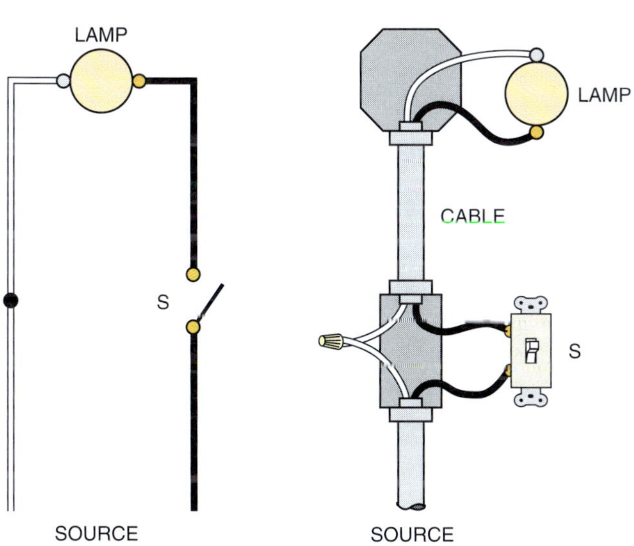

Figure 5-13 Single-pole switch in circuit with feed at switch.

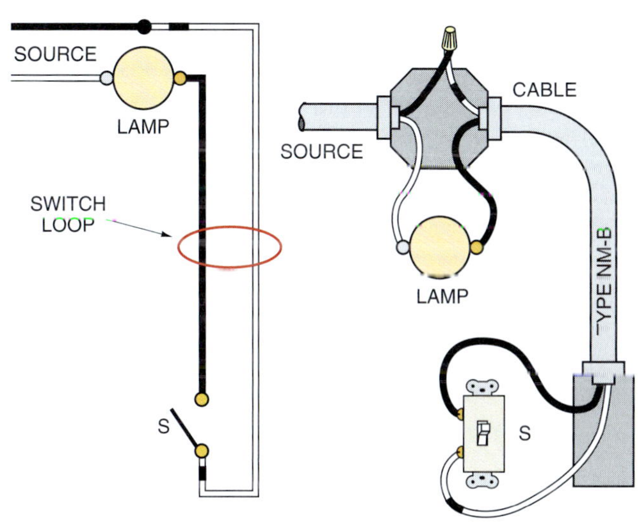

Figure 5-14 Single-pole switch in circuit with feed at light.

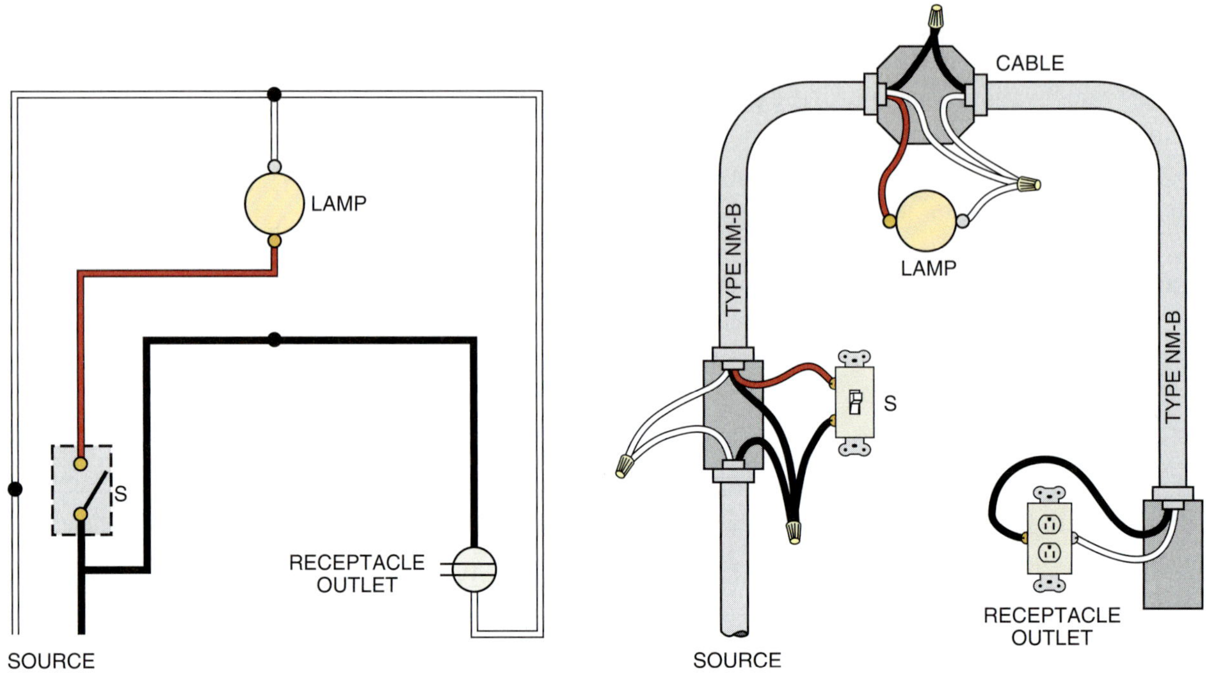

Figure 5-15 Ceiling outlet controlled by single-pole switch with live receptacle outlet and feed at switch.

Three-Way Switches. Three-way switches are used when a load is to be controlled from two locations. The term "three-way" is very misleading. Three-way switches have three terminals. Maybe they should have been named "three-terminal" switches. One terminal is called the "common" and is darker in color than the other two terminals. The other two terminals are called "traveler terminals."

Figure 5-16 shows the two positions of a three-way switch. Actually, a three-way switch is a single-pole, double-throw switch.

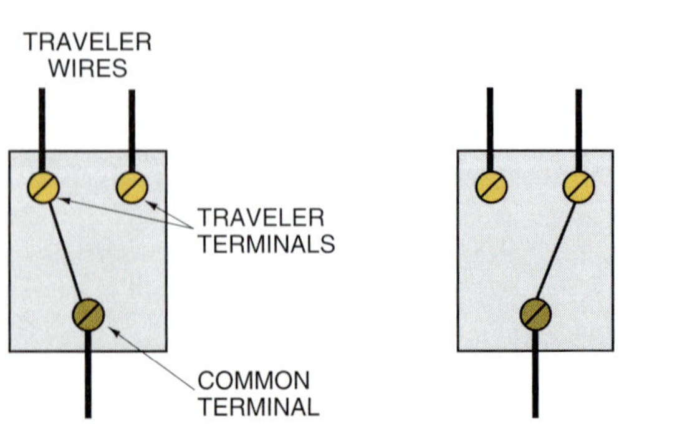

Figure 5-16 Two positions of a three-way switch.

There is no "ON/OFF" marking on a three-way switch, as can be seen in Figure 5-17.

Three-Way Switch Control, Feed at Switch. Figure 5-18 shows the 120-volt source entering at

Figure 5-17 Toggle switch: three-way snap switch. *Courtesy of* Pass & Seymour.

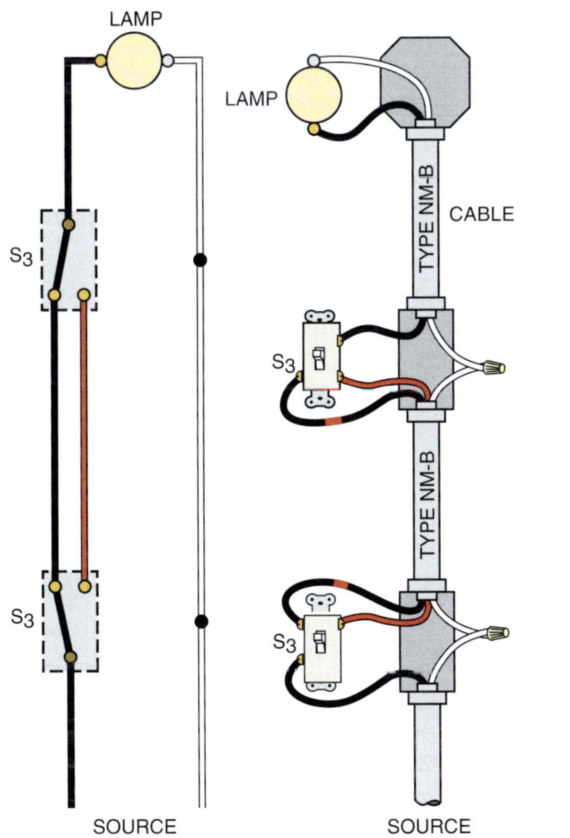

Figure 5-18 Circuit with three-way switch control. The feed is at the first switch. The load is connected to the second switch. The black and red conductors are used for the travelers. The black conductor has been reidentified with red tape.

the first switch location. A 3-wire cable is run between the two switches. A 2-wire cable is run from the second switch to the lamp. The white conductors in both switch boxes are spliced directly through to the lamp. The red and black conductors in the 3-wire cable are the "travelers." The black conductor in the 3-wire cable is reidentified with red tape, consistent with keeping both "travelers" red in color. The black conductor from the source is connected to the "common" terminal of the first switch. The black conductor in the cable coming from the outlet box at the lamp is connected to the "common" terminal of the second switch. The circuitry is such that no reidentification of the white conductor is necessary.

Three-Way Switch Control, Feed at Light. Figure 5-19 shows the 120-volt source feeding into the outlet box at the lamp. A 2-wire cable is run from the outlet box to the first switch location. A 3-wire cable is run from the first switch to the second switch. In all locations where the white wire is to be used as an ungrounded "hot" conductor, it must be reidentified, *200.7(C)(2)*. In this diagram, reidentification of the white conductor in the outlet box is with black tape.

The black conductor of the 2-wire cable is connected to the "common" terminal of the first switch. At the first switch, the white conductor in the 2-wire cable is reidentified with black tape. The white conductor of the 3-wire cable is reidentified with red tape. The red conductor and the reidentified white conductor in the 3-wire cable are the "travelers." The white conductor is reidentified with red tape, consistent with keeping both "travelers" red in color.

At the second switch location, the black conductor of the 3-wire cable is connected to the "common" terminal of the switch. The white conductor of the 3-wire cable is reidentified with red tape. The red

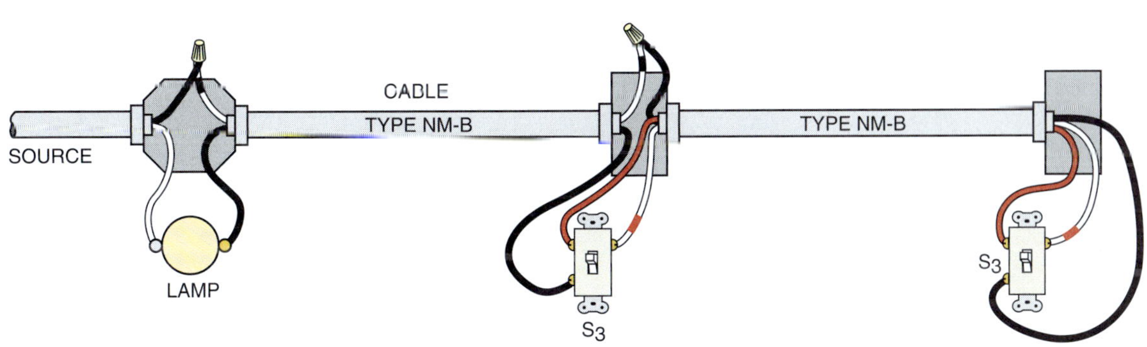

Figure 5-19 Circuit with three-way switch control and feed at light.

conductor and the reidentified white conductor in the 3-wire cable are the "travelers." Here again, the white conductor is reidentified with red tape, so that the "travelers" are red in color.

Three-Way Switch Control, Feed at Light (Alternate Connection). Figure 5-20 shows the 120-volt source entering at the outlet box. The white conductor from the 120-volt source at the outlet box goes directly to the lampholder. In all locations where the white wire is to be used as an ungrounded "hot" conductor, it must be reidentified, *200.7(C)(2)*. From the outlet box to the switch on the left, the black conductor in the 3-wire cable serves as the switch return to the lamp, and the red conductor and the reidentified white conductor are the "travelers." From the outlet box to the switch on the right, the black conductor serves as the feed to the three-way switch, and the red conductor and the reidentified white conductor are the "travelers." For uniformity, reidentification of the white conductors used for "travelers" through the outlet box and in the switch boxes is with red tape.

When wiring with cable, this connection is not the best way to run the cables. Always try to design your cable runs so the travelers run between switches, not through the outlet box at the luminaire.

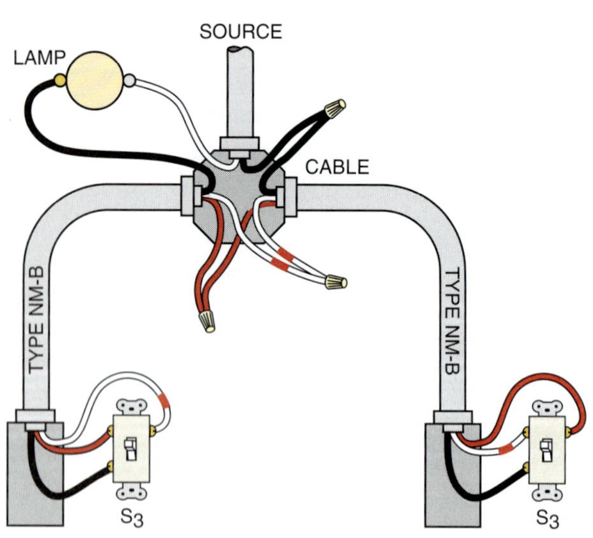

Figure 5-20 Circuit with a three-way switch control with feed at the lamp. This is not the best way to wire multiple switches when wiring with cable. It is best to run the travelers between switches, not through the outlet box. Less confusion—fewer connections.

Four-Way Switches. Four-way switches are used where switch control is needed from more than two locations. The term "four-way" is misleading. Four-way switches have four terminals. Maybe four-way switches should have been called "four-terminal" switches. A four-way switch does not have "ON" and "OFF" markings. Four-way switches are connected to the "travelers" *between* two three-way switches. One three-way switch is fed by the source—the other three-way switch is connected to the load. Make sure that the "travelers" are connected to the proper "pairs" of terminals on a four-way switch; otherwise the switching will not work.

Figure 5-21 shows the internal switching of a four-way switch.

Figure 5-22 shows a lamp controlled from three switching points. Because the white conductor from the source is connected straight through all of the switch boxes and on to the lamp, no reidentification of the white wire is necessary. The black conductor from the source is connected to the common terminal on the first three-way switch. The black conductor at the third switch is connected to the common terminal on the three-way switch. The black and red conductors in the 3-wire cables are the "travelers" and are connected to the proper "traveler" terminals of the three-way and four-way switches. The black conductors in the 3-wire cables have been reidentified with red tape, consistent with keeping both "travelers" red in color. At the lamp, the white conductor of the 2-wire cable connects to the white conductor (or silverish terminal) of the lampholder, and the black conductor connects to the black conductor (or dark brassy terminal) of the lampholder.

Figure 5-23 shows a lamp controlled from three switching points. The supply comes into the outlet

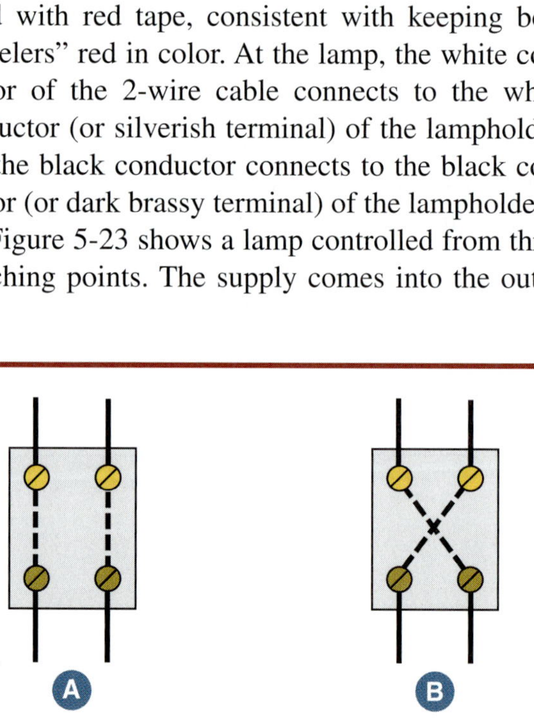

Figure 5-21 Two positions of a four-way switch.

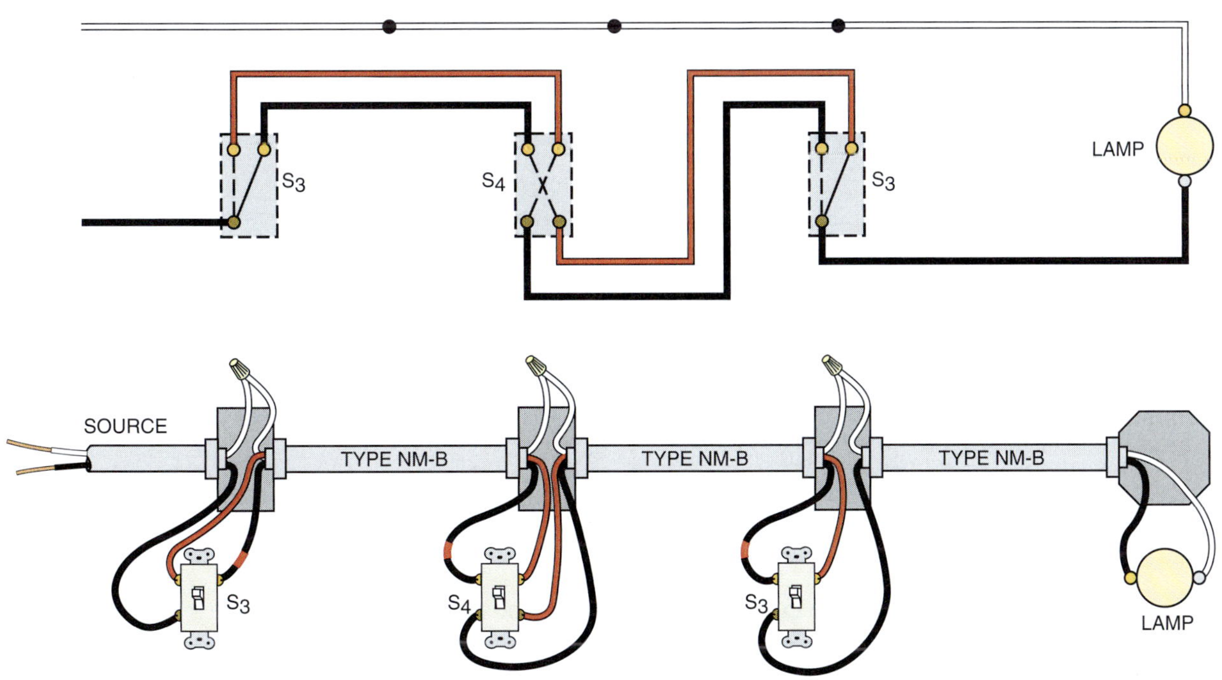

Figure 5-22 Circuit with switch control at three locations—feed at switch.

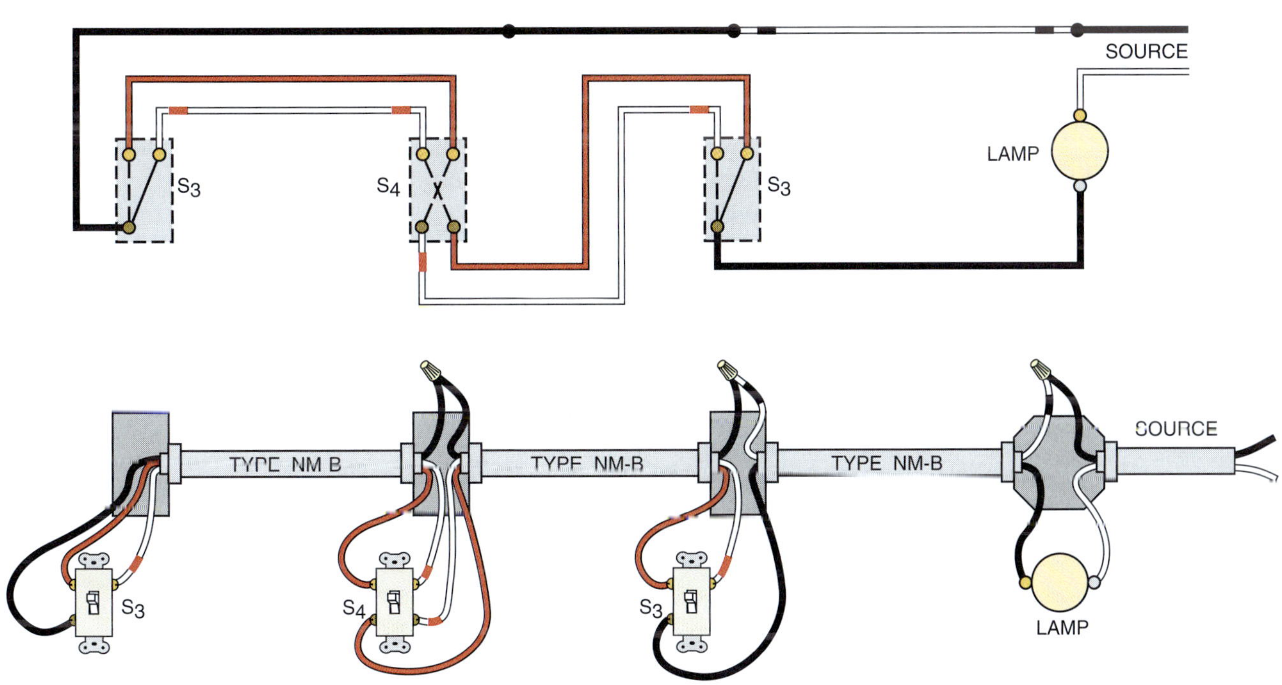

Figure 5-23 Circuit with switch control at three locations—feed at lamp.

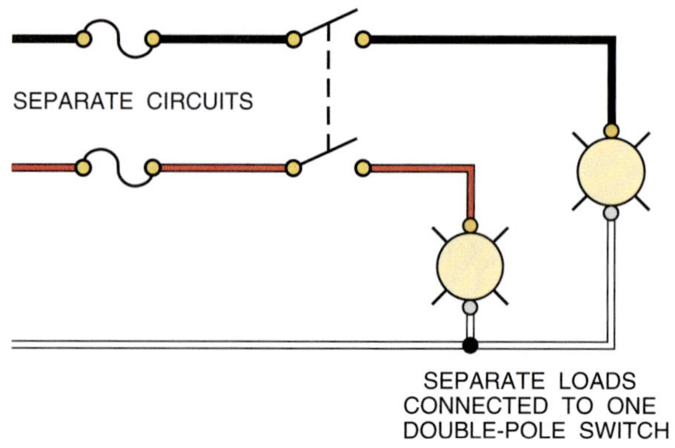

Figure 5-24 Application of a double-pole switch.

box where the lamp is located. The white conductor is required to be reidentified at every point where it is used as an ungrounded "hot" conductor, *200.7(C)(2)*.

Double-Pole Switches. Double-pole switches are not common in residential work. They can be used when two separate circuits must be controlled with one switch, as in Figure 5-24. They are also used to control 240-volt loads, such as electric heat, motors, electric clothes dryers, and similar 240-volt loads, as in Figure 5-25. When line-voltage thermostats for electric heat are double-pole, they switch both ungrounded "hot" conductors and are marked with "ON" and "OFF" positions.

Switches with Pilot Lights. There are instances when a pilot light is desired at the switch location. Figure 5-26 shows a "locator" type of switch where the lamp in the toggle glows when the switch is in the "OFF" position. *This is sometimes referred to as a "glow" or "lit-handle" switch.* A resistor inside the switch is connected in series with the pilot light. Be careful when working on this type of switch because when the switch is in the "OFF" position, the load and the pilot light are actually connected in "series." Even though these switches are marked with an "OFF" position, they are not truly off. The circuit's path through the switch and connected load is still complete. There is a voltage drop (almost full open circuit voltage) across the pilot light/resistor and an infinitesimal voltage drop across the connected load. Although there is not enough voltage at the light to light it, there may be enough voltage and current present to cause a person to "flinch," which might result in the person jerking back and falling off a ladder.

Figure 5-27 shows a true pilot light that is "on" when the light is on.

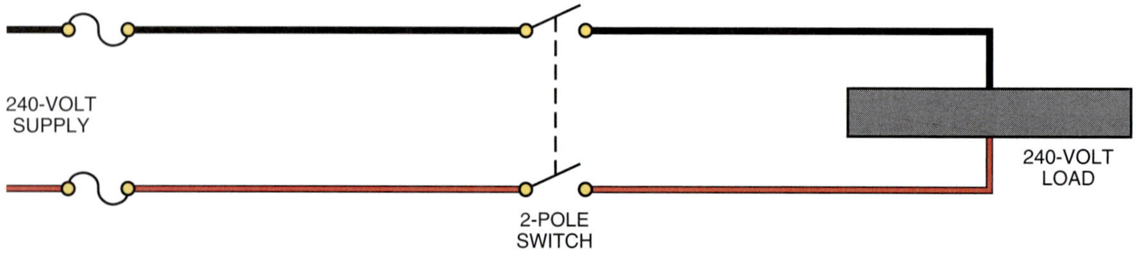

Figure 5-25 Double-pole (2-pole) disconnect switch.

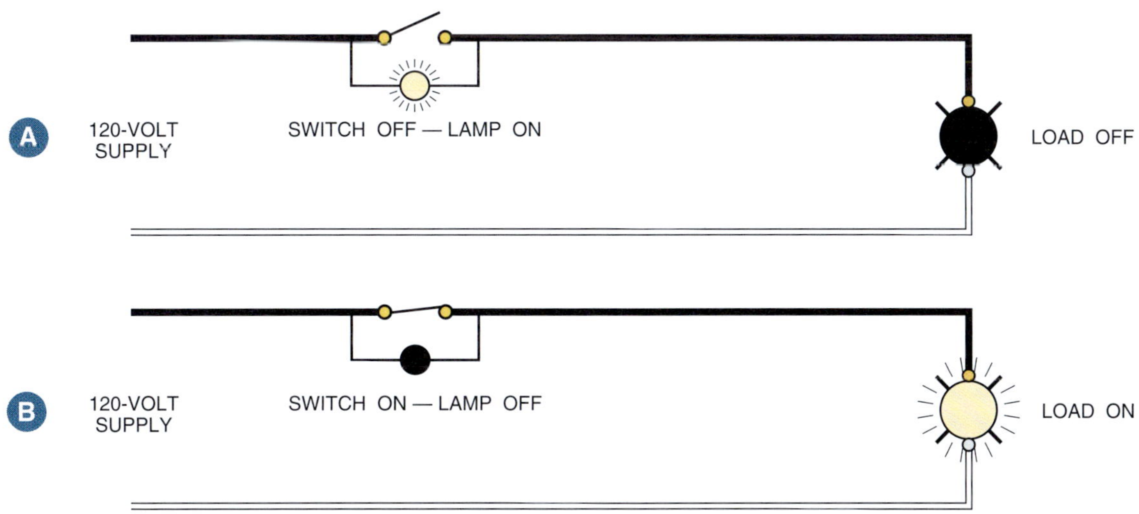

Figure 5-26 In (A) the switch is in the "OFF" position. The neon lamp in the handle of the switch glows and the load is off. This is a series circuit. The neon lamp has extremely high resistance. In a series circuit voltage divides proportionately to the resistance. Therefore, the neon lamp "sees" line voltage (120 volts) for all practical purposes and the load "sees" zero voltage. The neon lamp glows.

In (B) the switch is in the "ON" position. The neon lamp is shunted out and therefore has zero voltage across it. Thus, the neon lamp does not glow. Full voltage is supplied to the load. This type of switch might be referred to as a *locator* because it glows when the load is off and does not glow when the load is on.

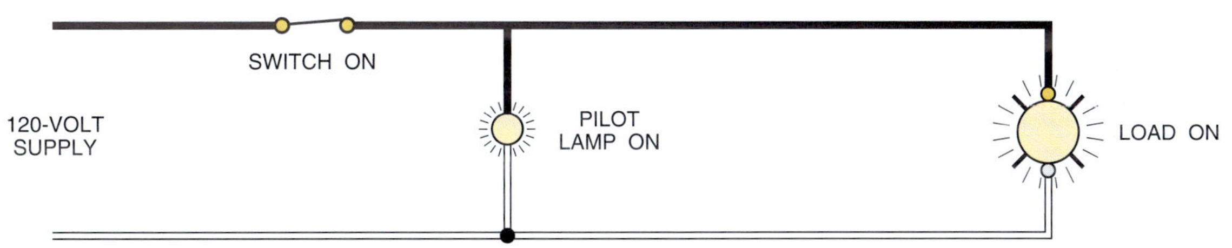

Figure 5-27 A true pilot light. The pilot lamp is an integral part of the switch. When the load is turned on, the pilot light is also on. When the load is turned off, the pilot light is also off. This switch has three terminals because it requires a grounded circuit conductor.

COMBINATION WIRING DEVICES

In the space of one standard wiring device, it is possible to install combination wiring devices. Figure 5-28A shows three types of combination wiring devices. Other combinations are available. Figure 5-28B shows an interchangeable line of wiring devices, assembled on the metal yoke by the electrician. Switches, receptacles, and neon and incandescent pilot lights are available. Combination wiring devices offer a neater appearance as opposed to having two-gang or three-gang faceplates at a given location. Another common use is where wall space is limited, such as between a door casing and a window casing where there is not enough space for a multigang faceplate. Be sure the wall box has plenty of room for the number of cable clamps, wiring devices, and conductors.

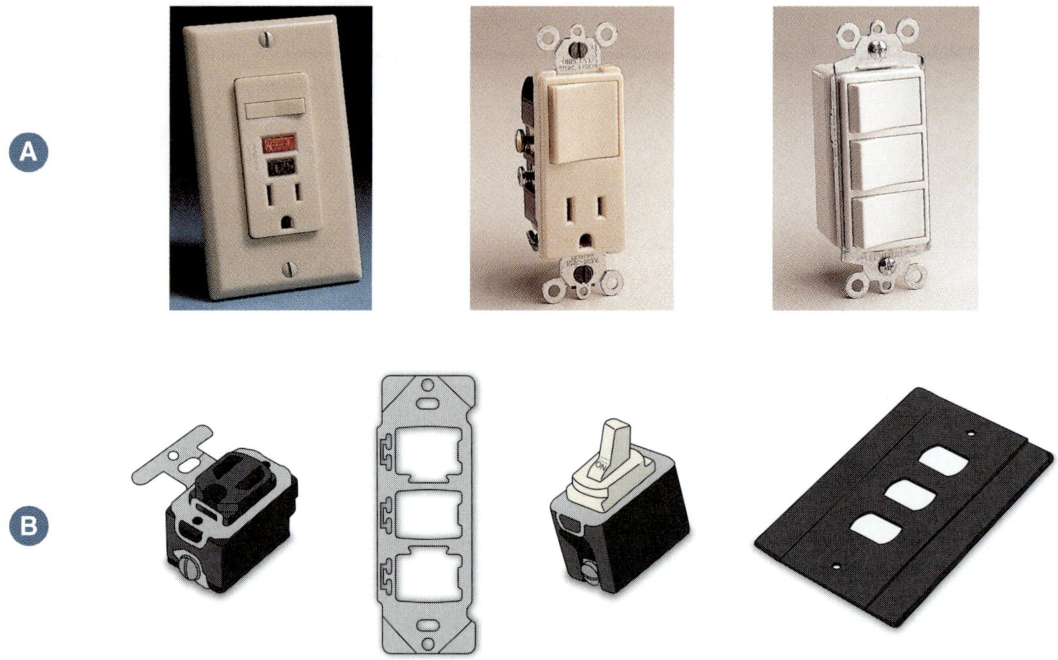

Figure 5-28 Combination wiring devices. Many combinations are available on a single yoke: slider, rocker, toggle, three-way plus two single poles, four single-pole switches, switches and pilot lights, switches and receptacles. ***Photos courtesy of*** **Leviton Manufacturing Co., Inc.**

Miscellaneous Connections. Figure 5-29 and Figure 5-30 are diagrams that somewhat combine parts of the previous wiring diagrams. These connections become rather complicated using cable because of the limitation on the available insulation colors. These connections are more suited to raceway wiring.

Do You Need the Grounded Circuit Conductor at the Switch? Maybe yes—maybe no.

Conventional switches operate on a mechanical principle and are simply connected "in series" with the load. The contacts of the switch close (on) and open (off). This type of switch does not require a grounded circuit conductor to be connected to the switch. See *404.2(A), Exception.*

Electronic control devices such as dimmers, motion sensors, occupational sensors, photoelectric devices, timers, and fan speed controls need a small voltage drop across them to operate. This type of switch (control) needs to have both the grounded and ungrounded circuit conductors connected to it.

►Recently introduced to the marketplace are listed wiring devices such as occupancy sensors that have internal electronic circuitry that allow a maximum of 0.5 milliampere (mA) "leakage" to ground. This tiny amount of "leakage" current is enough to powerup the electronic circuitry in the device, yet not pose a shock hazard. This is referred to as low-level standby current. The maximum leakage current of 0.5 mA is the same value of leakage current permitted for electric appliances. This type of device does not need the grounded circuit conductor to work.◄

Check the manufacturer's wiring diagram to determine if the grounded circuit conductor is required at the switch location. The next topic, "Does OFF Really Mean OFF?," discusses this in greater detail. See Figure 5-31.

Illuminated toggle switches, rocker switches, and illuminated faceplates do not require the grounded circuit conductor. These are merely "in series" with the load. Their operation is: load "ON," pilot lamp "OFF" or load "OFF," pilot lamp "ON." See Figure 5-26.

True pilot lights require the grounded circuit conductor. Their operation is: load "ON," pilot lamp "ON" or load "OFF," pilot lamp "OFF." See Figure 5-27.

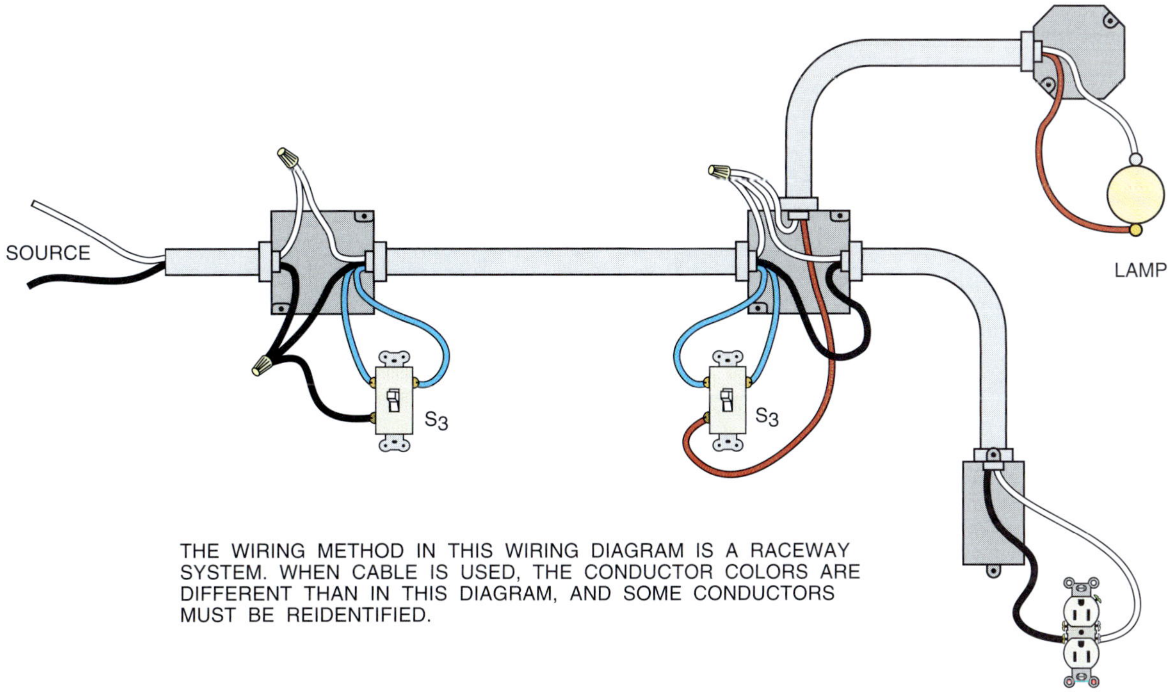

Figure 5-29 A lighting outlet controlled by two three-way switches. The receptacle is "live" at all times. The wiring method is a raceway. When cable is used, the conductor colors are different from those in this wiring diagram, and some conductors must be reidentified. A typical example of this might be between a house and a detached garage or other outbuilding.

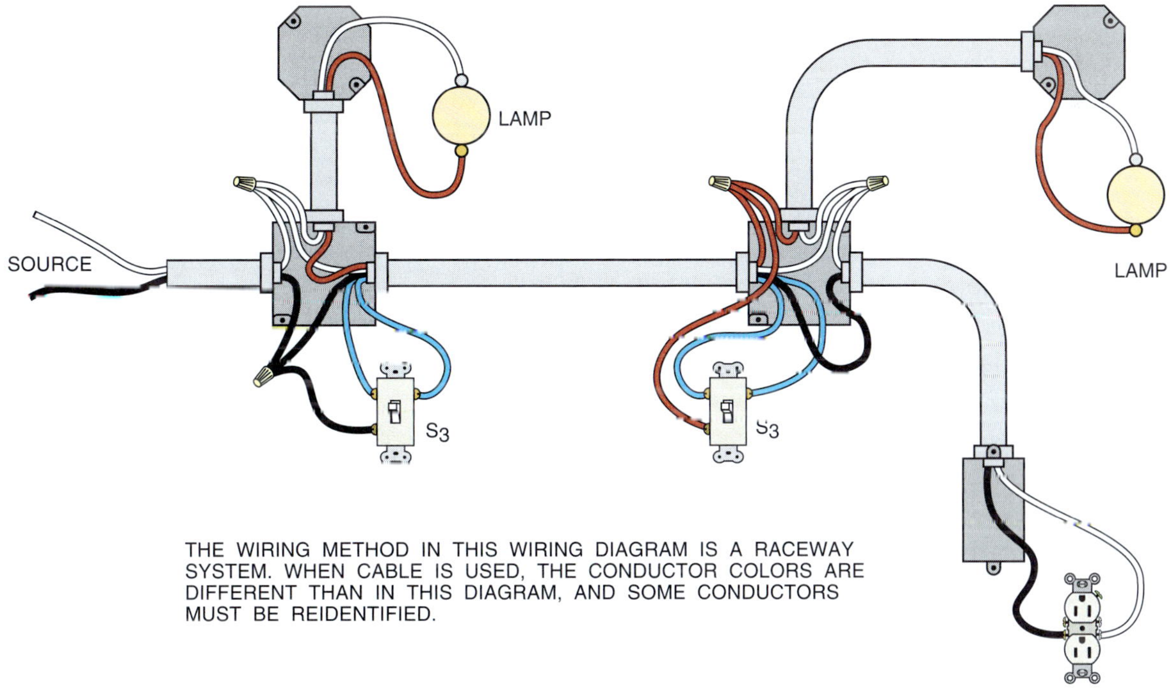

Figure 5-30 Two lighting outlets controlled by two three-way switches. The receptacle is "live" at all times. An example of this hookup might be between a house and a detached garage or other outbuilding, where one lighting outlet is on the house and the other lighting outlet is on or in the garage or outbuilding.

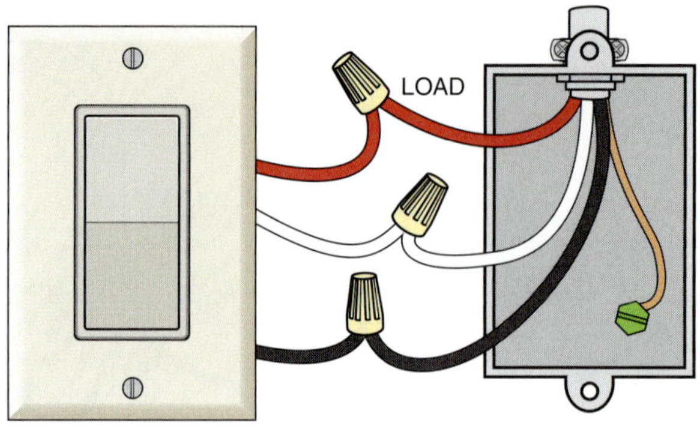

Figure 5-31 An X-10 switch. To operate properly, it requires the presence of the grounded circuit conductor. *Never* connect the white wire on the switch to an equipment grounding conductor in the box. This is hazardous and is a violation of *250.6(A)* and *250.24(A)(5)*.

What to do? Since this Catch-22 is always a concern, many electricians anticipate using electronic switching devices and always run the full branch circuit (grounded and ungrounded conductors) first to the switch location, then up to the lighting outlet as shown in Figure 5-13 and Figure 5-15. This also eliminates the need to reidentify a white conductor when used as a "hot" switch leg. This is a matter of choice. Not a bad idea!

Proposals to change the *NEC*® have been made to require that a branch-circuit grounded conductor be present at every switch location. To date, these proposals have been rejected by the Code-Making Panel (CMP) as being unrealistic because most switching locations do not need the grounded circuit conductor; what to do with the conductor when it is not used; and the possible need for a larger wall box because of the extra conductor.

Never use the equipment grounding conductor as a substitute for the circuit's grounded conductor. This could prove to be deadly.

As always, read the manufacturers' instructions.

Does "OFF" Really Mean "OFF?"

The answer is YES. When a switching device has a marked "OFF" position, it must completely disconnect the ungrounded conductor(s) to the load it serves when turned to the "OFF" position. UL Standards require this. Also see *404.15(B)*.

Electronic controls, such as some motion (occupancy) sensors, some dimmers, some fan speed controls, and X-10 transmitting and receiving devices (see Chapter 31), require a small voltage drop across the device to operate. When these devices are turned to what appears to be the "OFF" mode, there is still an ever-so-slight amount of voltage present at the load. The device is really not in a full "OFF" position. This can be hazardous to someone working on a luminaire, for example, thinking it is totally "OFF."

You will probably find instructions furnished with an electronic switch (control) that the load must be a minimum of "X" watts. This is to provide the proper voltage drop across the switch (control).

Compact fluorescent lamps will not operate on an electronic motion sensor or electronic timer because until voltage is applied to the lamp, there is no current draw. A fluorescent lamp is basically an open circuit until energized. The lamp cannot be energized because there will be no voltage across the electronic control to operate the electronic control.

Refer to Chapter 6 for additional information relating to the effects of an electrical shock.

Bonding and Grounding at Receptacles and Switches

A metal box is considered to be adequately grounded when the wiring method is armored cable, nonmetallic-sheathed cable with ground, or a metal raceway such as EMT, *250.118*. A separate equipment grounding conductor can also provide the required grounding, *250.134(B)*. Equipment grounding conductors may be bare or green.

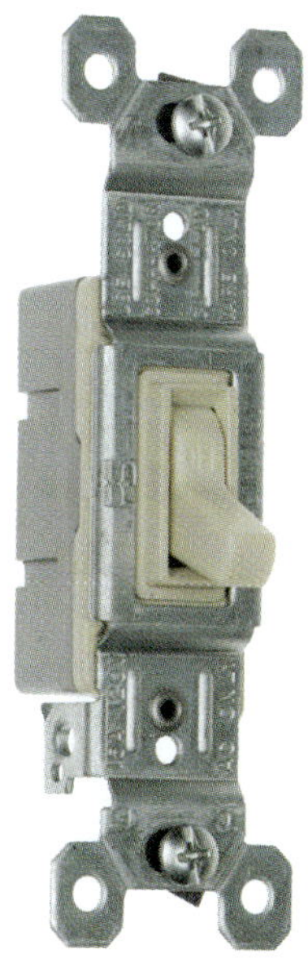

Figure 5-32 Single-pole toggle switch. Note that this switch has a terminal for the connection of an equipment ground conductor. Thus, when a metal faceplate is installed, it will be grounded. See *404.9(A)* and *(B)*. *Courtesy of* Pass & Seymour.

Figure 5-32 illustrates a switch that has an equipment grounding conductor terminal. Using a switch of this type provides an easy means for providing the required grounding of a metal faceplate when using nonmetallic boxes.

Grounding and bonding of the equipment grounding conductor to a metal box, switch, or receptacle is important. Figure 5-33, Figure 5-34, and Figure 5-35 show how an equipment grounding conductor of a nonmetallic-sheathed cable can be attached to a metal box and to the equipment grounding screw of a receptacle. Most metal boxes have a No. 10-32 tapped hole for securing a green hexagon-shaped equipment grounding screw.

Other than for special "isolated ground" receptacles, the metal yoke of a receptacle is integrally bonded to the equipment grounding terminal of the receptacle.

Figure 5-3 and Figure 5-4 show a receptacle that has a special listed "self-grounding" feature for the No. 6-32 mounting screws that results in effective grounding of the metal yoke and equipment grounding terminal without the use of a separate equipment grounding conductor.

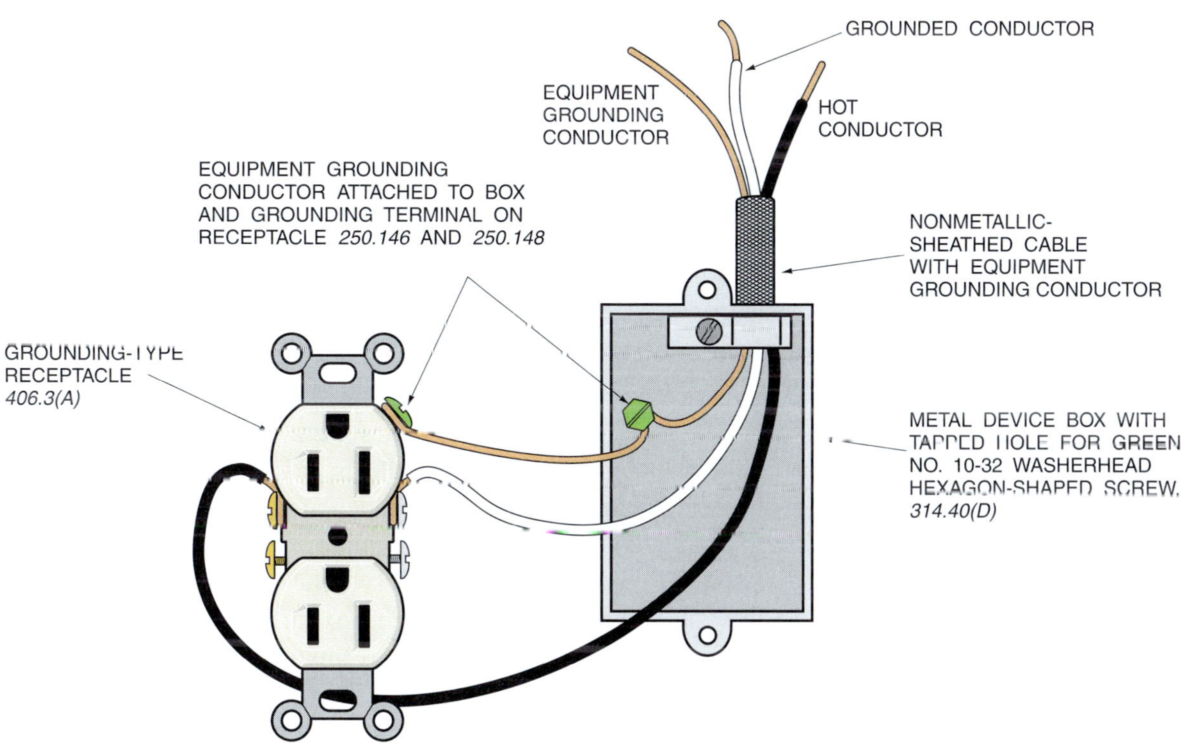

Figure 5-33 Connections for grounding-type receptacles.

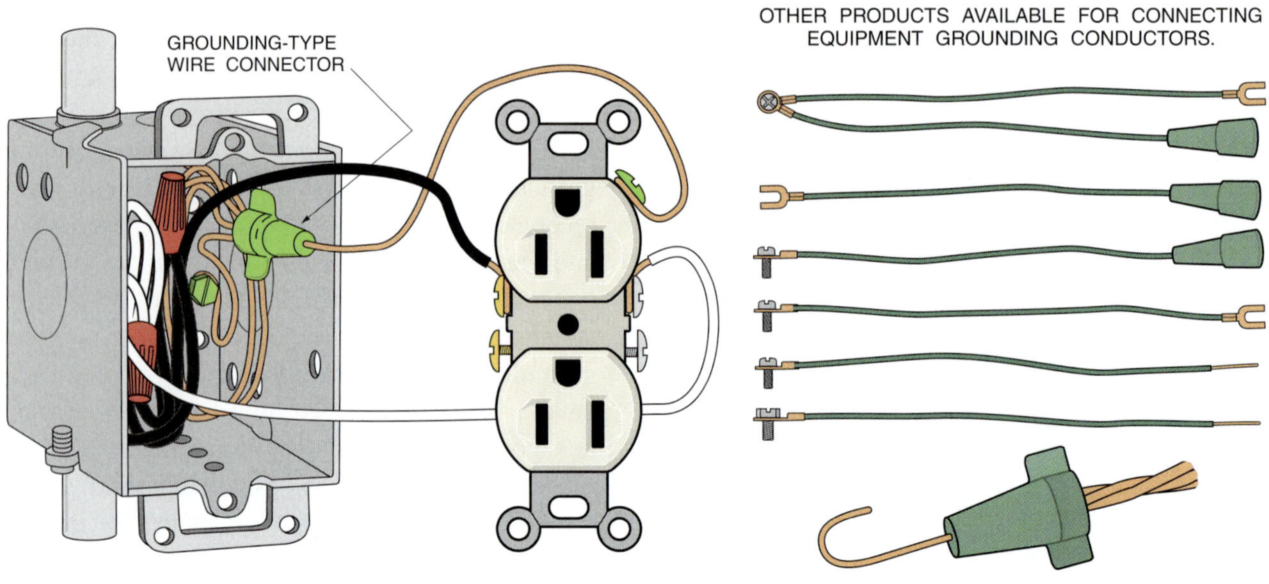

Figure 5-34 One method of connecting the grounding conductor using a special grounding-type wire connector. See *250.146* and *250.148*.

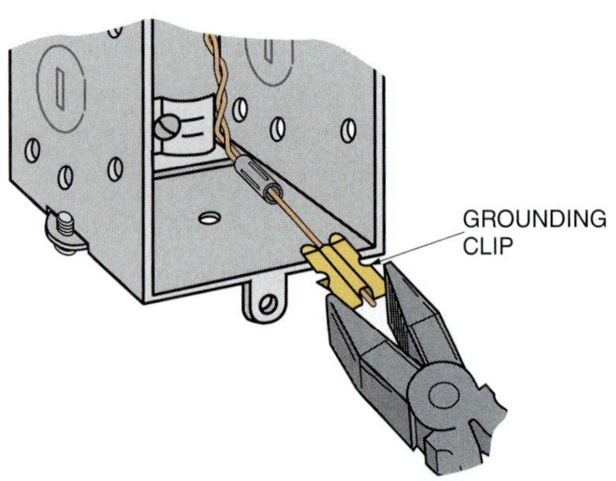

Figure 5-35 Method of attaching grounding clip to switch (device) box. See *250.146* and *250.148*.

To ensure the continuity of the equipment grounding conductor path, *250.148* requires that where more than one equipment grounding conductor enters a box, they shall be spliced with devices "suitable for the use." Splices shall not depend on solder. The splicing must be done so that if a receptacle or other wiring device is removed, the continuity of the equipment grounding path shall not be interrupted. This is clearly shown in Figure 5-34. Splicing must be done in accordance with *110.14(B)*.

Grounding Metal Faceplates and Switches

Assuming that an equipment grounding conductor has been carried to and properly connected at all metallic and nonmetallic boxes, we now need to be concerned with carrying that equipment grounding means to receptacles, switches, and metal faceplates.

Metal faceplates for receptacles shall be grounded, *406.5(B)*. This is accomplished through the No. 6-32 screw that secures the faceplate to the metal yoke on the receptacle.

A similar requirement for the grounding of metal faceplates is found in *314.25(A)*.

Snap switches and dimmer switches must provide a means to ground metal faceplates, *404.9(B)*. This is a requirement whether metallic or nonmetallic face plates are installed. The actual grounding of the faceplate is through the No. 6-32 screws that secure the faceplate to the metal yoke on the switch.

In *UL Standard 20*, we find the requirement that flush-type switches intended for mounting in a flush-device box shall provide a grounding means. In most cases this is a green hexagon-shaped screw connected to the metal yoke of the switch. This can be seen on the switches illustrated in Figure 5-8, Figure 5-17, and Figure 5-32. The grounding means could also be a special self-grounding clip on the metal yoke, as illustrated in Figure 5-3 and Figure

5-4, a bare copper wire, a copper wire with green insulation, or a copper wire with green insulation having one or more yellow stripes.

Connecting a bare equipment grounding conductor to the equipment grounding terminal on a switch complies with *406.5(B)* for the grounding of a metal faceplate. Where there are multiple switches, there is no need to attach an equipment grounding conductor on all of the switches. One connection is enough.

If the equipment grounding path is accomplished through a self-grounding clip on the metal yoke of a switch or receptacle, you do not have to connect an equipment grounding conductor to the green hexagon-shaped grounding screw on the switch or receptacle.

Many wiring devices have small pieces of cardboard holding the No. 6-32 mounting screws from falling out. Remove at least one of these small pieces of cardboard when direct metal-to-metal contact between the yoke of the wiring device and the box is needed, *250.146(A)*. An example of this would be a receptacle secured to a handy box. If there is no metal-to-metal contact, then an equipment grounding conductor must be connected to the grounding terminal on the wiring device or the wiring device must have the special self-grounding clips discussed above. See Figure 5-33 and Figure 5-34.

For surface-mounted boxes of the type shown in Figure 18-8 and Figure 18-9, where cover-mounted receptacles are used, the metal-to-metal requirement mentioned earlier is not acceptable. Some other "listed" means for providing satisfactory ground continuity must be used, *250.146(A)*. This section makes it clear that there must be direct metal to metal contact between the metal box and the device yoke to be considered an acceptacle means of grounding the receptacle equipment grounding terminal and the metal cover

To make sure that there is direct metal-to-metal contact between the metal yoke of a receptacle and a surface-mounted metal box, *250.146(A)* accepts the automatic self-grounding device on the yoke of the receptacle, or by removing at least one of the insulating washers. Automatic self-grounding devices on the yoke of a receptacle are clearly shown in Figure 5-3, Figure 5-4, and Figure 5-5.

In general, where no effective grounding means exists in the switch box, it is acceptable to replace a snap switch with another snap switch that does not have a provision for grounding.

However, in existing installations where no effective grounding means is present, and where the snap switch is located within reach of the earth, a conductive floor (i.e., concrete, tile), or other conductive surfaces (i.e., metal pipes, metal ducts), use nonmetallic faceplaces, or provide GFCI protection for the wiring to that particular snap switch. See *404.9(B), Exception*.

CAUTION: *Never* make connections (jumpering) between the different colored terminals on receptacles. Lives have been lost because of this!

- **Jumpering between the brass and silver terminals is a violation of *200.10* and *200.11*.**
- **Jumpering between the silver and green hexagon-shaped terminals is a violation of *250.24(A)(5)* and *250.142(B)*.**
- **Jumpering between the brass and green hexagon-shaped terminals is a violation of *250.126*.**

COMMON *CODE* VIOLATION— MAKING "TAPS"

As defined in *240.2*, a "tap" is a conductor that has overcurrent protection ahead of its point of supply that exceeds the ampacity of the conductor. In general, conductors shall be protected at their ampacities per *310.15*. Tap conductors are excluded from the basic rule, and this is found in *240.4(E)*. Some examples of "taps" are small luminaire wires. In some cases, taps can be cost-effective for hooking up electric ranges, counter-mounted cooktops, and wall-mounted ovens. This is discussed in Chapter 20.

Table 5-2 shows the maximum overcurrent protection for small conductors as permitted by *240.4(D)*.

Figure 5-36 illustrates a *Code* violation. The switch leg (loop) conductors are part of the branch-circuit wiring and are not to be considered a "tap."

CONDUCTOR SIZE	MAXIMUM OVERCURRENT PROTECTION
14 AWG copper	15 amperes
12 AWG copper	20 amperes
10 AWG copper	30 amperes

Table 5-2

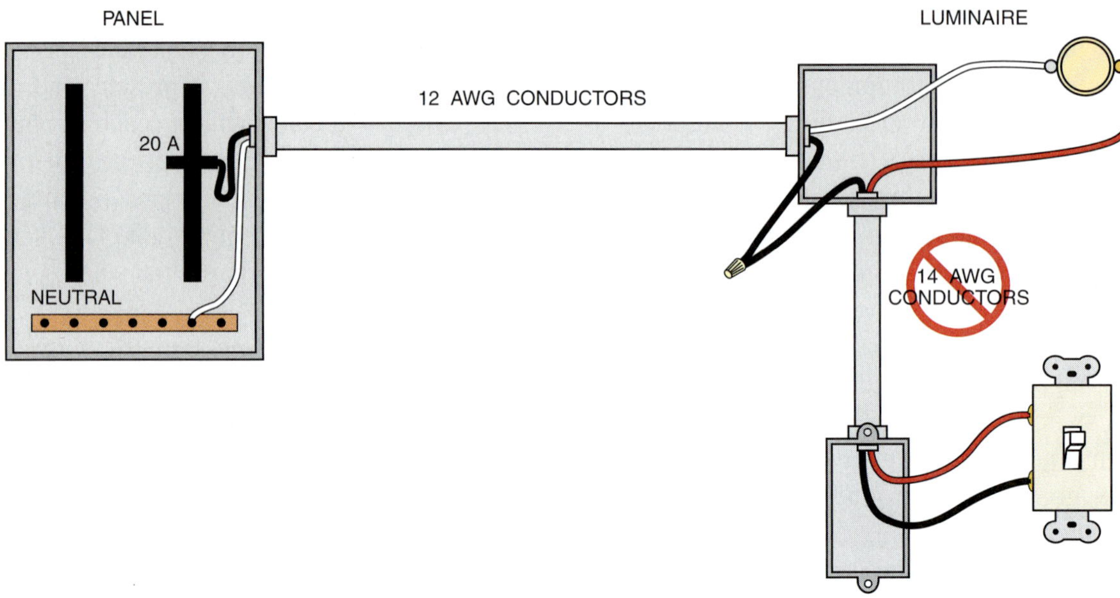

Figure 5-36 ***Violation:*** **The electrician has run a 20-ampere branch circuit consisting of 12 AWG conductors to the outlet box where a luminaire will be installed. 14 AWG conductors are run as the switch legs between the lighting outlet and the switch. The switch legs are part of the branch circuit and must have an ampacity equal to that of the branch-circuit ampere rating, 20 amperes. Switch legs are not "taps." For the same reasons, it is a *Code* violation to use short "pigtails" of 14 AWG wire to connect receptacles to the 12 AWG conductors fed from a 20-ampere branch circuit.**

Although the connected load may be well within the ampacity of the switch leg, the switch leg must also be capable of handling short circuits and ground faults. The switch leg shown in Figure 5-36 must be the same size as the branch-circuit conductors, which are 12 AWG 20-ampere conductors protected by a 20-ampere circuit breaker.

Connecting Receptacles to 20-Ampere Branch Circuits

Another very common *Code* violation is using short 14 AWG pigtails to connect receptacles to 20-ampere small-appliance branch-circuit conductors in a kitchen or dining room. These short pigtails must be rated 20 amperes because they are an *extension* of the 20-ampere branch-circuit wiring . . . they are not "taps." Figure 5-5 illustrates this type of connection.

Consider Using Larger Size Conductors for Home Runs

To minimize voltage drop, sometimes 12 AWG conductors are used for long "home runs" (50 ft or longer) even though the branch-circuit overcurrent device is rated 15 amperes. A "home run" is the branch-circuit wiring from the panel to the first outlet or junction box in that circuit. This is permitted by *210.3*, which states, *where conductors of higher ampacity are used for any reason, the ampere rating or setting of the specified overcurrent device shall determine the circuit rating.** In this case, 14 AWG conductors are permitted for the switch legs. But this leads to confusion later when someone removes the cover from the panel and wonders why 12 AWG branch-circuit conductors are connected to 15-ampere circuit breakers. For house wiring, it is best to use the same size conductor throughout a given branch circuit.

Specifications for commercial and industrial installations oftentimes will call for a "home run" of 50 ft or more to be 10 AWG conductors, even though the branch-circuit rating is 20 amperes.

Table 210.24 is a summary of branch-circuit requirements. This table lists branch-circuit ratings, branch-circuit conductor sizes, tap conductor sizes, overcurrent protection, outlet (lampholder and receptacle) ratings, maximum loads, and permissible loads.

TIMERS

Timers are unique in that they provide automatic control of electrical loads. Timers are also referred to as time clocks.

Timers are used where a load is to be controlled for specific "ON/OFF" times of the day or night. The capabilities of timers are endless.

Figure 5-37 shows two types of spring-loaded timers that are connected in series with the load—the same as a standard wall switch. A typical application is in a bathroom for the control of an exhaust fan or an electric heater. These timers install in a standard single-gang device box. Because they take up quite a bit of space, make sure the wall box is large enough to meet the box-fill requirements of *314.16*.

Figure 5-38 is a 24-hour time clock commonly used to control security lighting, decorative lighting, or energy management. This particular time clock has four adjustable and removable "pins" that control two "ON" and two "OFF" operations (additional "pins" can be added). There is an "override" switch for manual control.

Figure 5-39 is an electronic 24-hour, 7-day time clock. It can be programmed to skip certain days, and up to sixteen events can be programmed. There is an "override" switch for manual control.

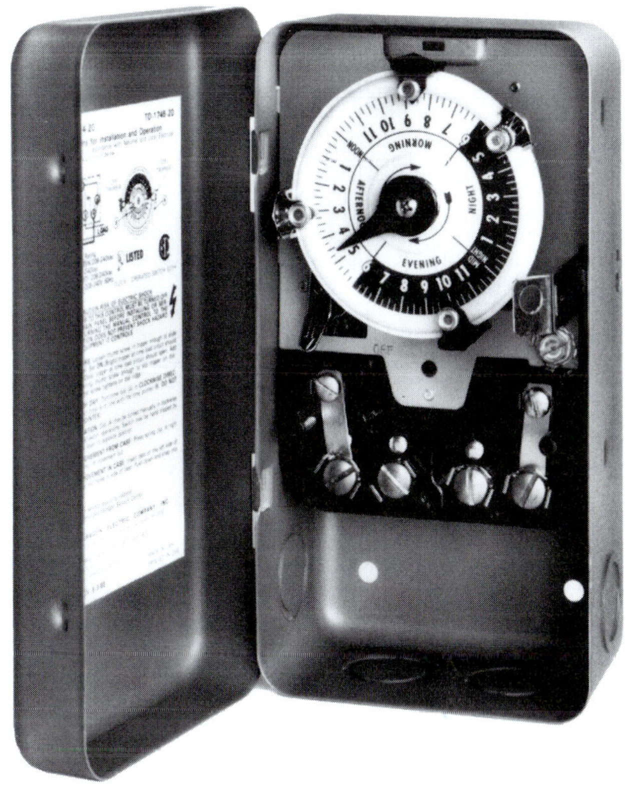

Figure 5-38 A 24-hour time clock. *Courtesy of* Invensys Climate Control.

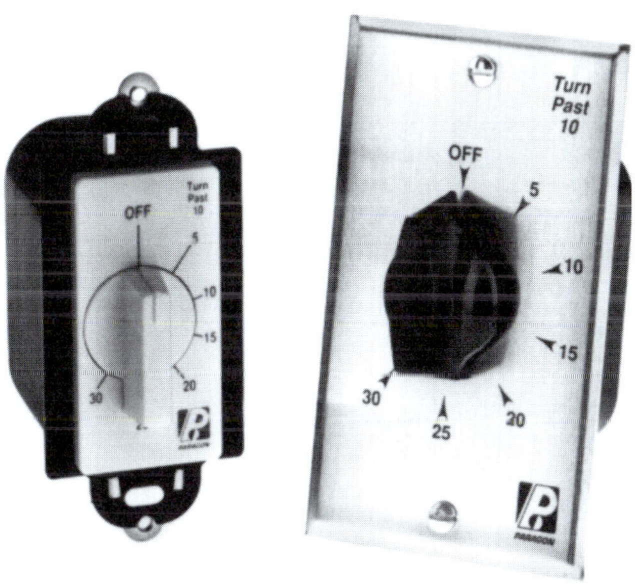

Figure 5-37 Spring-loaded timers. *Courtesy of* Invensys Climate Control.

Figure 5-39 An electronic time clock. *Courtesy of* Invensys Climate Control.

REVIEW

Note: Refer to the *Code* or the plans where necessary.

1. The identified grounded circuit conductor must be ______________ or ______________ in color.
2. Explain how lighting switches are rated. ______________
3. A T-rated switch may be used to its ______________ current capacity when controlling an incandescent lighting load.
4. What switch type and rating is required to control five 300-watt tungsten filament lamps on a 120-volt circuit? Show calculations. ______________
5. List four types of lighting switches.
   a. ______________ c. ______________
   b. ______________ d. ______________
6. To control a lighting load from one control point, what type of switch would be used? ______________
7. Single-pole switches are always connected to the ______________ wire.
8. Complete the connections in the following arrangement so that both ceiling light outlets are controlled from the single-pole switch. Assume the installation is in cable.

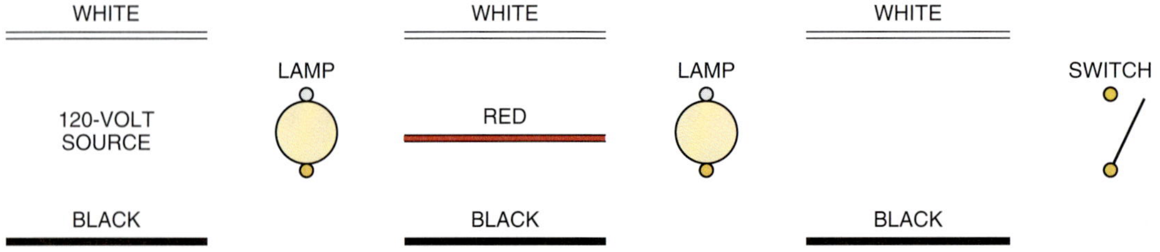

9. Complete the connections for the diagram. Installation is cable.

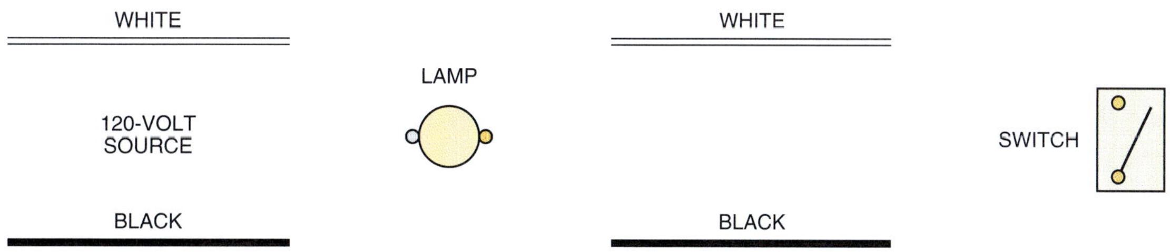

10. A three-way switch may be compared to a ______________________________ switch.

11. What type of switch is installed to control a luminaire from two different control points? How many switches are needed and what type are they? ________________
____

12. Complete the connections in the following arrangement so that the lamp may be controlled from either three-way switch.

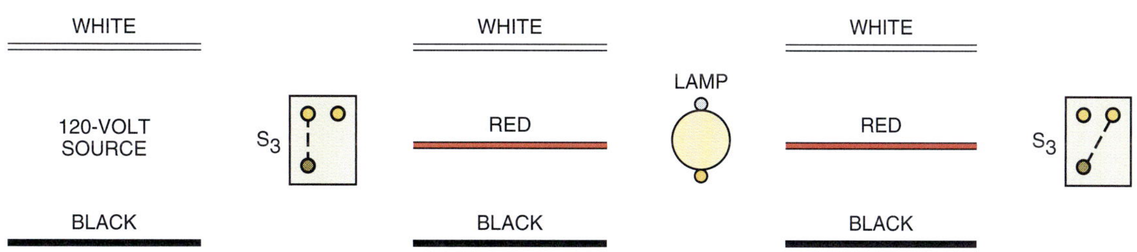

13. When connecting four-way switches, care must be taken to connect the "travelers" to the ______________________________ terminals.

14. Show the connections for a ceiling outlet that is to be controlled from any one of three switch locations. The 120-volt feed is at the light. Use color pens or pencils. Assume the installation is in cable.

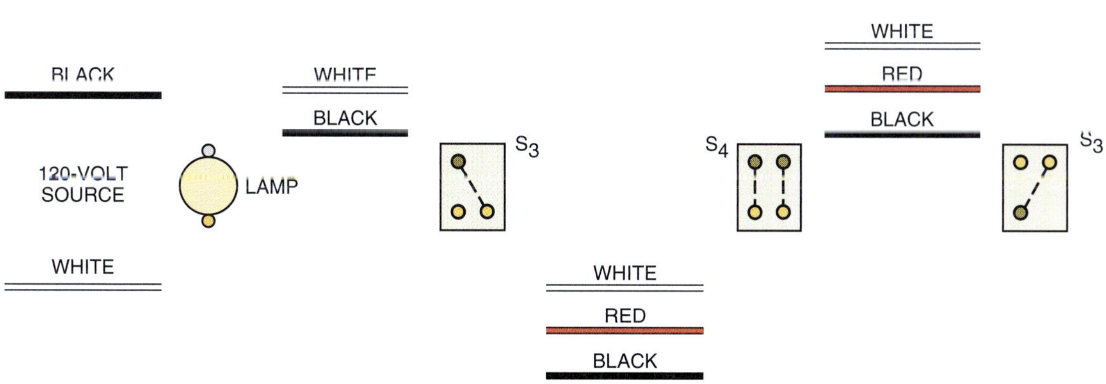

15. Match the following switch types with the correct number of terminals for each.

Three-way switch	Two terminals
Single-pole switch	Four terminals
Four-way switch	Three terminals

16. When connecting single-pole, three-way, and four-way switches, they must be wired so that all switching is done in the ____________________ circuit conductor.

17. What section of the *Code* emphasizes the fact that all circuiting must be done so as to avoid the damaging effects of induction heating? ____________________

18. If you had to install an underground 3-wire feeder to a remote building using three individual conductors, which of the following installations "meets Code"? Circle the correct installation.

19. Is it always necessary to attach the bare equipment grounding conductor of a nonmetallic-sheathed cable to the green hexagon-shaped grounding screw on a receptacle? Explain.

____

20. List the methods by which an equipment grounding conductor is connected to a device box.

____

21. When two nonmetallic-sheathed cables (Romex) enter a box, is it permitted to bring both of the bare equipment grounding conductors directly to the grounding terminal of a receptacle, using the terminal as a splice point? ____________________

22. This installation is in electrical metallic tubing. Receptacle outlet "B" is only a few feet from switch "C." Receptacle outlet "A" is only a few feet from switch "D." The electrician saved a considerable amount of wire by picking up the supply (feed) for switch "C" from receptacle "B," and the switch leg (return) from switch "D." What is wrong with this installation?

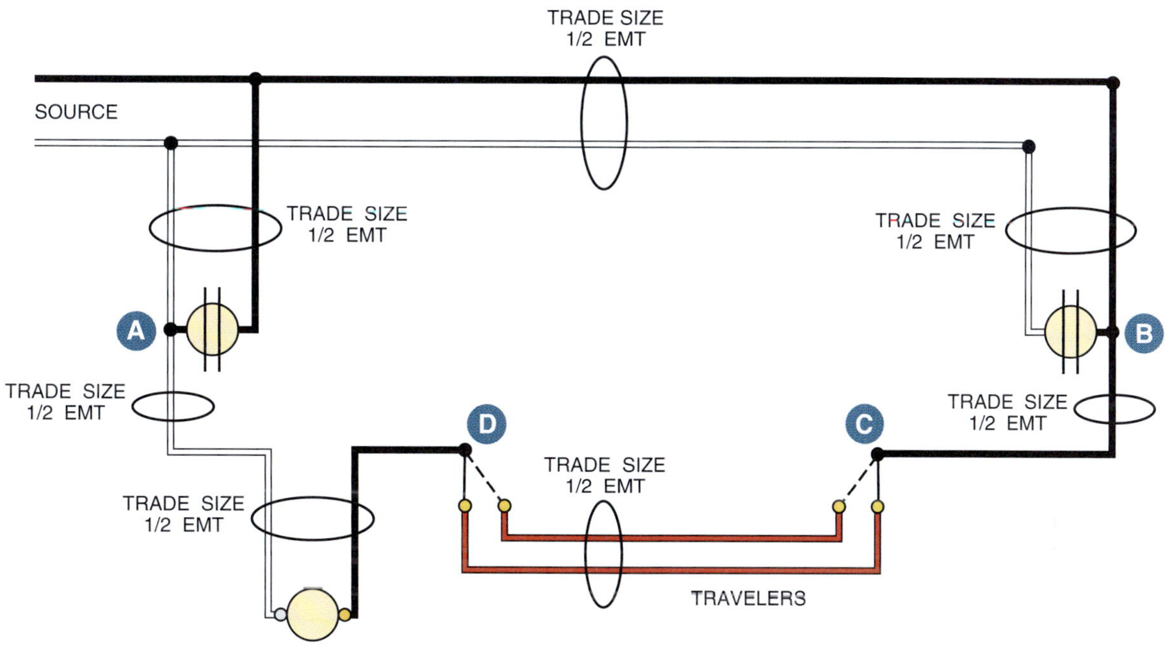

____

____

____

23. Define an *equipment grounding conductor*. ____

____

____

____

24. When metal toggle switchplates are used with nonmetallic boxes, the faceplate must be grounded according to *404.9(B)*. How is this accomplished?

____

25. Does the *Code* permit the ampacity of switch legs to be less than the ampere rating of the branch circuit? ____

26. Does the *Code* permit connecting receptacles to a 20-ampere branch circuit using short lengths of 14 AWG conductors as the "pigtail" between the receptacle terminals and the 12 AWG branch-circuit conductors? ____

27. Do receptacles that have back-wired "push-in" terminals accept 12 AWG conductors? Give a brief explanation for your answer. ____

____

____

____

CHAPTER 6

Ground-Fault Circuit Interrupters, Arc-Fault Circuit Interrupters, Transient Voltage Surge Suppressors, Immersion Detection Circuit Interrupters, and Appliance Leakage Current Interrupters

OBJECTIVES

After studying this chapter, you should be able to

- **understand how GFCIs, AFCIs, IDCIs, and ALCIs operate.**
- **understand *NEC*® requirements of where and how GFCIs and AFCIs are to be installed and connected.**
- **understand why AFCIs and GFCIs should not be used on a shared neutral branch circuit unless it is listed as such.**
- **understand the important *NEC*® requirements for replacing existing receptacles.**
- **know the rules for providing GFCI protection on construction sites.**
- **understand the basics of transient voltage surge suppressors.**

ELECTRICAL SHOCK HAZARDS

There can be no compromise where human life is involved!

Many injuries have occurred and many lives have been lost because of electrical shock. Coming in contact with live wires or with an appliance or other equipment that is "hot" spells danger. Problems arise in equipment when there is a breakdown of insulation because of wear and tear, defective construction, or misuse of the equipment. Insulation failure can result when the "hot" ungrounded conductor in the appliance comes in contact with the metal frame of the appliance. If the equipment is not properly grounded, the potential for an electrical shock is present.

The shock hazard exists whenever the user can touch both the defective equipment and grounded surfaces such as water pipes, stainless steel sinks, metal faucets, grounded metal luminaires, earth, concrete in contact with the earth, or water.

A severe shock can cause considerably more damage to the human body than is visible. A person may suffer internal hemorrhages, destruction of tissues, nerves, and muscles. Further injury can result from a fall, cuts, burns, or broken bones.

The effect of an electric current passing through

a human body varies, depending upon circuit characteristics (i.e., current, frequency [60 Hz is the worst], voltage, body contact resistance [open wounds are extremely hazardous as compared to a callused hand]), internal body resistance, the path of current, duration of contact, and environmental conditions (e.g., humidity).

Experts generally agree on values of 800 to 1000 ohms as typical body and contact resistance, but the resistance can vary from a few hundred ohms to many thousand ohms. Let's see how important the role of resistance is for a person coming in contact with a 120-volt circuit.

Take a dry hand, for example:

$$I = \frac{E}{R} = \frac{120 \text{ volts}}{100{,}000 \text{ ohms}} = \begin{array}{l}0.0012 \text{ ampere} \\ (1.2 \text{ milliamperes})\end{array}$$

This would probably be a little tingle.

Now take a wet hand and standing barefoot on the ground:

$$I = \frac{E}{R} = \frac{120 \text{ volts}}{1{,}000 \text{ ohms}} = \begin{array}{l}0.12 \text{ ampere} \\ (120 \text{ milliamperes})\end{array}$$

This would probably be fatal.

EFFECT OF ELECTRIC SHOCK	Current in milliamperes @ 60 hertz	
	Men	Women
• cannot be felt	0.4	0.3
• a little tingling—mild sensation	1.1	0.7
• shock—not painful—can still let go	1.8	1.2
• shock—painful—can still let go	9.0	6.0
• shock—painful—just about to point where you can't let go—called "threshold"—you may be thrown clear	16.0	10.5
• shock—painful—severe—can't let go—muscles immobilize—breathing stops	23.0	15.0
• ventricular fibrillation (usually fatal) length of time . . . 0.03 sec. length of time . . . 3.0 sec.	 1000 100	 1000 100

Table 6-1

Figure 6-1 shows a time/current curve that indicates the amount of current that a normal, healthy adult can stand for a certain time. Table 6-1 shows

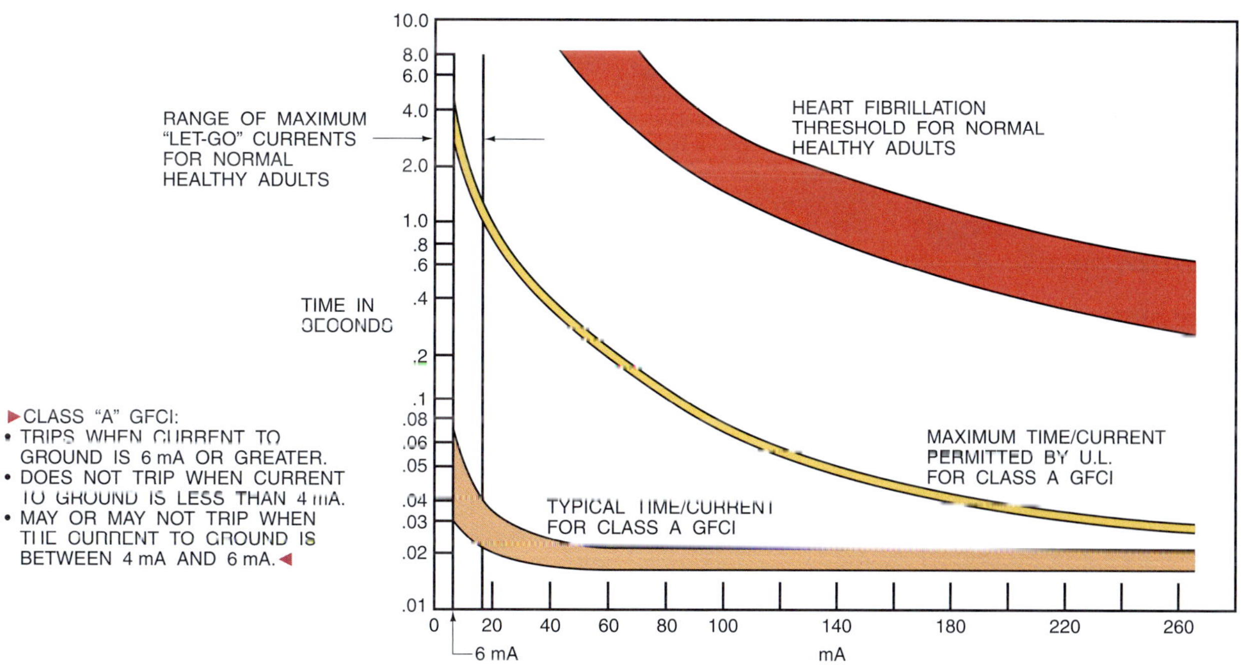

Figure 6-1 The time/current curve shows the tripping characteristics of a typical Class A GFCI. Note that if you follow the 6-mA line vertically to the crosshatched typical time/current curve, you will find that the GFCI will open in from approximately 0.035 second to just less than 0.1 second. One electrical cycle is 1⁄60 of a second (0.0167 second). An air bag in an automobile inflates in approximately 1⁄20 of a second (0.05 second).

expected sensations at various current levels in milliamperes.

The path of current is very important. Where and how is contact to the live conductor made? What are you touching with the other hand? Where and in what are you standing? The current flow might be finger to finger, hand to hand, head to hand, head to foot, or any other combination such as a hand holding a "hot" wire, a hand holding a pair of pliers, a hand holding an electric drill, a hand grasping a grounded metal pipe, two hands grasping a grounded metal pipe, a hand in water, standing in water, hand to foot, foot to foot, and so on. Hand to foot can be fatal since the current is probably passing through the heart and lungs.

Generally, voltages of less than 50 volts to ground are considered safe. Voltages 50 volts and greater are considered lethal. All ac systems (with few exceptions) of 50 volts to 1000 volts that supply premises wiring are required to be grounded, *250.20(B)*. This is covered in Chapter 1.

Some circuits of less than 50 volts must be grounded according to *250.20(A)*:

- if the circuit is supplied by a transformer where the primary exceeds 150 volts to ground
- if the circuit is supplied by a transformer where the primary supply is ungrounded
- if the circuit is overhead wiring outside of a building

CODE REQUIREMENTS FOR GROUND-FAULT CIRCUIT INTERRUPTERS *(210.8)*

►To protect against electric shocks, *210.8(A)* requires that ground-fault circuit interrupters (GFCI) be provided for *all* single-phase, 125-volt, 15- and 20-ampere receptacles in dwellings. GFCI protection can be provided with GFCI circuit breakers or with GFCI receptacles. The basic requirements for receptacle GFCI protection are as follows:

- **Bathrooms:** See Figure 10-7 for the definition of a bathroom.
- ►**Garages** (attached and detached) and in accessory buildings not habitable, such as sheds, workshops, storage buildings, or areas of similar use that have the floor at or below grade.◄
- **Outdoors:** An exception is that GFCI protection is not required for a receptacle not readily accessible and supplied by a dedicated branch circuit for snow melting or deicing equipment. Install these receptacles for snow melting or deicing equipment according to *426.28*.
- **Crawl spaces** that are at or below grade.
- **Unfinished basements:** An exception to this GFCI requirement is for a receptacle that serves a permanently installed fire alarm or burglar alarm system. See *760.41B* and *760.121(B)*. A receptacle on a porcelain or plastic lampholder must also be GFCI protected. Some individuals try to get around the requirement for GFCI protection in basements by calling the basement "finished," even though it is clearly evident that it is not "finished." If the basement is truly intended to be "finished," then the *Code* requirements for the spacing of receptacles, required lighting outlets, and switch controls must be followed.
- **Kitchens:** All receptacles that serve the countertop surfaces. This includes receptacles installed on islands and peninsulas, as in Figure 6-2. The key words here are *that serve the countertop surfaces*.

  GFCI protection is *not* required for receptacles that are obviously not intended to serve countertops, such as a receptacle:
  - installed solely for a clock.
  - installed inside of an upper kitchen cabinet for plugging in a microwave oven that is fastened to the underside of the cabinet.
  - installed below the kitchen sink for plugging in a food-waste disposer or dishwasher.
  - installed behind a range or refrigerator.
- ►**Laundry, utility, wet bar, and similar sinks:** Any receptacle within 6 ft (1.8 m) of the outside edge of a laundry, utility, wet bar, or similar sink. See Figure 6-2. This requirement is easy to understand. Just measure 6 ft (1.8 m) in any direction around a corner, even in another room or hallway.◄
- **Swimming pools:** See Chapter 30.
- For the branch circuit supplying heated floors in bathrooms, and hydromassage bathtub, spa, and hot tub locations, *424.44(G)*. This GFCI

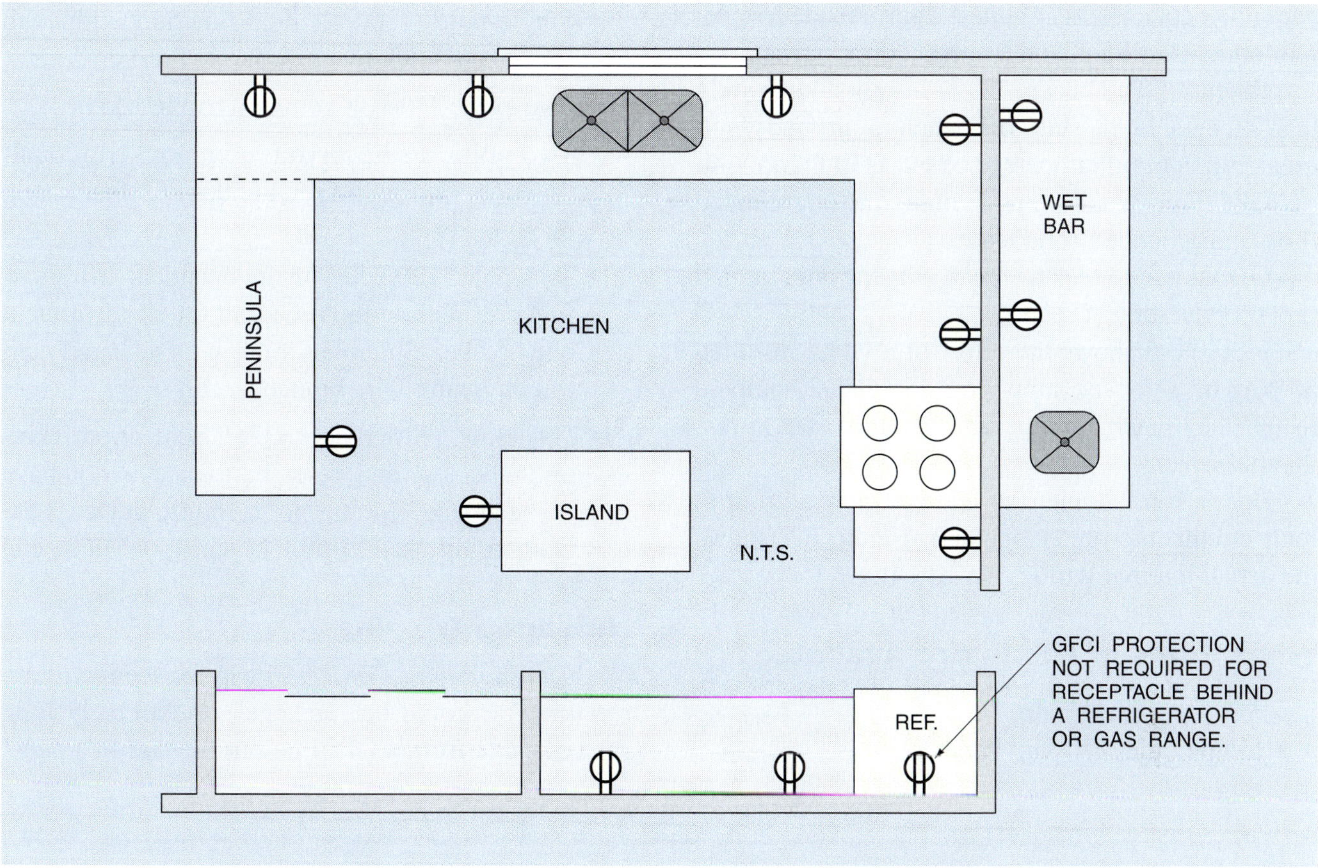

Figure 6-2 In kitchens, *all* 125-volt, single-phase, 15- and 20-ampere receptacles that serve countertop surfaces (walls, islands, or peninsulas) must be GFCI protected. The key words are *that serve countertop surfaces.* GFCI personnel protection is *not* required for the refrigerator receptacle, a receptacle under the sink for plugging in a food waste disposer, or a receptacle installed inside cabinets above the countertops for plugging in a microwave oven attached to the underside of the cabinets. ►All 125-volt, single-phase, 15- and 20-ampere receptacles within 6 ft (1.8 m) of a wet bar, laundry, or utility room sink must be GFCI protected. See *210.8(A)(6)* and *210.8(A)(7)*.◄ Drawing is not to scale.

requirement is regardless of the type of flooring or heating cables used.

GFCI Receptacles and Breakers

The *Code* requirements for ground-fault circuit protection can be met in many ways. Figure 6-3 illustrates a GFCI circuit breaker installed on a branch circuit. A ground fault in the range of 4 to 6 milliamperes or more shuts off the entire circuit. If, for example, a GFCI circuit breaker were to be installed on Circuit B14, a ground fault at any point in the circuit would shut off the garage lighting,

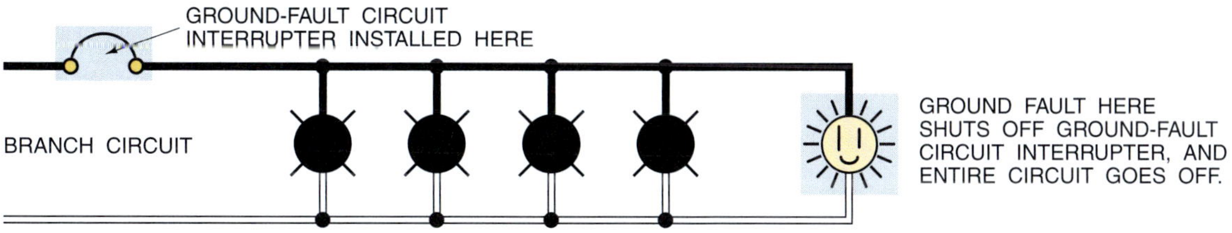

Figure 6-3 Ground-fault circuit interrupter as a part of the branch-circuit overcurrent device.

garage receptacles, rear garage door outside bracket luminaire, post light, and overhead door opener.

When a GFCI receptacle is installed, then only that receptacle is shut off when a ground fault greater than 6 milliamperes occurs, as in Figure 6-4.

GFCI receptacles break both the ungrounded (hot) and grounded conductors.

GFCI circuit breakers break only the ungrounded (hot) conductor.

Figure 6-5 shows the effect of a GFCI installed as part of a feeder supplying 15- and 20-ampere receptacle branch circuits. This is rarely used in residential wiring.

Figure 6-6 is a pictorial view of how a ground-fault circuit interrupter operates. Figure 6-7 shows the actual internal wiring of a GFCI.

What Kinds of GFCIs Are Available?

- 120-volt receptacles
- Single-pole, 120-volt breakers
- Single-pole, 120-volt dual-function with both GFCI and AFCI features in one breaker
- Two-pole, 240-volt common trip breakers
- Two-pole, 120/240-volt common trip dual-function with both GFCI and AFCI features in one breaker
- Two-pole, 120/240-volt independent trip dual-function with both AFCI and GFCI features in one breaker. Suitable for use with a shared neutral on a multiwire branch circuit
- "Faceless." Strictly for GFCI protection. Have only the test and reset buttons. Do not have a receptacle. Mount in a single-device box. Commonly used to protect whirlpool tubs, etc.

Nuisance Tripping

Occasionally, a GFCI will trip for seemingly no reason. This could be "leakage" in extremely long runs of cable from a GFCI circuit breaker in a panel

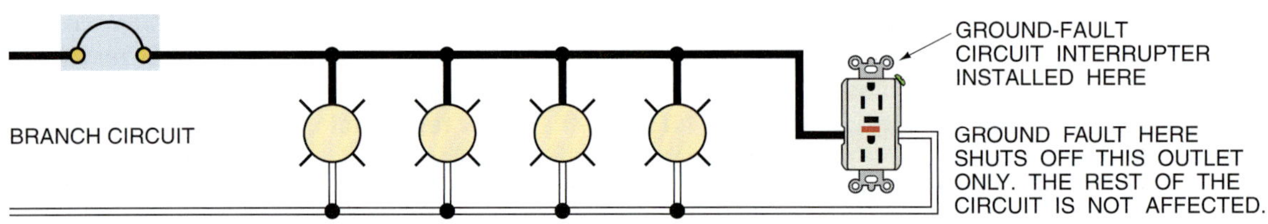

Figure 6-4 Ground-fault circuit interrupter as an integral part of a receptacle outlet.

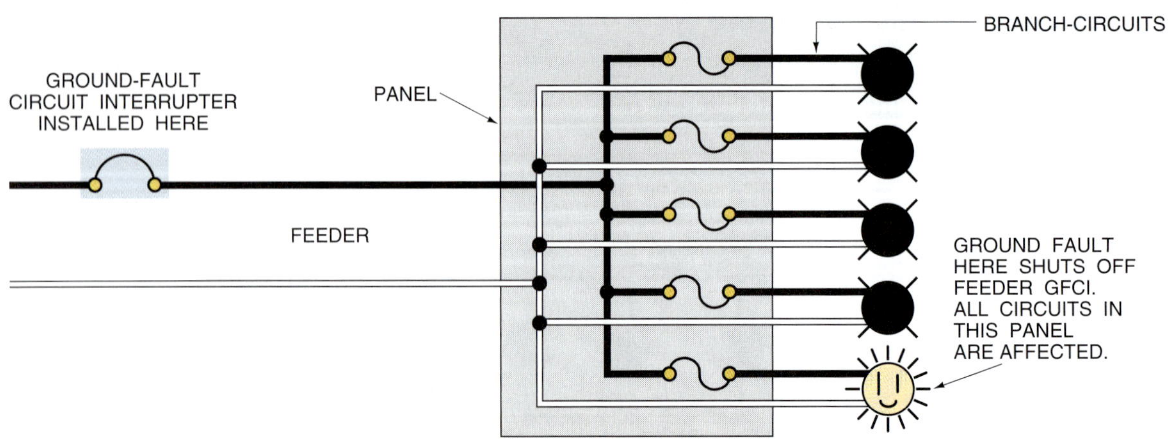

Figure 6-5 Ground-fault circuit interrupter as part of the feeder supplying a panel that serves a number of 15- and 20-ampere branch circuits. This is permitted by *215.9* but is rarely—if ever—used in residential wiring.

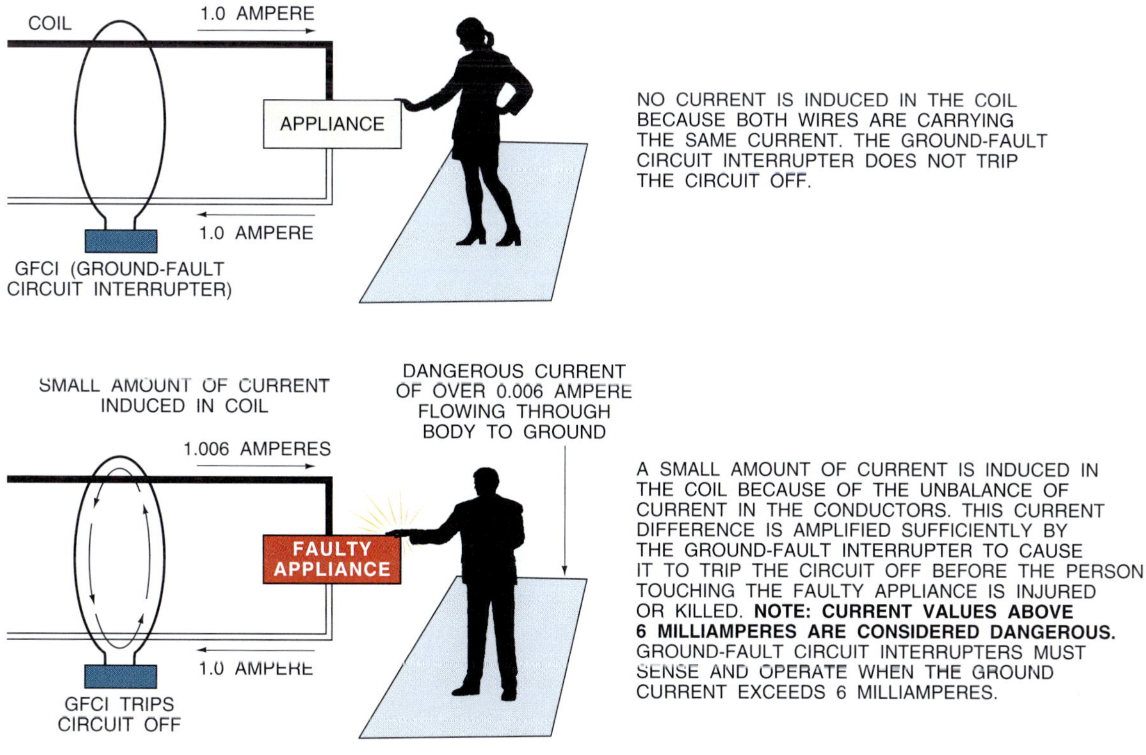

Figure 6-6 Basic principle of how a ground-fault circuit interrupter operates.

to the protected branch-circuit wiring. One manufacturer's literature specifies a maximum one-way length of 250 ft for the branch circuit.

The allowable "leakage current" for listed cord-and plug-connected appliances is so small that they should not cause nuisance tripping of GFCI devices. However, if nuisance tripping can be traced to an appliance, it might be a good idea to simply replace the GFCI circuit breaker or the GFCI receptacle before discarding the appliance. If the GFCI continues to nuisance trip, it probably is the appliance.

Nuisance tripping occasionally can be traced to moisture somewhere in the circuit wiring, receptacles, or lighting outlets.

Some electricians are of the opinion that using nonmetallic staples (see Figure 4-14[C]) will reduce the possibility of nuisance tripping. No actual testing has been done to prove or disprove this opinion.

What a GFCI Does

A GFCI monitors the current balance between the ungrounded "hot" conductor and the grounded conductor. As soon as the current flowing through the "hot" conductor is in the range of 4 to 6 milliamperes more than the current flowing in the "return" grounded conductor, the GFCI senses this unbalance and trips (opens) the circuit off. The unbalance indicates that part of the current flowing in the circuit is being diverted to some path other than the normal return path along the grounded return conductor. If the "other" path is through a human body, as illustrated in Figure 6-6, the outcome could be fatal.

UL Standard No. 943 covers ground-fault circuit interrupters.

- Class "A" GFCI devices are the most common. They are designed to:
  - trip when current to ground is 6 milliamperes (6/1000 of an ampere) or greater.
  - not trip when the current to ground is less than 4 milliamperes (4/1000 of an ampere).
  - may or may not trip when the current to ground is between 4 and 6 milliamperes.
- Class "B" GFCI devices are pretty much obsolete. They were designed to trip on ground faults of 20 milliamperes (20⁄1000 of an ampere)

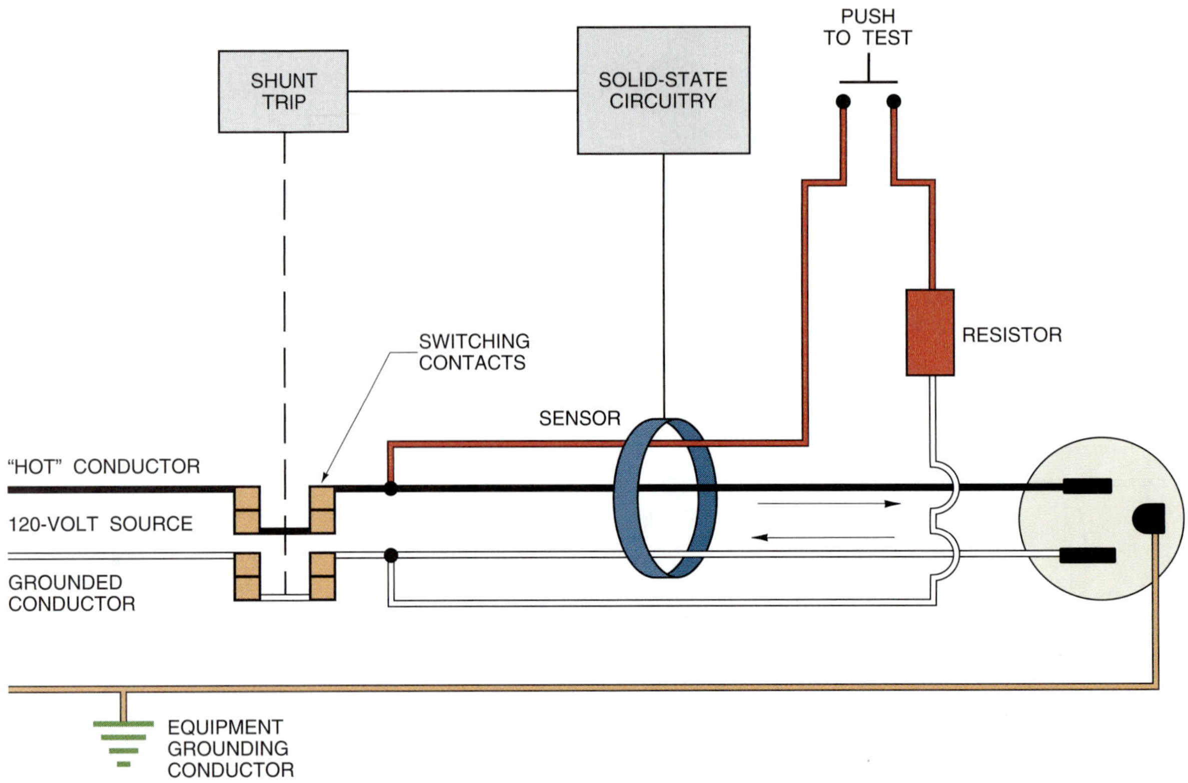

Figure 6-7 Ground-fault circuit interrupter internal components and connections. Receptacle-type GFCIs switch both the phase (hot) and grounded conductors. Note that when the test button is pushed, the test current passes through the test button, the sensor, then back around (bypasses, outside of) the sensor, then back to the opposite circuit conductor. This is how the "unbalance" is created then monitored by the electronic circuitry to signal the GFCI's contacts to open. Note that because both normal "load" currents pass through the sensor, no unbalance is present.

or more. They were used only for underwater swimming pool lighting installed before the adoption of the 1965 *NEC*.® For this application, Class "A" devices were too sensitive and would nuisance trip.

What a GFCI Does *Not* Do

- It *does not* protect against electrical shock when a person touches both circuit conductors at the same time (two "hot" wires, or one "hot" wire and one grounded neutral conductor) because the current flowing in both conductors is the same. Thus, there is no unbalance of current for the GFCI to sense and trip.
- It *does not* limit the magnitude of ground-fault current. It *does* limit the length of time that a ground fault will flow. In other words, you will still receive a severe shock during the time it takes the GFCI device to trip "off." See Figure 6-1.
- It *does not* sense solid short circuits between the "hot" conductor and the grounded "neutral" conductor. The branch-circuit fuse or circuit breaker provides this protection.
- It *does not* sense solid short circuits between two "hot" conductors. The branch-circuit fuse or circuit breaker provides this protection.
- It *does not* sense and protect against the damaging effects of arcing faults, such as would occur with frayed extension cords. This protection is provided by an arc-fault circuit interrupter (AFCI) discussed later in this chapter.
- It *does not* provide overload protection for the branch-circuit wiring. It provides *ground-fault protection only*.

GROUND-FAULT CIRCUIT INTERRUPTERS IN RESIDENCE CIRCUITS

In this residence, GFCI personnel protection must be provided for receptacle outlets installed outdoors, in the bathrooms, in the garage, in the workshop, specific receptacles in the basement area, and in the kitchen for those receptacles that serve countertops. All 125-volt, single-phase, 15- and 20-ampere receptacles within 6 ft (1.8 m) of a wet bar, laundry, or utility room sink must be GFCI protected. See *210.8(A)(6)* and *210.8(A)(7)*. The GFCI protection can be provided by GFCI circuit breakers or by GFCI receptacles of the type shown in Figure 6-8.

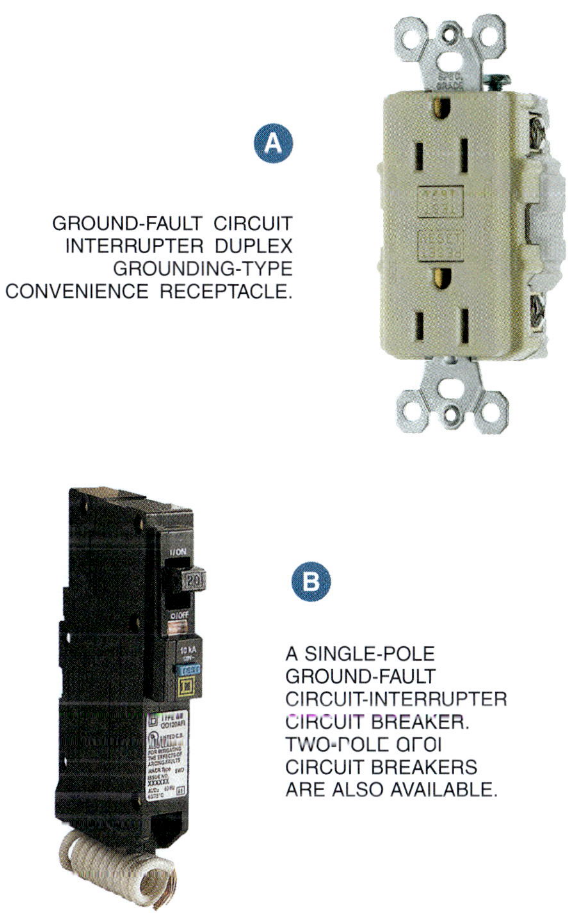

Figure 6-8 (A) A ground-fault circuit interrupter receptacle, *courtesy of* Pass & Seymour, and (B) a ground-fault circuit interrupter circuit breaker. The switching mechanism of a GFCI receptacle opens both the ungrounded "hot" conductor and the grounded conductor. The switching mechanism of a GFCI circuit breaker opens the ungrounded "hot" conductor only. *Courtesy of* Square D/Schneider Electric.

This is a design issue that confronts the electrician. The electrician must decide how to provide the GFCI personnel protection required by *210.8*. These receptacle outlets are connected to the circuits listed in Table 6-2.

Swimming pools also have special requirements for GFCI protection. These requirements are covered in Chapter 30.

GFCIs operate properly only on grounded electrical systems, as is the case in all residential, condo, apartment, commercial, and industrial wiring. The GFCI will operate on a two-wire circuit even though an equipment grounding conductor is not included with the circuit conductor. In this residence, equipment grounding conductors are in the cables. In the case of a metal raceway (EMT) or armored cable (Type AC or Type MC), the equipment

CIRCUITS	GFCI RECEPTACLE LOCATIONS
A15	Front porch receptacle
A16	Outdoor receptacle on front of residence outside of Front Bedroom
A18	Workbench receptacles
A19	Outdoor receptacle on rear of residence outside of Master Bedroom
A20	Workshop receptacles on window wall
A22	Master Bath receptacle
A23	Bath (off hall) receptacle
B9	Wet-bar (Recreation Room) receptacles
B13	Kitchen receptacles
B14	Garage receptacles
B15	Kitchen receptacles
B16	Kitchen receptacles
B17	Outdoor receptacle outside of Living Room next to sliding door
B18	Laundry Room receptacle for clothes washer
B20	Laundry Room receptacles (2) and weatherproof receptacle (1) outside of laundry
B21	Powder Room receptacle

Table 6-2 Circuit numbers and general locations of GFCI-protected receptacles. GFCI protection can be provided by using GFCI receptacles, GFCI circuit breakers, or GFCI/AFCI dual-function circuit breakers. Refer to Panel Schedules shown in Figure 27-11 and Figure 27-14.

grounding conductor is provided by the metal raceway or armored cable that contains a bonding strip.

Never ground a system neutral conductor except at the service equipment. A GFCI would be inoperative.

Never connect the neutral conductor of one circuit to the neutral conductor of another circuit.

When a GFCI feeds an isolation transformer (separate primary winding and separate secondary winding), as might be used for swimming pool underwater luminaires, the GFCI *will not* detect any ground faults on the secondary of the transformer.

Ground-fault circuit interrupters may be installed on other circuits, in other locations, and even when rewiring existing installations where the *Code* does not specifically call for GFCI protection.

Do not connect fire and smoke alarms to a circuit that is protected by a GFCI breaker. A nuisance tripping of the GFCI would render the fire alarm and smoke detectors inoperative. This requirement is found in *NFPA 72, The National Fire Alarm Code*.

FEEDTHROUGH GROUND-FAULT CIRCUIT INTERRUPTER

With rare exception, all GFCI receptacles on the market today have the "feedthrough" feature.

The decision to use more GFCIs rather than trying to protect many receptacles through one GFCI becomes one of economy and practicality. GFCI receptacles are more expensive than regular receptacles. Here is where knowledge of material and labor costs comes into play. The decision must be made separately for each installation, keeping in mind that GFCI protection is a safety issue recognized and clearly stated in the *Code*. However, the actual circuit layout is left up to the electrician.

Figure 6-9 illustrates how a feedthrough GFCI receptacle supplies many other receptacles. Should a ground fault occur anywhere on this circuit, all eleven receptacles lose power—not a good circuit layout. Attempting to locate the ground-fault problem, unless it's obvious, can be very time-consuming. The use of more GFCI receptacles is generally the more practical approach.

Figure 6-10 shows how a feedthrough receptacle is connected into a circuit. Figure 6-11 shows a feedthrough GFCI receptacle connected midway into a circuit. In both diagrams, the feedthrough GFCI receptacle and all downstream outlets are ground-fault protected.

In UL Standard 943, we find that a GFCI recep-

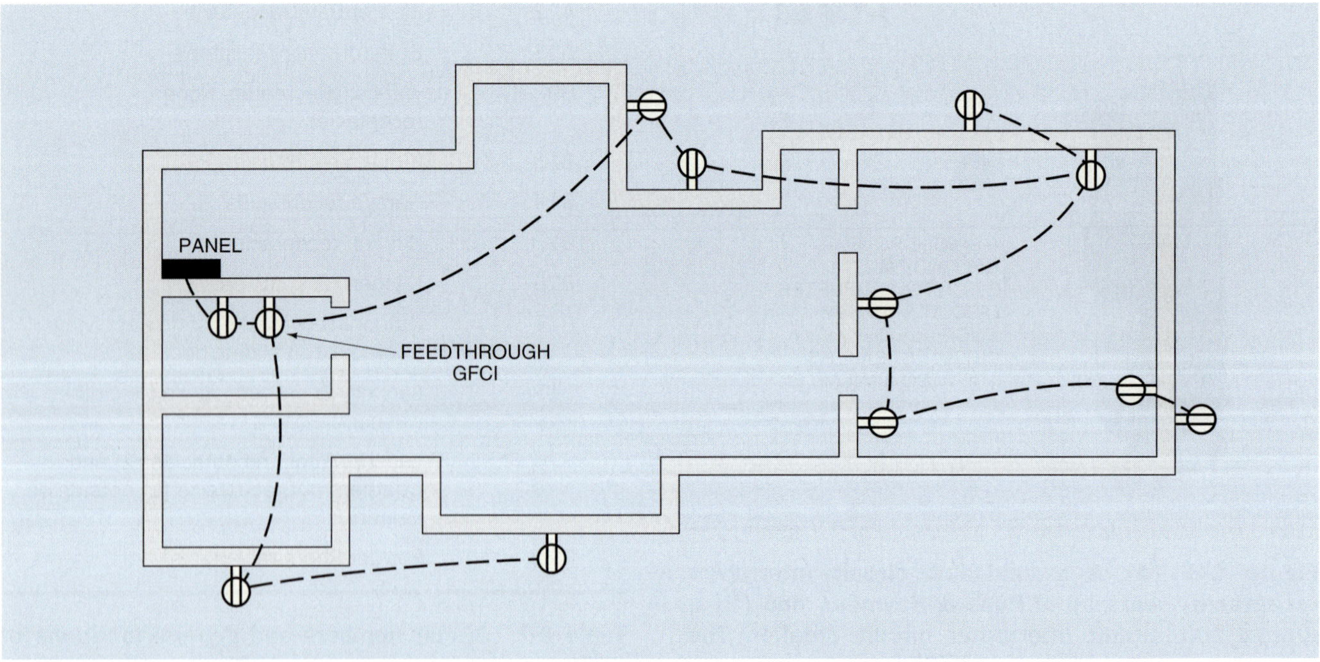

Figure 6-9 Illustration showing one GFCI feedthrough receptacle protecting other receptacles. Although this might be an inexpensive way to protect many other downstream receptacles outlets that require GFCI protection, it could be considered as "putting too many eggs in one basket." The same situation exists if a GFCI circuit breaker were to be installed in the panel. One major manufacturer of GFCI circuit breakers suggests that the maximum one-way length of a GFCI-protected branch circuit be limited to 250 feet.

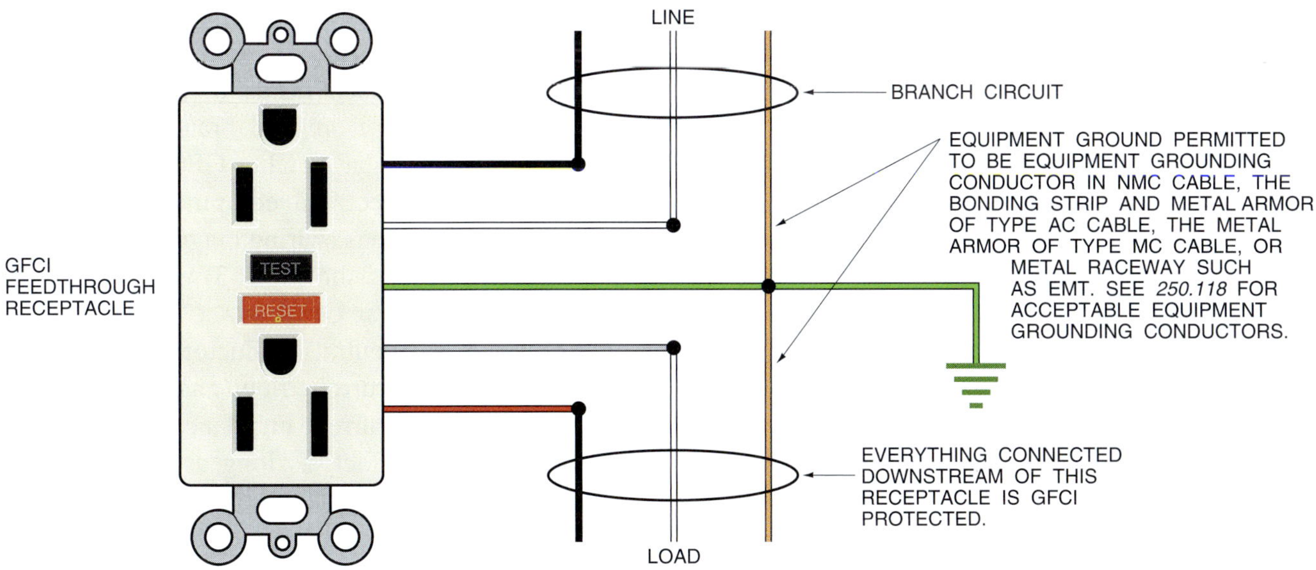

Figure 6-10 Connecting feedthrough ground-fault circuit interrupter into circuit.

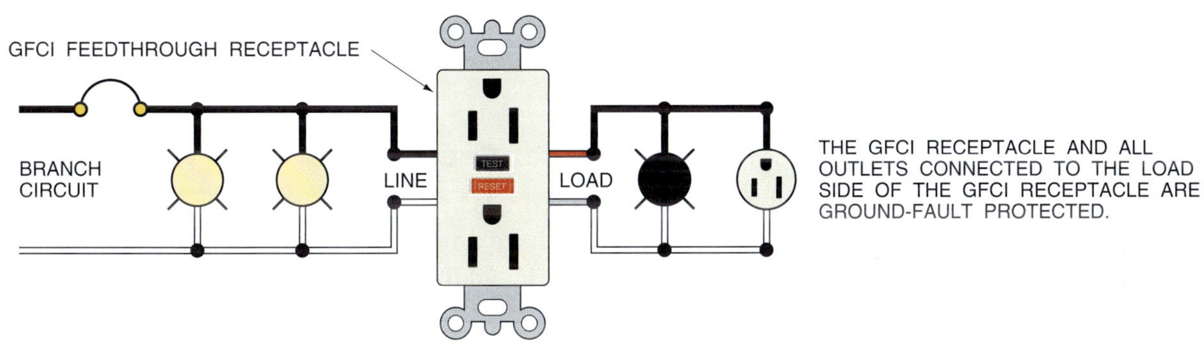

Figure 6-11 Feedthrough GFCI receptacle installed midway in a branch circuit.

tacle may have black-and-white line wire leads, red-and-gray load wire leads, and a green lead for the equipment grounding conductor as illustrated in Figure 6-10. GFCI receptacles may have ordinary screw terminals: brass color for the "hot" conductors, silver color for the grounded conductors, and a green hexagon-shaped screw for the equipment grounding conductor. The line and load connections are clearly marked.

Where the wiring method is a grounded method such as electrical metallic tubing, flexible metal conduit, or armored cable, the grounding terminal of the GFCI receptacle is considered adequately grounded by the metallic grounded wiring method, and a separate connection to the green lead or to the green hexagon-shaped screw is not necessary. This is discussed and illustrated in Chapter 5.

A "safety yellow" adhesive label must cover the load terminals, or be wrapped around the load wire leads. The label must be marked with wording like this: *"Attention! The load terminals under this label are for feeding additional receptacles. Miswiring can leave this outlet without ground-fault protection. Read instructions prior to wiring."*

The most important factors to be considered are the continuity of electrical power and the economy of the installation. The decision must be made separately for each installation.

WARNING: Be very careful when hooking up GFCI receptacles. It is extremely important that the LINE and LOAD connections are done correctly. On older style GFCI receptacles, it was possible to reverse the line and load connections. Under a ground-fault condition, this sort of misconnection would result in the GFCI receptacle itself still being "live" even though the GFCI mechanism has tripped "off." In the case of feedthrough receptacles, a ground-fault condition would shut off the circuit downstream, yet the feedthrough GFCI receptacle itself is still energized.

It is easy to tell if a GFCI receptacle has the line and load leads reversed. Push the test button. The GFCI will trip. If the GFCI receptacle is still "hot," it has been wired incorrectly.

The current UL Standard 943 requires that a GFCI receptacle must trip to the "OFF" position if the receptacle is miswired, such as a reversal of the line/load connections. In other words, if misconnected, the receptacle simply will not work!

WARNING: The circuitry in a GFCI detects any unbalance current in the circuit.

The circuitry in an AFCI detects various levels and types of arcing in the circuit.

Be extremely careful when hooking up GFCI and AFCI circuit breakers. AFCIs are discussed a little later in this chapter. A misconnection or misapplication could result in a fatal electrical shock! Before hooking up these devices, study the installation instructions (wiring diagrams, cautions, etc.).

Questions that need to be answered. Will all branch-circuit "home runs" be 2-wire? Will some "home runs" be 3-wire multiwire branch circuits in order to save "time and material"? You've got to think about this before you lay out your branch-circuit wiring. To "Meet Code," you must clearly understand the requirements in *NEC®* *210.8* and *210.12* for GFCIs and AFCIs.

These *NEC®* sections tell you "where" to install these devices. These sections do not tell you "how" to electrically install them.

What about Multiwire Branch Circuits? It's plain and simple. Some AFCI and GFCI devices are "listed" for use on multiwire branch circuits—others are not.

Those that are not "listed" for use on multiwire branch circuits have clear instructions warning "Never share a neutral." Using two single-pole AFCIs or GFCIs on a multiwire branch circuit will not work because each needs to have the white grounded conductor from that branch circuit connected to that particular AFCI or GFCI.

As with any electrical equipment, follow the installation instructions (wiring diagrams).

Figure 6-12(A) shows a 3-wire, multiwire circuit. This particular GFCI is not "listed" as suitable for sharing a neutral conductor in a multiwire branch. Trace the current flow and note that the GFCI will sense a current unbalance of 5 amperes and trip "OFF." In fact, as long as the unbalance exists, it will never be able to be turned "ON."

Figure 6-12(B) and Figure 6-12(C) show a 2-wire circuit. Figure 6-12(B) is an improper connection of a feedthrough GFCI receptacle. Note how the GFCI detects a current unbalance of 1 ampere and will trip "OFF." As long as the unbalance exists, the GFCI receptacle will continue to trip "OFF" until the misconnection is corrected. Figure 6-12(C) illustrates the proper connection of a GFCI receptacle.

Other Features for GFCI Receptacles

GFCIs have come a long way. All GFCI receptacles have a manual TEST button and a RESET button. In addition, look for GFCI receptacles that have:

- an LED that indicates that there is power to the receptacle.
- an LED that indicates that the device is not functioning properly.
- a built-in line/load reversal feature that prevents power to the receptacle face if the line/load connections are reversed.
- a lockout feature so the GFCI cannot be reset if the internal GFCI circuit is not functioning properly. This is referred to as the "End-of-Life" feature. This is self-testing circuitry that continuously checks for ground-fault conditions and confirms that the device is capable of sensing and tripping when a ground fault occurs. The user does not have to remember to test the device periodically.

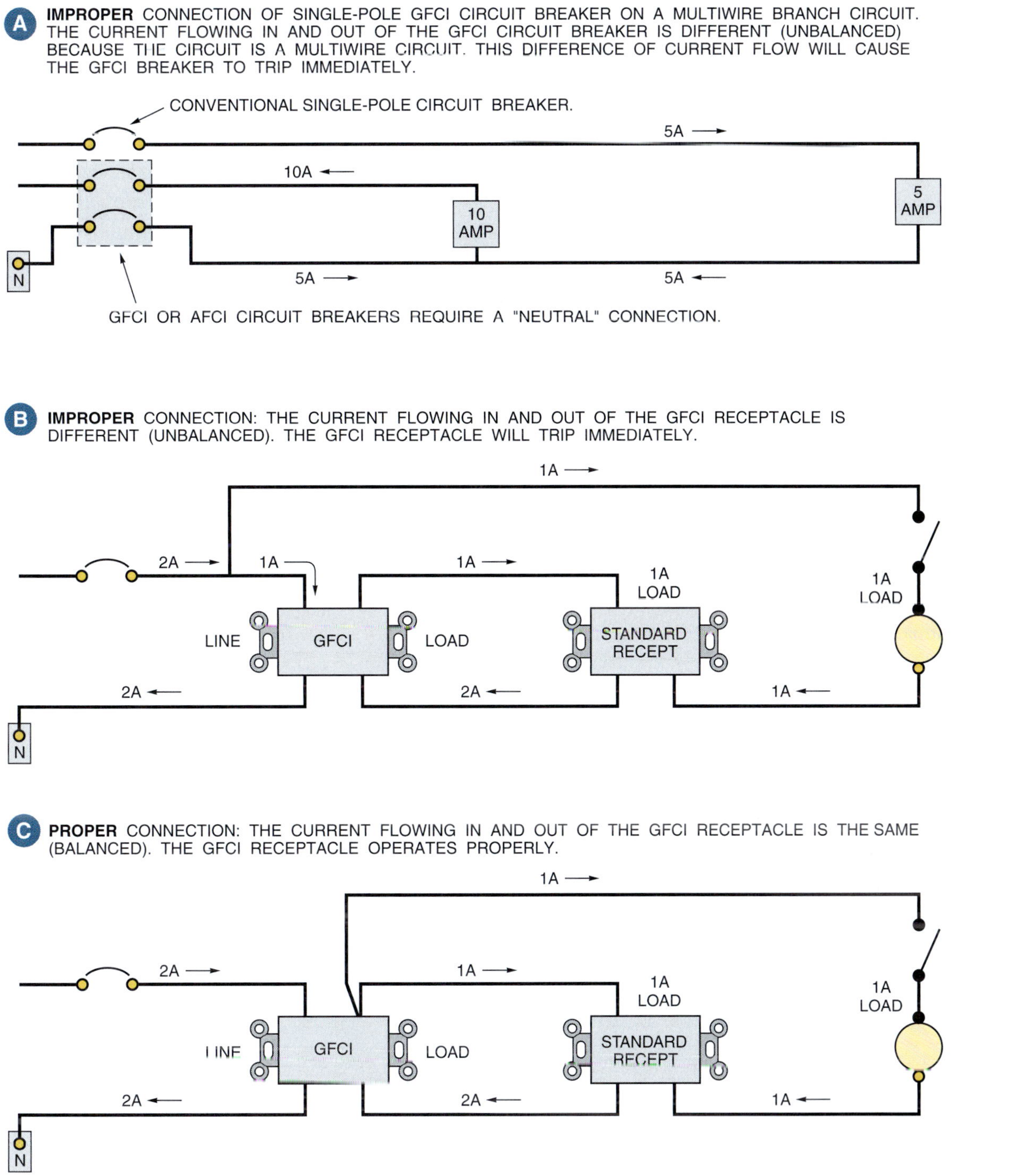

Figure 6-12 These diagrams show improper and proper connections of GFCI circuit breakers.

Nuisance Tripping

Occasionally, a GFCI will trip for seemingly no reason.

The maximum allowable "leakage" for listed cord- and plug-connected appliances is 0.5 milliampere (mA). However, some product standards, such as for computers and televisions permit higher values of leakage current—some as high as 3.5 mA. If nuisance tripping can be traced to an appliance, the appliance should be checked by a qualified person.

Nuisance tripping might be traced to moisture somewhere in the branch-circuit wiring, wiring devices, or lighting outlets.

"Leakage" in extremely long runs of cable from a GFCI circuit breaker in a panel to the protected branch-circuit wiring could result in nuisance tripping. This occurrence is very rare, but since this is a possibility, it is worth checking out. Of course, the problem could be a defective GFCI breaker or GFCI receptacle.

TESTING AND RECORDING OF TEST DATA FOR GFCI RECEPTACLES

Refer to Figure 6-8 and note that the GFCI receptacle has "T" (Test) and "R" (Reset) buttons. Pushing the test button places a small ground fault on the circuit. If operating properly, the GFCI receptacle should trip to the "OFF" position. Pushing the reset button will restore power. The operation is similar for the GFCI circuit breakers.

Because of the fragile nature of the electronic circuitry in GFCIs, test them often, particularly in high lightning strike areas of the country. GFCIs and other delicate electronic circuitry are susceptible to transient voltage surges.

"Things" are changing so fast in the electronic world, it is hard to keep up with the changes. At least one manufacturer recently announced the availability of a self-testing GFCI receptacle. Its circuitry automatically generates a simulated ground-fault leakage current every 60 seconds. Instead of relying on the homeowners to do the recommended monthly test of the GFCI receptacles in their homes, the test is performed automatically.

Underwriters Laboratories (UL) requires that detailed installation and testing instructions be included in the packaging for GFCI receptacles or circuit breakers. Instructions are not only for the electrician but also for homeowners, and must be left in a conspicuous place so homeowners can familiarize themselves with the receptacle, its operation, and its need for testing. Figure 6-13 shows a chart homeowners can use to record monthly GFCI testing.

OCCUPANT'S TEST RECORD

TO TEST, depress the "TEST" button. The "RESET" button should extend. Should the "RESET" button not extend, the GFCI will not protect against electrical shock. Call qualified electrician.

TO RESET, depress the "RESET" button firmly into the GFCI unit until an audible click is heard. If reset properly, the "RESET" button will be flush with the surface of the "TEST" button.

This label should be retained and placed in a conspicuous location to remind the occupants that for maximum protection against electrical shock, each GFCI should be tested monthly.

Year	Jan	Feb	Mar	Apr	May	Jun	Jul	Aug	Sep	Oct	Nov	Dec

Figure 6-13 Homeowner's testing chart for recording GFCI testing dates. UL requires that the instructions furnished with GFCIs be marked and that testing be done at least once each month and after severe lightning storms.

ARC-FAULT CIRCUIT INTERRUPTERS (AFCIs)

Arc-fault circuit interrupters are "the new kids on the street." First came ground-fault circuit interrupters (GFCIs), then came arc-fault circuit interrupters (AFCIs). As you will learn later in this chapter, dual-function circuit breakers are available that provide both AFCI and GFCI protection, making it very easy to "Meet Code."

▶*NEC® 210.12(A)* defines an arc-fault circuit interrupter as: *A device intended to provide protection from the effects of arc faults by recognizing characteristics unique to arcing and by functioning to de-energize the circuit when an arc fault is detected.*◀

▶*NEC® 210.12(B)* states that in dwelling units, *All 120-volt, single-phase, 15- and 20-ampere branch circuits supplying outlets installed in dwelling unit family rooms, dining rooms, living rooms, parlors, libraries, dens, bedrooms, sun rooms, recreation rooms, closets, hallways , or similar rooms or areas shall be protected by a listed arc-fault circuit interrupter, combination-type, installed to provide protection of the branch circuit.*◀

Certain rooms and areas are exempt from the AFCI requirement:

- Attics—AFCI protection not required, but no problem if you do provide AFCI protection.
- Bathrooms—The receptacle(s) require GFCI protection. You could put the lighting on an AFCI-protected circuit.
- Garages—The receptacle(s) require GFCI protection. You could put the lighting on an AFCI-protected circuit.
- Kitchens—Receptacles serving countertops require GFCI protection. You could put the lighting on an AFCI-protected circuit.
- Outdoors—Outdoor receptacle(s) require GFCI protection. Outdoor lighting is probably connected to indoor branch circuits that are AFCI-protected.
- Unfinished basements—Unfinished basement receptacle(s) require GFCI protection. You could put the lighting on an AFCI-protected circuit.

Note the last few words in *210.12(B) installed to provide protection of the branch circuit.*

By definition, a branch circuit is *The circuit conductors between the final overcurrent device protecting the circuit and the outlet(s).* These are the branch-circuit conductors that connect to the circuit breaker (or fuse) in the panelboard. There are two exceptions.

▶The first exception to *210.12(B)* is *Where RMC, IMC, EMT, or steel armored cable, Type AC meeting the requirements of 250.118 using metal outlet and junction boxes is installed for the portion of the branch circuit between the branch circuit overcurrent device and the first outlet, it shall be permitted to install a combination AFCI at the first outlet to provide protection for the remaining portion of the branch circuit.*◀ This permits a combination AFCI receptacle to be installed downstream (any distance) from the panel, but only if the wiring method is all metal.

▶The second exception to *210.12(B)* is that AFCI protection is not required for the branch circuit that supplies a fire alarm system installed in accordance with *760.41(B)* and *760.121(B)*.◀ See Chapter 26 in this text. Fire alarm system requirements are found in NFPA 72.

Don't Get Confused

Don't confuse an AFCI with a GFCI. These two devices protect against two different kinds of electrical hazards.

- An AFCI device is designed to sense and respond to an arcing fault that could develop into a fire. Some AFCI devices also provide personnel GFCI protection (6 mA). Some AFCI devices provide equipment ground-fault protection (GFP—30 mA). A typical application for equipment GFP in dwellings is for outdoor electric deicing and snow melting equipment, covered in *Article 426*.

  Always read the label and the instructions of an AFCI device to be sure you know where and how to connect it.
- A GFCI device is designed to sense and respond to a ground fault, protecting people from severe electrical shock that could lead to death.
- Dual-function AFCI/GFCI breakers provide arcing and ground-fault protection.

Smoke Alarms and AFCI Protection

As you will learn in Chapter 26, smoke alarms are required to have secondary battery backup protection. Permanently installed fire alarm systems shall not be GFCI- or AFCI-protected, *760.41(B)* and *760.121(B)*.

Why AFCI Protection?

Electrical arcing is an "early" event in the history of a typical electrical fire. Arcing is considered one of the leading causes of electrical fires in homes. Think about frayed cords, cords under carpets, cords pinched under legs of furniture, and nails being driven through plaster into cables in the wall. The Consumer Product Safety Commission recently cited 150,000 residential electrical fires annually in the United States, 850 deaths, 6000 injuries, and more than $1.5 billion in property loss. These statistics are pretty convincing of the need for greater electrical protection. The heat of an arc is extremely high, known to reach 10,000°F or more. Hot particles of metal expelled by the arc are enough to ignite most surrounding combustible materials.

We have all been guilty of blaming electrical fires on overloaded circuits, overloaded extension cords, and too many extension cords plugged into a receptacle. The heat of an overloaded cord by itself is generally not hot enough to ignite surrounding combustible materials. An overload condition can cause the breakdown of the insulation on the conductors, allowing the conductors to touch one another. This sets the stage for an arcing condition between the conductors, or between the "hot" conductor and ground. We now have the ingredients of an electrical fire.

For example, let's say that the cord on an electric iron becomes frayed and the conductor(s) break. The iron draws 10 amperes. The arcing of 10 amperes trying to bridge the gap in the broken conductor(s) develops the tremendous heat capable of igniting surrounding combustible material, yet 10 amperes flowing in the circuit will not trip a 15-ampere circuit breaker or open a 15-ampere fuse. This condition is not an overload and initially is not a short circuit. Conventional overcurrent devices "sees" this as normal. They are not designed to detect and open under current levels below their trip setting. What is needed is a device that can detect the unique characteristics of an arcing condition—an AFCI.

Types of Arcs

Arcing is current flowing outside of the intended path. Arcing is a function of voltage and the amount of current flowing in the arc.

Taking the liberty of using familiar terms, we could say that arcs come in two varieties—*good* and *bad*.

Good arcs are not dangerous. For example, the slight arcing that occurs between the contacts of a switch when turned ON and OFF, or when a male attachment plug cap is inserted into a receptacle is not considered hazardous. This type of arcing creates a unique "signature."

Bad arcs are dangerous. Arcs develop a tremendous amount of heat (I^2R) at the point of arcing (sputtering). Arcing could be line-to-line, line-to-neutral, or line-to-ground. This type of arcing also creates a "signature."

To avoid nuisance tripping, the sophisticated electronic circuitry in an AFCI has the ability to recognize the "signature," and distinguish between *good* (harmless) and *bad* (dangerous) arcs. It makes a decision if the arcing or glowing is dangerous or harmless.

Arcs are classified as:

Series Arcs: When a conductor that is carrying current breaks, or when a loose connection occurs, a "series" arcing fault is created. The current draw of the connected load is trying to jump across the open created by the break or loose connection. Table 6-3 gives you a good idea of how fast an AFCI circuit breaker trips for various values of arcing current as specified in UL Standard 1699. Remember, there are 60 cycles in 1 second.

Parallel Arcs: When arcing occurs between the black ("hot") and white grounded (neutral) circuit conductors, or between the black ("hot") conductor and ground, it is referred to as a "parallel" arc. These conditions might be caused by a nail being driven through a cable, a staple driven too tightly, or a clamp or connector squeezing the cable too tightly. The current is traveling outside of its intended path. A broken or frayed cord could result in a "series" or "parallel" arc, or both.

Table 6-4 shows UL Standard 1699 specified current values for "parallel" arc testing of an AFCI device.

Ampere Rating of AFCI Circuit Breaker	ARCING CURRENT IN AMPERES			
	5	10	Rated Current of the AFCI Circuit Breaker	150% of Rated Current of the AFCI Circuit Breaker
15 amperes	1 second	0.40 second	0.28 second	0.16 second
20 amperes	1 second	0.40 second	0.20 second	0.11 second
30 amperes	1 second	0.40 second	0.14 second	0.10 second

Table 6-3 Clearing times for listed AFCI combination-type circuit breakers when subjected to various values of arcing-fault current.

ARCING CURRENT IN AMPERES					
75	100	150	200	300	500
FOR EACH OF THE ABOVE ARCING CURRENT VALUES, THE TOTAL ARCING TIME SHALL NOT EXCEED 8 HALF-CYCLES IN 0.5 SECOND. THE 8 HALF-CYCLES OF ARCING COULD BE CONSECUTIVE OR INTERMITTENT.					

Table 6-4 Arcing current values for parallel arcing tests.

Types of AFCI Devices

The *NEC*® tells us where to install AFCIs in homes. UL Standard 1699 specifies the sensing and tripping characteristics of AFCIs.

AFCIs are available in the following types:

1. *Combination AFCI:* ▶This type of AFCI is mandatory in *210.12(B)*.◀ It is installed in the panel where the branch circuit originates. It provides arc-fault protection as specified in the UL Standard for both *Branch/feeder AFCIs* and *Outlet AFCIs*.

   Note: Don't get confused. A *combination AFCI* means that the device has been tested and listed as meeting the requirements for both *Branch/feeder AFCIs* and *Outlet AFCIs*. When referring to a device that provides both AFCI and GFCI personnel protection, think of it as having *dual-function* characteristics. Don't use the word *combination*!

2. *Branch/feeder AFCI:* This type of AFCI circuit breaker is installed in a panel. It provides arc-fault protection for the branch-circuit wiring. It is not quite as sensitive as an *Outlet AFCI* although it does provide limited protection for extension cords plugged into receptacles on the circuit. The time permitted for the use of this type ended on January 1, 2008.

3. *Outlet AFCI:* This is an AFCI receptacle. It provides protection for cord sets that are plugged into the receptacle. It is more sensitive than a *Branch/feeder AFCI*. A feedthrough AFCI receptacle installed at the first receptacle is permitted by *210.12(B), Exception*. ▶There is no limitation on the length of the branch-circuit overcurrent device to the first receptacle. However, the branch-circuit wiring method must be RMC, IMC, EMT, or steel armored cable (AC).◀ Everything downstream from the feedthrough AFCI receptacle is AFCI-protected.

4. *Portable AFCI:* A plug-in device with one or more receptacles. It provides AFCI protection for cords that are plugged to it. This type of AFCI device is a "must" for workers using electrical tools on the job.

5. *Cord AFCI:* A plug-in device that provides AFCI protection to the power cord connected to it. It has no additional outlets. An example of this would be the AFCI device required to be an integral part of room air-conditioning equipment in accordance with *440.65*.

How Do You Know What Type It Is? The marking is found on the device. When installed in a panelboard, the marking must be visible after you remove the cover from the panelboard.

What Kinds of AFCIs Are Available?

- Single-pole, 120-volt breaker
- Single-pole, 120-volt dual-function with both AFCI and GFCI features in one breaker

- Two-pole, 240-volt, common trip breaker
- Two-pole, 120/240-volt breaker
- Two-pole, 120/240-volt common trip dual-function with both AFCI and GFCI features in one breaker.
- Two-pole, 120/240-volt independent trip dual-function with both AFCI and GFCI features in one breaker; suitable for use with a shared neutral on a multiwire branch circuit
- 120-volt feedthrough receptacles

UL Standards for AFCIs and GFCIs

Type	Conforms to requirements of	If circuit breaker type, also conforms to requirements of
AFCI	UL 1699	UL489
GFCI	UL 943	UL 489
AFCI/GFCI combination	UL 1699 and 943	UL 489

What Types of AFCI Devices Do Electricians Install?

The most common AFCIs that electricians install today are the circuit-breaker type. Circuit-breaker AFCIs are the same width as a standard circuit breaker so they will fit into a standard electrical panel. See Figure 6-14.

Figure 6-14 ►A listed combination-type arc-fault circuit-interrupter (AFCI) circuit breaker. *Courtesy of Square D/Schneider.*◄

How to Connect AFCIs

When installing a 125-volt, single-pole AFCI circuit breaker, you first "snap" the breaker into the panel. Then the white lead from the AFCI circuit breaker is connected to the neutral bar in the panel. The black branch-circuit conductor is connected to the brass-colored load side terminal on the breaker. The white branch-circuit conductor is connected to the silver-colored load side terminal on the breaker. This is the same as for GFCI circuit breakers discussed earlier in this chapter.

Never share the neutral conductor of a multiwire branch circuit when using GFCIs and AFCIs unless they are listed for sharing a neutral. See Figure 6-12. Two-pole AFCIs and GFCIs are available. Always follow the instructions furnished with these devices.

May I Use a GFCI Receptacle on a Circuit Protected by an AFCI?

Yes! There should be no problem installing GFCI receptacles downstream from an AFCI circuit breaker in those locations where GFCI protection is required.

On branch circuits that are required by *210.12(B)* to be AFCI-protected, you might want to pick up a receptacle(s) that requires GFCI protection. This occurs a few times in the residence discussed in this book. The Front Bedroom branch circuit A16 picks up an outdoor receptacle on the front of the house. The Master Bedroom branch circuit A19 picks up an outdoor receptacle on the back of the house. The Living Room branch circuit B17 picks up an outdoor receptacle on the back of the house.

You could also install a dual-function AFCI/GFCI circuit breaker in the panel, which would provide arc-fault and ground-fault protection for an entire branch circuit with one device. It is a matter of choice and availability of AFCI, GFCI, and AFCI/GFCI dual-function breakers.

AFCIs in Existing Homes

The mandatory requirement in *210.12* for AFCI protection is for new work only. It is not retroactive. But it's not a bad idea to consider installing AFCIs on existing installations. It is easy to do. Just replace existing circuit breaker(s) with an AFCI circuit breaker(s). In older homes, the insulation on the original wiring is rated 140°F (60°C). Over the years, the insulation becomes brittle. For example, in and above a luminaire, the heat from the luminaire literally bakes and chars the insulation on the conductors. AFCI protection could "catch" an arcing problem in its early stages. Today, conductors used in house wiring are rated 194°F (90°C), so the deterioration of conductor insulation because of heat has become a thing of the past.

Testing AFCIs and GFCIs

AFCI/GFCI testers are used to test AFCI and GFCI receptacles and circuit breakers to make sure they are working properly. These devices simulate arc faults and ground faults. Figure 6-15A shows an arc-fault tester that also tests for proper polarity. Figure 6-15B shows a combination arc-fault/ground-fault tester that also tests for shared neutrals and verifies proper wiring connections.

REPLACING EXISTING RECEPTACLES

The *NEC*® is very specific on the type of receptacle permitted to be used as a replacement for an existing receptacle. These *Code* rules are found in *406.3(D)*.

In *406.3(D)(2)* we find a retroactive ruling requiring that when an existing receptacle is replaced in *any* location where the present code requires GFCI protection (bathrooms, kitchens, outdoors, unfinished basements, garages, etc.), the replacement receptacle must be GFCI-protected. This could be a GFCI-type receptacle, or the branch circuit could be protected by a GFCI-type circuit breaker.

It is important to note that on existing wiring systems, such as "knob and tube," or older nonmetallic-sheathed cable wiring that did not have an equipment grounding conductor, that a GFCI receptacle will still properly function. It does not need an equipment grounding conductor. Thus, protection against lethal shock is still provided. See Figure 6-7.

Replacing Existing Two-Wire Receptacles Where Grounding Means Does Exist

When replacing an existing receptacle (Figure 6-16[A]) where the wall box is properly grounded (Figure 6-16[E]) or where the branch-circuit wiring contains an equipment grounding conductor (Figure 6-16[D]), at least two easy choices are possible for the replacement receptacle:

1. The replacement receptacle must be of the grounding type (Figure 6-16[B]) unless . . .
2. The replacement receptacle is of the GFCI type (Figure 6-16[C]).

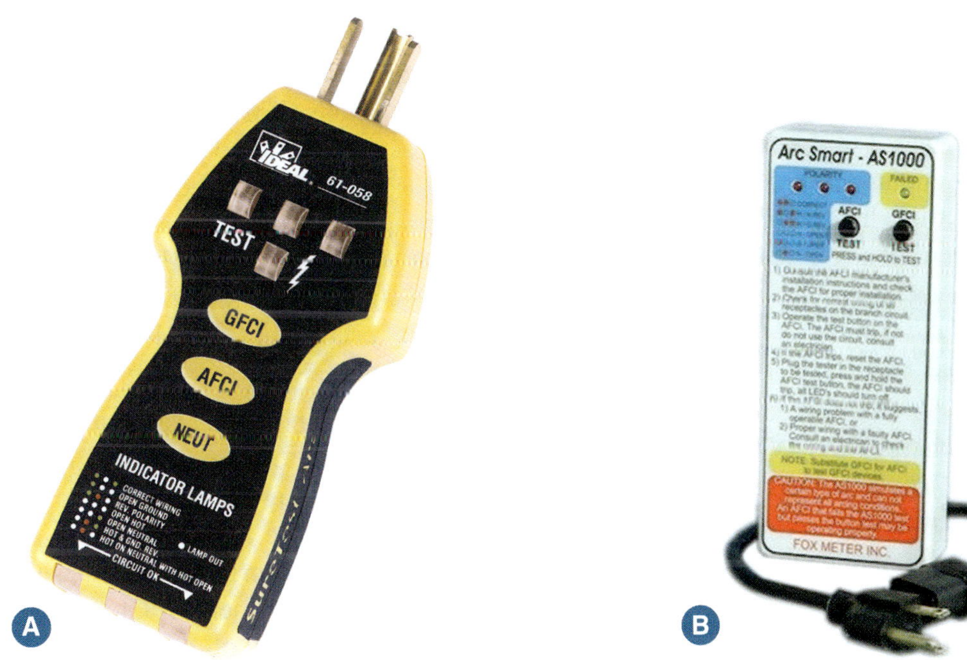

Figure 6-15 (A) An arc-fault tester that also tests for proper polarity. (B) A combination arc-fault/ground-fault tester that also tests for shared neutrals and verifies proper wiring connections.

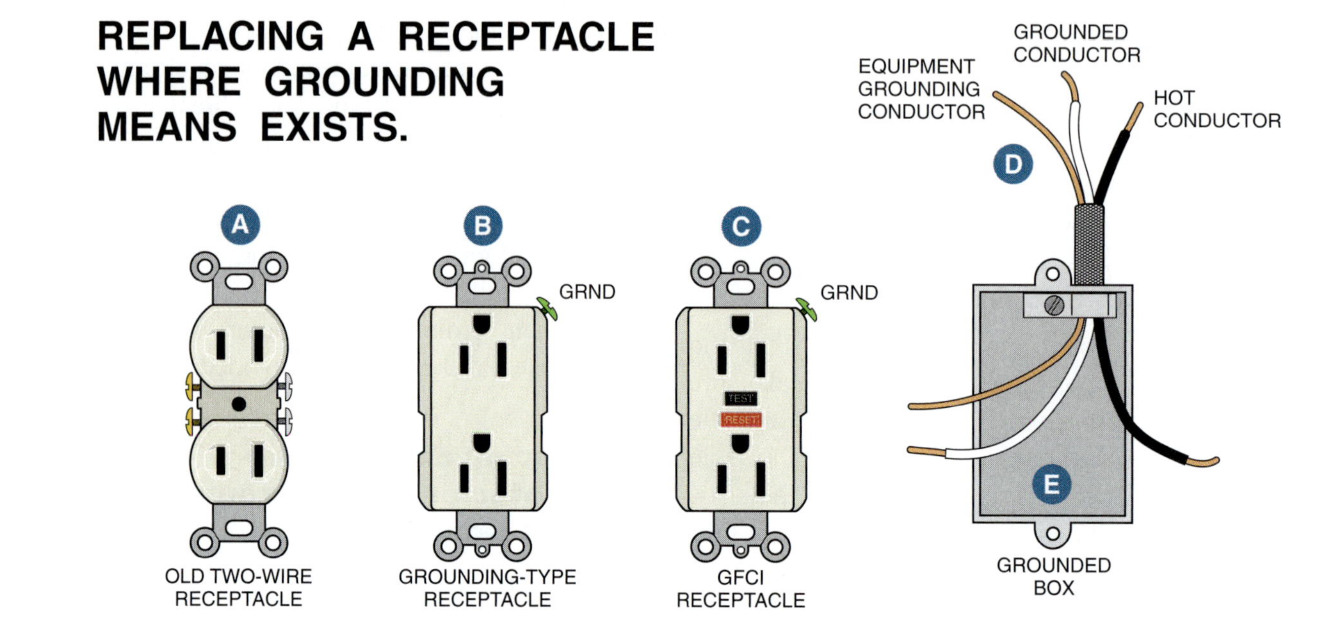

Figure 6-16 If a wall box (E) is properly grounded by any of the methods specified in *250.118*, or if the branch-circuit wiring contains an equipment grounding conductor (D), an existing receptacle of the type shown in (A) must be replaced with a grounding-type receptacle (B) or with a GFCI receptacle (C). See *406.3(D)(1)*.

If the enclosure is not grounded, *250.130(C)* permits an equipment grounding conductor to be run from the enclosure to be grounded, or from the green hexagon grounding screw of a grounding-type receptacle, to any accessible point on the grounding electrode system or to any accessible point on the grounding electrode conductor. Note, however, that this permission is only for existing installations. See Figure 6-19.

Be sure that the equipment grounding conductor of the circuit is connected to the receptacle's green hexagon-shaped grounding terminal.

Do not connect the white grounded circuit conductor to the green hexagon-shaped grounding terminal of the receptacle.

Do not connect the white grounded circuit conductor to a metal box.

Replacing Existing Two-Wire Receptacles Where Grounding Means Does Not Exist

When replacing an existing 2-wire nongrounding-type receptacle (Figure 6-17[A]), where the box is not grounded (Figure 6-17[E]), or where an equipment grounding conductor has not been run with the circuit conductors (Figure 6-17[D]), four choices are possible for selecting the replacement receptacle:

1. The replacement receptacle may be a non-grounding type (Figure 6-17[A]).
2. The replacement receptacle may be a GFCI type (Figure 6-17[C]).
   - The GFCI replacement receptacle must be marked "*No Equipment Ground*," as in Figure 6-18.
   - The green hexagonal grounding terminal of the GFCI replacement receptacle does not have to be connected to any grounding means. It can be left "unconnected." The GFCI's trip mechanism will operate properly when ground faults occur anywhere on the load side of the GFCI replacement receptacle. Ground-fault protection is still there. Refer to Figure 6-7.
   - Do not connect an equipment grounding conductor from the green hexagonal grounding terminal of a replacement GFCI receptacle (see Figure 6-18) to any other downstream receptacles that are fed through the replacement GFCI receptacle.

     The reason this is not permitted is that if at a later date someone saw the conductor connected to the green hexagonal grounding terminal of the downstream

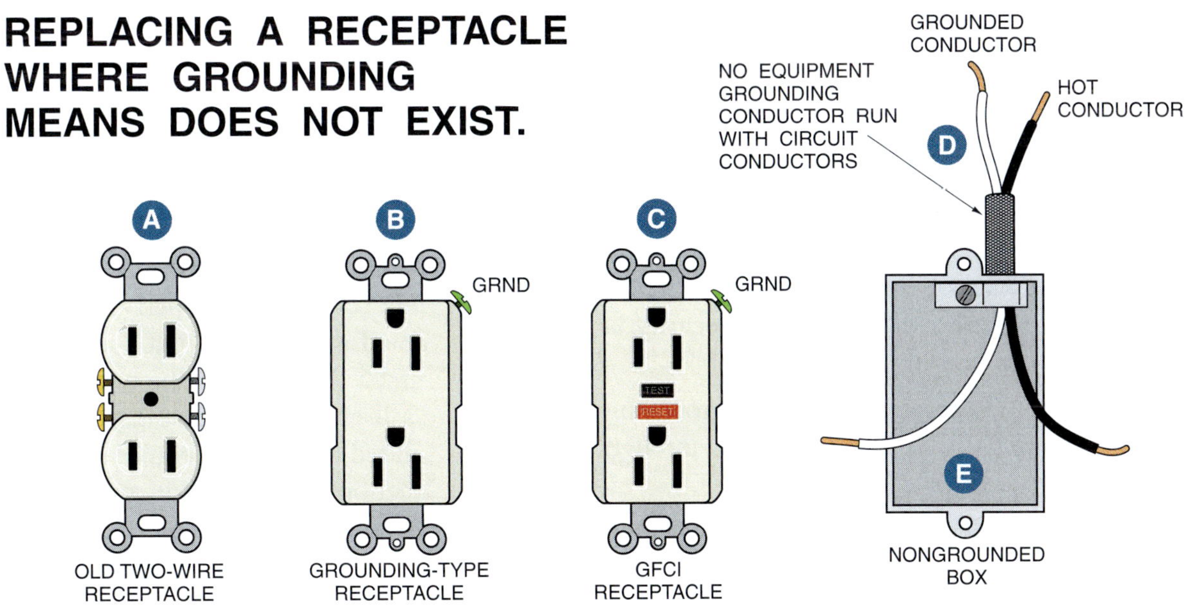

Figure 6-17 If a box (E) is *not* grounded, or if in an equipment grounding conductor has not been run with the circuit conductors (D), an existing nongrounding-type receptacle (A) may be replaced with a nongrounding-type receptacle (A), a GFCI-type receptacle (C), a grounding-type receptacle (B) if supplied through a GFCI receptacle (C), or a grounding-type receptacle (B) if a separate equipment grounding conductor is run from the receptacle to any accessible point on the grounding electrode system, *250.130(C)*. See Figure 6-19. Most electricians would replace an existing nongrounding-type receptacle with a GFCI type rather than install an equipment grounding conductor, which could be very labor-intensive. See *406.3(D)(3)*.

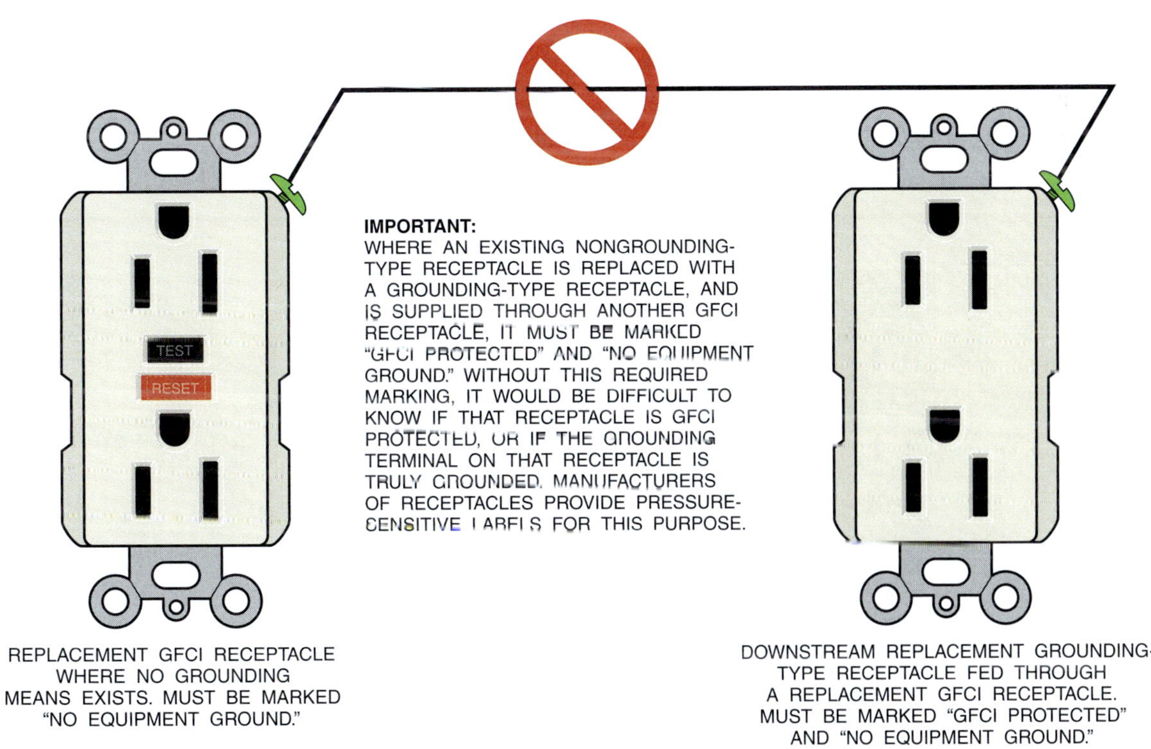

Figure 6-18 Where a grounding means does not exist, there are certain marking requirements as presented in this diagram. *Do not* connect an equipment grounding conductor between these receptacles. See *406.3(D)(3)*.

receptacle, there would be an immediate assumption that the other end of that conductor had been properly connected to an acceptable grounding point of the electrical system. The fact is that the so-called equipment grounding conductor had been connected to the replacement GFCI receptacle's green hexagonal grounding terminal that was not grounded in the first place. We now have a false sense of security, a real shock hazard.

3. The replacement receptacle may be a grounding type (Figure 6-17[B]) if it is supplied through a GFCI-type receptacle (Figure 6-17[C]).
   - The replacement receptacle must be marked "*GFCI Protected*" and "*No Equipment Ground*," as in Figure 6-18.
   - The green hexagonal equipment grounding terminal of the replacement grounding-type receptacle (Figure 6-17[B]) need not be connected to any grounding means. It may be left "unconnected." The upstream feedthrough GFCI receptacle (Figure 6-17[C]) trip mechanism will work properly when ground faults occur anywhere on its load side. Ground-fault protection is still there. Refer to Figure 6-7.
   - Do not connect an equipment grounding conductor from the green hexagonal grounding terminal of a replacement GFCI receptacle (Figure 6-18) to any other downstream receptacles that are fed through the replacement GFCI receptacle.
4. The replacement receptacle may be a grounding type (Figure 6-17[B]) if:
   - an equipment grounding conductor, sized per *Table 250.122*, is run from the replacement receptacle's green hexagonal grounding screw and properly connected to a listed ground clamp at some point on the first 5 ft (1.5 m) of the metal water piping as it enters the building. You are *not* permitted to make the equipment ground connection to the interior metal water piping anywhere beyond the first 5 ft (1.5 m). See *250.130(C)* and the *FPN*. Also read *250.50* for the explanation of a "grounding electrode system." This permission is only for replacing a receptacle in existing installations. See Figure 6-19.

PERSONNEL GROUND-FAULT PROTECTION FOR ALL TEMPORARY WIRING

Because of the nature of construction sites, there is a continual presence of shock hazard that can lead to serious personal injury or death through electrocution. Workers are standing in water, standing on damp or wet ground, or in contact with steel framing

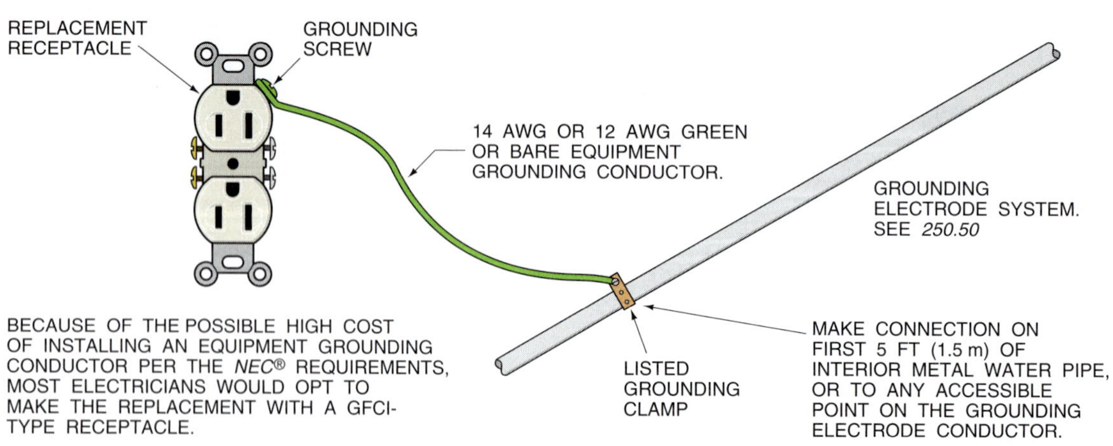

Figure 6-19 In old installations where no equipment ground exists, one option is to run an equipment grounding conductor to an accessible point on the grounding electrode system per *250.130(C)*. This can be very expensive laborwise. The better choice is to make the replacement with a GFCI receptacle. Label it "No Equipment Ground" using the pressure-sensitive label furnished with the GFCI receptacle. See Figure 6-17 and Figure 6-18.

members. Electric cords and cables are lying on the ground, subject to severe mechanical abuse. All of these conditions spell danger.

All 125-volt, single-phase, 15-, 20- and 30-ampere receptacle outlets that are not part of the permanent wiring of the building and that will be used by the workers on the construction site must be GFCI protected, *590.6(A)*. Receptacle outlets that are part of the actual permanent wiring of a building and are used by personnel for temporary power are also required to be GFCI-protected.

Figure 6-20 A temporary power box used on construction sites. This particular type is connected with a 50-ampere, 120/240-volt power cord. It has six 20-ampere, GFCI-protected, 125-volt receptacles plus additional 30-ampere and 50-ampere Twist-Lock® receptacles. *Courtesy of* Hubbell Incorporated, Wiring Device Division.

For receptacles *other* than 125-volt, single-phase, 15-, 20-, and 30-ampere receptacles, there are two options for providing personnel protection. In *590.6(B)(1)*, GFCI protection is one of the choices. In *590.6(B)(2)*, a written *Assured Equipment Grounding Conductor Program* is the second choice. This program shall be continuously enforced on the construction site. A designated person must keep a written log, ensuring that all electrical equipment is properly installed and maintained according to the applicable requirements of *250.114*, *250.138*, *406.3(C)*, and *590.4(D)*. Because this option is difficult to enforce, many Authorities Having Jurisdiction (AHJs) require GFCI protection as stated in *590.6(B)(1)*.

Figure 6-20 is a listed manufactured power outlet for providing GFCI-protected temporary power on construction sites. It meets the requirements of *590.6(A)*.

Most electricians and other construction site workers carry their own listed portable ground-fault circuit-interrupter cord sets to be sure they are protected against shock hazard. These are shown in Figure 6-21 and also meet the requirements of *590.6(A)*.

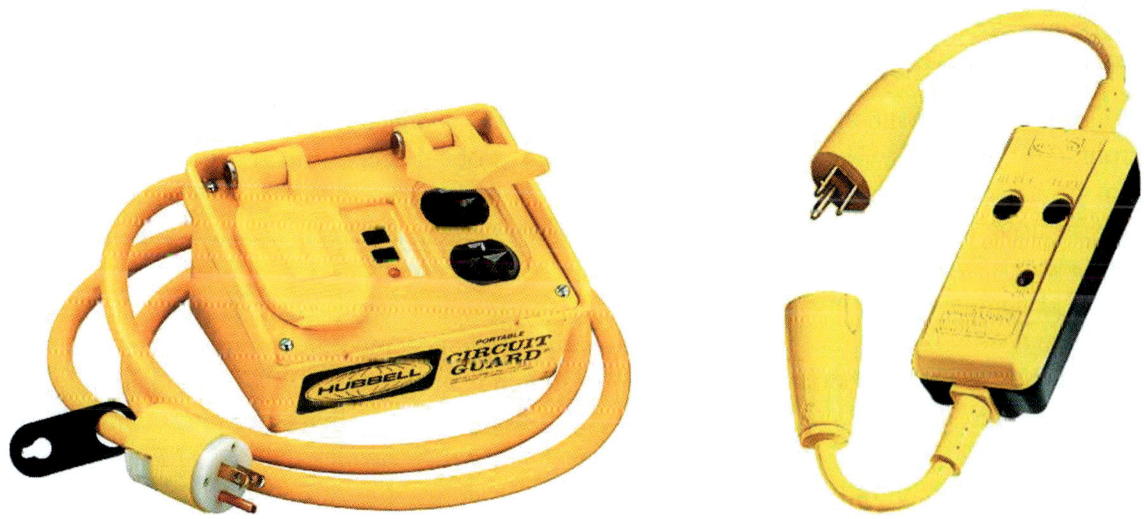

Figure 6-21 Plug- and cord-connected "portable" GFCI devices are easy to carry around. They can be used anywhere when working with electrical tools and extension cords. These devices operate independently and are not dependent upon whether or not the branch circuit is GFCI protected. These portable GFCI in-line cords are relatively inexpensive and should always be used when using portable electric tools. *Courtesy of* Hubbell Incorporated, Wiring Device Division.

Portable GFCI devices are easy to carry around. They have "open neutral" protection should the neutral conductor in the circuit supplying the GFCI open for whatever reason.

Portable GFCI devices are available with manual reset, which is advantageous should a power outage occur or if the GFCI is unplugged, so that equipment (drills, saws, etc.) will not start up again when the power is restored. This could cause injury to anyone using the equipment when the power is restored.

Portable devices are also available that reset automatically. These should be used on lighting, engine heaters, water (sump) pumps, and similar equipment where it would be advantageous to have the equipment start up as soon as power is restored.

Temporary Power for Construction Sites

In many parts of the country, it is common for the electrical contractor to furnish and install a panel for all trades to use at a construction site of a new home. Figure 6-22 shows a typical pedestal that might be secured to a pole or set in the ground. It contains a meter base, a main breaker, and GFCI branch breakers for 120-volt receptacles.

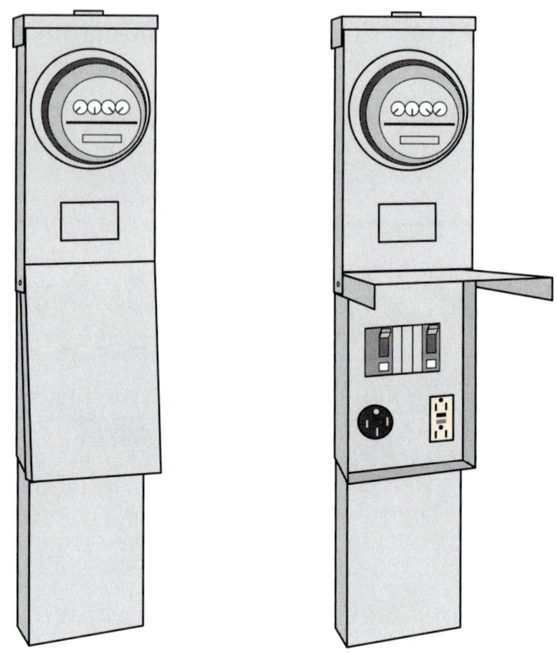

Figure 6-22 An example of a temporary construction site combination meter, breakers, and receptacles. The breakers and receptacles are under the lift-up cover.

IMMERSION DETECTION CIRCUIT INTERRUPTERS (IDCIs) AND APPLIANCE LEAKAGE CURRENT INTERRUPTERS (ALCIs)

Major culprits for electrical shock in the home are personal grooming appliances. The worst offender was found to be hand-held hair-drying appliances, most commonly used near a wash basin, or even worse, next to a water-filled bathtub with a person in it. Accidentally dropping or pulling the appliance into the tub can be deadly.

Because older homes probably do not have GFCI receptacles in bathrooms, *immersion detection circuit interrupters (IDCIs)* and *appliance leakage current interrupters (ALCIs)* were introduced to provide people with shock protection.

IDCI- and ALCI-protected appliances are easily recognized by the large attachment plug cap on the cord. IDCI and ALCI devices are an integral part of the attachment plug cap on hand-held hair-drying appliances such as electric hair dryers, stylers, and heated air combs. These devices might be manually resettable or nonresettable.

The operation of an IDCI or ALCI device depends upon a "third" wire probe in the cord, which is connected to a sensor inside the appliance. This probe detects leakage current in the range of 4 to 6 milliamperes when conductive liquid (e.g., water) enters the appliance and makes contact with any live part inside the appliance and the internal "sensor." IDCI and ALCI devices cut off power to the appliance regardless of whether the appliance switch is in the "ON" or "OFF" position.

UL requires that the plug cap be marked: *"Warning: To Reduce the Risk of Electric Shock, Do Not Remove, Modify, or Immerse This Plug."*

Never replace the special attachment plug cap on these appliances with a standard plug cap. That would make the appliance unsafe!

IDCIs and ALCIs are a requirement of *NEC® 422.41* and UL Standard 859.

TRANSIENT VOLTAGE SURGE SUPPRESSOR (TVSS)

Transient voltage surge suppressors (TVSSs) are also known as Surge-Protective Devices (SPDs).

The *Code* requirements for these devices that are permanently installed are found in *Article 285* in the *NEC*.® Always install TVSS devices that are listed under the requirements of UL Standard 1449. Carefully read and follow the instructions furnished with the TVSS.

In today's homes, we find many electronic appliances (television, stereo, personal computer, fax equipment, word processor, VCR, VDR, CD player, digital stereo equipment, microwave oven), all of which contain many sensitive, delicate electronic components (printed circuit boards, chips, microprocessors, transistors, etc.).

Voltage transients, called *surges* or *spikes*, can stress, degrade, and/or destroy these components. They can cause loss of memory in the equipment or "lock up" the microprocessor.

The increased complexity of electronic integrated circuits makes this equipment an easy target for "dirty" power that can and will affect the performance of the equipment.

Voltage transients cause abnormal current to flow through the sensitive electronic components. This energy is measured in joules. A *joule* is the unit of energy when 1 ampere passes through a 1-ohm resistance for 1 second (like wattage, only on a much smaller scale).

Line surges can be line-to-neutral, line-to-ground, and line-to-line.

Transients

Transients are generally grouped into two categories:

- **Ring wave:** These transients originate within the building and can be caused by copiers, computers, printers, HVAC cycling, spark igniters on furnaces, water heaters, dryers, gas ranges, ovens, motors, and other inductive loads.
- **Impulse:** These transients originate outside of the building and are caused by utility company switching, lightning, and so on.

To minimize the damaging results of these transient line surges, service equipment, panelboards, load centers, feeders, branch circuits, and individual receptacle outlets can be protected with a TVSS, as shown in Figure 6-23.

A TVSS contains one or more metal-oxide varistors (MOV) that clamp the transients by absorbing the major portion of the energy (joules) created by the surge, allowing only a small, safe amount of energy to enter the actual connected load.

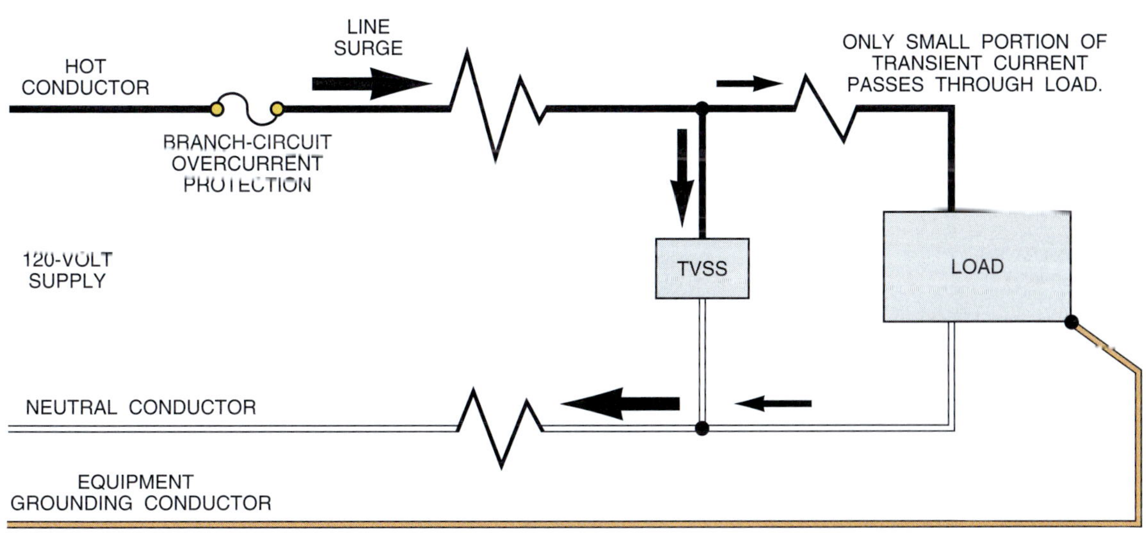

Figure 6-23 A transient voltage surge suppressor absorbs and bypasses (shunts) transient currents around the load. The MOV dissipates the surge in the form of heat.

The MOV clamps the transient in times of less than 1 nanosecond, which is one billionth of a second, and keeps the voltage spike passed through to the connected load to a maximum range of 400 to 500 peak volts.

Typical TVSS devices for homes are available as an integral part of receptacle outlets that mount in the same wall boxes as regular receptacles. They look the same as a normal receptacle and may have an audible alarm that sounds when an MOV has failed. The TVSS device may also have a visual indication, such as a light-emitting diode (LED) that glows continuously until an MOV fails. Then the LED starts to flash on and off, as in Figure 6-24.

TVSS devices are available in plug-in strips (Figure 6-25) and as part of desktop computer hardware power direction stands commonly placed under a monitor for plugging in a monitor, printer, scanner, and other peripheral equipment. These minimize the accumulation of the multitude of cords under and behind the equipment.

A TVSS on a branch circuit will provide surge suppression for all of the receptacles on the same circuit. These surges are classified as Category A low-level surges.

"Whole-house" surge protectors are available that offer surge protection for the entire house. See Figure 6-26. These are generally available at electrical supply houses and are installed at the main electrical panel of a home.

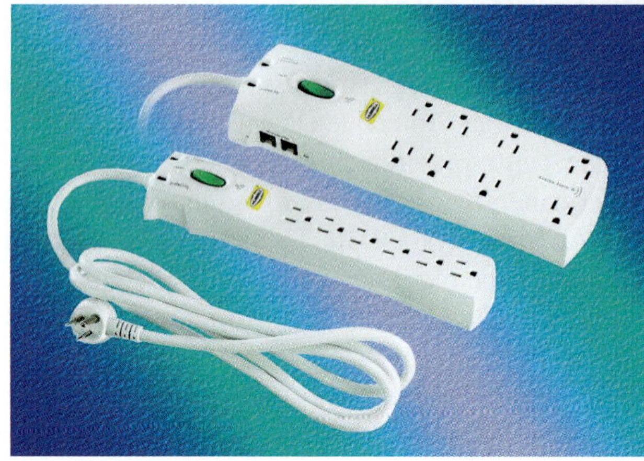

Figure 6-25 Surge suppressors. ***Courtesy of*** **Hubbell Incorporated, Wiring Device Division.**

When a whole-house surge protector is installed, it is still a good idea to install surge protectors at the plug-in locations to more closely protect against low-level surges at the computer or other delicate electronic equipment location.

Noise

Electromagnetic "noise," not to be confused with audible noise, is external interference that can be generated in varying degrees by all types of electrical and electronic equipment. You might recognize "noise" as snow on a TV screen, or as humming/buzzing/static on a radio or telephone. Some typical

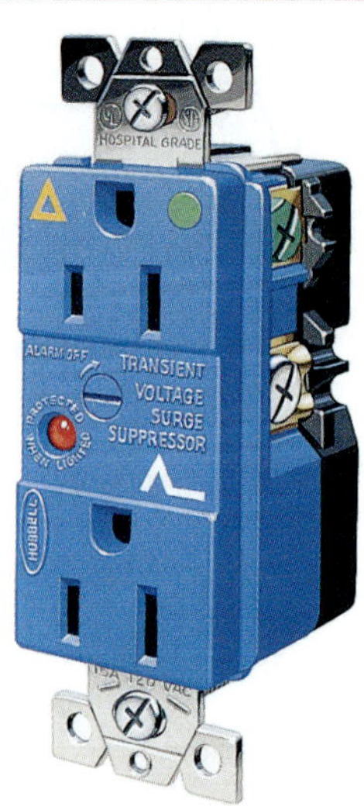

Figure 6-24 Surge suppressor protector. ***Courtesy of*** **Hubbell Incorporated, Wiring Device Division.**

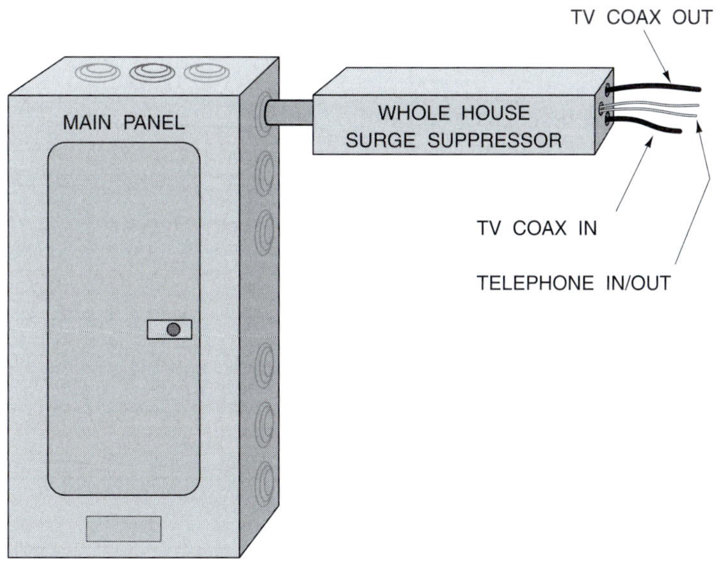

Figure 6-26 A whole-house transient voltage surge suppressor installed next to the main service panel. *Article 285* in the *NEC®* requires that these devices be listed and have their short-circuit rating marked on the device. Be sure to follow the manufacturer's installation and connection instructions.

sources of noise are fluorescent lamps and ballasts, motors running or being switched "ON" and "OFF," loose electrical connections, or improper grounding. Even equipment running in the area such as X-ray equipment can be the culprit.

Although low-level noise is not physically damaging to electronic equipment, computers can lose memory, perform wrong calculations, have program malfunction, or lose Internet connection.

Noise comes from electromagnetic interference (EMI) and radio frequency interference (RFI).

EMI is usually caused by ground currents of very low values from such things as motors, utility switching loads, and lightning, and is transmitted through metal conduits.

RFI is noise, like the buzzing heard on a car radio when driving under a high-voltage transmission line. This interference "radiates" through the air from the source. Noise can be radiated or conducted from one residence to another. In commercial buildings, this radiated noise can be picked up by the grounding system of the building.

Consumer and commercial products today must meet Federal Communication Commission requirements for emission of electromagnetic and electronic noise so as not to interfere with communications equipment. Note: A cell phone has very limited amount of transmitting power.

In commercial work, *isolated ground receptacles* are installed in computer rooms to minimize "noise."

In residential work, isolated ground receptacles are rarely, if ever, used.

Various types of electronic "noise' eliminators are available from electronic stores that filter out and virtually eliminate undesirable interference.

Here are some related UL Standards:

- UL 498 Attachment Plugs and Receptacles
- UL 943 Ground Fault Circuit Interrupters
- UL 1283 Electromagnetic Interference Filters
- UL 1363 Relocatable Power Taps
- UL 1449 Transient Voltage Surge Suppressors
- UL 1644 Immersion Detection Circuit Interrupters
- UL 1699 Arc-Fault Circuit Interrupters

REVIEW

1. Explain the operation of a ground-fault circuit interrupter. Why are GFCI devices used? Where are GFCI receptacles required? ______

2. Residential GFCI devices are set to trip a ground-fault current above ______ milliamperes.
3. Where must GFCI receptacles be installed in residential garages? ______

4. The *Code* requires GFCI protection for certain receptacles in the kitchen. Explain where these are required. ______

5. Is it a *Code* requirement to install GFCI receptacles in a fully carpeted, finished recreation room in the basement? ______
6. A homeowner calls in an electrical contractor to install a separate circuit in the basement (unfinished) for a freezer. Is a GFCI receptacle required? ______
7. GFCI protection is available as (a) branch-circuit breaker GFCI, (b) feeder circuit breaker GFCI, (c) individual GFCI receptacles, (d) feedthrough GFCI receptacles. In your opinion, for residential use, what type would you install? ______
8. Extremely long circuit runs connected to a GFCI branch-circuit breaker might result in
   a. nuisance tripping of the GFCI.
   b. loss of protection.
   c. the need to reduce the load on the circuit.

   Circle the correct answer.
9. If a person comes in contact with the "hot" and grounded conductors of a 2-wire branch circuit that is protected by a GFCI, will the GFCI trip "OFF"? Why?

10. What might happen if the line and load connections of a feedthrough GFCI receptacle were reversed? ______________________________

11. May a GFCI receptacle be installed as a replacement in an old installation where the 2-wire circuit has no equipment grounding conductor? ______________

12. What two types of receptacles may be used to replace a defective receptacle in an older home that is wired with knob-and-tube wiring where no equipment grounding means exists in the box? ______________________________

13. You are asked to replace a receptacle. Upon checking the wiring, you find that the wiring method is conduit and that the wall box is properly grounded. The receptacle is of the older style 2-wire type that does not have a grounding terminal. You remove the old receptacle and replace it with (circle the letter of the correct answer)
    a. the same type of receptacle as the type being removed.
    b. a receptacle that is of the grounding type.
    c. a GFCI receptacle.

14. What color are the terminals of a standard grounding-type receptacle? ______________

15. What special shape and color are the grounding terminals of receptacle outlets and other devices? ______________________________

16. Construction sites can be dangerous because of the manner in which extension cords, portable electrical tools, and other electrical equipment are used and abused. To reduce this hazard, *590.6(A)* of the *NEC*® requires that all 125-volt, single-phase, 15-, 20-, and 30-ampere receptacle outlets used for temporary wiring during construction must be ______________ protected.

17. In your own words, explain why the *Code* does not require certain receptacle outlets in kitchens, garages, and basements to be GFCI protected. ______________

18. Circuit A1 supplies GFCI receptacles ① and ②. Circuit A2 supplies GFCI receptacles ③ and ④. Receptacles ① and ③ are feed-through type. Using colored pencils or marking pens, complete all connections.

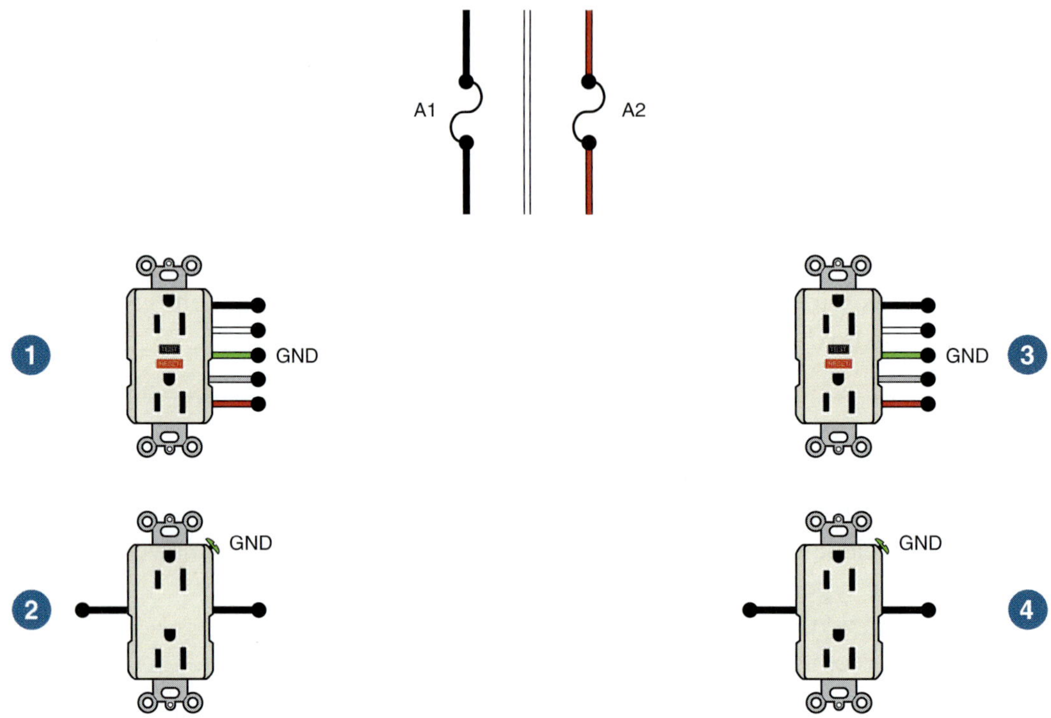

19. The term *TVSS* is becoming quite common. What do the letters stand for? ________

____

____

20. Transients (surges) on a line can cause spikes or surges of energy that can damage delicate electronic components. A TVSS device contains one or more ________ ________ ________ that bypass and absorb the energy of the transient.

21. Undesirable "noise" on a circuit can cause computers to lock up, lose their memory, and/or cause erratic performance of the computer. This "noise" does not damage the equipment. The two types of this "noise" are EMI and RFI. What do these letters mean?

____

____

____

____

22. Can TVSS receptacles be installed in standard device boxes? ________

23. Some line transients are not damaging to electronic equipment but can cause the equipment to operate improperly. The effects of these transients can be minimized by installing ________ ________ ________ ________ .

24. Briefly explain the operation of an immersion detection circuit interrupter (IDCI).

____

____

____

____

____

____

25. What range of leakage current must trip an IDCI? ____________________

____

____

26. What amount of current flowing through a male human being will cause muscle contractions that will keep him from letting go of the live wire? _______ milliamperes

27. Other than for a few exceptions, the *NEC*® requires that all systems having a voltage of over _________ volts shall be grounded.

28. In an old house, an existing nongrounding non-GFCI-type receptacle in a bathroom needs to be replaced. According to *406.3(D)*, this replacement receptacle shall be (circle the letter of the correct answer):

    a. a nongrounding-type receptacle.

    b. a GFCI-type receptacle or be GFCI protected in some other way, such as changing the breaker that supplies the receptacle to a GFCI type.

29. Do all receptacle outlets in kitchens have to be GFCI protected? Explain. __________

____

____

____

30. *NEC*® *210.12(B)* requires AFCI protection for the branch-circuit wiring that supplies all electrical outlets in specific rooms in dwellings. The branch circuits serving what areas, locations, or rooms in dwellings are not required to have AFCI protection?

____

____

____

31. When installing GFCI and AFCI circuit breakers in a panel, it is permissible to connect them to a multiwire branch circuit. (True) (False). Circle the correct answer.

Specifications for Electrical Work—Single-Family Dwelling

1. **GENERAL:** The "General Clause and Conditions" shall be and are hereby made a part of this division.
2. **SCOPE:** The electrical contractor shall furnish and install a complete electrical system as shown on the drawings and/or in the specifications. Where there is no mention of the responsible party to furnish, install, or wire for a specific item on the electrical drawings, the electrical contractor will be responsible completely for all purchases and labor for a complete operating system for this item.
3. **WORKMANSHIP:** All work shall be executed in a neat and workmanlike manner. All exposed conduits shall be routed parallel or perpendicular to walls and structural members. Junction boxes shall be securely fastened, set true and plumb, and flush with finished surface when wiring method is concealed.
4. **LOCATION OF OUTLETS:** The electrical contractor shall verify location, heights, outlet and switch arrangements, and equipment prior to rough-in. No additions to the contract sum will be permitted for outlets in wrong locations, in conflict with other work, and so on. The owner reserves the right to relocate any device up to 10 ft (3.0 m) prior to rough-in, without any charge by the electrical contractor.
5. **CODES:** The electrical installation is to be in accordance with the latest edition of the *National Electrical Code*,® all local electrical codes, and the utility company's requirements.
6. **MATERIALS:** All materials shall be new and shall be listed and bear the appropriate label of Underwriters Laboratories, Inc., or another nationally recognized testing laboratory for the specific purpose. The material shall be of the size and type specified on the drawings and/or in the specifications.
7. **WIRING METHOD:** Wiring, unless otherwise specified, shall be nonmetallic-sheathed cable, armored cable, or electrical metallic tubing (EMT), adequately sized and installed according to the latest edition of the *National Electrical Code*® and local ordinances.
8. **PERMITS AND INSPECTION FEES:** The electrical contractor shall pay for all permit fees, plan review fees, license fees, inspection fees, and taxes applicable to the electrical installation and shall be included in the base bid as part of this contract.
9. **TEMPORARY WIRING:** The electrical contractor shall furnish and install all temporary wiring for handheld tools and construction lighting per latest OSHA standards and *Article 590, NEC*,® and include all costs in base bid.
10. **WORKSHOP:** Workshop wiring is to be installed in EMT using steel compression gland fittings.
11. **NUMBER OF OUTLETS PER CIRCUIT:** In general, not more than ten (10) lighting and/or receptacle outlets shall be connected to any one lighting branch circuit. Exceptions may be made in the case of low-current-consuming outlets.

12. **CONDUCTOR SIZE:** General lighting branch circuits shall be 14 AWG copper protected by 15-ampere overcurrent devices. Small-appliance circuits shall be 12 AWG copper protected by 20-ampere overcurrent devices. Conductors shall be Type THHN. For service-entrance conductors, see Clause 28.

    All other circuits: conductors and overcurrent devices as required by the *Code*.

13. **LOAD BALANCING:** The electrical contractor shall connect all loads, branch circuits, and feeders per the Panel Schedule, but shall verify and modify these connections as required to balance connected and calculated loads to within 10% variation.

14. **SPARE CONDUITS:** Furnish and install two empty trade size 1 EMT conduits between workshop and attic for future use.

15. **GUARANTEE OF INSTALLATION:** The electrical contractor shall guarantee all work and materials for a period of one full year after final acceptance by the architect/engineer, electrical inspector, and owner.

16. **APPLIANCE CONNECTIONS:** The electrical contractor shall furnish all wiring materials and make all final electrical connections for all permanently installed appliances such as, but not limited to, the furnace, water heater, water pump, built-in ovens and ranges, food waste disposer, dishwasher, and clothes dryer.

    These appliances are to be furnished by the owner.

17. **CHIMES:** Furnish and install two (2) two-tone door chimes where indicated on the plans, complete with two (2) push buttons and a suitable chime transformer. Allow $150.00 for above items. Chimes and buttons to be selected by owner.

18. **DIMMERS:** Furnish and install dimmer switches where indicated.

19. **EXHAUST FANS:** Furnish, install, and provide connections for all exhaust fans indicated on the plans, including, but not limited to, ducts, louvers, trims, speed controls, and lamps. Included are the recreation room, laundry, rear entry powder room, range hood, and bedroom hall ceiling fans. Allow a sum of $700.00 in the base bid for this. This allowance does not include the two bathroom heat/vent/light units.

20. **LUMINAIRES:** A luminaire allowance of $1,500.00 shall be included in the electrical contractor's bid for all surface-mounted luminaires and post lanterns, not including the ceiling paddle fans. Luminaires to be selected by owner. This allowance includes the three (3) medicine cabinets.

    The electrical contractor shall:

    a. furnish and install all incandescent and fluorescent recessed luminaires.
    b. install all surface, recessed, track, strip, pendant, and hanging luminaires, and post lanterns.
    c. furnish and install two 2-lamp fluorescent luminaires above the workbench.
    d. furnish and install all lamps except as noted. Fluorescent lamps and incandescent lamps shall be energy-efficient type. Lamps for ceiling paddle fans to be furnished by owner.
    e. furnish and install all porcelain pull-chain and keyless lampholders.

    This luminaire allowance does not include the two bathroom ceiling heat/vent/light units. See Clause 21.

21. **HEAT/VENT/LIGHT CEILING UNITS:** Furnish and install two heat/vent/light units where indicated on the plans, complete with switch assembly, ducts, and louvers required to perform the heating, venting, and lighting operations as recommended by the manufacturer.

22. **PLUG-IN STRIP:** Where noted in the workshop, furnish and install a multioutlet assembly with six outlets.

23. **SWITCHES, RECEPTACLES, AND FACEPLATES:** All flush switches shall be of the quiet ac-rated toggle type. They shall be mounted 46 in. (1.15 m) to center above the finished floor unless otherwise noted.

    Receptacle outlets shall be mounted 12 in. (300 mm) to center above the finished floor unless otherwise noted. All convenience receptacles shall be of the grounding type. Furnish and install, where indicated, ground-fault circuit interrupter (GFCI) receptacles to provide ground-fault circuit protection as required by the *National Electrical Code*.® All wiring devices are to be provided with ivory handles or faces and shall be trimmed with ivory faceplates except in the kitchen, where chrome-plated steel faceplates shall be used.

    Receptacle outlets, where indicated, shall be of the split-circuit design.

24. **TELEVISION OUTLETS:** Furnish and install 4-in. square, 1½-in.-deep outlet boxes with single-gang raised plaster covers at each television outlet where noted on the plans. Mount at the same height as receptacle outlets. Furnish and install 75-ohm coaxial cable to each television outlet from a point in the workshop near the main service-entrance switch. Allow 6 ft (1.8 m) of cable in workshop. Furnish and install television plug-in jacks at each location. Faceplates are to match other faceplates in home. All remaining work done by others.

25. **TELEPHONES:** Furnish and install a 3-in.-deep device box or 4-in. square box, 1½ in. deep, with a suitable single-gang raised plaster cover at each telephone location, as indicated on the plans.

    Furnish and install four-conductor 18 AWG copper telephone cables from the telephone company's point of demarcation near the service-entrance panel to each designated telephone location. Terminate in a proper modular jack, complete with faceplates that match the electrical device faceplates. Allow 6 ft (1.8 m) of cable to hang below ceiling joists. Telephone company to furnish, install, and connect any and all equipment (including grounding connection) up to and including their Standard Network Interface (SNI) device.

    Installation shall be in accordance with any and all applicable *National Electrical Code*® and local code regulations.

26. **MAIN SERVICE PANEL:** Furnish and install in the Workshop where indicated on the plans one (1) 200-ampere, 120/240-volt, single-phase, 3-wire panelboard with a 200-ampere main circuit breaker. Panelboard shall be series-rated for 22,000 amperes available fault current.

    Furnish and install all active and spare breakers as indicated on the Panel Schedule.

    Circuit breakers shall be AFCI, GFCI, or dual-function AFCI/GFCI as required by the *NEC*.®

27. **SERVICE-ENTRANCE UNDERGROUND LATERAL CONDUCTORS:** To be furnished and installed by the utility. Meter enclosure (pedestal type) to be furnished by the utility and installed by the electrical contractor where indicated on plans. Electrical contractor to furnish and install all panels, conduits, fittings, conductors, and other materials required to complete the service-entrance installation from the demarcation point of the utility's equipment to and including the Main Panel.

28. **SERVICE-ENTRANCE CONDUCTORS:** Service-entrance conductors supplied by the electrical contractor shall be two 2/0 AWG THHN/THWN phase conductors and one 1 AWG bare neutral conductor. Install trade size 1½ EMT from Main Panel A to the meter pedestal.

29. **BONDING AND GROUNDING:** Bond and ground service-entrance equipment in accordance with the latest edition of the *National Electrical Code*,® local, and utility code requirements. Install one 4 AWG copper grounding electrode conductor.

30. **SUBPANEL:** Furnish and install in the Recreation Room where indicated on the plans one (1) 20-circuit, 125-ampere, 120/240-volt, single-phase, 3-wire MLO load center. Panelboard shall be series-rated for 22,000 amperes available fault current.

    Furnish and install all active and spare breakers as indicated on the Panel Schedule.

    Circuit breakers shall be AFCI, GFCI, or dual-function AFCI/GFCI as required by the *NEC*.®

    Feed panelboard with three 3 AWG THHN or THWN conductors from a 100-ampere, two-pole breaker in Main Panel A. Install conductors in trade size 1 EMT.

31. **CIRCUIT IDENTIFICATION:** All panelboards shall be furnished with typed-card directories with proper designation of the branch-circuit loads, feeder loads, and equipment served. The directories shall be located in the panel in a holder for clear viewing.

32. **SEALING PENETRATIONS:** The electrical contractor shall seal and weatherproof all penetrations through foundations, exterior walls, and roofs.

33. **FINAL SITE CLEAN-UP:** Upon completion of the installation, the electrical contractor shall review and check the entire installation, clean equipment and devices, and remove surplus materials and rubbish from the owner's property, leaving the work in neat and clean order and in complete working condition. The electrical contractor shall be responsible for the removal of any cartons, debris, and rubbish for equipment installed by the electrical contractor, including equipment furnished by the owner or others and removed from the carton by the electrical contractor.

34. **SMOKE DETECTORS:** Furnish and install all smoke detectors and associated wiring per manufacturer's instructions and all codes. See Clause 5. Detectors to be of the ac/dc type. Interconnect to provide simultaneous signaling.

35. **SPECIAL-PURPOSE OUTLETS:** Install, provide, and connect all wiring for all special-purpose outlets. Upon completion of the job, all luminaires and appliances shall be operating properly. See plans and other sections of the specifications for information as to who is to furnish the luminaires and appliances.

36. **AFCI AND GFCI:** Furnish and install ground-fault circuit interrupter (GFCI) and arc-fault circuit interrupter (AFCI) protection as required by the latest edition of the *National Electrical Code*.®

37. **CEILING PADDLE FANS:** The electrical contractor shall furnish and install outlet boxes identified as suitable for fan support at all locations where a ceiling suspended paddle fan is likely to be installed. The ceiling suspended paddle fans, controls, timers, lamps for same to be furnished by the owner and installed by the electrical contractor.

SCHEDULE OF SPECIAL-PURPOSE OUTLETS

SYMBOL	DESCRIPTION	VOLTS	HORSE-POWER	APPLIANCE AMPERE RATING	TOTAL APPLIANCE WATTAGE RATING (OR VA)	CIRCUIT AMPERE RATING	POLES	WIRE SIZE THHN	CIRCUIT NUMBER	COMMENTS
A	Hydromassage tub, master bedroom	120	½	10	1200	15	1	14	A9	Connect to separate circuit. Class "A" GFCI circuit breaker.
B	Water pump	240	1	8	1920	20	2	12	A(5–7)	Run circuit to disconnect switch on wall adjacent to pump. Install 10-ampere dual-element fuses as "back-up" protection. Pump controller has integral overload protection.
C	Water heater: top element 2000 W. Bottom element 3000 W.	240	–0–	12.5	3000	20	2	12	A(6–8)	Connected for limited demand. Both elements cannot operate at the same time.
D	Dryer	120/240	120 V ⅙ Motor Only	23.75	5700 Total	30	2	10	B(1–3)	Provide flush-mounted 30-A dryer receptacle.
E	Overhead garage door opener	120	See Unit 16 for explanation of overhead door operator horsepower rating	5.8	696	15	1	14	B14	Unit comes with 3-W cord. Provide box-cover unit (fuse/switch). Install Fustat Type S fuse, 8 amperes. Unit has integral protection. Fustat fuses are additional "back-up" protection. Connect to garage lighting circuit. Shall be GFCI protected
F	Wall-mounted oven	120/240	–0–	27.5	6600	30	2	10	B(6–8)	
G	Countertop range	120/240	–0–	31	7450	40	2	8	B(2–4)	
H	Food waste disposer	120	⅓	7.2	864	20	1	12	B19	Controlled by S.P. switch on wall to the right of sink.
I	Dishwasher	120	⅓	9.2 Includes 875-W heater	1104	20	1	12	B5	
J	Heat/vent/light master B.R. bath	120	–0–	12.5	1500	20	1	12	A12	
K	Heat/vent/light front B.R. bath	120	0	12.5	1500	20	1	12	A11	
L	Attic exhaust fan	120	¼	5.8	696	15	1	14	A10	Run circuit to 4-in. square box. Locate near fan in attic. Provide box-cover unit. Install Fustat Type S fuse, 8 amperes. Unit has integral protection. Fustat fuses provide additional back-up protection.
M	Electric furnace	240	⅓ Motor Only	Motor 3.5 Htr. 50.7 Total 54.2	13000	70	2	4	A(1–3)	The overcurrent device and branch-circuit conductors shall not be less than 125% of the total load of the heaters and motor. 54.2 × 1.25 = 67.75 *(424.3(B))*.
N	Air conditioner	240	–0–	26.4	6336	45	2	10	A(2–4)	
O	Freezer	120	¼	5.8	696	15	1	14	A13	Install single receptacle outlet.

Appendix

USEFUL FORMULAS

TO FIND	SINGLE PHASE	THREE PHASE	DIRECT CURRENT
AMPERES when kVA is known	$\frac{kVA \times 1000}{E}$	$\frac{kVA \times 1000}{E \times 1.73}$	not applicable
AMPERES when horsepower is known	$\frac{HP \times 746}{E \times \%\ eff. \times pf}$	$\frac{HP \times 746}{E \times 1.73 \times \%\ eff. \times pf}$	$\frac{HP \times 746}{E \times \%\ eff.}$
AMPERES when kilowatts are known	$\frac{kW \times 1000}{E \times pf}$	$\frac{kW \times 1000}{E \times 1.73 \times pf}$	$\frac{kW \times 1000}{E}$
HORSEPOWER	$\frac{I \times E \times \%\ eff. \times pf}{746}$	$\frac{I \times E\ 1.73 \times \%\ eff. \times pf}{746}$	$\frac{I \times E \times \%\ eff.}{746}$
KILOVOLT AMPERES	$\frac{I \times E}{1000}$	$\frac{I \times E \times 1.73}{1000}$	not applicable
KILOWATTS	$\frac{I \times E \times pf}{1000}$	$\frac{I \times E \times 1.73 \times pf}{1000}$	$\frac{I \times E}{1000}$
WATTS	$E \times I \times pf$	$E \times I \times 1.73 \times pf$	$E \times I$

$$\text{ENERGY EFFICIENCY} = \frac{\text{Load Horsepower} \times 746}{\text{Load Input kVA} \times 1000}$$

$$\text{POWER FACTOR (pf)} = \frac{\text{Power Consumed}}{\text{Apparent Power}} = \frac{W}{VA} = \frac{kW}{kVA} = \cos\varnothing$$

I = Amperes
HP = Horsepower
E = Volts
% eff. = Percent Efficiency
e.g., 90% eff. is 0.90
kW = Kilowatts
kVA = Kilovolt-amperes
pf = Power Factor
e.g., 95% pf is 0.95

EQUATIONS BASED ON OHM'S LAW:

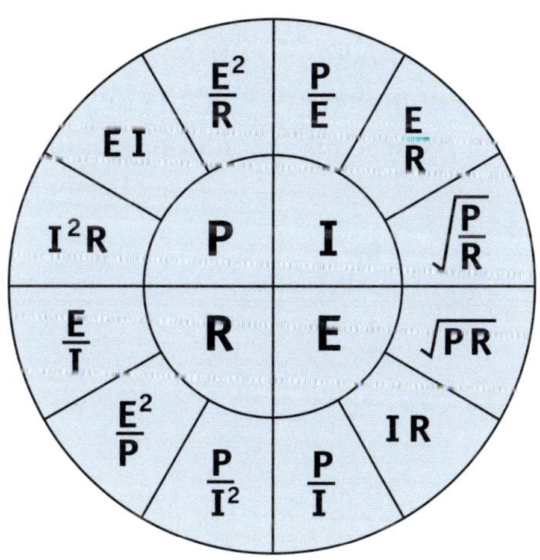

P = POWER, IN WATTS
I = CURRENT, IN AMPERES
R = RESISTANCE, IN OHMS
E = ELECTROMOTIVE FORCE, IN VOLTS

METRIC SYSTEM OF MEASUREMENT

The metric system is known as the International System of Units (SI), taken from the French Le Système International d'Unites. The following conversion table was developed from the latest National Institute of Standards and Technology (NIST) publications. In the table, whenever the slant line (/) is found, say it as "per."

The NIST Web site is http://www.nist.gov.

The *NEC*® shows both inch-pound and metric units. The term *inch-pound* refers to the way dimensions (i.e., inches, feet, yards), weights (i.e., ounces, pounds), and volume (i.e., cubic inches, cubic feet) are given in the United States. Inch-pound units are also called U.S. Customary units. Whenever possible, use the measurements found in the *NEC*® instead of making your own conversions.

Throughout the *NEC*,® inch-pound values were converted to metric units in accordance to specific rules established by the National Fire Protection Association.®

Soft Metric Conversion

A *soft conversion* is a direct mathematical conversion. A soft conversion is the result of taking a product already designed, manufactured to inch-pound values, then converting those values to metric units. The products dimension does not change in any way. Only the measurement units change.

Converting an inch-pound measurement to a metric measurement always results in bizarre, fractional values. The same holds true when converting a metric measurement to an inch-pound measurement.

In the *NEC*,® to obtain a more convenient numerical expression and eliminate awkward values, an "exact metric conversion" is often rounded (up or down) to some value within acceptable tolerances of the original value, making sure that the final measurement does not violate a "maximum" or "minimum" *Code* requirement. This is called a *soft conversion*.

Here is an example of a soft conversion where there is a real safety issue.

EXAMPLE: The minimum clearance from combustible material for a NON-IC recessed luminaire is ½ in. (13 mm). One-half inch is exactly 12.70 mm. The *NEC*® rounded this measurement up to 13 mm to obtain a more convenient, easy-to-use numerical expression.

Here is an example of a soft conversion where safety is not an issue.

EXAMPLE: Type NM cable shall be secured at intervals of 4½ ft (1.4 m) and not more than 12 in. (300 mm) from an electrical box. The exact conversion of 4½ ft is 1.3716 m and of ½ in. is 304.8 mm. These values would be cumbersome to use, so the *NEC*® rounded off the measurements to obtain convenient numerical expressions.

Hard Metric Conversion

A *hard metric conversion* involves a change in physical size of a product or measurement. An inch-pound standard size is replaced with an accepted metric standard size for a particular purpose.

A hard metric dimension is attained by designing a product to metric dimensions. No conversion from inch-pound units is involved. For example, a box is designed to measure 50 × 100 × 100 mm. It's a done deal.

Multiply This Unit(s)	By This Factor	To Obtain This Unit(s)
acre	4 046.9	square meters (m^2)
acre	43 560	square feet (ft^2)
ampere hour	3 600	coulombs (C)
angstrom	0.1	nanometer (nm)
atmosphere	101.325	kilopascals (kPa)
atmosphere	33.9	feet of water (at 4°C)
atmosphere	29.92	inches of mercury (at 0°C)
atmosphere	0.76	meter of mercury (at 0°C)
atmosphere	0.007 348	ton per square inch
atmosphere	1.058	tons per square foot
atmosphere	1.0333	kilograms per square centimeter
atmosphere	10 333	kilograms per square meter
atmosphere	14.7	pounds per square inch
bar	100	kilopascals (kPa)

Multiply This Unit(s)	By This Factor	To Obtain This Unit(s)
barrel (oil, 42 U.S. gallons)	0.158 987 3	cubic meter (m^3)
barrel (oil, 42 U.S. gallons)	158.987 3	liters (L)
board foot	0.002 359 737	cubic meter (m^3)
bushel	0.035 239 07	cubic meter (m^3)
Btu	778.16	foot-pounds
Btu	252	gram-calories
Btu	0.000 393 1	horsepower-hour
Btu	1 054.8	joules (J)
Btu	1.055 056	kilojoules (kJ)
Btu	0.000 293 1	kilowatt-hour (kWh)
Btu per hour	0.000 393 1	horsepower (hp)
Btu per hour	0.293 071 1	watt (W)
Btu per degree Fahrenheit	1.899 108	kilojoules per kelvin (kJ/K)
Btu per pound	2.326	kilojoules per kilogram (kJ/kg)
Btu per second	1.055 056	kilowatts (kW)
calorie	4.184	joules (J)
calorie, gram	0.003 968 3	Btu
candela per feet squared (cd/ft^2)	10.763 9	candelas per meter squared (cd/m^2)

Note: The former term *candlepower* has been replaced with the term *candela*.

Multiply This Unit(s)	By This Factor	To Obtain This Unit(s)
candela per meter squared (cd/m^2)	0.092 903	candela per feet squared (cd/ft^2)
candela per meter squared (cd/m^2)	0.291 864	footlambert*
candela per square inch (cd/in^2)	1 550.003	candelas per square meter (cd/m^2)
Celsius = (Fahrenheit − 32) × 5/9		
Celsius = (Fahrenheit − 32) × 0.555555		
Celsius = (0.556 × Fahrenheit) − 17.8		

Note: The term *centigrade* was officially discontinued in 1948, and was replaced by the term *Celsius*. The term *centigrade* may still be found in some publications.

Multiply This Unit(s)	By This Factor	To Obtain This Unit(s)
centimeter (cm)	0.032 81	foot (ft)
centimeter (cm)	0.393 7	inch (in.)
centimeter (cm)	0.01	meter (m)
centimeter (cm)	10	millimeters (mm)
centimeter (cm)	393.7	mils
centimeter (cm)	0.010 94	yard
circular mil	0.000 005 067	square centimeter (cm^2)
circular mil	0.785 4	square mil
circular mil	0.000 000 785 4	square inch (in^2)
cubic centimeter (cm^3)	0.061 02	cubic inch (in^3)
cubic foot per second	0.028 316 85	cubic meter per second (m^3/s)
cubic foot per minute	0.000 471 947	cubic meter per second (m^3/s)
cubic foot per minute	0.471 947	liter per second (L/s)
cubic inch (in^3)	16.39	cubic centimeters (cm^3)
cubic inch (in^3)	0.000 578 7	cubic foot (ft^3)
cubic meter (m^3)	35.31	cubic feet (ft^3)
cubic yard per minute	12.742 58	liters per second (L/s)
cup (c)	0.236 56	liter (L)
decimeter	0.1	meter (m)
dekameter	10	meters (m)
Fahrenheit = (9/5 Celsius) + 32		
Fahrenheit = (Celsius × 1.8) + 32		
fathom	1.828 804	meters (m)
fathom	6.0	feet
foot	30.48	centimeters (cm)
foot	12	inches
foot	0.000 304 8	kilometer (km)
foot	0.304 8	meter (m)
foot	0.000 189 4	mile (statute)
foot	304.8	millimeters (mm)
foot	12 000	mils
foot	0.333 33	yard
foot, cubic (ft^3)	0.028 316 85	cubic meter (m^3)
foot, cubic (ft^3)	28.316 85	liters (L)
foot, board	0.002 359 737	cubic meter (m^3)
cubic feet per second (ft^3/s)	0.028 316 85	cubic meter per second (m^3/s)
cubic feet per minute (ft^3/min)	0.000 471 947	cubic meter per second (m^3/s)
cubic feet per minute (ft^3/min)	0.471 947	liter per second (L/s)

Multiply This Unit(s)	By This Factor	To Obtain This Unit(s)
foot, square (ft^2)	0.092 903	square meter (m^2)
footcandle	10.763 91	lux (lx)
footlambert*	3.426 259	candelas per square meter (cd/m^2)
foot of water	2.988 98	kilopascals (kPa)
foot-pound	0.001 286	Btu
foot-pound-force	1 055.06	joules (J)
foot-pound-force per second	1.355 818	joules (J)
foot-pound-force per second	1.355 818	watts (W)
foot per second	0.304 8	meter per second (m/s)
foot per second squared	0.304 8	meter per second squared (m/s^2)
gallon (U.S. liquid)	3.785 412	liters (L)
gallons per day	3.785 412	liters per day (L/d)
gallons per hour	1.051 50	milliliters per second (mL/s)
gallons per minute	0.063 090 2	liter per second (L/s)
gauss	6.452	lines per square inch
gauss	0.1	millitesla (mT)
gauss	0.000 000 064 52	weber per square inch
grain	64.798 91	milligrams (mg)
gram (g) (a little more than the weight of a paper clip)	0.035 274	ounce (avoirdupois)
gram (g)	0.002 204 6	pound (avoirdupois)
gram per meter (g/m)	3.547 99	pounds per mile (lb/mile)
grams per square meter (g/m^2)	0.003 277 06	ounces per square foot (oz/ft^2)
grams per square meter (g/m^2)	0.029 494	ounces per square yard (oz/yd^2)
gravity (standard acceleration)	9.806 65	meters per second squared (m/s^2)
quart (U.S. liquid)	0.946 352 9	liter (L)
horsepower (550 ft•lbf/s)	0.745 7	kilowatt (kW)
horsepower	745.7	watts (W)
horsepower hours	2.684 520	megajoules (MJ)
inch per second squared ($in./s^2$)	0.025 4	meter per second squared (m/s^2)
inch	2.54	centimeters (cm)
inch	0.254	decimeter (dm)
inch	0.083 3	feet
inch	0.025 4	meter (m)
inch	25.4	millimeters (mm)
inch	1 000	mils
inch	0.027 78	yard
inch, cubic ($in.^3$)	16 387.1	cubic millimeters (mm^3)
inch, cubic ($in.^3$)	16.387 06	cubic centimeters (cm^3)
inch, cubic ($in.^3$)	645.16	square millimeters (mm^2)
inches of mercury	3.386 38	kilopascals (kPa)
inches of mercury	0.033 42	atmosphere
inches of mercury	1.133	feet of water
inches of water	0.248 84	kilopascal (kPa)
inches of water	0.073 55	inch of mercury
joule (J)	0.737 562	foot-pound-force (ft•lbf)
kilocandela per meter squared (kcd/m^2)	0.314 159	lambert*
kilogram (kg)	2.204 62	pounds (avoirdupois)
kilogram (kg)	35.274	ounces (avoirdupois)
kilogram per meter (kg/m)	0.671 969	pound per foot (lb/ft)
kilogram per square meter (kg/m^2)	0.204 816	pound per square foot (lb/ft^2)
kilogram-meter-squared ($kg•m^2$)	23.730 4	pounds-foot squared ($lb•ft^2$)
kilogram-meter-squared ($kg•m^2$)	3 417.17	pounds-inch squared ($lb•in.^2$)
kilogram per cubic meter (kg/m^3)	0.062 428	pound per cubic foot (lb/ft^3)
kilogram per cubic meter (kg/m^3)	1.685 56	pound per cubic yard (lb/yd^3)
kilogram per second (kg/s)	2.204 62	pounds per second (lb/s)
kilojoule (kJ)	0.947 817	Btu
kilometer (km)	1 000	meters (m)
kilometer (km)	0.621 371	mile (statute)
kilometer (km)	1 000 000	millimeters (mm)
kilometer (km)	1 093.6	yards
kilometer per hour (km/h)	0.621 371	mile per hour (mph)
kilometer squared (km^2)	0.386 101	square mile ($mile^2$)
kilopound-force per square inch	6.894 757	megapascals (MPa)
kilowatts (kW)	56.921	Btus per minute
kilowatts (kW)	1.341 02	horsepower (hp)
kilowatts (kW)	1 000	watts (W)

Multiply This Unit(s)	By This Factor	To Obtain This Unit(s)
kilowatt-hour (kWh)	3 413	Btus
kilowatt-hour (kWh)	3.6	megajoules (MJ)
knots	1.852	kilometers per hour (km/h)
lamberts*	3 183.099	candelas per square meter (cd/m^2)
lamberts*	3.183 01	kilocandelas per square meter (kcd/m^2)
liter (L)	0.035 314 7	cubic foot (ft^3)
liter (L)	0.264 172	gallon (U.S. liquid)
liter (L)	2.113	pints (U.S. liquid)
liter (L)	1.056 69	quarts (U.S. liquid)
liter per second (L/s)	2.118 88	cubic feet per minute (ft^3/min)
liter per second (L/s)	15.850 3	gallons per minute (gal/min)
liter per second (L/s)	951.022	gallons per hour (gal/hr)
lumen per square foot (lm/ft^2)	10.763 9	lux (lx)
lumen per square foot (lm/ft^2)	1.0	footcandles
lumen per square foot (lm/ft^2)	10.763	lumens per square meter (lm/m^2)
lumen per square meter (lm/m^2)	1.0	lux (lx)
lux (lx)	0.092 903	lumen per square foot (foot-candle)
maxwell	10	nanowebers (nWb)
megajoule (MJ)	0.277 778	kilowatt-hours (kWh)
meter (m)	100	centimeters (cm)
meter (m)	0.546 81	fathom
meter (m)	3.2809	feet
meter (m)	39.37	inches
meter (m)	0.001	kilometer (km)
meter (m)	0.000 621 4	mile (statute)
meter (m)	1 000	millimeters (mm)
meter (m)	1.093 61	yards
meter, cubic (m^3)	1.307 95	cubic yards (yd^3)
meter, cubic (m^3)	35.314 7	cubic feet (ft^3)
meter, cubic (m^3)	423.776	board feet
meter per second (m/s)	3.280 84	feet per second (ft/s)
meter per second (m/s)	2.236 94	miles per hour (mph)
meter, squared (m^2)	1.195 99	square yards (yd^2)
meter, squared (m^2)	10.763 9	square feet (ft^2)
mho per centimeter (mho/cm)	100	siemens per meter (S/m)

Note: The older term *mho* has been replaced with *siemens*. The term *mho* may still be found in some publications.

Multiply This Unit(s)	By This Factor	To Obtain This Unit(s)
micro inch	0.025 4	micrometer (µm)
mil	0.002 54	centimeters
mil	0.000 083 33	feet
mil	0.001	inches
mil	0.000 000 025 40	kilometers
mil	0.000 027 78	yards
mil	25.4	micrometers (µm)
mil	0.025 4	millimeter (mm)
miles per hour	1.609 344	kilometers per hour (km/h)
miles per hour	0.447 04	meter per second (m/s)
miles per gallon	0.425 143 7	kilometer per liter (km/L)
miles	1.609 344	kilometers (km)
miles	5 280	feet
miles	1 609	meters (m)
miles	1 760	yards
miles (nautical)	1.852	kilometers (km)
miles squared	2.590 000	kilometers squared (km^2)
millibar	0.1	kilopascal (kPa)
milliliter (mL)	0.061 023 7	cubic inch (in^3)
milliliter (mL)	0.033 814	fluid ounce (U.S.)
millimeter (about the thickness of a dime)	0.1	centimeter (cm)
millimeter (mm)	0.003 280 8	foot
millimeter (mm)	0.039 370 1	inch
millimeter (mm)	0.001	meter (m)
millimeter (mm)	39.37	mils
millimeter (mm)	0.001 094	yard
millimeter squared (mm^2)	0.001 550	square inch (in^2)
millimeter cubed (mm^3)	0.000 061 023 7	cubic inches (in^3)
millimeter of mercury	0.133 322 4	kilopascal (kPa)

Multiply This Unit(s)	By This Factor	To Obtain This Unit(s)
ohm	0.000 001	megohm
ohm	1 000 000	micro ohms
ohm circular mil per foot	1.662 426	nano ohms meter (nΩ•m)
oersted	79.577 47	amperes per meter (A/m)
ounce (avoirdupois)	28.349 52	grams (g)
ounce (avoirdupois)	0.062 5	pound (avoirdupois)
ounce, fluid	29.573 53	milliliters (mL)
ounce (troy)	31.103 48	grams (g)
ounce per foot squared (oz/ft^2)	305.152	grams per meter squared (g/m^2)
ounces per gallon (U.S. liquid)	7.489 152	grams per liter (g/L)
ounce per yard squared (oz/yd^2)	33.905 7	grams per meter squared (g/m^2)
pica	4.217 5	millimeters (mm)
pint (U.S. liquid)	0.473 176 5	liter (L)
pint (U.S. liquid)	473.177	milliliters (mL)
pound (avoirdupois)	453.592	grams (g)
pound (avoirdupois)	0.453 592	kilograms (kg)
pound (avoirdupois)	16	ounces (avoirdupois)
poundal	0.138 255	newton (N)
pound-foot (lb•ft)	0.138 255	kilogram-meter (kg•m)
pound-foot per second	0.138 255	kilogram-meter per second (kg•m/s)
pound-foot squared (lb•ft^2)	0.042 140 1	kilogram-meter squared (kg•m^2)
pound-force	4.448 222	newtons (N)
pound-force foot	1.355 818	newton-meters (N•m)
pound-force inch	0.112 984 8	newton-meter (N•m)
pound-force per square inch	6.894 757	kilopascals (kPA)
pound-force per square foot	0.047 880 26	kilopascal (kPa)
pound per cubic foot (lb/ft^3)	16.018 46	kilograms per cubic meter (kg/m^3)
pound per foot (lb/ft)	1.488 16	kilograms per meter (kg/m)
pound per foot squared (lb/ft^2)	4.882 43	kilograms per meter squared (kg/m^2)
pound per foot cubed (lb/ft^3)	16.018 5	kilograms per meter cubed (kg/m^3)
pound per gallon (U.S. liquid)	119.826 4	grams per liter (g/L)
pound per second (lb/s)	0.453 592	kilogram per second (kg/s)
pound-inch squared (lb•in^2)	292.640	kilograms-millimeter squared (kg•mm^2)
pound per mile	0.281 849	gram per meter (g/m)
pound-square foot (lb•ft^2)	0.042 140 11	kilogram square meter (kg/m^2)
pound per cubic yard (lb/yd^3)	0.593 276	kilogram per cubic meter (kg/m^3)
quart (U.S. liquid)	946.353	milliliters (mL)
square centimeter (cm^2)	197 300	circular mils
square centimeter (cm^2)	0.001 076	square foot (ft^2)
square centimeter (cm^2)	0.155	square inch (in^2)
square centimeter (cm^2)	0.000 1	square meter (m^2)
square centimeter (cm^2)	0.000 119 6	square yard (yd^2)
square foot (ft^2)	144	square inches (in^2)
square foot (ft^2)	0.092 903 04	square meter (m^2)
square foot (ft^2)	0.111 1	square yard (yd^2)
square inch (in^2)	1 273 000	circular mils
square inch (in^2)	6.4516	square centimeters (cm^2)
square inch (in^2)	0.006 944	square foot (ft^2)
square inch (in^2)	645.16	square millimeters (mm^2)
square inch (in^2)	1 000 000	square mils (m^2)
square meter (m^2)	10.764	square feet (ft^2)
square meter (m^2)	1 550	square inches (in^2)
square meter (m^2)	0.000 000 386 1	square mile
square meter (m^2)	1.196	square yards (yd^2)
square mil	1.273	circular mils
square mil	0.000 001	square inch (in^2)
square mile	2.589 988	square kilometers (km^2)
square millimeter (mm^2)	1 973	circular mils
square yard (yd^2)	0.836 127 4	square meter (m^2)
tablespoon (tbsp)	14.786 75	milliliters (mL)
teaspoon (tsp)	4.928 916 7	milliliters (mL)
therm	105.480 4	megajoules (MJ)
ton (long) (2 240 lb)	1 016.047	kilograms (kg)
ton (long) (2 240 lb)	1.016 047	metric tons (t)
ton, metric	2 204.62	pounds (avoirdupois)
ton, metric	1.102 31	tons, short (2 000 lb)

Multiply This Unit(s)	By This Factor	To Obtain This Unit(s)
ton, refrigeration	12 000	Btus per hour
ton, refrigeration	4.716 095 9	horsepower-hours
ton, refrigeration	3.516 85	kilowatts (kW)
ton (short) (2 000 lb)	907.185	kilograms (kg)
ton (short) (2 000 lb)	0.907 185	metric ton (t)
ton per cubic meter (t/m^3)	0.842 778	ton per cubic yard (ton/yd^3)
ton per cubic yard (ton/yd^3)	1.186 55	tons per cubic meter (ton/m^3)
torr	133.322 4	pascals (Pa)
watt (W)	3.412 14	Btus per hour (Btu/hr)
watt (W)	0.001 341	horsepower
watt (W)	0.001	kilowatt (kW)
watt-hour (Wh)	3.413	Btus
watt-hour (Wh)	0.001 341	horsepower-hour
watt-hour (Wh)	0.001	kilowatt-hour (kW/h)
yard	91.44	centimeters (cm)
yard	3	feet
yard	36	inches
yard	0.000 914 4	kilometer (km)
yard	0.914 4	meter (m)
yard	914.4	millimeters
yard, cubic (yd^3)	0.764 55	cubic meter (m^3)
yard, squared (yd^2)	0.836 127	meter squared (m^2)

* These terms are no longer used, but may still be found in some publications.

ARCHITECTURAL DRAFTING SYMBOLS

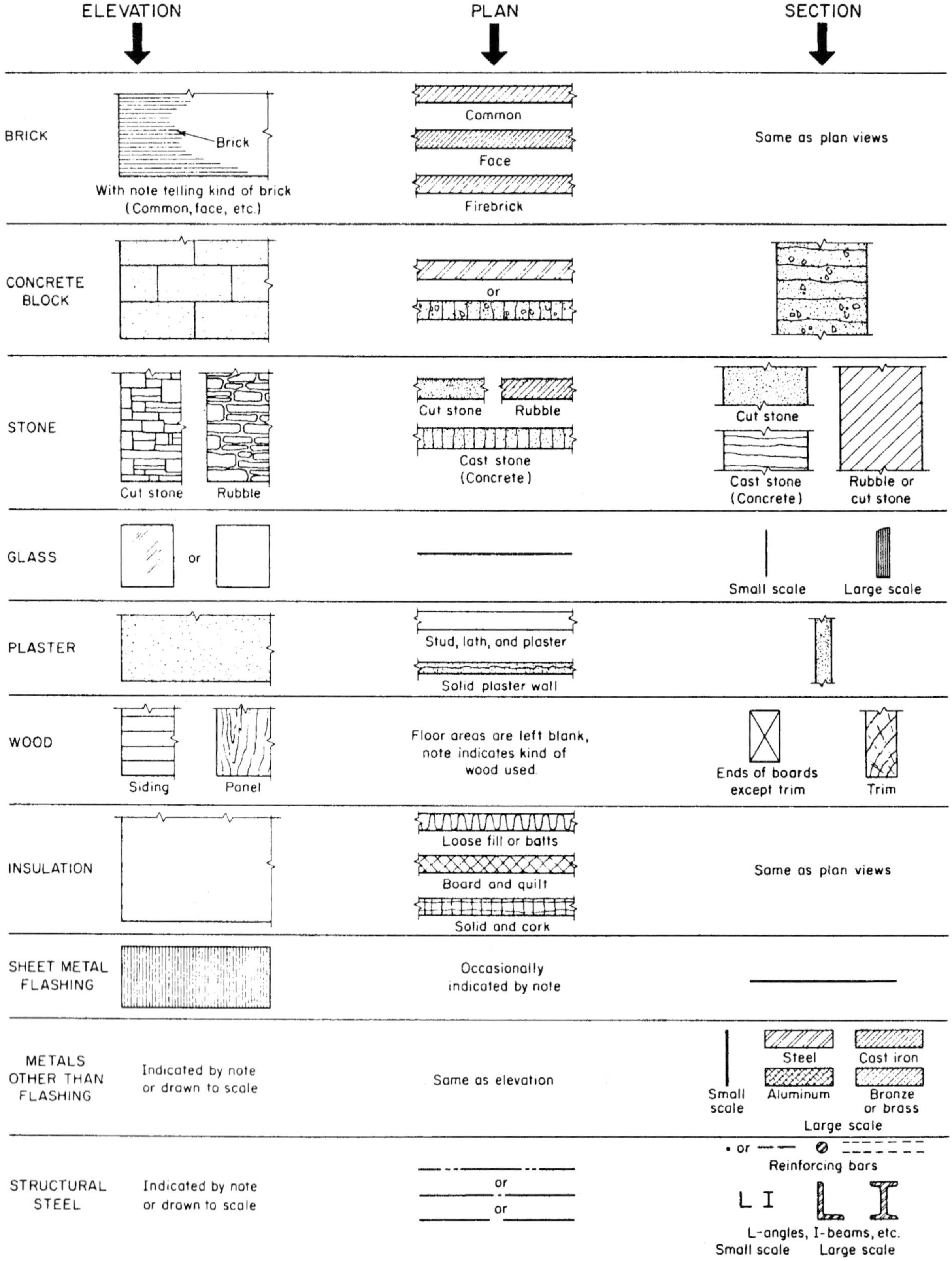

ARCHITECTURAL DRAFTING SYMBOLS (continued)

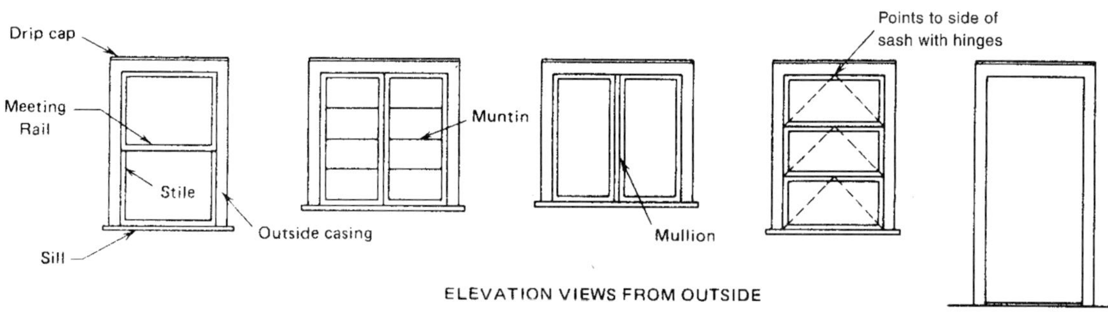

ELEVATION VIEWS FROM OUTSIDE

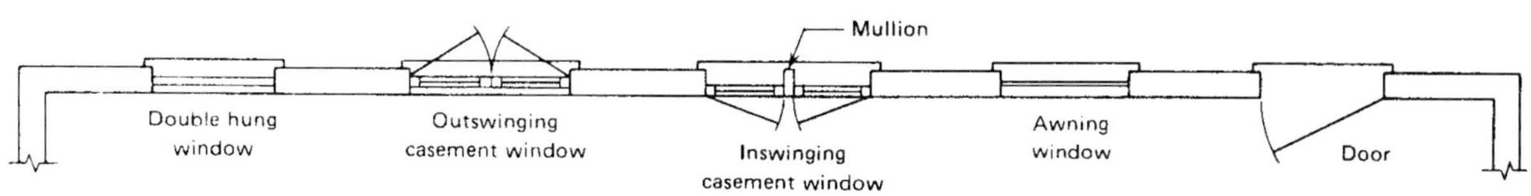

OPENINGS IN A FRAME WALL

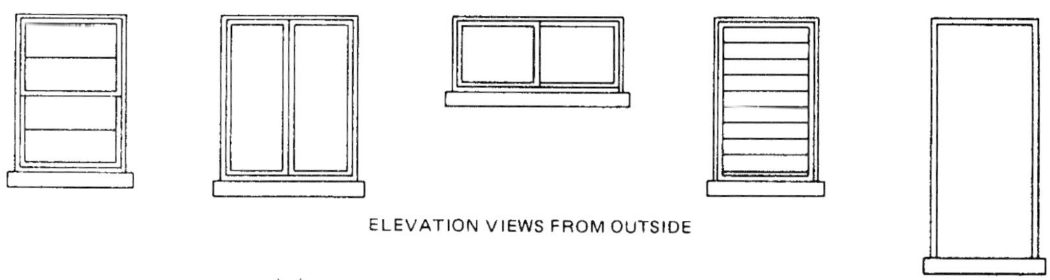

ELEVATION VIEWS FROM OUTSIDE

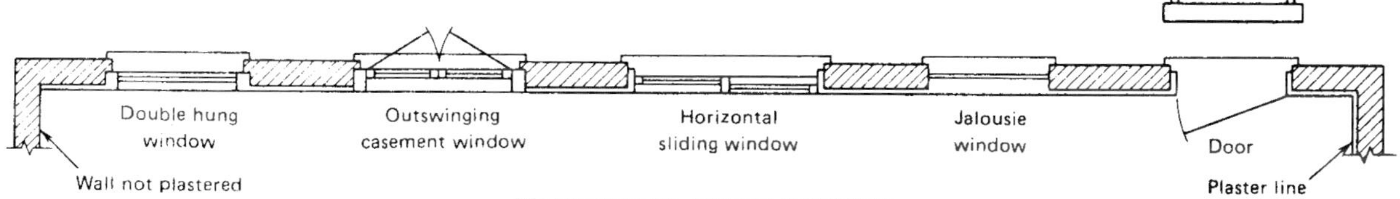

OPENINGS IN 8 in. (203 mm) BRICK WALL

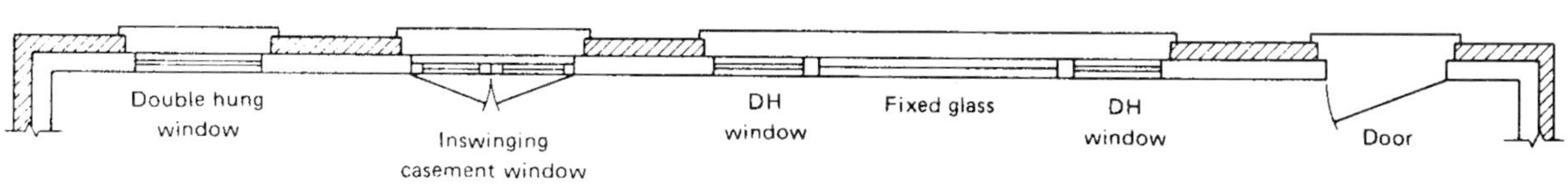

OPENINGS IN BRICK VENEER WALL
ELEVATIONS SIMILAR TO BRICK WALL

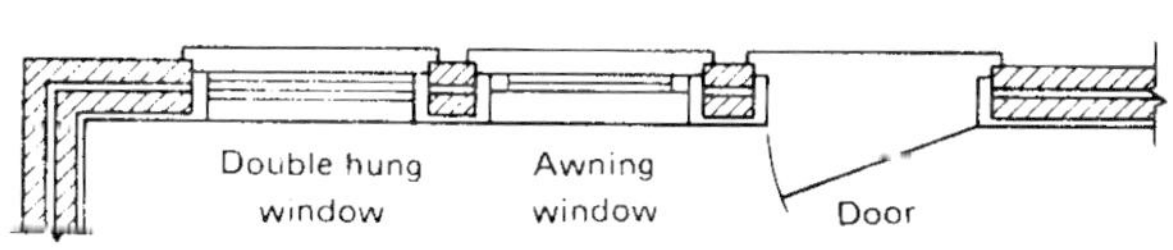

OPENINGS IN A BRICK CAVITY WALL

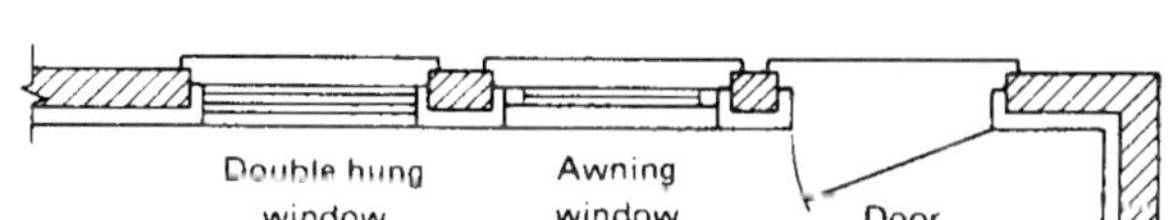

OPENINGS IN AN SCR BRICK WALL

ELEVATIONS SIMILAR TO BRICK WALL

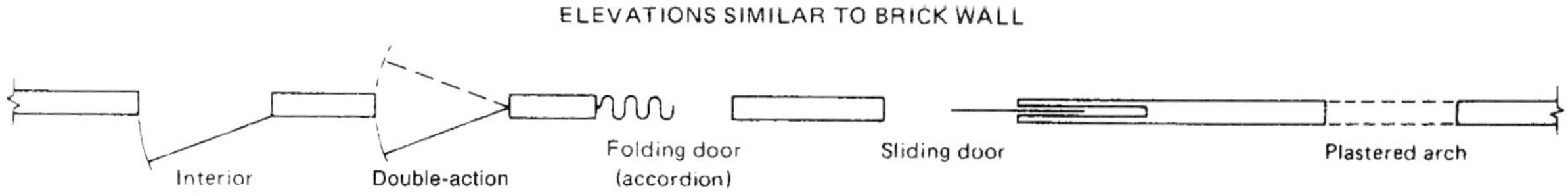

OPENINGS IN INTERIOR PARTITIONS

STANDARD SYMBOLS FOR PLUMBING, PIPING, AND VALVES

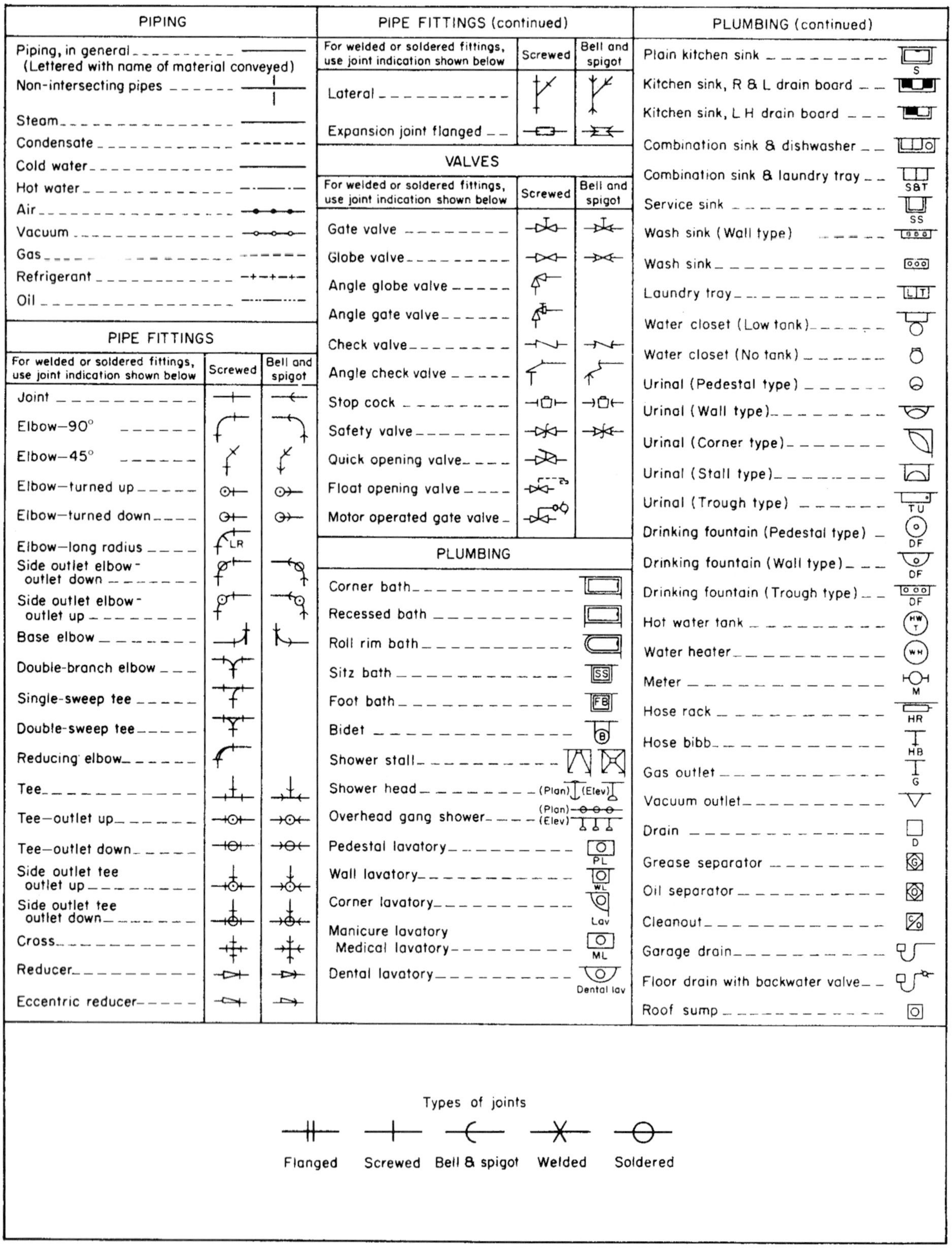

SHEET METAL DUCTWORK SYMBOLS

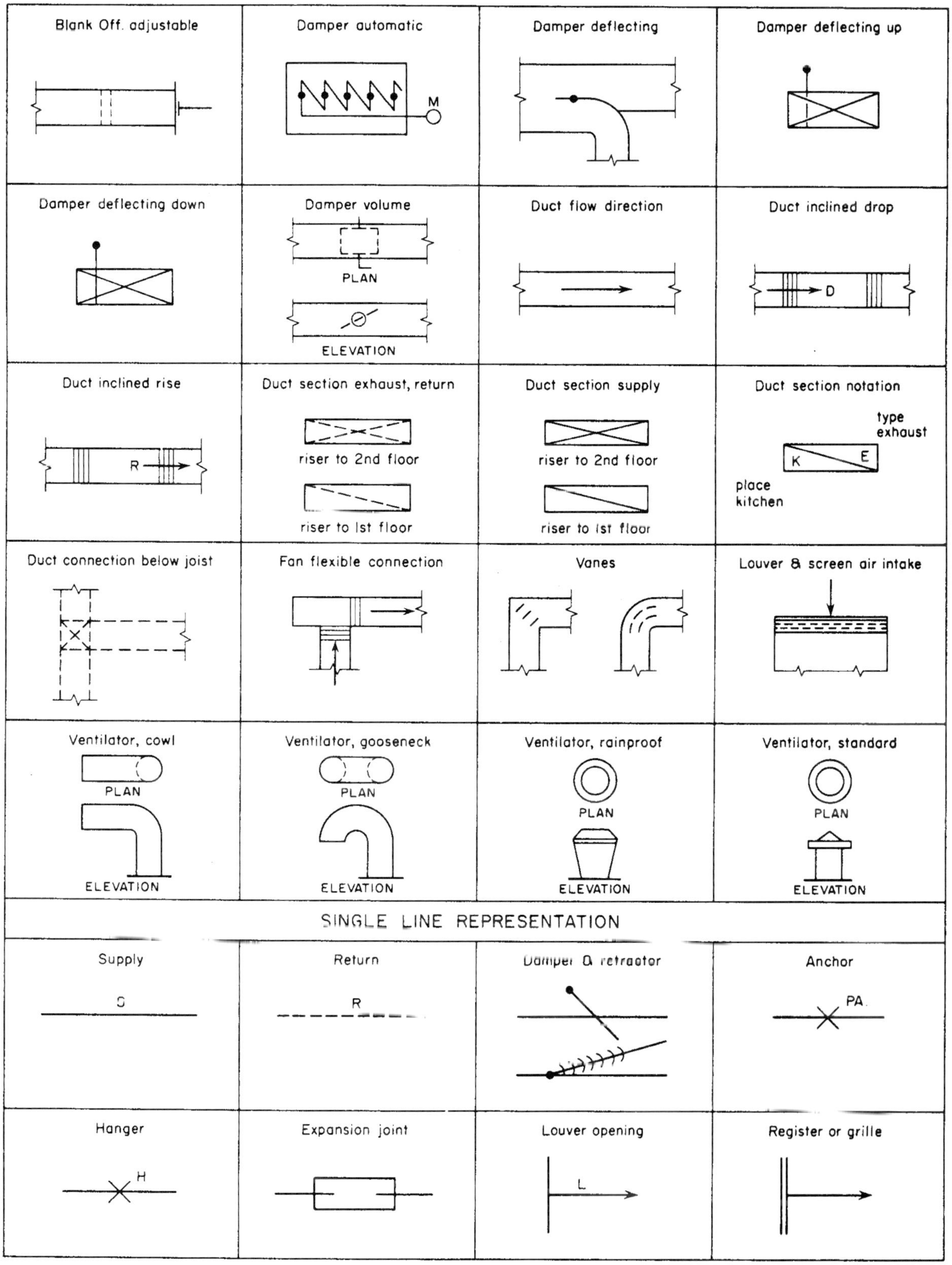

SINGLE-FAMILY DWELLING SERVICE-ENTRANCE CALCULATIONS

1. General Lighting Load (*220.12*).

__________________ ft^2 @ 3 VA per ft^2 = ____________ VA

Note: Included in this floor area calculation are all lighting outlets and general-use receptacles. Do not include open porches, garages, or unused or unfinished spaces not adaptable for future use. See *NEC*® *220.12*, *Table 220.12*, and *220.14(J)*.

2. Minimum Number of 15-ampere Lighting Branch Circuits.

$\frac{\text{Line 1}}{120} = \frac{\qquad\qquad}{120}$ = ____________ amperes

then, $\frac{\text{amperes}}{15} = \frac{\qquad\qquad}{15}$ = ____________ 15-ampere branch circuits

3. Small-Appliance Load [*210.11(C)(1)*, *220.52(A)*, and *210.52(B)*].
(Minimum of two 20-ampere branch circuits)

__________________ branch circuits @ 1500 VA each = ____________ VA

4. Laundry Branch Circuit [*210.11(C)(2)*, *220.52(B)*, and *210.52(F)*].
(Minimum of one 20-ampere branch circuit)

__________________ branch circuit(s) @ 1500 VA each = ____________ VA

5. Total General Lighting, Small-Appliance, and Laundry Load.

Lines 1 + 3 + 4 = ____________ VA

6. Net Calculated General Lighting, Small-Appliance, and Laundry Loads (less ranges, ovens, and "fastened-in-place" appliances). Apply demand factors from *Table 220.42*.

a. First 3000 VA @ 100% = 3000 VA

b. Line 5 ____________ – 3000 = ____________ @ 35% = ____________ VA

Total a + b = ____________ VA

7. Electric Range, Wall-Mounted Ovens, Counter-Mounted Cooking Units *(Table 220.55)*. = ____________ VA

8. Electric Clothes Dryer *(Table 220.51)*. = ____________ VA

9. Electric Furnace *(220.54)*.
Air Conditioner, Heat Pump *(Article 440)*.
(Enter largest value, *220.60*) = ____________ VA

10. Net Calculated General Lighting, Small-Appliance, Laundry, Ranges, Ovens, Cooktop Units, HVAC.

Lines 6 + 7 + 8 + 9 = ____________ VA

11. List "Fastened-in-Place" Appliances *in addition* to Electric Ranges, Electric Clothes Dryers, Electric Space Heating, and Air-Conditioning Equipment.

Appliance		**VA Load**	
Water heater:	=	________	VA
Dishwasher:	=	________	VA
Garage door opener:	=	________	VA
Food waste disposer:	=	________	VA
Water pump:	=	________	VA
Gas-fired furnace:	=	________	VA
Sump pump:	=	________	VA
Other: ________	=	________	VA
________	=	________	VA
________	=	________	VA
________	=	________	VA
Total	=	________	VA

12. Apply 75% Demand Factor (*220.53*) if Four or More "Fastened-in-Place" Appliances. If Less Than Four, Figure @ 100%. Do not include electric ranges, electric clothes dryers, electric space heating, or air-conditioning equipment.

Line 11 Total: ________ × 0.75 = ________ VA

13. Total Calculated Load (Lighting, Small-Appliance, Ranges, Dryer, HVAC, "Fastened-in-Place" Appliances).

Line 10 ________ + Line 12 ________ = ________ VA

14. Add 25% of Largest Motor (*220.50* and *430.24*).

________ × 0.25 = ________ VA

Note: The largest motor can be difficult to determine since nothing is in place when service-entrance load calculations are made. It might be an air-conditioning unit or a heat pump. If the dwelling is cooled by an evaporative cooler, the largest motor might be a water pump, a large attic exhaust fan, a large food waste disposer, or a sump pump. For simplicity in this example, the water pump was chosen. The additional 25% of the largest motor is a small portion of the total service-entrance load calculation.

15. Grand Total Line 13 + Line 14. = ________ VA

16. Minimum Ampacity for Ungrounded Service-Entrance Conductors.

$$\text{Amperes} = \frac{\text{Line 15}}{240} = \frac{\_\_\_\_\_\_\_\_}{240} = \_\_\_\_\_\_\_\_ \text{ amperes}$$

17. Ungrounded Conductor Size (copper). ____________ AWG

Note: *Table 310.15(B)(6)* may be used only for 120/240-volt, 3-wire, residential single-phase service-entrance conductors, service lateral conductors, and feeder conductors that serve as the main power feeder to a dwelling unit.

18. Minimum Ampacity for Neutral Service-Entrance Conductor, *220.61* and *310.15(B)(6)*. Do Not Include Straight 240-Volt Loads.

a. Line 6: = ____________ VA

b. Line 7: ____________ @ 0.70 = ____________ VA

c. Line 8: ____________ @ 0.70 = ____________ VA

d. Line 11: (Include only 120-volt loads.)

____________	____________	VA
____________	____________	VA
____________	____________	VA
____________	____________	VA
____________	____________	VA
Total	____________	VA

e. Line d total @ 75% demand factor if four or more per *220.53*, otherwise use 100%.

____________ × 0.75 = ____________ VA

f. Add 25% of largest 120-volt motor.

____________ × 0.25 = ____________ VA

Total = ____________ VA

g. Total a + b + c + e + f. = ____________ VA

$$\text{Amperes} = \frac{\text{Line g}}{240} = \frac{\qquad\qquad}{240} = \underline{\qquad\qquad} \text{ amperes}$$

19. Neutral Conductor Size (copper) (*220.61*). ____________ AWG

Note: *NEC® 310.15(B)(6)* permits the neutral conductor to be smaller than the ungrounded "hot" conductors if the requirement of *215.2, 220.61*, and *230.42* are met. *NEC® 220.61* states that a feeder or service neutral load shall be the maximum unbalance of the load determined by *Article 220*. When bare conductors are used with insulated conductors, the conductors' ampacity is based on the ampacity of the other insulated conductors in the raceway, *310.15(B)(3)*. The neutral conductor shall not be smaller than the grounding electrode conductor, *250.24(C)(1)*.

20. Grounding Electrode Conductor Size (copper) *(Table 250.66)*. ____________ AWG

21. Raceway Size. ________ Trade Size

Obtain dimensional data from *Table 1*, *Table 4*, *Table 5*, and *Table 8*, *Chapter 9*, *NEC®*

SINGLE-FAMILY DWELLING SERVICE-ENTRANCE CALCULATIONS

JOB ____________________

Note: See back of page for line item instructions.

1. **General Lighting Load** ________ ft^2 @ 3 VA per ft^2 = ________ VA
2. **Minimum Number of 15-Ampere Lighting Branch Circuits.**

   $\frac{\text{Line 1}}{120} = \frac{\_\_\_\_}{120} = \_\_\_\_$ *amperes, then* $\frac{\text{amperes}}{15} = \frac{\_\_\_\_}{15} = \_\_\_\_$ *15 ampere lighting branch circuits*
3. **Small-Appliance Load** ________ branch circuits @ 1,500 VA each = ________ VA
4. **Laundry Branch Circuit** ________ branch circuit(s) @ 1,500 VA each = ________ VA
5. **Total General Lighting, Small-Appliance, and Laundry Load. Lines 1 + 3 + 4** = ________ VA
6. **General Lighting, Small-Appliance, Laundry.**
   a. First 3000 VA @ 100% = 3,000 VA
   b. Line 5 ________ – 3000 = ________ @ 35% = ________ VA
   Total a + b = ________ VA
7. **Electric Range, Ovens, Counter-Mounted Cooking Units** = ________ VA
8. **Electric Clothes Dryer** = ________ VA
9. **Electric Furnace, Air Conditioner, Heat Pump (Enter largest)** = ________ VA
10. **Add Lines 6 + 7 + 8 + 9** = ________ VA
11. **List "Fastened-in-Place" Appliances *in addition* to Electric Ranges, Electric Clothes Dryers, Electric Space Heating, and Air-Conditioning Equipment.**

Appliance	**VA Load**
Water heater:	________ VA
Dishwasher:	________ VA
Garage door opener:	________ VA
Food waste disposer:	________ VA
Water pump:	________ VA
Gas-fired furnace:	________ VA
Sump pump:	________ VA
Other: ________	________ VA
________	________ VA
________	________ VA
Total	________ VA

12. **Apply 75% Demand Factor (220.53) if Four or More "Fastened-in-Place" Appliances. If Less Than Four, Figure @ 100%.**
   Line 11 Total: ________ × 0.75 = ________ VA
13. **Total Calculated Load (Lighting, Small-Appliance, Ranges, Dryer, HVAC, "Fastened-in-Place" Appliances).**
   Line 10 ________ + Line 12 ________ = ________ VA
14. **Add 25% of Largest Motor (*220.50* and *430.24*).**
   ________ × 0.25 = ________ VA
15. **Grand Total Line 13 + Line 14.** = ________ VA
16. **Minimum Ampacity for Ungrounded Service-Entrance Conductors.**

   Amperes $= \frac{\text{Line 15}}{240} = \frac{\_\_\_\_}{240} = \_\_\_\_$ *amperes*
17. **Ungrounded Conductor Size (copper).** ________ AWG
18. **Minimum Ampacity for Neutral Service-Entrance Conductor**
   a. Line 6 total: ________ VA
   b. Line 7: ________ @ 0.70 ________ VA
   c. Line 8: ________ @ 0.70 ________ VA
   d. Line 11: (Include only 120-volt loads.)
   ________ VA ________ VA
   ________ VA ________ VA
   Total VA ________ VA
   e. Line d total @ 75% demand factor if four or more per *220.53*, otherwise use 100%.
   ________ × 0.75 = ________ VA
   f. Add 25% of largest 120-volt motor. ________ × 0.25 = ________ VA
   g. Total a + b + c + e + f Total = ________ VA
19. **Neutral Conductor Size (copper)** ________ AWG
20. **Grounding Electrode Conductor Size (copper)** ________ AWG
21. **Raceway Size.** ________ Trade Size (inch)

SINGLE-FAMILY DWELLING SERVICE-ENTRANCE CALCULATIONS

Line item instructions.

1. Included in this floor area calculation are all lighting outlets and general-use receptacles. Do not include open porches, garages, or unused or unfinished spaces not adaptable for future use. See *NEC® 220.12*, *Table 220.12*, and *220.14(J)*.
2. No further explanation needed.
3. Minimum of two 20-ampere branch-circuits. See *210.11(C)(1)*, *210.52(B)*, and *220.52(A)*.
4. Minimum of one 20-ampere branch-circuit. See *210.11(C)(2)*, *210.52(F)*, and *220.52(B)*.
5. No further explanation needed.
6. Apply the 100% and 35% demand factors from *Table 220.42*.
7. See *Table 220.55* for load values. Typical household electric ranges come under the 8 kW level.
8. See *Table 220.54* for load values. 5000 VA minimum or nameplate rating whichever is larger.
9. Enter largest value, *220.60*. Also see *220.51* and *Article 440*.
10. This is the total for General Lighting, Small-Appliance, Laundry, Ranges, Ovens, Cooktop Units, HVAC.
11. List fastened in places appliances. See *220.53*.
12. Apply 75% demand factor. Do not include electric ranges, electric clothes dryers, electric space heating, or air-conditioning equipment. See *220.53*.
13. No further explanation needed.
14. What is the largest motor? The largest motor can be difficult to determine since nothing is in place when service-entrance load calculations are made. It might be an air-conditioning unit or a heat pump. If the dwelling is cooled by an evaporative cooler, the largest motor might be the evaporative cooler motor. It could also be a furnace fan motor, a water pump, a large attic exhaust fan, a sump pump, or a large food waste disposer. Don't waste valuable time quibbling. Enter a large volt-ampere value to be on the safe side.
15. No further explanation needed.
16. No further explanation needed.
17. Shall not be smaller than 100 amperes, *230.42(B)* and *230.79*. Special conductor sizing might be permitted. See *Table 310.16* or *Table 310.15(B)(6)* may be used only for 120/240-volt, three-wire, residential single-phase service-entrance conductors, service lateral conductors, and feeder conductors that serve as the main power feeder to a dwelling unit. Check if this is permitted in your locality.
18. See *220.61* and *310.15(B)(6)*. Do Not Include Straight 240-Volt Loads.
19. See *220.61*. *NEC® 310.15(B)(6)* permits the neutral conductor to be smaller than the ungrounded "hot" conductors if the requirement of *215.2*, *220.61*, and *230.42* are met. *NEC® 220.61* states that a feeder or service neutral load shall be the maximum unbalance of the load determined by *Article 220*. When bare conductors are used with insulated conductors, the conductors' ampacity is based on the ampacity of the other insulated conductors in the raceway, *310.15(B)(3)*. The neutral conductor must not be smaller than the grounding electrode conductor, *250.24(B)(1)*.
20. See *Table 250.66*. Grounding electrode conductor based on size of service-entrance conductors.
21. Obtain dimensional data from *Table 1*, *Table 4*, *Table 5*, and *Table 8*, *Chapter 9, NEC®*

MEMBERSHIP APPLICATION

For Inspector Member/Associate Member

Annual Membership Dues $90

Services from the IAEI for you and your organization include all this and more:

- IAEI News magazine subscription
- Educational Opportunities
- Networking
- Career Advancement
- Great Discount Savings

PLEASE PRINT

Name - Last	First	M.I.	Chapter, where you live or work, if known
Title			(Division, where appropriate)
E-mail Address			
Employer			For Office Use Only — Section No. / Ch. No. / Div. No.
Address of Applicant			If previous member, give last membership number
City	State or Province	Zip or Postal Code	and last year of membership
Endorsed by RAY C. MULLIN			Endorser's Membership Number 533800
Applicant's Signature			(Area Code) Telephone Number - -

☐ Check ☐ Money Order ☐ Diners Club ☐ MasterCard ☐ Visa ☐ Amex ☐ Discover

Name on Card	Charge Card Number	Exp. Date

☐ Inspector $90 ☐ Associate $90

Inspector Members MUST sign below:

☐ I,______________________________ ______, meet the qualifications for inspector member type as described below.

Inspector members must regularly make electrical inspections for preventing injury to persons or damage to property on behalf of a governmental agency, insurance agency, rating bureau, recognized testing laboratory or electric light and power company.

Contact the IAEI Customer Service Department for information on our special membership categories - Section, National, and International Member; Sustaining Member (Bronze, Silver, Gold, or Platinum); and Inspection Agency Member.

Email addresses and telephone numbers are not required but are requested to facilitate IAEI's communicating with members and conducting IAEI/member business.

Mail to: IAEI, P. O. Box 830848 Richardson, TX 75083-0848 For information call: (972) 235-1455 (8-5 CT)
http://www.iaei.org • email: iaei@iaei.org

MA2007

Key Terms

The following is a list of terms used extensively in the electrical trades. Many of these terms are unique to the electrical industry. Words marked with an * are defined in the *National Electrical Code*.® Definitions are found in *Article 100, NEC*.®

Accent Lighting: Directional lighting to emphasize a particular object or to draw attention to a part of the field in view.

Accessible (equipment)*: Admitting close approach: not guarded by locked doors, elevation, or other effective means.

Accessible, Readily*: Capable of being reached quickly for operation, renewal, or inspections, without requiring those to whom ready access is requisite to climb over or remove obstacles or to resort to portable ladders, chairs, and so forth.

Accessible (wiring methods)*: Capable of being removed or exposed without damaging the building structure or finish, or not permanently closed in by the structure or finish of the building.

Addendum: Modification (change) made to the construction documents (plans and specifications) during the bidding period.

Adjustment Factor: A multiplier (penalty) that is applied to conductors when there are more than three current-carrying conductors in a raceway or cable. These multipliers are found in *Table 310.15(B)(2)*. An *adjustment factor* is also referred to as a *derating factor*.

AL/CU: Terminal marking on switches and receptacles rated 30 amperes and greater suitable for use with aluminum, copper, and copper-clad aluminum conductors. If not marked, suitable for copper conductors only.

Alternate Bid: Amount stated in the bid to be added or deducted from the base bid amount proposed for alternate materials and/or methods of construction.

Ambient Lighting: Lighting throughout an area that produces general illumination.

Ambient Temperature: The environmental temperature surrounding the object under consideration.

American National Standards Institute (ANSI): An organization that identifies industrial and public requirements for national consensus standards and coordinates and manages their development, resolves national standards problems, and ensures effective participation in international standardization. ANSI does not itself develop standards. Rather, it facilitates development by establishing consensus among qualified groups. ANSI ensures that the guiding principles—consensus, due process, and openness—are followed.

Ampacity*: The current, in amperes, that a conductor can carry continuously under the conditions of use without exceeding its temperature rating.

Ampere: The measurement of intensity of rate of flow of electrons in an electric circuit. An ampere is the amount of current that will flow through a resistance of 1 ohm under a pressure of 1 volt.

Appliance*: Utilization equipment, generally other than industrial, normally built in standardized sizes or types, that is installed or connected as a unit to perform one or more functions such as clothes washing, air conditioning, food mixing, deep frying, and so forth.

Approved*: Acceptable to the authority having jurisdiction (AHJ).

Arc-Fault Circuit-Interrupter (AFCI)*: A device intended to provide protection from the effects of arc faults by recognizing characteristics unique to arcing and by functioning to de-energize a circuit when an arcing fault is detected. See *210.12(A)*.

Architect: One who designs and supervises the construction of buildings or other structures.

Architectural Drawing: A line drawing showing plan and/or elevation views of the proposed building for the purpose of showing the overall appearance of the building.

As-Built Drawings: Contract drawings that reflect changes made during the construction process.

As-Built Plans: When required, a modified set of working drawings that are prepared for a construction project that includes all variances from the original working drawings that occurred during the project construction.

Authority Having Jurisdiction (AHJ): The organization, office, or individual responsible for approving equipment, materials, an installation, or a procedure. An AHJ is usually a governmental body that has legal jurisdiction over electrical installations. The AHJ has the responsibility for making interpretations of the rules, for deciding upon the approval of equipment and materials, and for granting special permission if required. Where a specific interpretation or deviation from the *NEC*® is given, get it in writing. See *90.4* of the *NEC*.®

Average Rated Life (lamp): How long it takes to burn out the lamp, for example, a 60-watt lamp is rated 1000 hours. The 1000-hour rating is based on the point in time when 50% of a test batch of lamps burn out and 50% are still burning.

AWG: The American Wire Gauge. Previously known as the Brown & Sharpe Gauge. The smaller the AWG number, the larger the conductor. There are forty electrical conductor sizes from 36 AWG through 0000 AWG. Starting from the smallest size, 36 AWG, each successive size is approximately 1.26 times larger than the previous AWG size. *Table 8* of *Chapter 9* in the *NEC*® lists conductor sizes commonly found in the electrical industry. Conductor sizes through 0000 AWG are shown using the AWG designation. Conductors larger than 0000 AWG are shown in circular mil area. The 1.26 relationship between sizes is easily confirmed in *Table 8* by checking conductor sizes 4 AWG through 0000 AWG.

Backlight: Illumination from behind a subject directed substantially parallel to a vertical plane through the optical axis of the camera.

Ballast: Used for energizing fluorescent lamps. It is constructed of a laminated core and coil windings or electronic components.

Ballast Factor: A measure of the light output (lumens) of a ballast and lamp combination in comparison to an ANSI Standard "reference" ballast operated with the same lamp. It is a measure of how well the ballast performs when compared to the "reference ballast."

Bare Lamp: A light source with no shielding.

Bid: An offer or proposal of a price.

Bid Bond: A written form of security executed by the bidder as principal and by a surety for the purpose of guaranteeing that the bidder will sign the contract, if awarded the contract, for the stated bid amount.

Bid Price: The stipulated sum stated in the bidder's bid.

Black Line Print: Another term for a photocopy or computer-aided drawing (CAD).

Blueprints: A term used to refer to a plan or plans. A photographic print in white on a bright blue ground or blue on a white ground used especially for copying maps, mechanical drawings, and architects' plans. See text for further explanation.

▶**Bonded (bonding)*:** Connected to establish electrical continuity and conductivity.◀

Bonding Jumper*: A reliable conductor to ensure the required electrical conductivity between metal parts required to be electrically connected.

Bonding Jumper, Equipment*: The connection between two or more portions of the equipment grounding conductor.

Bonding Jumper, Main*: The connection between the grounded circuit conductor and the equipment grounding conductor at the service.

Branch Circuit*: The circuit conductors between the final overcurrent device protecting the circuit and the outlet(s).

Branch Circuit, Appliance*: A branch circuit supplying energy to one or more outlets to which appliances are to be connected; such circuits are to have no permanently connected luminaires not a part of an appliance.

Branch Circuit, General Purpose*: A branch circuit that supplies a number of outlets for lighting and appliances.

Branch Circuit, Individual*: A branch circuit that supplies only one utilization equipment.

Branch Circuit—Multiwire*: A branch circuit consisting of two or more ungrounded conductors having a voltage between them, and a grounded conductor having equal voltage between it and each ungrounded conductor of the circuit and that is connected to the neutral or grounded conductor of the system.**

►**Branch-Circuit Overcurrent Device*:** A device capable of providing protection for service, feeder, and branch circuits and equipment over the full range of overcurrent between its rated current and the interrupting rating. Branch-circuit overcurrent protective devices are provided with interrupting ratings appropriate for the intended use but no less than 5000 amperes.◄

Branch Circuit Selection Current*: Branch circuit selection current is the value in amperes to be used instead of the rated-load current in determining the ratings of motor branch-circuit conductors, disconnecting means, controllers, and branch-circuit short-circuit and ground-fault protective devices wherever the running overload protective device permits a sustained current greater than the specified percentage of the rated-load current. The value of branch-circuit selection current will always be equal to or greater than the marked rated-load current. This definition is found in *Article 440*.

Brightness: In common usage, the term "brightness" usually refers to the strength of sensation that results from viewing surfaces or spaces from which light comes to the eye.

Building Code: The legal requirements set up by the prevailing various governing agencies covering the minimum acceptable requirements for all types of construction.

Building Inspector/Official: A qualified government representative authorized to inspect construction for compliance with applicable building codes, regulations, and ordinances.

Building Permit: A written document issued by the appropriate governmental authority permitting construction to begin on a specific project in accordance with drawings and specifications approved by the governmental authority.

Candela: The international (SI) unit of luminous intensity. Formerly referred to as a "candle," as in "candlepower."

Candlepower: A measure of intensity mathematically related to lumens.

Carrier: A wave having at least one characteristic that may be varied from a known reference value by modulation.

Carrier Current: The current associated with a carrier wave.

CC: A marking on wire connectors and soldering lugs indicating they are suitable for use with copper-clad aluminum conductors only.

CC/CU: A marking on wire connectors and soldering lugs indicating they are suitable for use with copper or copper-clad aluminum conductors only.

**Reprinted with permission from NFPA 70-2008.

Change Order: A written document signed by the owner and the contractor authorizing a change in the work or an adjustment in the contract sum or the contract time. A contract sum and the contract time may be changed only by a change order.

Circuit Breaker*: A device designed to open and close a circuit by nonautomatic means and to open the circuit automatically on a predetermined overcurrent without damage to itself when properly applied within its rating.

▶**Clothes Closet*:** A non-habitable room or space intended primarily for the storage of garments and apparel.◀

CO/ALR: Terminal marking on switches and receptacles rated 15 and 20 amperes that are suitable for use with aluminum, copper, and copper-clad aluminum conductors. If not marked, they are suitable for copper or copper-clad conductors only.

Conductor*:

Bare: A conductor having no covering or electrical insulation whatsoever. (See *Conductor, Covered*)

Covered: A conductor encased within material of a composition or thickness that is not recognized by this *Code* as electrical insulation. (See *Conductor, Bare*)

Insulated: A conductor encased within material of a composition and thickness that is recognized by this *Code* as electrical insulation.

Construction Documents: A term used to represent all drawings, specifications, addenda, and other pertinent construction information associated with the construction of a specific project.

Construction Drawing: See *Drawings*.

Construction Types: (Also see *Annex E, NEC®*)

Type I: Fire-resistive construction. A building constructed of noncombustible materials such as reinforced concrete, brick, stone, etc., and having any metal members properly "fireproofed" with major structural members designed to withstand collapse and to prevent the spread of fire. Type I construction is subdivided into Types IA and IB.

Type II: Noncombustible construction. A building having all structural members, including walls, floors, and roofs, of noncumbustible materials such as reinforced concrete, brick, stone, etc., and not qualifying as fire-resistive construction. Type II construction is divided into Types IIA, IIB, and IIC.

Type III: Construction where the exterior walls are of concrete, masonry, or other noncombustible material. The interior structural members are constructed of any approved materials such as wood or other combustible materials. Type III construction is subdivided into Types IIIA and IIIB.

Type IV: Construction where the exterior walls are constructed of approved noncombustible materials. The interior structural members are of solid or laminated wood. Type V construction is divided into Types VA and VB.

Type V: Construction where the exterior walls, loadbearing walls, partitions, floors, and roofs are constructed of any approved material. This is wood construction as found in typical residential construction.

Continuous Load*: A load where the maximum current is expected to continue for 3 hours or more.

Contract: An agreement between two or more parties, especially one that is written and enforceable by law.

Contract Modifications: After the agreement has been signed, any additions, deletions, or modifications of the work to be done are accomplished by change order, supplemental instruction, and field order. They can be issued at any time during the contract period.

Contractor: A properly licensed individual or company that agrees to furnish labor, materials, equipment, and associated services to perform the work as specified for a specified price.

Correction Factor: A multiplier (penalty) that is applied to conductors when the ambient temperature is greater than 86°F (30°C) . These multipliers are found at the bottom of *Table 310.16* of the *NEC®*

CSA: This is the Canadian Standards Association that develops safety and performance standards in Canada for electrical products, similar to but not always identical to those of (Underwriters Laboratories) UL in the United States.

CU: A marking on wire connectors and soldering lugs indicating they are suitable for use with copper conductors only.

Current: The flow of electrons through an electrical circuit, measured in amperes.

Derating Factor: A multiplier (penalty) that is applied to conductors when there are more than three current-carrying conductors in a raceway or cable. These multipliers are found in *Table 310.15(B)(2)*. A *derating factor* is also referred to as an *adjustment factor*.

Details: Plans, elevations, or sections that provide more specific information about a portion of a project component or element than smaller scale drawings.

▶**Device*:** A unit of an electrical system that carries or controls electric energy as its principal function.◀

Diagrams: Nonscaled views showing arrangements of special system components and connections not possible to clearly show in scaled views. A *schematic diagram* shows circuit components and their electrical connections without regard to actual physical locations. A *wiring diagram* shows circuit components and the actual electrical connections.

Dimmer: A switch with components that permits variable control of lighting intensity. Some dimmers have electronic components; others have core and coil (transformer) components.

Dimming Ballast: Controls light output of fluorescent lamps.

Direct Glare: Glare resulting from high luminances or insufficiently shielded light sources in the field of view. Usually associated with bright areas, such as luminaires, ceilings, and windows that are outside the visual task of the region being viewed.

Disconnecting Means*: A device, or group of devices, or other means by which the conductors of a circuit can be disconnected from their source of supply.

Downlight: A small, direct lighting unit that guides the light downward. It can be recessed, surface-mounted, or suspended.

Drawings: (1) A term used to represent that portion of the contract documents that graphically illustrates the design, location, and dimensions of the components and elements contained in a specific project. (2) A line drawing.

Dry Niche Luminaire*: A luminaire intended for installation in the wall of a pool or fountain in a niche that is sealed against the entry of pool water. This definition is found in *Article 680*.

▶**Dwelling Unit:** A single unit, providing complete and independent living facilities for one or more persons, including permanent provisions for living, sleeping, cooking, and sanitation.◀

Effective Ground-Fault Current Path: See *Ground-Fault Current Path, Effective*.

Efficacy: The total amount of light energy (lumens) emitted from a light source divided by the total lamp and ballast power (watts) input, expressed in lumens per watt.

Elevations: Views of vertical planes, showing components in their vertical relationship, viewed perpendicularly from a selected vertical plane.

▶**Equipment*:** A general term including material, fittings, devices, appliances, luminaires, apparatus, machinery, and the like used as a part of, or in connection with, an electrical installation.◀

Feeder*: All circuit conductors between the service equipment, the source of a separately derived system, or other power-supply source and the final branch-circuit overcurrent device.

Fill Light: Supplementary illumination to reduce shadow or contract range.

Fine Print Note (FPN)*: Explanatory material is in the form of Fine Print Notes (FPN). Fine Print Notes are informational only and are not enforceable as a requirement by the *Code*.

Fire Rating: The classification indicating in time (hours) the ability of a structure or component to withstand fire conditions.

Flame Detector: A radiant energy-sensing fire detector that detects the radiant energy emitted by a flame.

Fluorescent Lamp: A lamp in which electric discharge of ultraviolet energy excites a fluorescing coating (phosphor) and transforms some of that energy to visible light.

Footcandle: The unit used to measure how much total light is reaching a surface. One lumen falling on 1 ft^2 of surface produces an illumination of 1 footcandle.

Fully Rated System: Panelboards are marked with their short-circuit rating in RMS symmetrical amperes. In a fully-rated system, the panelboard short-circuit current rating will be equal to the lowest interrupting rating of any branch-circuit breaker or fuse installed. All devices installed shall have an interrupting rating greater than or equal to the specified available fault-current. (See *Series-Rated System.*)

Fuse: An overcurrent protective device with a fusible link that operates to open the circuit on an overcurrent condition.

General Conditions: A written portion of the contract documents set forth by the owner, stipulating the contractor's minimum acceptable performance requirements including the rights, responsibilities, and relationships of the parties involved in the performance of the contract. General conditions are usually included in the book of specifications but are sometimes found in the architectural drawings.

General Lighting: Lighting designed to provide a substantially uniform level of illumination throughout an area, exclusive of any provision for special lighting.

Glare: The sensation produced by luminance within the visual field that is sufficiently greater than the luminance to which the eyes are adapted to cause annoyance, discomfort, or loss of visual performance and visibility.

►**Ground*:** The earth.◄

►**Grounded (Grounding)*:** Connected (connecting) to ground or to a conductive body that extends the ground connection.◄

►**Grounded, Solidly*:** Connected to ground without inserting any resistor or impedance device.◄

►**Grounded Conductor:** A conductor used to connect equipment or the grounded circuit of a wiring system to a grounding electrode or electrodes.◄

►**Ground Fault*:** An unintentional, electrically conducting connection between a normally current-carrying conductor of an electrical circuit, and the normally non-current-carrying conductors, metallic enclosures, metallic raceways, metallic equipment, or earth.◄ This definition found in *NEC® 250.2.*

Ground-Fault Circuit-Interrupter (GFCI)*: A device intended for the protection of personnel that de-energizes a circuit or portion thereof within an established period of time when a current to ground exceeds the values established for a Class A device.

►FPN: Class A ground-fault circuit interrupter trip when the current to ground is 6 mA or higher and do not trip when the current to ground is less than 4 mA. For further information, see UL 943, *Standard for Ground-Fault Circuit Interrupters.*◄

Ground-Fault Current Path*: An electrically conductive path from the point of a ground fault on a wiring system through normally non-current-carrying conductors, equipment, or the earth to the electrical supply source. This definition found in *NEC® 250.2.*

Ground-Fault Current Path, Effective*: An intentionally constructed, permanent, low-impedance electrically conductive path designed and intended to carry current under ground-fault conditions from the point of a ground fault on a wiring system to the electrical supply source and that facilitates the operation of the overcurrent protective device or ground fault detectors on high-impedance grounded systems. See *NEC*® *250.2* and *250.4(A)(5)*.

Ground-Fault Protection of Equipment*: A system intended to provide protection of equipment from damaging line-to-ground fault currents by operating to cause a disconnecting means to open all ungrounded conductors of the faulted circuit. This protection is provided at current levels less than those required to protect conductors from damage through the operation of a supply circuit overcurrent device.

Grounding Conductor: A conductor used to connect equipment or the grounded circuit of a wiring system to a grounding electrode or electrodes.

▶**Grounding Conductor, Equipment (EGC)*:** *The conductive path installed to connect normally non-current carrying metal parts of equipment together and to the system grounded conductor or to the grounding electrode conductor, or both.*

▶**Grounding Electrode*:** A conducting object through which a direct connection to earth is established.◀

▶**Grounding Electrode Conductor*:** A conductor used to connect the system grounded conductor or the equipment to a grounding electrode or to a point on the grounding electrode system.◀

HACR: This term has become obsolete. In the past, when a circuit breaker was subjected to additional tests unique to HVAC equipment, it was marked with the letters HACR. The letters stood for Heating, Air Conditioning, and Refrigeration. The HVAC equipment would also be marked with the letters HACR if that is the type of overcurrent protection required by the manufacturer of the HVAC equipment.

Today, all standard molded case circuit breakers tested and listed to UL 489 are suitable for use on HVAC equipment. The letters *HACR* will disappear from the scene as time goes on.

Habitable Room*: A room in a residential occupancy used for living, sleeping, cooking, and eating, but excluding bath, storage and service area, and corridors. (NFPA definition)

Halogen Lamp: An incandescent lamp containing a halogen gas that recycles tungsten back onto the tungsten filament surface. Without the halogen gas, the tungsten would normally be deposited onto the bulb wall.

Heat Alarm: A single or multiple station alarm responsive to heat.

Hermetic Refrigerant Motor-Compressor: A combination consisting of a compressor and motor, both of which are enclosed in the same housing, with no external shaft or shaft seals; the motor operating in the refrigerant. This definition is found in *Article 440*.

High-Intensity Discharge Lamp (HID): A general term for a mercury, metal-halide, or high-pressure sodium lamp.

High-Pressure Sodium Lamp: A high-intensity discharge light source in which the light is primarily produced by the radiation from sodium vapor.

Horsepower (tools): Horsepower is a measurement of motor torque multiplied by speed. Horsepower also refers to the rate of work (power) an electric motor is capable of delivering. See *Torque*, *Rated Horsepower*, and *Maximum Developed Horsepower*.

Horsepower, Rated: Rated horsepower is a motor's running torque at its rated running speed. The motor can be run continuously at its rated horsepower without overheating. If the motor is required to give an extra spurt of effort while running, the motor is overloaded and develops extra horsepower to compensate. The most horsepower that can be drawn from a motor to handle this extra effort is its maximum developed horsepower. See *Torque*, *Horsepower* and *Maximum Developed Horsepower*.

Horsepower, Maximum Developed: If a motor is required to work harder than its idle speed, it will be overloaded and must develop extra horsepower. The most horsepower that can be expected from a motor to handle this extra effort is referred to as its maximum developed horsepower. See *Horsepower*, *Torque*, and *Rated Horsepower*.

Household Fire Alarm System: A system of devices that produces an alarm signal in the household for the purpose of notifying the occupants of the presence of a fire so that they will evacuate the premises.

Identified* (conductor): The identified conductor is the insulated grounded conductor.

- For sizes 6 AWG or smaller, the insulated grounded conductor shall be identified by a continuous white or gray outer finish or by three continuous white stripes on other than green insulation along its entire length.
- For sizes larger than 6 AWG, the insulated grounded conductor shall be identified either by a continuous white or gray outer finish or by three continuous white stripes on other than green insulation along its entire length, or at the time of installation by a distinctive white marking at its terminations.

Identified* (equipment): Recognizable as suitable for the specific purpose, function, use, environment, application, and so forth, where described in a particular *Code* requirement.

Identified* (terminal): The identification of terminals to which a grounded conductor is to be connected shall be substantially white in color. The identification of other terminals shall be of a readily distinguishable different color. See *NEC® 200.10*.

IEC: The International Electrotechnical Commission is a worldwide standards organization. These standards differ from those of Underwriters Laboratories. Some electrical equipment might conform to a specific IEC Standard but may not conform to the UL Standard for the same item.

Illuminance: The amount of light energy (lumens) distributed over a specific area expressed as footcandles (lumens/ft^2) or lux (lumens/m^2).

Illumination: The act of illuminating or the state of being illuminated.

Immersion Detection Circuit Interrupter (IDCI): A device integral with grooming appliances that will shut off the appliance when the appliance is dropped in water.

Incandescent Filament Lamp: A lamp that provides light when a filament is heated to incandescence by an electric current. Incandescent lamps are the oldest form of electric lighting technology.

Indirect Lighting: Lighting by luminaires that distribute 90% to 100% of the emitted light upward.

Inductive Load: A load that is made up of coiled or wound wire that creates a magnetic field when energized. Transformers, core and coil ballasts, motors, and solenoids are examples of inductive loads.

In Sight*: Where this *Code* specifies that one equipment shall be "in sight from," "within sight from," or "within sight," and so forth, of another equipment, the specified equipment is to be visible and not more than 50 ft (15 m) from the other.

Instant Start: A circuit used to start specially designed fluorescent lamps without the aid of a starter. To strike the arc instantly, the circuit utilizes higher open-circuit voltage than is required for the same length preheat lamp.

International Association of Electrical Inspectors (IAEI): A not-for-profit and educational organization cooperating in the formulation and uniform application of standards for the safe installation and use of electricity, and collecting and disseminating information relative thereto. The IAEI is made up of electrical inspectors, electrical contractors, electrical apprentices, manufacturers, and governmental agencies.

Interrupting Rating*: The highest current at rated voltage that a device is intended to interrupt under standard test conditions.

Ionization Detector: This type of detector triggers an alarm when oxygen and nitrogen particles are ionized in the ionization chamber. The internal circuitry measures a minute amount of electrical current between two plates.When smoke enters the ionization chamber the current is reduced, triggering the alarm. This type of detector works well for detecting small amoutns of smoke such as that resulting from gasoline fires. Consult the manufacturer's literature for more information.

Isolated Ground Receptacle: A grounding type device in which the equipment ground contact and terminal are electrically isolated from the receptacle mounting means.

Kilowatt (kW): One thousand watts equals 1 kilowatt.

Kilowatt-hour (kWh): One thousand watts of power in 1 hour. One 100-watt lamp burning for 10 hours is 1 kilowatt-hour. Two 500-watt electric heaters operated for 1 hour is 1 kilowatt-hour.

►**Kitchen*:** An area with a sink and permanent facilities for food preparation and cooking.◄

Labeled*: Equipment or materials to which has been attached a label, symbol, or other identifying mark of an organization that is acceptable to the authority having jurisdiction (AHJ) and concerned with product evaluation that maintains periodic inspection of production of labeled equipment or materials and by whose labeling the manufacturer indicates compliance with appropriate standards or performance in a specified manner.

Labor and Material Payment Bond: A written form of security from a surety (bonding) company to the owner, on behalf of an acceptable prime or main contractor or subcontractor, guaranteeing payment to the owner in the event the contractor fails to pay for all labor, materials, equipment, or services in accordance with the contract. (see *Performance Bond* and *Surety Bond*).

Lamp: A generic term for a man-made source of light.

Light: The term generally applied to the visible energy from a source. Light is usually measured in lumens or candlepower. When light strikes a surface, it is either absorbed, reflected, or transmitted.

Lighting Outlet*: ►An outlet intended for the direct connection of a lampholder or luminaire.◄

Listed*: Equipment, materials, or services included in a list published by an organization that is acceptable to the authority having jurisdiction (AHJ) and concerned with evaluation of products or services, that maintains periodic inspection of production of listed equipment or materials or periodic evaluation of services, and whose listing states that either the equipment, material, or services meets appropriate designated standards or has been tested and found suitable for a specified purpose.

Load: The electric power used by devices connected to an electrical system. Loads can be figured in amperes, volt-amperes, kilovolt-amperes, or kilowatts. Loads can be intermittent, continuous intermittent, periodic, short-time, or varying. See the definition of "Duty" in the *NEC*®

Load Center: A common name for residential panelboards. A load center may not be as deep as a panelboard and generally does not contain relays or other accessories as are available for panelboards. Circuit breakers "plug in" as opposed to the "bolt-in" types used in panelboards. Manufacturers' catalogs will show both load centers and panelboards. The UL standards do not differentiate.

Location, Damp*: Locations protected from weather and not subject to saturation with water or other liquids but subject to moderate degrees of moisture. Examples of such locations include partially protected locations under canopies, marquees, roofed open porches, and like locations, and interior locations subject to moderate degrees of moisture, such as some basements, some barns, and some cold-storage warehouses.

Location, Dry*: A location not normally subject to dampness or wetness. A location classified as dry may be temporarily subject to dampness or wetness, as in the case of a building under construction.

Location, Wet*: Installations under ground or in concrete slabs or masonry in direct contact with the earth; in locations subject to saturation with water or other liquids, such as vehicle washing areas; and in unprotected locations exposed to weather.

Locked Rotor Current (LRC): The steady-state current taken from the line with the rotor locked and with rated voltage and frequency applied to the motor.

Low-Pressure Sodium Lamp: A discharge lamp in which light is produced from sodium gas operating at a partial pressure.

Lumens: The SI unit of luminous flux. The units of light energy emitted from the light source.

►**Luminaire*:** A complete lighting unit consisting of a light source such as a lamp or lamps, together with the parts designed to position the light source and connect it to the power supply. It may also include parts to protect the light source, ballast, or distribute the light. A lampholder itself is not a luminaire.◄ Prior to the *National Electrical Code*® adopting the International System (SI) definition of *luminaire*, the commonly used term in the United States was and in most instances still is "lighting fixture." It will take years for the electrical industry to totally change and feel comfortable with the term *luminaire*.

Luminaire Efficiency: The total lumen output of the luminaire divided by the rated lumens of the lamps inside the luminaire.

Lux: The SI (International System) unit of illumination. One lumen uniformly distributed over an area 1 square meter in size.

Mandatory Rules: Required. The terms *shall* or *shall not* are used when a *Code* statement is mandatory.

Maximum Continuous Current (MCC): A value that is determined by the manufacturer of hermetic refrigerant motor compressors under high load (high refrigerant pressure) conditions. This value is established in the *NEC*® as being no greater than 156% of the marked rated amperes or the branch-circuit selection current.

Maximum Overcurrent Protection (MOP): A term used with equipment that has a hermetic motor compressor(s). MOP is the maximum ampere rating for the equipment's branch-circuit overcurrent protective device. The ampere rating is determined by the manufacturer and is marked on the nameplate of the equipment. The nameplate will also indicate if the overcurrent device can be a circuit breaker, a fuse, or either.

Mercury Lamp: A high-intensity discharge light source in which radiation from the mercury vapor produces visible light.

Metal-Halide Lamp: A high-intensity discharge light source in which the light is produced by the radiation from mercury together with the halides of metals such as sodium and candium.

Minimum Circuit Ampacity (MCA): A term used with equipment that has a hermetic motor compressor(s). MCA is the minimum ampere rating value used to determine the proper size conductors, disconnecting means, and controllers. MCA is determined by the manufacturer and is marked on the nameplate of the equipment.

***National Electrical Code*® (*NEC*®):** The electrical code published by the National Fire Protection Association. This *Code* provides for practical safeguarding of persons and property from hazards arising from the use of electricity. It does not become law until adopted by federal, state, and local laws and regulations.

National Electrical Manufacturers Association (NEMA): NEMA is a trade organization made up of many manufacturers of electrical equipment. They develop and promote standards for electrical equipment.

National Fire Protection Association (NFPA): Located in Quincy, MA. The NFPA is an international Standards Making Organization dedicated to the protection of people from the ravages of fire and electric shock. The NFPA is responsible for developing and writing the

National Electrical Code,® the *Installation of Sprinkler Systems in One- and Two-Family Dwellings and Manufactured Homes,*® the *Life Safety Code,*® the *National Fire Alarm Code,*® and over 300 other codes, standards, and recommended practices. The NFPA phone number is (800) 344-3555. Its Web site is http://www.nfpa.org.

Nationally Recognized Testing Laboratory (NRTL): The term used to define a testing laboratory that has been recognized by OSHA; for example, Underwriters Laboratories (UL).

▶**Neutral Conductor*:** The conductor connected to the neutral point of a system that is intended to carry current under normal conditions.◀

In residential wiring, the neutral conductor is the grounded conductor in a circuit. A neutral conductor is always a grounded conductor. A grounded conductor is not always a neutral conductor, such as a "grounded B phase" system discussed in *Electrical Wiring—Commercial*.

▶**Neutral point*:** The common point on a wye-connection in a polyphase system or midpoint on a single-phase, 3-wire system, or midpoint of a single-phase portion of a 3-phase delta system, or a midpoint of a 3-wire, direct current system.◀

No Niche Luminaire*: A luminaire intended for installation above or below the water without a niche. The definition is found in *Article 680*.

Noncoincidental Loads: Loads that are not likely to be on at the same time. Heating and cooling loads would not operate at the same time. See *220.21* of the *NEC.*®

Notations: Words found on plans to describe something.

Occupational Safety and Health Act (OSHA): This is the code of federal regulations developed by the Occupational Safety and Health Administration, U.S. Department of Labor. The electrical regulations are covered in *Part 1910, Subpart S*. In order to shorten and simplify the regulations, *Part 1920, Subpart S* contains only the most common performance requirements of the *NEC.*® The *NEC*® must still be referred to in conjunction with OSHA regulations.

Ohm: A unit of measure for electric resistance. An ohm is the amount of resistance that will allow 1 ampere to flow under a pressure of 1 volt.

Outlet*: A point on the wiring system at which current is taken to supply utilization equipment.

Overcurrent*: Any current in excess of the rated current of equipment or the ampacity of a conductor. It may result from overload, short circuit, or ground fault.

Overcurrent Device: Also referred to as an overcurrent protection device. A form of protection that operates when current exceeds a predetermined value. Common forms of overcurrent devices are circuit breakers, fuses, and thermal overload elements found in motor controllers.

Overload*: Operation of equipment in excess of the normal, full-load rating, or of a conductor in excess of rated ampacity that, when it persists for a sufficient length of time, would cause damage or dangerous overheating. The current flow is contained in its normal intended path. A fault, such as a short circuit or a ground fault, is not an overload.

Owner: An individual or corporation that owns a real property.

Panelboard*: A single panel or group of panel units designed for assembly in the form of a single panel, including buses and automatic overcurrent devices; equipped with or without switches for the control of light, heat, or power circuits; designed to be placed in a cabinet or cutout box placed in or against a wall or partition and accessible only from the front.

Performance Bond: (1) A written form of security from a surety (bonding) company to the owner, on behalf of an acceptable prime or main contractor or subcontractor, guaranteeing payment to the owner in the event the contractor fails to perform all labor, materials, equipment, or services in accordance with the contract. (2) The surety companies generally reserve the right to have the original prime or main or subcontractor remedy any claims before paying on the bond or hiring other contractors.

Permissive Rules: Allowed but not required. Terms such as *shall be permitted* or *shall not be required* are used when a *Code* statement is permissive.

Photoelectric Detector: This type of detector triggers an alarm when light is blocked between its internal light source and sensor. Typically, heavy smoke will block the light. The action of blocking light is similar to that of the safety feature on a garage door operator. Consult the manufacturer's literature for more information.

Photometry: The pattern and amount of light that is emitted from a luminaire, normally represented as a cross-section through the luminaire distribution pattern.

Plan: (1) A line drawing (by floor) representing the horizontal geometrical section of the walls of a building. The section (a horizontal plane) is taken at an elevation to include the relative positions of the walls, partitions, windows, doors, chimneys, columns, pilasters, etc. (2) A plan can be thought of as cutting a horizontal section through a building at an eye level elevation.

Plan Checker: A term sometimes used to describe a building department official who examines the building permit documents.

Plans: A term used to represent all drawings, including sections and details and any supplemental drawings, for complete execution of a specific project.

Power Factor: A ratio of actual power (W or kW) being used to apparent power (VA or kVA) being drawn from the power source.

Power Supply: A source of electrical operating power including the circuits and terminations connecting it to the dependent system components.

Preheat: A type of ballast that is easily identified because it has a starter. One type of starter is automatic with two buttons on one end; the other type is a manual ON/OFF switch that has a momentary "make" postion jsut beyond the "ON" position.

Preheat Fluorescent Lamp Circuit: A circuit used on fluorescent lamps wherein the electrodes are heated or warmed to a glow stage by an auxiliary switch or starter before the lamps are lighted.

Preliminary Drawings: The drawings that precede the final approved drawings. Usually stamped "PRELIMINARY."

Prime Contractor: Any contractor having a contract directly with the owner. Usually the main (general) contractor for a specific project.

Prints: A term used to refer to a plan or plans.

Project: A word used to represent the overall scope of work being performed to complete a specific construction job.

Proposal: A written offer from a bidder to the owner, preferably on a prescribed proposal form, to perform the work and to furnish all labor, materials, equipment and/or service for the prices and terms quoted by the bidder.

Punch List (Inspection List): A list prepared by the owner or his or her authorized representative of items of work requiring immediate corrective or completion action by the contractor.

►**Qualified Person*:** One who has skills and knowledge related to the construction and operation of the electrical equipment and installations and has received safety training to recognize and avoid the hazards involved.◄

Raceway*: An enclosed channel of metallic or nonmetallic materials designed expressly for holding wires, cables, or busbars, with additional functions as permitted in this *Code*. Raceways include, but are not limited to, rigid metal conduit, rigid PVC conduit, intermediate metal conduit, liquidtight flexible conduit, flexible metallic tubing, flexible metal conduit, electrical nonmetallic tubing, electrical metallic tubing, underfloor raceways, cellular concrete floor raceways, cellular metal floor raceways, surface raceways, wireways, and busways.

Rapid Start: The most common type of ballast used today that does not require a starter.

Rapid Start Fluorescent Lamp Circuit: A circuit designed to start lamps by continuously heating or preheating the electrodes. Lamps must be designed for this type of circuit. This is the modern version of the "trigger start" system. In a rapid-start two-lamp circuit, one end of each lamp is connected to a separate starting winding.

Rate of Rise Detector: A device that responds when the temperature rises at a rate exceeding a predetermined value.

Rated-Load Current: The rated-load current for a hermetic refrigerant motor-compressor is the current resulting when the motor-compressor is operated at the rated load, rated voltage, and rated frequency of the equipment it serves. See *NEC® Article 440.*

Receptacle*: A receptacle is a contact device installed at the outlet for the connection of an attachment plug. A single receptacle is a single contact device with no other contact device on the same yoke. A multiple receptacle is two or more contact devices on the same yoke.

Receptacle Outlet*: An outlet where one or more receptacles are installed.

Resistive Load: An electric load that opposes the flow of current. A resistive load does not contain cores or coils of wire. Some examples of resistive loads are the electric heating elements in an electric range, ceiling heat cables, and electric baseboard heaters.

Root-Mean-Square (RMS): The square root of the average of the square of the instantaneous values of current or voltage. For example, the RMS value of voltage, line to neutral, in a home is 120 volts. During each electrical cycle, the voltage rises from zero to a peak value ($120 \times 1.4142 = 169.7$ volts), back through zero to a negative peak value, then back to zero. The RMS value is 0.707 of the peak value ($169.7 \times 0.707 = 120$ volts). The root-mean-square value is what an electrician reads on an ammeter or voltmeter.

Schedules: Tables or charts that include data about materials, products, and equipment.

Scope: A written range of view or action; outlook; hence, room for the exercise of faculties or function, capacity for achievement; all in connection with a designated project.

Sections: Views of vertical cuts through and perpendicular to components showing their detailed arrangement.

Series-Rated System: Panelboards are marked with their short-circuit rating in RMS symmetrical amperes. A series-rated panelboard will be determined by the main circuit breaker or fuse, and branch-circuit breaker combination tested in accordance to UL Standard 489. The series rating will be less than or equal to the interrupting rating of the main overcurrent device, and greater than the interrupting rating of the branch-circuit overcurrent devices. (See "Fully Rated System.")

Service*: The conductors and equipment for delivering energy from the serving utility to the wiring system of the premises served.

Service Conductors*: The conductors from the service point to the service disconnecting means.

Service Drop*: The overhead service conductors from the last pole or other aerial support to and including the splices, if any, connecting to the service-entrance conductors at the building or other structure.

Service Equipment*: The necessary equipment, usually consisting of a circuit breaker or switch and fuses and their accessories, located near the point of entrance of supply conductors to a building or other structure, or an otherwise defined area, and intended to constitute the main control and means of cutoff of the supply.

Service Lateral Conductor*: The underground service conductors between the street main, including any risers at a pole or other structure or from transformers, and the first point of connection to the service-entrance conductors in a terminal box or meter or other enclosure with adequate space, inside or outside the building wall. Where there is no terminal box, meter, or other enclosure with adequate space, the point of connection shall be considered to be the point of entrance of the service conductors into the building.

Service Point*: The point of connection between the facilities of the serving utility and the premises wiring.

Shall: Indicates a mandatory requirement.

Short Circuit: A connection between any two or more conductors of an electrical system in such a way as to significantly reduce the impedance of the circuit. The current flow is outside of its intended path, thus the term "short circuit." A short circuit is also referred to as a fault.

►**Short-Circuit Current Rating:** The prospective symmetrical fault current at a nominal voltage to which an apparatus or system is able to be connected without sustaining damage exceeding defined acceptance criteria.◄

Should: Indicates a recommendation or that which is advised but not required.

Site: The place where a structure or group of structures was, or is, to be located (as in construction site).

Smoke Alarm: A single or multiple station alarm responsive to smoke.

Smoke Detector: A device that detects visible or invisible particles of combustion.

Sone: A unit of loudness equal to the loudness of a sound of 1 kilohertz at 40 decibels above the threshold of hearing of a given listener.

Specifications: Text setting forth details such as description, size, quality, performance, workmanship, and so forth. Specifications that pertain to all of the construction trades involved might be subdivided into "General Conditions" and "Supplemental General Conditions." Further subdividing the specifications might be specific requirements for the various contractors such as electrical, plumbing, heating, masonry, and so forth. Typically, the electrical specifications are found in Division 16.

Split-Circuit Receptacle: A receptacle that can be connected to two branch circuits. These receptacles may also be used so that one receptacle is live at all times, and the other receptacle is controlled by a switch. The terminals on these receptacles usually have breakaway tabs so the receptacle can be used either as a split-circuit receptacle or as a standard receptacle.

Standard Network Interface (SNI): A device usually installed by the telephone company at the demarcation point where their service leaves off and the customer's service takes over. This is similar to the service point for electrical systems.

Starter: A device used in conjunction with a ballast for the purpose of starting an electric discharge lamp.

Structure*: That which is built or constructed.

Subcontractor: A qualified subordinate contractor to the prime or main contractor.

Surety Bond: A legal document issued to ensure the completion of an act by another person.

Contractors usually are required to purchase surety bonds, if they are working on public projects. A surety bond guarantees to one party that another (the contractor) will perform specified acts, usually within a stated period of time. The surety company typically becomes responsible for fulfillment of a contract if the contractor defaults. In the case of a public works project, such as a road, that means that the surety bond protects taxpayers should a contractor go out of business.

Surface-Mounted Luminaire: A luminaire mounted directly on the ceiling.

Surge Suppressor: A device that limits peak voltage to a predetermined value when voltage spikes or surges appear on the connected line.

Suspended (pendant) Luminaire: A luminaire hung from a ceiling by supports.

Switches*:

General-Use Snap Switch: A form of general-use switch constructed so that it can be installed in device boxes or on box covers, or otherwise used in conjunction with wiring systems recognized by this *Code*.

General-Use Switch: A switch intended for use in general distribution and branch circuits. It is rated in amperes, and it is capable of interrupting its rated current at its rated voltage.

Motor-Circuit Switch: A switch, rated in horsepower, capable of interrupting the maximum operating overload current of a motor of the same horsepower rating as the switch at the rated voltage.

Symbols: Graphic representations that stand for or represent other things. A symbol is a simple way to show such things as lighting outlets, switches, and receptacles on an electrical plan. The American Institute of Architects has developed a very comprehensive set of symbols that represent just about everything used by all building trades. When an item cannot be shown using a symbol, then a more detailed explanation using a notation or inclusion in the specifications is necessary.

T & M: An abbreviation for a contracting method called Time and Material. A written agreement between the owner and the contractor wherein payment is based on the contractor's actual cost for labor equipment, materials, and services plus a fixed add-on amount to cover the contractor's overhead and profit.

Task Lighting: Lighting directed to a specific surface or area that provides illumination for visual tasks.

Terminal: A screw or a quick-connect device where a conductor(s) is intended to be connected.

Thermocouple: A pair of dissimilar conductors so joined at two points that an electromotive force is developed by the thermoelectric effects when the junctions are at different temperatures.

Thermopile: More than one thermocouple connected together. The connections may be series or parallel, or both.

Torque: A measurement of rotation or turning force. Torque is measured in ounce-inches (oz.-in.), ounce-feet (oz.-ft) and pound-feet (lb.-ft). See *Horsepower*, *Rated Horsepower*, and *Maximum Developed Horsepower*.

Transient Voltage Surge Suppressor (TVSS): A device that clamps transient voltages by absorbing the major portion of the energy (joules) created by the surge, allowing only a small, safe amount of energy to enter the actual connected load.

Troffer: A recessed lighting unit, usually long and installed with the opening flush with the ceiling. The term is derived from "trough" and "coffer."

UBC (Uniform Building Code): One of the family of codes and related publications published by the International Conference of Building Officials (ICBO) and other organizations, such as the International Association of Plumbing and Mechanical Officials (IAPMO) and the National Fire Protection Association (NFPA), which have similar goals as far as code publications are concerned. The Uniform Building Code is designed to be compatible with these other codes, as together they make up the enforcement tools of a jurisdiction.

UL: Underwriters Laboratories (UL) is an independent not-for-profit organization that develops standards and tests electrical equipment to these standards.

UL-Listed: Indicates that an item has been tested and approved to the standards established by UL for that particular item. The UL Listing Mark may appear in various forms, such as the letters UL in a circle. If the product is too small for the marking to be applied to the product, the marking must appear on the smallest unit container in which the product is packaged.

UL-Recognized: Refers to a product that is incomplete in construction features or limited in performance capabilities. A "Recognized" product is intended to be used as a component part of equipment that has been "listed." A "Recognized" product must not be used by itself. A UL product may contain a number of components that have been "Recognized."

▶**Ungrounded:** Not connected to ground or a conductive body that extends the ground connection.◀

Ungrounded Conductor: The conductor of an electrical system that is not intentionally connected to ground. This conductor is referred to as the "hot" or "live" conductor.

Volt: The difference of electric potential between two points of a conductor carrying a constant current of 1 ampere, when the power dissipated between these points is equal to 1 watt. A voltage of 1 volt can push 1 ampere through a resistance of 1 ohm.

Voltage (of a circuit)*: The greatest root-mean-square (effective) difference of potential between any two conductors of the circuit concerned.

Voltage (nominal)*: A nominal value assigned to a circuit or system for the purpose of conveniently designating its voltage class (e.g., 120/240 volts, 480Y/277 volts, 600 volts).

The actual voltage at which a circuit operates can vary from the nominal within a range that permits satisfactory operation of equipment.

Voltage to Ground*: For grounded circuits, the voltage between the given conductor and that point or conductor of the circuit that is grounded; for ungrounded circuits, the greatest voltage between the given conductor and any other conductor of the circuit.

Voltage Drop: Also referred to as IR drop. Voltage drop is most commonly associated with conductors. A conductor has resistance; when current is flowing through the conductor, a voltage drop will be experienced across the conductor. Voltage drop across a conductor can be calculated using Ohm's law: $E = IR$.

Volt-ampere: A unit of power determined by multiplying the voltage and current in a circuit. A 120-volt circuit carrying 1 ampere is 120 volt-amperes.

Watt: A measure of true power. A watt is the power required to do work at the rate of 1 joule per second. Wattage is determined by multiplying voltage times amperes times the power factor of the circuit: $W = E \times I \times PF$.

Watertight: Constructed so that moisture will not enter the enclosure under specified test conditions.

Weatherproof*: Constructed or protected so that exposure to the weather will not interfere with successful operation.

(FPN): Rainproof, raintight, or watertight equipment can fulfill the requirements for weatherproof where varying weather conditions other than wetness, such as snow, ice, dust, or temperature extremes, are not a factor.

Wet Niche Luminaire*: A luminaire intended for installation in a forming shell mounted in a pool. This definition is found in *Article 680.*

Working Drawing(s): A drawing sufficiently complete with plan and section views, dimensions, details, and notes, so that whatever is shown can be constructed and/or replicated without instructions but subject to clarifications, see drawings.

Work Order: A written order, signed by the owner or his or her representative, of a contractual status requiring performance by the contractor without negotiation of any sort.

Zoning: Restrictions of areas or regions of land within specific geographical areas based on permitted building size, character, and uses as established by governing urban authorities.

Web Sites

The following list of Internet World Wide Web sites has been included for your convenience. These are current as of the time of printing. Web sites are a "moving target" with continual changes. We do our utmost to keep these Web sites current. If you are aware of Web sites that should be added, deleted, or that are different than shown, please let us know. Most manufacturers will provide catalogs and technical literature upon request either electronically or by mail. You will be amazed at the amount of electrical and electronic equipment information that is available on these Web sites.

You can search the Web using a search engine such as http://www.google.com, http://www.dogpile.com, http://www.yahoo.com, or http://www.askjeeves.com. Just type in a key word (for example: fuses) and you will be led to many Web sites relating to fuses. It's easy!

Web sites marked with an asterisk * are closely related to the "home automation" market.

ACCUBID	http://www.accubid.com
Acme Electric Corporation	http://www.acmepowerdist.com
ActiveHome*	http://www.X10-beta.com/activehome/
Active Power	http://www.activepower.com
Adalet	http://www.adalet.com
Advance Transformer Co.	http://www.advancetransformer.com
Advanced Cable Ties	http://www.advancedcableties.com
AEMC Instruments	http://www.aemc.com
AFC Cable Systems	http://www.afcweb.com
Air-Conditioning & Refrigeration Association	http://www.ari.org
Alcan Cable	http://www.cable.alcan.com
Alflex	http://www.alflex.com
Allen-Bradley	http://www.automation.rockwell.com
Allen-Bradley	http://www.ab.com
Allied Moulded Products	http://www.alliedmoulded.com
Allied Support Products	http://www.alliedsupport.com
Allied Tube & Conduit	http://www.alliedtube.com
Alpha Wire	http://www.alphawire.com
ALTO Lamps	http://www.altolamp.com
The Aluminum Association, Inc.	http://www.aluminum.org
American Council for an Energy-Efficient Economy	http://www.aceee.org
American Gas Association	http://www.aga.org
American Heart Association	http://www.americanheart.org
American Institute of Architects	http://www.aia.org
American Insulated Wire Corp.	http://www.aiwc.com
American Lighting Association	http://www.americanlightingassoc.com
American National Standards Institute	http://www.ansi.org
American Pipe & Plastics, Inc.	http://www.ampipe.com
American Power Conversion	http://www.apcc.com
American Public Power Assoc.	http://www.appanet.org

American Red Cross	http://www.redcross.org
American Society of Heating, Refrigerating, and Air-Conditioning Engineers	http://www.ashrae.org
American Society for Testing and Materials	http://www.astm.org
American Society of Mechanical Engineers	http://www.asme.org
American Society of Safety Engineers	http://www.asse.org
AMP*	http://www.amp.com
Amprobe	http://www.amprobe.com
Angelo	http://www.angelobrothers.com
Anixter (data & telecommunications cabling)*	http://www.anixter.com
Appleton Electric Co.	http://www.appletonelec.com
ArcWear	http://www.arcwear.com
Arlington Industries, Inc.	http://www.aifittings.com
Arrow Fasteners	http://www.arrowfastener.com
Arrow Hart Wiring Devices	http://www.arrowhart.com
Assisted Living: The World of Assisted Technology	http://www.abledata.com
Associated Builders & Contractors	http://www.abc.org
Association of Cabling Professions	http://www.wireville.com
Association of Home Appliance Manufacturers	http://www.aham.org
Automated Home Technologies*	http://www.autohometech.com
Automatic Switch Co. (ASCO)	http://www.asco.com
AVO Training Institute	http://www.avotraining.com
Baldor Motors & Drives	http://www.baldor.com
R. W. Beckett Corporation (oil burner technical info.)	http://www.beckettcorp.com
Belden Wire & Cable Co.	http://www.belden.com
Bell, Hubbell Inc.	http://www.hubbell-bell.com
Bender	http://www.bender.org
Best Power	http://www.bestpower.com
BICC General	http://www.generalcable.com
BICSI (Building Industry Consulting Services International, a telecommunications assoc.)*	http://www.bicsi.org
BidStreet	http://www.BidStreetUSA.com
Black and Decker	http://www.blackanddecker.com
The Blue Book (construction)	http://www.thebluebook.com
Bodine Company	http://www.bodine.com
BOCA	http://www.bocai.org
boltswitch, inc.	http://www.boltswitch.com
Brady Worldwide, Inc.	http://www.whbrady.com
Bridgeport Fittings Inc.	http://www.bptfittings.com
Broan	http://www.broan.com
Bryant – Hubbell Inc.	http://www.hubbell-bryant.com
Building Industry Consulting Service International, Inc.	http://www.bisci.org
Builder Online—a source for the home building industry.	http://www.builderonline.com
BuildPoint	http://www.buildpoint.com
Burndy Electrical Products	http://www.fciconnect.com
Bussmann, Cooper Industries	http://www.bussmann.com
Cable Telecommunications Engineers*	http://www.scte.org

Caddy	http://www.erico.com
Cadweld	http://www.erico.com
California Title 24	http://www.energy.ca.gov/title24
Canadian Standards Association	http://www.csa-international.org
Cantex	http://www.cantexinc.com
Carlon, A Lamson & Sessions Co.	http://www.carlon.com
Carol Cable	http://www.generalcable.com
Casablanca Fan Company	http://www.casablancafanco.com
Caterpillar	http://www.cat.com
Caterpillar	http://www.cat-engines.com
CEBus Industry Council*	http://www.cebus.org
CEDIA (Custom Electronic Design & Installation Association)	http://www.cedia.net
CEE News magazine	http://www.ceenews.com
Cengage Delmar Learning	http://www.delmarlearning.com
Cengage Delmar Learning (electrical)	http://www.delmarelectric.com
Center for Disease Control (CDC)	http://www.cdc.gov
Centralite*	http://www.centralite.com
CEPro*	http://www.ce-pro.com
Channellock Inc	http://www.channellock.com
ChannelPlus*	http://www.multiplextechnology.com/channelplus/
Chromalox	http://www.chromalox.com
Circon Systems Corporation*	http://www.circon.com
Clifford of Vermont*	http://www.cliffordvt.com
CNA Insurance (many safety bulletins about use of tools, electricity, and other equipment that are downloadable free)	http://www.CNA.com
Coleman Cable	http://www.colemancable.com
Columbia Lighting	http://www.columbia-ltg.com
CommScope* (coax cable mfg.)	http://www.commscope.com
Communications Systems, Inc.	http://www.commsystems.com
Computer and Telecommunications Page*	http://www.cmpcmm.com/cc/
ConnectHome*	http://www.connecthome.com
Construction Specifications Institute	http://www.csinet.org
Construction Terms/Glossary	http://www.constructionplace.com/glossary.html
Consumer Electronic Association (CEA)*	http://www.ce.org
Consumer Product Safety Commission (CPSC)	http://www.cpsc.gov
Continental Automated Buildings Association (CABA)*	http://www.caba.org
Contrast Lighting (recessed)	http://www.contrastlighting.com
Copper (technical information)	http://energy.copper.org
Copper Development Assoc.	http://www.copper.org
Cooper Industries Here you will find links to all Cooper Divisions for electrical products, lighting, wiring devices, power and hand tools.	http://www.cooperindustries.com
Craftsman Tools	http://www.craftsman.com
Crouse-Hinds	http://www.crouse-hinds.com
Cummins Power Generation*	http://www.cumminspower.com

Custom Electronic Design & Installation Association*	http://www.cedia.net
Custom Electronic Professional*	http://www.ce-pro.com
Cutler-Hammer	http://www.cutler-hammer.com
DABMAR	http://www.dabmar.com
Daman Tools	http://www.damantools.com
Danaher Power Solutions	http://www.danaherpoersolutions.com
Daniel Woodhead Company	http://www.danielwoodhead.com
Day-Brite Lighting	http://www.daybrite.com
Dept. of Energy	http://www.energy.gov
Dimension Express (to obtain roughing-in dimensions from all appliance manufacturers)	http://www.dexpress.com
F. W. Dodge	http://www.fwdodge.com
DOMOSYS Corporation*	http://www.domosys.com
Douglas Lighting Control	http://www.douglaslightingcontrol.com
Dremel	http://www.dremel.com
Dual-Lite	http://www.dual-lite.com
Dynacom Corporation	http://www.dynacomcorp.com
Eaton (links to all divisions)	http://www.eatonelectrical.com
Edison Electric Institute	http://www.eei.org
EC Online	http://www.econline.com
EC & M magazine	http://www.ecmweb.com
Edwards Signaling and Security Products	http://www.edwards-signals.com
ELAN Home Systems*	http://www.elanhomesystems.com
Electric-Find	http://www.electric-find.com
Electric Smarts	http://www.electricsmarts.com
Electri-flex	http://www.electriflex.com
Electrical Apparatus Service Assoc.	http://www.easa.com
Electrical Contracting & Engineering News	http://www.ecenmag.com
Electrical Contractor Magazine	http://www.ecmag.com
The Electrical Contractor Network	http://www.electrical-contractor.net
Electrical Designers Reference	http://www.edreference.com
Electrical Distributor Magazine	http://www.tedmag.com
Electrical Reliability Services, Inc. (formerly Electro-Test)	http://www.electro-test.com
Electrical Safety	http://www.electrical-safety.com
Electrical Safety Foundation International (ESFI)	http://www.esfi.org
Electrician.com	http://www.electrician.com
Electro-Test Inc.	http://www.electro-test.com
Electronic Design Technology*	http://www.edt.biz
Electronic House*	http://www.electronichouse.com
Electronic Industry Alliance*	http://www.eia.org
Emerson	http://www.emersonfans.com
Encore Wire Limited	http://www.encorewire.com
Energy Efficiency & Renewable Energy Network (U.S. Dept. of Energy)	http://www.eere.energy.gov
Energy Star	http://www.energystar.gov
Environmental Protection Agency	http://www.epa.gov
Erico	http://www.erico.com
Essex Group, Inc.*	http://www.essexgroup.com

Estimation Inc.	http://www.estimation.com
ETL Semko	http://www.etlsemko.com
Exide Technologies	http://www.exide.com
Factory Mutual Insurance Co.	http://www.fmglobal.com
Faraday	http://www.faradayfirealarms.com
FCI/Burndy (telecom connectors)	http://www.fciconnect.com
Federal Communications Commission*	http://www.fcc.gov
Federal Pacific	http://www.federalpacific.com
Federal Signal Corp.	http://www.federalsignal.com
Ferraz-Shawmut	http://www.ferrazshawmut.com
Fiber Optic Association, Inc.*	http://www.thefoa.org
Fibertray	http://www.ditel.net
First Alert	http://www.firstalert.com
Flex-Core	http://www.flex-core.com
Fluke Corporation	http://www.fluke.com
Fluke Networks*	http://www.flukenetworks.com
Fox Meter Inc.	http://www.arcfaulttester.com
Fox Meter Inc.	http://www.foxmeter.com
Gardner Bender	http://www.gardnerbender.com
GE Appliances	http://www.geappliances.com
GE Consumer and Industrial	http://www.geelectrical.com
GE Electrical Distribution & Control	http://www.ge.com/edc
GE Industrial Systems	http://www.geindustrial.com
GE Lighting	http://www.gelighting.com
GE Total Lighting Control	See Horton Control
General Cable	http://www.generalcable.com
Generators:	
Coleman Powermate	http://www.colemanpowermate.com
Cummins Power Generation	http://www.cumminspowergeneration.com
Generac Power Systems	http://www.generac.com
Gen-X	http://www.genxnow.com
Gillette Generators, Inc.	http://www.gillettegenerators.com
Kohler Power Systems	http://www.kohlergenerators.com
Onan Corporation	http://www.onan.com
Reliance Electric	http://www.reliance.com
Genesis Cable Systems*	http://www.genesiscable.com
Global Engineering Documents	http://www.global.ihs.com
Grayline, Inc. (tubing)	http://www.graylineinc.com
Greenlee Inc.	http://www.greenlee.com
Greyfox Systems*	http://www.greyfox.com
Guth Lighting	http://www.guth.com
The Halex Company	http://www.halexco.com
Hand Tools Institute	http://www.hti.org.
Handicapped Suggestions The World of Assisted Technology	http://www.abledata.com
Hatch Transformers, Inc	http://www.hatchtransformers.com
Heavy Duty	http://www.milwaukeetool.com
Heyco Products, Inc.	http://www.heyco.com
Hilti Corporation	http://www.hilti.com
Hinkley Lighting	http://www.hinkleylighting.com
HIOKI (measuring instruments)	http://www.hioki.co.jp/

Hitachi Cable Manchester, Inc.*	http://www.hcm.hitachi.com
Hoffmann	http://www.hoffmanonline.com
Holophane	http://www.holophane.com
Holt, Mike Enterprises	http://www.mikeholt.com
Home Automation and Networking Association*	http://www.homeautomation.org
Home Automation, Inc.*	http://www.homeauto.com
Home Automation Links*	http://www.asihome.com
Home Automation Systems*	http://www.smarthome.com
Home Controls, Inc.*	http://www.homecontrols.com
Home Director, Inc.*	http://www.homedirector.net
Home Seer	http://www.homeseer.com
HomeStar*	http://www.homestar.net
Homestore*	http://www.homestore.com
Home Touch*	http://www.home-touch.com
Home Toys*	http://www.hometoys.com
Honeywell	http://www.honeywell.com
Honeywell*	http://www.honeywell.com/yourhome
Housing Urban Development	http://www.hud.gov.
Houston Wire & Cable Company	http://www.houwire.com
Hubbell Incorporated (links to all divisions)	http://www.hubbell.com
Hubbell Incorporated	http://www.hubbell-premise.com
Hubbell Lighting Incorporated	http://www.hubbell-ltg.com
Hubbell Wiring Devices	http://www.hubbell-wiring.com
Hunt Control Systems, Inc.	http://www.huntdimming.com
Hunter Fans	http://www.hunterfan.com
Husky	http://www.mphusky.com
ICBO	http://www.icbo.org
Ideal Industries, Inc.	http://www.idealindustries.com
Illuminating Engineering Society of North America	http://www.iesna.org
ILSCO	http://www.ilsco.com
Independent Electrical Contractors	http://www.ieci.org
Institute of Electrical and Electronic Engineers, Inc.	http://www.ieee.org
Instrumentation, Systems, and Automation Society	http://www.isa.org
Insulated Cable Engineers Association (ICEA)	http://www.icea.net
Insulated Tools (certified insulated products)	http://www.insulatedtools.com
Intel's Home Network	http://www.intel.com/anypoint
Intermatic. Inc.	http://www.intermatic.com
International Association of Electrical Inspectors (IAEI)	http://www.iaei.org
International Association of Plumbing & Mechanical Officials	http://www.iapmo.org
International Brotherhood of Electrical Workers	http://www.ibew.org
International Code Council (ICC)	http://www.iccsafe.org
International Dark-Sky Association	http://www.darksky.org
International Electrotechnical Commission (IEC)	http://www.iec.ch/

International Organization for Standardization (ISO)	http://www.iso.org
Intertec Testing Services (ETL)	http://www.etlsemko.com
Jacuzzi	http://www.jacuzzi.com
Jefferson Electric	http://www.jeffersonelectric.com
Johnson Controls, Inc.	http://www.johnsoncontrols.com
Joslyn	http://www.joslynmfg.com
Juno Lighting, Inc.	http://www.junolighting.com
KatoLight	http://www.katolight.com
Kenall Lighting	http://www.kenall.com
Kichler Lighting	http://www.kichler.com
Kidde (home safety)	http://www.kiddeus.com
King Safety Products	http://www.kingsafety.com
King Wire Inc.	http://www.kingwire.com
Klein Tools, Inc.	http://www.kleintools.com
Kohler Generators	http://www.kohler.com
LEDS Magazine	http://www.ledsmagazine.com
Leviton Mfg. Co., Inc. (links to all divisions)	http://www.leviton.com
Lew Electric	http://www.lewelectric.com
Liebert	http://www.liebert.com
Lighting	http://www.lightsearch.com
Lighting Design Forum	http://www.qualitylight.com
Lighting Research Center	http://www.lrc.rpi.edu
Lightning Protection Institute	http://www.lightning.org
Lightolier	http://www.lightolier.com
Lightolier Controls*	http://www.lolcontrols.com
Litetouch*	http://www.litetouch.com
Lithonia Lighting	http://www.lithonia.com
Littelfuse, Inc.	http://www.littelfuse.com
LonWorks *	http://www.lonworks.echelon.com
Lucent Technologies*	http://www.lucent.com
Lumisistemas, S.A. de C.V.	http://www.lumisistemas.com
Lutron Electronics Co., Inc.	http://www.lutron.com
Lutron Home Theater*	http://www.ultimatehometheater.com
MagneTek (links to all divisions)	http://www.magnetek.com
Makita Tools	http://www.makita.com
Manhattan/CDT	http://www.manhattancdt.com
McGill	http://www.mcgillelectrical.com
Megger	http://www.megger.com/us/index.asp
MET Laboratories, Inc.	http://www.metlabs.com
MI Cable Company	http://www.micable.com
Midwest Electric Products, Inc.	http://www.midwestelectric.com
Milbank Manufacturing Co.	http://www.milbankmfg.com
Milwaukee Electric Tool	http://www.milwaukeetool.com
Minerallac	http://www.minerallac.com
Molex Inc.	http://www.molex.com
Motor Control	http://www.motorcontrol.com
Motorola Lighting Inc.	http://www.motorola.com
National Association of Electrical Distributors	http://www.naed.org
National Association of Fire Marshalls (NASFM)	http://www.firemarshals.org
National Association of Home Builders	http://www.nahb.org

National Association of Home Inspectors	http://www.nahi.org
National Association of Mfg.	http://www.nam.org
National Association of Radio and Telecommunications Engineers, Inc.	http://www.narte.com
National Conference of States on Building Codes and Standards	http://www.ncsbcs.org
National Electrical Contractors Association (NECA)	http://www.necanet.org
National Electrical Manufacturers Association (NEMA)	http://www.nema.org
National Electrical Manufacturers Association (AFCI information)	http://www.afcisafety.org
National Electrical Safety Foundation	http://www.nesf.org
National Fire Protection Association	http://www.nfpa.org
National Fire Protection Association *National Electrical Code®* information	http://www.nfpa.org/nec/
National Institute for Occupational Safety & Health	http://www.cdc.gov/niosh
National Institute of Standards and Technology (NIST)	http://www.nist.gov
National Joint Apprenticeship and Training Committee (NJATC)	http://www.njatc.org
National Lighting Bureau	http://www.nlb.org
National Resource for Global Standards	http://www.nssn.org
National Safety Council	http://www.nsc.org
National Spa and Pool Institute	http://www.nspi.org
National Systems Contractors Association*	http://www.nsca.org
NECDirect	http://www.necdirect.org
Newton's Electrician	http://www.electrician.com
Nora Lighting	http://www.noralighting.com
NuTone	http://www.nutone.com
Occupation Health & Safety	http://www.ohsonline.com
Occupational Safety & Health Administration	http://www.osha.gov
Okonite Co.	http://www.okonite.com
Olflex Cable	http://www.olflex.com
Onan Corporation	http://www.onan.com
ONEAC Corporation	http://www.oneac.com
OnQ Technologies*	http://www.onqtech.com
Optical Cable Corporation*	http://www.occfiber.com
Ortronics Inc.	http://www.ortronics.com
Osram Sylvania Products, Inc.	http://www.sylvania.com
Overhead door information: Door & Access System Manufacturers Association	http://www.dasma.com
OZ/Gedney	http://www.o-zgedney.com
Panasonic Lighting	http://www.panasonic.com/lighting
Panasonic Technologies	http://www.panasonic.com
Panduit Corporation	http://www.panduit.com
Pass and Seymour, Legrand	http://www.passandseymour.com
Pelican Rope Works	http://www.pelicanrope.com
Penn-Union Corp.	http://www.penn-union.com
Phase-A-Matic, Inc.	http://www.phase-a-matic.com

Philips	http://www.philips.com
Philips Lamps	http://www.ALTOlamp.com
Philips Lighting Company	http://www.philipslighting.com
Philtek Power Corporation	http://www.philtek.com
Phoenix Contact	http://www.phoenixcon.com
Pigeon Hole, The	http://www.thepigeonhole.com
Plant Engineering On-Line	http://www.plantengineering.com
Popular Home Automation*	http://www.pophome.com
Porter Cable	http://www.porter-cable.com
Power Quality Monitoring	http://www.pqmonitoring.com
Power-Sonic Corporation	http://www.power-sonic.com
Premise Wiring Products	http://www.unicomlink.com
Prescolite	http://www.prescolite.com
Pringle Electrical Mfg. Co.	http://www.pringle-elec.com
Progress Lighting	http://www.progresslighting.com
Radix Wire Company	http://www.radix-wire.com
RCA*	http://www.rca.com
RACO	http://www.racoinc.com
Rayovac Corporation	http://www.rayovac.com
Red Cross	http://www.redcross.org
Refrigeration Service Engineering Society	http://www.rses.org
Regal Fittings	http://www.regalfittings.com
Reliable Power Meters	http://www.reliablemeters.com
Remke Industries, Inc.	http://www.remke.com
Rhodes, M. H. (timers)	http://www.mhrhodes.com
Rigid Tool Company	http://www.ridgid.com
Robertson Transformer Co.	http://www.robertsontransformer.com
Robicon	http://www.robicon.com
Robroy Industries – Conduit Div.	http://www.robroy.com
Romex Cable	http://www.biccgeneral.com
RotoZip Tool Corp.	http://www.rotozip.com
Russelectric	http://www.russelectric.com
Safety Technology International, Inc.	http://www.sti-usa.com
S&C Electric Company	http://www.sandc.com
SBCCI	http://www.sbcci.org
Schneider Electric Square D	http://www.us.squared.com
Sea Gull Lighting	http://www.seagulllighting.com
Seatek, Inc.	http://www.SeatekCo.com
SECURITY*	
Caddx*	http://www.caddx.com
Digital Monitoring Products*	http://www.dmpnet.com
Home Automation*	http://www.homeauto.com
Honeywell Security*	http://www.security.honeywell.com/sce
NAPCO Security Systems*	http://www.napcosecurity.com
Sensor Switch Inc.	http://www.sensorswitchinc.com
Siemens (main site)	http://www.siemens.com
Siemens Energy & Automation	http://www.sea.siemens.com
The Siemon Company*	http://www.siemon.com
Shat-R-Shield	http://www.shat-r-shield.com
Silent Knight	http://www.silentknight.com
Simplex Grinnell	http://www.simplexgrinnell.com

Simpson Electric Co.	http://www.simpsonelectric.com
Skil Tools	http://www.skil.com
Smart Home*	http://www.smarthome.com
Smart Home Pro*	http://www.smarthomepro.com
Smart House, Inc.*	http://www.smart-house.com
Smoke & Fire Extinguisher Signs	http://www.smokesign.com
Sola/Hevi Duty	http://www.sola-hevi-duty.com
Southwire Co.	http://www.mysouthwire.com
SP Products, Inc.	http://www.spproducts.com
A.W. Sperry Instruments, Inc.	http://www.awsperry.com
Square D, Groupe Schneider	http://www.squared.com
Square D (Homeline)	http://www.squared.com/retail
Square D, Power Logic	http://www.powerlogic.com
Stanley Tools	http://www.stanleyworks.com
Starfield Controls*	http://www.starfieldcontrols.com
Steel Tube Institute	http://www.steeltubeinstitute.org
Steel Tube Institute—Conduit Committee	http://www.steelconduit.org
Straight Wire*	http://www.straightwire.com
Sunbelt Transformers	http://www.sunbeltusa.com
Superior Electric	http://www.superiorelectric.com
Superior Essex Group	http://www.superioressex.com
Suttle	http://www.suttleonline.com
Sylvania	http://www.sylvania.com
Sylvania Lighting Int'l.	http://www.sli-lighting.com
Technical Consumer Products Inc.	http://www.springlamp.com
Telecommunications Industry Association (TIA)*	http://www.tiaonline.org
Terms /Construction /Glossary	http://www.constructionplace.com/glossary.html
Thermostats, Communicating*	http://www.homeauto.com
This Old House	http://www.thisoldhouse.org
Thomas & Betts Corporation	http://www.tnb.com
Thomas Lighting	http://www.thomaslighting.com
Thomas Register	http://www.thomasregister.com
3M Electrical Products	http://www.3m.com/elpd
Tork	http://www.tork.com
Touch-Plate Lighting Controls	http://www.touchplate.com
Trade Service Corporation	http://www.tradeservice.com
Trade Service Systems	http://www.tradepower.com
The Training Dept.	http://www.trainingdept.com
Triplett Corporation	http://www.triplett.com
TYCO (links to all divisions)	http://www.tyco.com
Tyton Hellermann	http://www.tytonhellermann.com
UEI Test Equipment	http://www.ueitest.com
Underwriters Laboratories	http://www.ul.com
UL Standards Dept	http://ulstandardsinfonet.ul.com
Unistrut Corp	http://www.unistrut.com
Unity Manufacturing	http://www.unitymfg.com
Universal Lighting Technologies	http://www.universalballast.com
USA Wire and Cable, Inc.	http://www.usawire-cable.com
U.S. Department of Energy (DOE)	http://www.doe.gov

U.S. Department of Labor	http://www.dol.gov
U.S. Department of Labor, Employment & Training Administration	http://www.doleta.gov
U.S. Environment Protection Agency (EPA)	http://www.epa.gov
Ustec*	http://www.ustecnet.com
Vantage Automation & Lighting Control*	http://www.vantagecontrols.com
Watt Stopper	http://www.wattstopper.com
Waukesha Electric Systems	http://www.waukeshaelectric.com
Werner Ladder Company	http://www.wernerladder.com
Westinghouse Lighting	http://www.westinghouselighting.com
Wheatland Tube Company	http://www.wheatland.com
Wireless Industry*	http://www.wireless.about.com
Wireless Thermostats*	http://www.wirelessthermostats.com
Wiremold Company, The	http://www.wiremold.com
Woodhead Industries	http://www.danielwoodhead.com
X-10*	http://www.x10.com
X-10 Pro Automation Products*	http://www.x10pro.com
Zenith Controls, Inc.*	http://www.geindustrialsystems.com
Zeus Home Control	http://www.zeushome.com
Zircon	http://www.zircon.com